THE MYTHS AND GODS OF INDIA

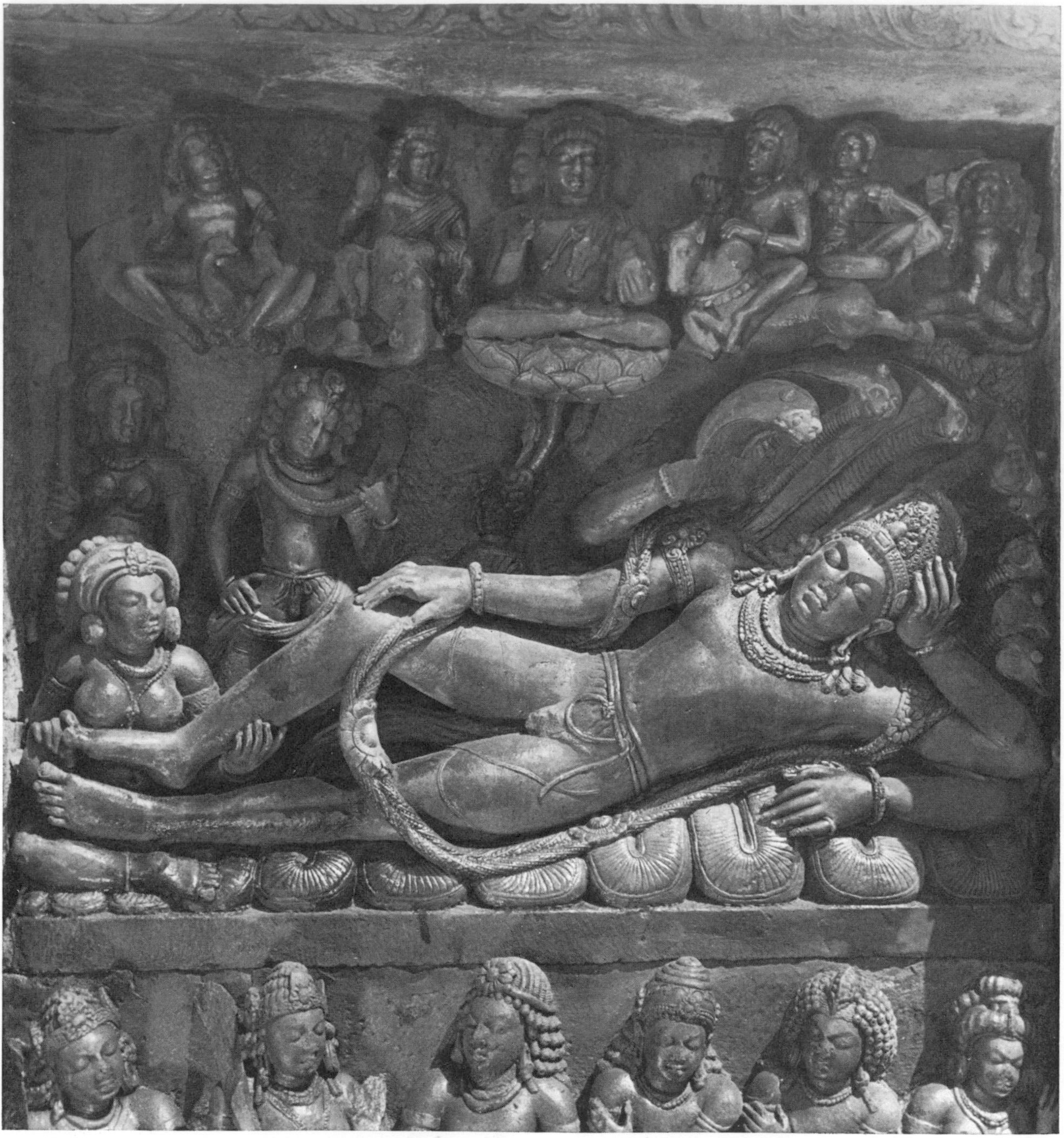

Viṣṇu sleeping on the serpent Śeṣa

Daśāvatāra temple, Deogaṛh (Central India), 7th century

THE MYTHS AND GODS OF INDIA

The Classic Work on Hindu Polytheism

ALAIN DANIÉLOU

INNER TRADITIONS INTERNATIONAL
ROCHESTER, VERMONT

Inner Traditions International
One Park Street
Rochester, Vermont 05767
www.InnerTraditions.com

Library of Congress Cataloging-in-Publication Data
Daniélou, Alain.
[Hindu polytheism]
The myths and gods of India : the classic work on Hindu polytheism / Alain Daniélou
p. cm.
Originally published: Hindu polytheism. New York : Bollingen Foundation, 1964, in series: Bollingen series ; 73.
Includes bibliographical references and index.
ISBN 978-089281354-4
ISBN 0-89281-354-7
1. Polytheism—Hinduism. 2. Hinduism—Doctrines. 3. Gods, Hindu.
I. Title
BL 1213.32.D36 1991
294.5'211—dc20 91-26265
CIP

Printed and bound in India

10 9

I WISH TO EXPRESS
MY GRATITUDE TO

Pandit N. Ramachandra Bhatt

FOR HIS CONSTANT AND UNTIRING HELP
IN THE LATER STAGES OF THE PREPARATION
OF THIS WORK AND FOR HIS MOST VALUABLE
CRITICISMS AND SUGGESTIONS

The One without color appears
by the manifold application of his power
with many colors in his hidden purpose.
May the Being of Splendor in whom the world dissolves
and from whom it rises
grant us a clear understanding.

He is Agni, the lord-of-fire,
and he is the Sun, and the Wind, and Moon.
He is the Seed, the Immense-Being,
He is the Lord-of-Progeny.

You are woman, and you are man,
You are the youth and the maiden,
and the old man tottering with a staff.
You are born again facing all directions.

You are the bluefly and the red-eyed parrot,
the cloud pregnant with lightning.
You are the seasons and the seas,
the Beginningless, the Abiding Lord
from whom the spheres are born.

Śvetāśvatara Upaniṣad 4.1–4. [1]

FOREWORD

This study of Hindu mythology is not an exhaustive one. It is a mere attempt at explaining the significance of the most prominent Hindu deities in the way in which they are envisaged by the Hindus themselves.

The mystery of creation and the destiny of man can be approached from various points of view. All religions are based on cosmological and metaphysical theories attempting to offer some explanation of the riddle of the universe. The complexity of Hindu polytheism is mainly due to the number of attempts at explaining in different ways the universal laws and the nature of the all-pervading principles from which the universe may appear to have arisen.

The names of the deities and the forms of the symbols used to represent universal principles have changed whenever this could help to make these principles more easily grasped. Historical iconography can, therefore, in no way be taken to represent the development of Hindu religious ideas. The apparent origins of the various gods and the histories of their names should not be taken as indisputable evidence of an evolution in religious ideas.

The outlook of modern people is, in the main, analytical. It tends to differentiate and isolate the various elements, religious, social, philosophical, which have combined to give its present form to the Hindu pantheon. The Hindu approach, on the other hand, being basically cosmological, tries to find an equivalent, a sort of legal precedent in its own tradition, for any new idea or system which it wants to understand or assimilate. Thus the Western approach tends to present us with a clear picture of original systems which become confused and mixed in the mass of Hindu thought, while the Hindu approach wants us to see a coherent, all-inclusive, ever-evolving knowledge with its roots in ancient systems which tried to express, more or less successfully, the complex structure of the cosmos, a structure which came to be better and better analyzed in the elaborate mythology of the later ages.

The word "Hindu," used for convenience, can be misleading, for it may convey the idea that Hinduism belongs to a country, to a particular human group, to a particular time. Hinduism, according to Hindu tradition and belief, is the remnant of a universal store of knowledge which, at one time, was accessible to the whole of mankind. It claims to represent the sum of all that has come to be known to man through his own effort or through revelation from the earliest age of his existence.

The development of the mutually exclusive creeds which now claim membership of the greater number of human beings seems to be, in the Hindu view, a comparatively recent phenomenon, which appeared only during the Kali Yuga, the "Age of Conflicts." [1] Whatever value we attribute to more recent religions, we should not attempt to equate Hinduism with them. Hinduism cannot be opposed to any creed, to any prophet, to any incarnation, to any way of realization, since one of its fundamental principles is to acknowledge them all and many more to come.

Hinduism, or rather the "eternal religion" (*sanātana dharma*), as it calls itself, recognizes for each age and each country a new form of revelation and for each man, according to his stage of development, a different path of realization, a different mode of worship, a different morality, different rituals, different gods.

The duty of the man of knowledge, of the realized being, is to teach to a worthy student what he has himself experienced and nothing more. He cannot claim that his is the only truth, because he cannot know what may be true to others. He cannot claim his way to be the only way, for the number of ways leading from the relative to the absolute is infinite. The teacher expounds what he knows and must leave the seeker to make his own discoveries, to find the path of his own development, for which each individual can be responsible finally only to himself.

There is therefore little room in Hinduism for dogmas, for proselytism, for set rules of behavior. Although the practice of certain virtues or restrictions may be, in many cases, a useful instrument of self-development, none can set a norm for others to follow. The rules of morality are a matter of social convenience, but have little to do with spiritual development. They can be mixed up with spiritual values only in religious creeds the main purpose of which is to codify the rules of conduct of a particular group, or race, or culture, whose "god" is a tribal chief enforcing a human code of behavior with superhuman threats. The multiplicity of

[1] The Kali Yuga started after the conclusion of the war depicted in the *Mahābhārata*, a contest which Hindu tradition variously dates between 3000 B.C. and 1500 B.C.

such "gods" in a polytheistic system, which ever opposes one divinity to another, has been a useful instrument in preventing the social code of human action from taking the place of the search for a higher truth. In this respect many of the civilized nations of today are just as primitive in their beliefs and in the picture of the "god" who guides their wars and approves of their social habits and prejudices as are the most primitive tribes of India. To them the message of Hindu polytheism can be one of tolerance and understanding.

THERE ARE some Hindu deities whose symbolism is not clear to me. I could not trace with certainty the tradition of their significance; available ancient texts and modern studies only mention their myths.

In such cases, and so as not to leave out entirely some important divinities, I have merely given a description of the form of the deity and a brief summary of the myth. This, however, creates an incomplete and eventually misleading picture. More contacts with the living pandits in the different parts of India may allow us one day to find the key to their significance.

I have written a French version of this book which differs from the English version in minor points. It is also less complete, containing only a few photographs and no index. It was published in Paris in 1960 by Buchet/Chastel under the title *Le Polythéisme Hindou.*

Throughout the text, numbers in brackets [ ] following the quotations translated from the Sanskrit refer to the Devanagari transcripts given in the appendix.

CONTENTS

TWO: The Gods of the Vedas

FOUR: The Divine Power (Śakti) as the Goddess

FIVE: Secondary Gods

SIX: The Representation and the Worship of Deities

LIST OF ILLUSTRATIONS

PLATES

All the plates are reproduced from photographs by Raymond Burnier. References are given to the pages on which the subjects represented are mentioned or discussed. Plates 1–32 follow p. 192.

Frontispiece. Viṣṇu sleeping on the serpent Śeṣa (p. 151).
Daśāvatāra temple, Deogaṛh (Central India), 7th century

1. Śiva manifested in the trinity (pp. 22 ff.) and in the dualism of Person and Nature (p. 35).
Brahmeśvara temple, Bhuvaneśvara (Orissa province), 11th century
2. The yogi fighting the power of Nature (pp. 33 f.) represented as a lion.
Khajuraho, 10th century
3. The yogi master of the power of Nature (p. 33).
Rājarānī temple, Bhuvaneśvara, 12th century
4. A sacrifice in Bengal (cf. pp. 70 ff.).
5. A ritual sacrifice, or *yajña* (pp. 68, 71 f.), at Benares. The *yajña* hall during an interruption of the rites.
6. Agni, or Fire (pp. 87 ff.).
Rājarānī temple, Bhuvaneśvara, 12th century
7. Sūrya, or the Sun (pp. 92 ff.).
Rāmgaṛh (Rajputana), 12th century
8. Yama, god of death (pp. 132 ff.).
Brahmeśvara temple, Bhuvaneśvara, 12th century
9. Varuṇa, the mysterious law of the gods (pp. 118 ff.).
Brahmeśvara temple, Bhuvaneśvara, 12th century
10. The man-lion, or Nṛsiṁha, an incarnation of Viṣṇu as courage (pp. 168 f.).
Paṭṭadkal, 7th century

FIGURES IN THE TEXT

Illustrations in the margins are not listed.

CHARTS AND DIAGRAMS

NOTE ON TRANSLATION OF THE SANSKRIT

In searching for expressions suitable to convey the meaning of the names of deities or of cosmic entities, I have tried to remain as close as possible to the images these names may evoke in spoken Sanskrit and to the notions they convey to the mind of a student of traditional philosophy.

One should keep in mind that, in the fields of religion and philosophy, for Sanskrit words the Hindus make use of symbolic etymologies distinct from the grammatical ones. A basic meaning is attributed to each syllabic sound, and the meanings of the syllables that form a word combine to express an idea that can be completely different from the etymological meaning of the word. In translating certain terms I have often chosen this symbolic meaning since this is the meaning that is important in practice and that alone can explain the use of those words in a particular context.

Since there exist authoritative texts explaining the symbolic etymologies of all important words, particularly all the names of deities (e.g., the *Viṣṇu-sahasra-nāma*, *Rudra-sahasra-nāma*, *Devī-sahasra-nāma*, and works such as the *Nirukta*), in most cases I omitted references which would have justified my translations, in order not to overburden the book with technical notes. For example, I translated Vinatā as "she before whom knowledge bows." The name Vinatā means "bowed to"; it is in the feminine gender, which therefore indicates the feminine deity, but from tradition one knows that it is knowledge that bows before her (Vinatā is the mother of Garuḍa, who represents the hermetic utterances of the Vedas, the essence of knowledge). Therefore I incorporated in the translation of the term the explanatory commentary that the Brahman student would give immediately.

In translating texts I have sometimes maintained a Sanskrit name although it was already translated, so that the meaning might appear together with the name. Thus I may translate "Viṣṇu, the Pervader" when in the text there is only the name Viṣṇu, which means "pervader."

I could not give complete references for all of the quotations; some of them were taken from texts of which I saw only incomplete manuscripts without chapter divisions. Since many of the texts I quote differ from those found in the printed versions available to Western scholars, I wanted to give in an appendix the texts I had translated. I am extremely happy that this could be realized in the present edition.

I beg to be forgiven for having given the references to the *Mahābhārata* sometimes in one recension, sometimes in another. I happened to have at my disposal first one version and later the other. I did not find the time or the courage to try to co-ordinate the two versions of this enormous work, which show endless variants.

NOTE ON PRONUNCIATION

VOWELS

Simple			*Mixed*	
Guttural	*a*	*ā*	Guttural-palatal	*e*
Palatal	*i*	*ī*		*ai*
Labial	*u*	*ū*	Guttural-labial	*o*
Lingual	*ṛ*	*ṝ*		*au*
Dental	*ḷ*	*ḹ*		

CONSONANTS

Guttural	*k*	*kh*	*g*	*gh*	*ṅ*	*h*	[*ḥ*: visarga]
Palatal	*c*	*ch*	*j*	*jh*	*ñ*	*y*	*ś*
Lingual	*ṭ*	*ṭh*	*ḍ*	*ḍh*	*ṇ*	*r*	*ṣ*
Dental	*t*	*th*	*d*	*dh*	*n*	*l*	*s*
Labial	*p*	*ph*	*b*	*bh*	*m*	*v*	[*ḥ*: upadhmānīya]

[*ṁ* or *ṅ*: anusvara]

All the Indian scripts follow the classical Sanskrit classification of the letters; only the shapes of the written characters vary.

The ancient Indian grammarians (Nandikeśvara, Bhartṛhari, Pāṇini, Patañjali, etc.) built up an alphabet that aimed at classifying the various possibilities of articulation (cf. p. 336, n. 3) and at standarizing the Sanskrit language; for then, as now, accurate pronunciation of the sounds was essential for the effectiveness of the magic formulae and for the symbolic significance of the names of the deities (see p. xxvii). A certain amount of degradation in the common pronunciation of some of the elements of this classification of articulate sounds has taken place since it was first established, more than two thousand five hundred years ago, disrupting in some cases its logic and its ordinance.

The classical grammarians recognize five places of articulation. There are therefore five groups of consonants and five "pure" vowels.

VOWELS are traditionally defined as continuous sounds that can be held without any movement of the lips or tongue while singing. In general, the vowels are pronounced somewhat as in Italian; short *a*, however, is a "neutral" vowel, like the vowel-sound of *but*.

Of the SIMPLE VOWELS, only three are used today in most Indian languages: the guttural *a*, the palatal *i*, the labial *u*.

The "lost" vowels are two: first, the lingual vowel transcribed as *ṛ*, which corresponds to the German *ö* (as in *böse*) or the French *eu* (as in *beurre*). The grammarians defined *ṛ* as the sound produced when one thinks of an *i* but utters it at the place where *r* is articulated. However, *ṛ* has come to be pronounced *ri* (as in *ri*ver) in most parts of India, so that Kṛṣṇa is now usually pronounced *Krishna*, although the older rendering *Köshna* is still current in several North Indian dialects.

The other "lost" vowel, the dental vowel transcribed as *ḷ*, corresponds to the French *u* (as in *lune*) or the German *ü* (as in *über*). The grammarians defined *ḷ* as the sound produced when one thinks of *r* but utters it at the place where *l* is made. However, it is now usually pronounced *lri* (approximately as in ax*le*-*r*im).

The so-called MIXED VOWELS are traditionally regarded as using two places of articulation at the same time. Thus they are sometimes mistaken by Western students for diphthongs. The first two, transcribed as *e* and *ai*, comprise the sounds represented phonetically as *a* with *i*: (guttural) *a* with (palatal) *i*; the *e* is pronounced as in French *fée*, and the *ai* as in French *fête*. The two other mixed vowels, transcribed as *o* and *au*, are the sounds represented phonetically as *a* with *u*: (guttural) *a* with (labial) *u*; the *o* is pronounced about as in n*o*te, the *au* as in *or*chid.

CONSONANTS, according to tradition, are formed in each place of articulation by a push or a pull (in Western terms, unvoiced or voiced) which can be dry or aspirate, thus giving in each position four kinds of occlusion, besides a fifth quality, a nasal. In addition, there are four semivowels (*y*, *r*, *l*, *v*), three sibilants (*ś*, *ṣ*, *s*), and a pure aspirate (*h*). Thus we obtain the thirty-three consonants defined by tradition (p. 336, n. 3); they exclude the terminal and nasalizing sounds bracketed in the above table.

The aspirate consonants, written as single characters in Sanskrit, are transcribed with an *h* following. Thus *h* after another consonant is always aspirated and audible; for example, *th* is pronounced as in boa*th*ook, *ph* as in ha*p*-*h*azard, *dh* as in ma*dh*ouse, and *bh* as in a*bh*or.

The guttural series contains the ordinary European *k*- and *g*-sounds and their aspirates (*kh* and *gh*), with a nasal *ṅ* which is pronounced as *ng* in si*ng*ing.

In the palatal series, *c* is pronounced about like *ch* in church (Sanskrit *ch*, consequently, sounds like chur*ch-h*ouse) and *j* about as in *j*udge. The nasal *ñ* is like *ñ* in Spanish *señor*. An exception is *jña*, which as pronounced by a modern Hindu sounds like *gñah* (or, vulgarly, *gyah*) with hard *g*. The palatal semivowel *y* is about as in English, and *ś*, the sibilant, approximately *sh*.

Linguals are pronounced with the tip of the tongue bent back and placed against the roof of the mouth instead of against the teeth. The *r* is untrilled. The *ṣ* is a harsh (semiguttural) sibilant, sometimes turned into *kh* in popular language. Hence *ṛṣabha* (bull) comes to be pronounced *ökhabh* or *rikhabh*.

The dentals and labials are about as in English.

Visarga and upadhmānīya, both transliterated *ḥ*, are final *h*-sounds uttered in the articulating position of the preceding syllable—visarga with gutturals, upadhmānīya with labials. Anusvara, *ṁ* or *ṅ*, is a nasal occurring at the end of a syllable.

ONE

Philosophy

The Theory of Polytheism

The Language of Symbols

Any attempt at representing something in terms of something else requires a system of equivalences. The representation of one order of things in terms of another is made with the help of real or arbitrary equivalents known as symbols. To represent a crop in terms of quantity we have to use symbols which are numbers. To represent ideas in terms of sounds we must use symbols which are words; to represent words graphically we have to use symbols which are characters. A symbol is a perceptible, analogical representation of a thing or an idea. Language is merely a particular form of symbolism. Writing, probably everywhere originally conceived as ideograms, is essentially symbolical.

A symbol can be natural or conventional. The direct relation of one order of things with another, the intersection of two worlds, of two aspects of existence, is the origin of natural symbols.

In the Hindu cosmological theory symbolism is conceived as the expression of a reality, as a search for the particular points where different worlds meet and where the relation between entities belonging to different orders of things may become apparent.

According to the Hindu view, all the aspects of the manifest world spring from similar principles—have, we might say, a common ancestry. There is of necessity some sort of equivalence between sounds, forms, numbers, colors, ideas, as there is also between the abstractions of the subtle and transcendent worlds on one side and the forms of the perceptible universe on the other.

The astronomical phenomena can be considered as basic symbols. We can find in them a figuration of universal principles. True symbolism, far from being invented by man, springs from Nature (*prakṛti*) [1] itself. The whole of Nature is but the symbol of a higher reality.

What we picture as the aspects of divinity are essentially the abstract prototypes of the forms of the manifest world. These must, by their very nature, have equivalents in all the aspects of the perceptible universe. Each divine aspect thus may appear to us as having affinities with some particular form, number, color, plant, animal, part of the body, vital energy, particular moments of the cycles of the day, of the year, of aeons, particular constellations, sounds, rhythms, etc.

The conception of the Hindu pantheon and its iconographical theory are based on the belief that such affinities exist. Thus an aspect of divinity can be represented and worshiped in forms which are extremely diverse and yet strictly equivalent, such as a mental figuration, a geometrical diagram (*yantra*), an anthropomorphic image (*mūrti*), a spoken formula (*mantra*), a particular human being (mother, teacher, etc.), a particular fruit, an animal, a mineral, etc. Any of these forms can be used indifferently as a support through which ritual or meditation can reach the Principle of which they are the images, the manifest aspects.

The Representation of the Transcendent

ALL RELIGIONS, all religious philosophies, are ultimately attempts at finding out the nature of the perceptible world—and of ourselves who perceive it—the process of the world's manifestation, and the purpose of life, so that we may discover the means of fulfilling our destiny. All mythologies are ways of representing transcendent or suprahuman states of Being conceived as deities or perceived as symbols.

Some ancient Hindu sages discovered that, through the diversity of our faculties and of our senses, and according to the postulates or methods we are ready to accept, we can find different channels through which to conduct our investigation into the extrasensorial world. Each of these channels, leading into distant spheres, has narrow limits, has its own distinct characteristics and methods. Each may bring us to conclusions that appear different from those arrived at through other channels.

Transcendent reality is, by definition, beyond the limitations that condition our means of knowledge. Yet, even if we cannot understand its nature, we

1 On the term Nature (including human nature and the physical universe), see pp. 31–32; for other aspects of its meaning, see pp. 33, 34 f., 253, 265 f., and passim.

may indirectly conclude that some form of being beyond the sphere of our perceptions must exist. Whenever he carries any form of experience to its farthest limit, man has a glimpse of an unknowable "Beyond" which he calls divinity. This divinity cannot be grasped nor understood, for it begins where understanding fails, yet it can be approached from many sides; any attempt at understanding its nature can merely be called a "near approach," an Upa-niṣad. We can only point to the necessity for a substratum, we never experience it directly, although it is ever near; for, at the limit of each form of experience, we apprehend some aspect of it. The more we can seize of the different aspects of the phenomenal world, often apparently contradictory, through which the Divine may be approached, the more we come near to a general, a "real," insight into the mysterious entity we call God.

We can look at a sculpture from different angles. We grasp its whole form only when we have observed the front, the back, the profiles. Each of these views is different from the others; some of the elements of their description may seem incompatible. Yet from these contradictory reports of our eyes we can build up a general conception of the sculpture which we could hardly do if we had seen it from one angle only.

The apparent contradiction between the transcendent forms glimpsed through the diverse means of approach is really the key to the comprehension of the "Immense" reality, which can never be grasped as a whole. Thus divinity has been defined as "that in which opposites coexist." The more insights we can get, the more aspects of the Divine we can perceive, the more we see of divinities beyond the different aspects of the universe, the more elements we can assemble to build up some conception of the origin of things, of the destiny and purpose of life, the nearer we are to understanding something of what divinity is.

There are certain curves whose equations cannot be stated. In such a case the mathematician searches for particular examples in which the formula is simpler; then, with the help of the data so obtained, he plots an outline and arrives at an approximate idea of the curve. This would have been impossible through one point of view, one approach, only. The theory of polytheism is based on a similar attempt. It is only through the multiplicity of approaches that we can draw a sort of outline of what transcendent reality may be. The multiple manifested entities that underlie existing forms alone are within the reach of our understanding. Any conception we may have of something beyond will be a mental projection, an imaginary link established between various perceptible data.

Hindu philosophy studies the mystery of the universe from three main outlooks. These are: (1) the experimental outlook, or Vaiśeṣika,[2] and its corroborating method, logic, or Nyāya, which envisages the "impermanent" or destructible form of things; (2) the cosmological outlook, or Sāṅkhya, and its corroborating method, direct supramental perception, or Yoga, which studies the "enduring" or permanent laws of things; and (3) the metaphysical outlook, or Vedānta, and its corroborating method, the dialectic and semantic study of language, which tries to grasp the nature of the changeless substratum of all forms and laws. We shall see, when studying the nature of the Cosmic Being, that these three approaches refer to the three orders of manifestation: the "Destructible Person" (*kṣara puruṣa*) or the perceptible universe, the "Indestructible Person" (*akṣara puruṣa*) or the body of permanent laws which rule manifestation, and the "Changeless Person" (*avyaya puruṣa*), the unmanifest substratum of existence beyond cause and effect.

It will make us ponder over the nature of transcendent reality to discover that, according to their own logic and their means of proof, some of the "points of view" (*darśana*) must be atheistic, others pantheistic, others deistic, moralistic, mystical. Yet we should not hastily conclude that these are the conflicting beliefs of philosophers. They are only the logical conclusions drawn from the premises and reached through the methods acceptable for each approach, each "point of view." Each one is real within its own field and aims toward the utmost limit of the reach of our faculties in a particular direction. The builders of the "points of view" are not spoken of as thinkers or prophets but as seers (*ṛṣi*).[3]

The Nondual Principle

A SUPREME CAUSE has to be beyond number, otherwise Number would be the First Cause. But the number one, although it has peculiar properties, is a number like two, or three, or ten, or a million. If "God" is one, he is not beyond number any more than if he is two or three or ten or a million. But, although a million is not any nearer to infinity than one or two or ten, it seems to be so

2 The meanings of the names are: Vaiśeṣika, "the particular"; Nyāya, "rule"; Sāṅkhya, "enumeration"; Yoga, "link"; Vedānta, "end of knowledge."

3 Sight is considered the most reliable of our perceptions. Hence the perception of ideas, the reality of thought, is represented as a mental vision.

"Verily, truth is sight. Therefore if two people should come disputing, saying, 'I have seen,' 'I have heard,' we should trust the one who says, 'I have seen.' " (*Bṛhad-āraṇyaka Upaniṣad* 5.14.4. [2])

from the limited point of view of our perceptions. And we may be nearer to a mental representation of divinity when we consider an immense number of different gods than when we try to stress their unity; for the number one is in a way the number farthest removed from infinity.[4]

"The nature of illusion (*māyā*) is [represented by] the number one." [5]

To speak of the manifest form of a unique God implies a confusion between different orders. God manifest cannot be one, nor can the number one apply to an unmanifest causal aspect. At no stage can unity be taken as the cause of anything, since the existence implies a relation and unity would mean existence without relation.[6]

Though, in its manifest form, divinity is of necessity multiple, in its ultimate essence it cannot be said to be either one or many. It cannot be in any way defined. Divinity is represented as that which remains when the reality of all that can be perceived has been denied. It is *Neti neti*, "Neither this nor that," nothing that the mind can know or words can express. We cannot say that it is one, yet we can say that it is not-one, not-two, not-many. The expression selected by the Vedāntists is that it is "not-two." Hence a nondual principle was pictured as existing beyond all the forms of manifest divinity.

"Whatever remains when the mind realizes that the concept of a 'living being' and that of a 'divinity' are mere illusions, and the reality of all appearances is denied, is [known as] the nondual Immensity." (*Advaya-tāraka Upaniṣad* 3. [3])

Nonduality, the essence of the unmanifest, cannot exist on the manifest plane. Although the doctrine of nonduality is kept as the goal of our efforts toward realization, this goal is ever beyond our reach. It is on a plane different from that of existence and is in no way real from the point of view of manifestation. We cannot imagine, we cannot name, we cannot describe the nondual Immensity, the Brahman. It is a mere abstraction which cannot act nor be experienced or propitiated. It can therefore have nothing whatever to do with any form of worship, of religion, of morality, or of mystical experience.

Existence is multiplicity. That which is not multiple does not exist. We may conceive of an underlying, all-pervading continuum, but it remains shape-

4 The inverted form $1/n$, the reflection of a number n, tends toward zero when n increases indefinitely. Zero is therefore the reflection or image of infinity and was taken as such in some branches of Indian philosophy. Yet one is the number farthest removed from both infinities, the infinitely small and the infinitely great.

5 *Ekaśabdātmikā māyā*. (*Maudgala Purāṇa* 1. Quoted in Karapātrī's *Śrī Bhagavat tattva*, p. 642.)

6 This is said to be evident from the property of the number one that, whenever multiplied by itself, it always remains unchanged.

less, without quality, impersonal, nonexistent. From the moment we envisage divinity in a personal form, or we attribute to it any quality, that divinity belongs to the multiple, it cannot be one; for there must be an entity embodying the opposite of its quality, a form complementary to its form, other deities.

Whenever we imagine a god, personify him, picture him, pray to him, worship him, this god, of necessity, is but one among many. Whenever we call him "the one God" we do not raise his status, but merely blind ourselves to other realities. We do not come in any way nearer to the nondual Immensity, the Brahman. In that sense, any form of monotheism takes man away from the path of knowledge and realization, substituting a simple but inaccurate postulate for the attempt to understand the divine multiplicity.

The gods are but the representations of the causal energies from which each aspect of the subtle and the visible worlds is derived. Deities should therefore be thought of as transcendent powers. Each of these manifests itself in a particular aspect of the perceptible universe, or, if we start our investigation from the perceptible end, each deity appears as a subtle entity presiding over the functioning of one aspect of the universe.

In truth, these divine aspects, which, from the point of view of man, seem more or less remote, may appear, from the point of view of divinity, as the mere modalities of the same essence. They are compared to the notes of the flute whose differences are the basis of music although they may be envisaged as mere modalities of air vibration.

"By the action of the undifferentiated air, the different notes, known as do, etc., are produced through the several holes of the flute. So, also, arising from the undifferentiated supreme Self, many states of being appear to exist." (*Viṣṇu Purāṇa* 2.14.32. [4])

But, although the different notes appear to be mere modalities in vibration, it is in their difference, in their relation, that the nature of music lies; the oneness of the air, their medium, is but an incidental factor. Similarly from the point of view of existence it is the divine multiplicity, not the unity, which is the source of the universe and the source of knowledge as well as the means of reintegration.

Monotheism and Polytheism

IN OUR time monotheism is often considered a higher form of religion than polytheism. People speak of God, pray to God, search for God rather than speak of gods, pray to a particular god, or acknowledge various divine incarnations. Individual monotheistic worshipers, however, usually worship a particularized form of their god and not his causal, unmanifest, formless aspect. There is a nearness, a response, in the formal aspect which is lacking in the abstract conception. But a causal, formless, all-pervading divinity, cause and origin of all forms, cannot be manifest in a particular form and would of necessity be equally at the root of all types of form. Divinity can only be reached through its manifestations, and there are as many gods as there are aspects of creation. The gods and the universe are two aspects—the conscious powers and the unconscious forms—of an indefinite multiplicity.

In the polytheistic religion each individual worshiper has a chosen deity (*iṣṭa-devatā*) and does not usually worship other gods in the same way as his own, as the one he feels nearer to himself. Yet he acknowledges other gods. The Hindu, whether he be a worshiper of the Pervader (Viṣṇu), the Destroyer (Śiva), Energy (Śakti), or the Sun (Sūrya), is always ready to acknowledge the equivalence of these deities as the manifestations of distinct powers springing from an unknowable "Immensity." He knows that ultimate Being or non-Being is ever beyond his grasp, beyond existence, and in no way can be worshiped or prayed to. Since he realizes that other deities are but other aspects of the one he worships, he is basically tolerant and must be ready to accept every form of knowledge or belief as potentially valid. Persecution or proselytization of other religious groups, however strange their beliefs may seem to him, can never be a defensible attitude from the point of view of the Hindu.

From the vast and solid basis for experience formed by the multiplicity of divine manifestation the polytheist can rise toward the goal beyond reach that is nondualism and toward the illusion of an ultimate identification. At every step he finds within the multiplicity a lesser degree of differentiation suitable to his stage of development as he travels from the outward forms of ritual and morality toward the more abstract aspects of knowledge and nonaction. These are outwardly represented by different groups of static symbols, that is, deities, and active symbols, that is, rites. The seeker chooses at each stage the deities and rites which are within his reach as he progresses on the path that leads toward liberation.

During the pilgrimage of life he goes from one temple to another, adopts different forms of ritual, different modes of living, and various means of self-development. He is constantly aware of the coexistence of different approaches to divinity, suitable for people at stages of realization different from his own.

It is considerably more difficult, within a monotheist creed, for an individual to establish the hierarchy of his attitudes to divinity at different stages of his development; and it is almost impossible for him not to mix planes and methods, for relative truth is different at each stage and yet its thorough understanding is essential if a particular stage is to be outgrown.

Since he cannot clearly see side by side, illustrated in different symbols, in different cults or philosophies—and in the attitude of their followers—the different stages of his own development, past as well as future, any attempt at looking beyond the limits of his creed makes the monotheist lose his balance. It is because of this precarious equilibrium that, in monotheist creeds, we find so little room between proselytizing and irreligion, so little place for tolerance, so little respect for modes of thought, or worship, or behavior different from the "norm." The monotheist, as a rule, confuses the religious and the moral planes, conventional practices with self-development. He mixes up faith with proselytism, mystical emotion with spiritual progress.

The man who finds himself at a stage of development different from that for which a given monistic system was devised has hardly any alternative but to abandon it, which often means, if he has no contact with other religious forms, abandoning religion and spiritual search altogether or devising some system of his own unlikely to lead him toward modes of thought and understanding of which he has not already an idea.

Monotheism is always linked with a culture, a civilization. It is not through its forms but in spite of them that gifted individuals may reach spiritual attainment. We shall see that monotheism is the projection of the human individuality into the cosmic sphere, the shaping of "god" to the image of man. Hence the monotheist commonly visualizes his "god" as an anthropomorphic entity who shares his habits, patronizes his customs, and acts according to his ideals. Religion becomes a means of glorifying his culture or his race, or of expanding his influence. He is one of the elect who follows the "Way of God" as if there could be a Way that did not lead to "God." We can see all monotheistic religions fighting to impose their god and destroy other gods as if God were not one as they claim. Monotheism is basically the absolute exaltation of the worshiper's own deity over all other aspects of the Divine, all other gods, who must be considered false and dangerous. The very notion of a false god is, however, an obvious fallacy. If there is an all-powerful, all-pervading divinity, how can there be a false god? How can we worship anything that is not Him? Whatever form we try to worship, the worship ultimately goes to Him who is everything.

"Those who piously worship other gods of whom they are the devotees, it is but myself they worship, [though] ignorant of the proper rites." (*Bhagavad-gītā* 9.23. [5])

Monotheism thus appears to be the opposite of nondualism, which might as well be called nonmonism, and which leads to the conception of an all-pervading —that is, from the point of view of our perceptions, an infinitely multiple—divinity.

Nondualism and Monism

THE TERM "nondualism" has proved, in many instances, to be a dangerous one, since it can easily be thought to rest on a monistic concept. The Hindu philosophical schools which made an extensive use of this term opened the way for religious monism, which is always linked with a "humanism" that makes of man the center of the universe and of "god" the projection of the human ego into the cosmic sphere. Monism sporadically appears in Hinduism as an attempt to give a theological interpretation to the theory of the substrata (see pp. 20–22, 40). Nondualism was, however, to remain a conception of philosophers. It never reached the field of common religion.

The tendency toward monism never has had in practice a deep influence on the forms of Hindu worship. A simplified system could never accommodate the multifaced, complex unity that characterizes the Hindu pantheon, where, although every element can, from a certain point of view, be equated with every other, the whole can never be brought back to numerical unity.

In the general picture of later Hinduism an exaggerated importance has been attributed to some philosophical schools of monistic Hinduism which developed mainly under the impact of Islamic and Christian influences and which aim at reinterpreting Vedic texts in a new light.

The Equivalence of Religions

THE CLASSIFICATION of the basic energies, of which the cosmological pantheon is an expression, is not an arbitrary creation of the mind but a rational effort to define the component elements of existence. As is the case for any form of knowledge, the classifications first chosen in a particular country or time may have been inadequate, they may constitute a first working hypothesis which can be perfected through deeper insight or later experience, or they may have defined all the essentials from the start. The only important thing, however, is the nature of the permanent realities that these classifications try to represent. This is the story of every science, of every philosophy, of all the ancient religions.

In the ancient world the Vedic Rudra could be equated with the Dravidian (?) Śiva, the Greek Dionysos, or the Egyptian Osiris. Just as we can say, "The French call a spoon a *cuiller*," the Hindu will say, "The Christians worship a form of Viṣṇu named Christ," because for him Viṣṇu is not an individual god pertaining to a particular religion but a general principle, as inevitably represented in any theology, in any code of symbols, as words representing objects (nouns), actions (verbs), and qualities (adjectives) are inevitably found in any language.

Hindu mythology acknowledges all gods. Since all the energies at the origin of all the forms of manifestation are but aspects of the divine power, there can exist no object, no form of existence, which is not divine in its nature. Any name, any shape, that appeals to the worshiper can be taken as a representation or manifestation of divinity.

The gods mentioned in the Vedas form only a small part of the Hindu pantheon, which gradually incorporated, and still is ready to incorporate, all the conceptions of divinity, all the gods, of all the religious groups, all new "incarnations" or representations of the supranatural powers which pervade the universe.

Many of the deities worshiped by the Hindus are not mentioned in the Vedas under their present names, and many Vedic gods are today known mostly to scholars. But it would be wrong to see a change in religion or a deviation from the Vedic idea of divinity in what is merely a matter of fashion, a way of representing the Divine that suited a particular time or country, a particular set of habits, or a different conception of the universe. The gods are universal principles; they are all-pervading realities. The words or forms we use to represent them are mere approximations, which can vary like the words of different languages used to represent the same object or like the different symbols used to represent the same mathematical facts.

All religions are based on the recognition of the existence of a suprasensorial reality. Very rarely can we find in any religion a positive assertion which is not to some extent justifiable. Error and conflict arise from exclusion, from negative elements. They appear whenever the door is closed to new discoveries, to the "revelation" of a new age. A religion reduced to a faith centered around fixed dogmas and refusing to equate its data with those of other creeds is to religion what the art of the primitive medicine man is to medical science, the mere practical utilization of some elements of knowledge accidentally assembled and used more for social supremacy than for real cure. This remains very short of the total search for the whole of truth. Thus, in many countries, the man of science, if he be true to himself, finds he has had to choose between reason and faith. This dilemma does not arise for the Hindu, for Hinduism does not claim any of its discoveries to be more than an approach. It rejects all dogma, all belief that reason and experience cannot justify; it remains ever ready to accept new and better expressions of the universal laws as they can be grasped through individual experience.

There is no doubt that superstition and ignorance have often superseded reason and enlightened thought in India just as elsewhere. Some of the modern Indian creeds have as little to be envied as foreign ones, so inadequate is their thinking. But the principle of a multiple approach, the recognition of the fundamental right of the individual to follow his own gods, his own code of behavior and ritual practice, has spared India so far the standardization of beliefs which is by its very nature the greatest obstacle on the path of Divine discovery.

The Nature of the Ultimate

The Origin of Existence

"IN THE BEGINNING, my dear, this world was just nondual Being (*sat*). To be sure, some people say that in the beginning this world was just nondual non-Being (*a-sat*), and that Being arose from non-Being. But how could that be? How could Being be produced from non-Being? In the beginning this world must have been pure Being, one and without a second." (*Chāndogya Upaniṣad* 6.2.1–2. [6])

Thus did the sage Āruṇi state the question of the ultimate origin of gods, men, and the cosmos.

The methods of yoga, which the Aryans had probably learned from earlier inhabitants of India, had made them conscious, through introspection, of an ultimate void within themselves, of a stage beyond thought and dream, beyond perception, beyond knowledge, motionless, indescribable, unbounded by space and time. Was this the causal principle? Was there a motionless substratum for matter, one for time, as there seemed to be one for thought? Were these different substrata the forms of a still more subtle one? The philosophers of the Upaniṣads pondered over these problems.

The Perceptible Continua: Space, Time, and Thought

WHEN ATTEMPTING to reach the root of any aspect of the manifest world we are led to imagine that there must exist beyond its form, beyond its appearance, some sort of causal state, some undifferentiated continuum, of which that particularized form would be an apparent development.

The first of the continua underlying all perceptible forms appears to be space. Absolute empty space is defined by Indian philosophers as a limitless, undifferentiated, indivisible continuum in which are built the imaginary divisions of relative space. The apparent localization of heavenly bodies and their movements creates the illusion of a division of space. But, according to the traditional example: "Space within a pitcher is not really separated from the space outside. It was not distinct before the pitcher was made; it will not be distinct once the pitcher is broken and is not therefore really distinct while the pitcher exists." [1] All the divisions of space into atoms and heavenly spheres are mere appearances. The space within the atom can be as immense as that within a solar system, and there can be no limit to the number of possible worlds contained in another.

Similarly time was called an "indivisible rod" (*akhaṇḍa-daṇḍāyamāna*),[2] or continuum. This absolute time is an ever-present eternity which seems inseparable from space. Relative time results from the apparent division of space by the rhythm of heavenly bodies.

The third perceptible continuum is thought. Everything that exists appears with a form, within a co-ordinated system. It seems to be the realization of a plan, the materialization of an organized dream. Hence the visible universe was conceived as the form of the thought of its creator. Whenever we go to the root of anything we find no longer a substance but a mere form, a concept, whose nature can be identified with that of thought.

The Three Modes of Being: the Substrata of Space, Time, and Consciousness

IF WE envisage the cosmos not merely as an unconscious mechanism but as a creative process, as the manifestation of a conscious power, we are led to search for an active or conscious substratum for each of the perceptible continua.

The substratum of space is existence (*sat*), the substratum of time is experience or enjoyment (*ānanda*), the substratum of thought is consciousness (*cit*).

Before there can be location, place, dimension, there must be something to locate, some sort of existence. There can be no location of the nonexistent. Hence existence must pre-exist space.

Time exists only in relation to perception. A nonperceived time can have no extension, cannot be the measure of anything. The principle of perception

1 Cited in Karapātrī's "Ahamartha aur ātmā," *Siddhānta*, II, 1941–42. I could not trace the original.

2 This term is used by Yogatrayānanda in his "Kāla tattva," *Śiva-rātrī*, but must come from an ancient work on Sāṅkhya.

must therefore pre-exist time. That first undifferentiated potential perception, that first principle of experience, is said to correspond to pure, absolute enjoyment, the innermost nature of existence.

"Know the Principle (*brahman*) to be enjoyment. From enjoyment are all beings born; once born they are sustained by enjoyment and leave this world to return into enjoyment." (*Taittirīya Upaniṣad* 3.6. [7])

"There is no experience, no enjoyment, without being, and no being without experience (enjoyment). When we speak of enjoyment (*ānanda*) as 'self-illumined existence' (*svaprakāśa-sattā*), enjoyment is shown as something other than sensation, and by saying that existence is the form of enjoyment, existence is freed from the notion of inertia." (Karapātrī, "Liṅgopāsanā-rahasya," *Siddhānta*, II, 1941–42, 153.)

The lord-of-sleep (Śiva), who is the principle of disintegration (*tamas*), the source of an ever-expanding (disintegrating) universe, is the principle of time, the destroyer, and at the same time the embodiment of experience, of enjoyment, whose symbol is the fount of life, the source of pleasure, the phallus (*liṅga*). Thus enjoyment that is life and time that is death are shown as the two aspects of one entity. The source of life and immortality (*a-mṛta*) is the same as that of death (*mṛta*), a symbol that expresses itself in all traditions as the oneness of love and death (*a-mor* and *mor-tis*).

Enjoyment being the form of experience, the enjoyment continuum, basis of experience, is also known as "feeling" (*rasa*) or "emotion." "He [the Total Being] verily is but feeling."[3] (*Taittirīya Upaniṣad* 2.7.)

The experience of pure, unbounded enjoyment as the innermost nature of things implies the realization of absolute time, which is ever-present eternity. The being who reaches that stage is freed from the bonds of action.

"He who knows the enjoyment of the Immensity does not know fear from any quarter. He is not tormented by the thought 'Why did not I act rightly? why did I sin?' He who knows that [right and wrong are relative things] reaches the Soul." (*Taittirīya Upaniṣad* 2.9. [8])

The substratum of thought is consciousness. Thought can exist only in a conscious mind. There can be no thought independent of a thinker, of someone conscious of the existence of thought. Consciousness is therefore the fundamental substratum of thought and is linked with the notion of individual existence, of an individual monad, or self, or being.

The formless Immensity that appears to be the innermost nature of things can be grasped as the void, the silence, the absolute darkness, which lies beyond

3 *Raso vai saḥ.*

mind, beyond intellect, and can be realized as the substratum of man's own nature, as his own Self, his own Soul (*ātman*).

"Vast, resplendent, of unthinkable form, it shines forth more subtly than what is subtlest. Farther than the far, it is here at hand, hidden in the hearts of the seers." (*Muṇḍaka Upaniṣad* 3.1.7. [9])

"That Soul is not 'this' nor 'that'; unseizable, it cannot be grasped; indestructible, it cannot be destroyed; unattached, it has no contacts; unbound, it knows no anguish; it cannot be injured." (*Bṛhad-āraṇyaka Upaniṣad* 3.9.26 and 4.5.15. [10])

Unbounded by space and time, the individual soul is as small as an atom, as vast as the universe. "He who realizes the sphere of space hidden in the cavern of his heart grasps all that may be desired and comes into contact with the Immensity." (*Taittirīya Upaniṣad* 2.1. [11])

The Soul is the unity that links all individual beings. It is the indivisible continuum in which beings appear as individual conscious units. Every existing thing contains a part of the universal Soul, just as every form encloses a part of space and every duration a part of time. But, although this individual fragment of the Soul, like the fragment of space in the pitcher, gives existence to the living being, at no moment is the individual soul really separated from the universal continuum of consciousness, the Ātman.

The experience of the universal Soul is an experience of identity; hence absolute consciousness is spoken of as the Self, the own self of each being. "For, where there is a duality, one sees another, one smells another, one tastes another, one speaks to another, one hears another, one thinks of another, one touches another, one understands another. But where everything has become just one's own self, then who can be seen by what? who can be smelt by what? who can be tasted by what? who can speak to what? who can hear what? who can think of what? who can touch what? who can understand what? who can understand that through which all things are understood?" (*Bṛhad-āraṇyaka Upaniṣad* 4.5.15. [12])

As the substratum of consciousness, the Ātman is the Self, the innermost nature of all divinities, of all the forms of the manifest universe, of all living beings.

The Soul is the sum of all the gods. "All the gods are this one Soul, and all dwell in the Soul." (*Manu Smṛti* 12.119. [13])

"The ruler-of-heaven (Indra) and all the gods are the Supreme Soul. It is supreme because it includes all." (Kullūka Bhaṭṭa, commentary on ibid. [14])

As the one [inner] Fire pervading the worlds takes the endless forms of things,
the one Soul within all beings fills their forms and the space around.

As the one Air pervading the worlds takes the endless forms of things,
the one Soul within all beings fills their forms and the space around.

As the one Sun, the eye of the worlds, is not affected by defects of sight,
the one Soul within all beings is not defiled by suffering.

There is but one Self for all beings, [one Power] that controls all, one Form that creates all forms.
The strong who witness it within their hearts alone know everlasting joy.

It is the eternity of things eternal, the consciousness of the conscious,
the unity of multiplicity, the fulfillment of desire.
The strong who witness it in their hearts alone know everlasting peace.

(*Kaṭha Upaniṣad* 5.9–13. [15])

The Soul, the all-pervading continuum of consciousness, becomes the sole object of the meditation of the realized sage.

"This Soul indeed is below, this Soul is above, this Soul is to the west and to the east. This Soul is to the south. This Soul is to the north. This Soul indeed is the whole world." (*Chāndogya Upaniṣad* 7.25.2. [16])

"It is not born, nor does it die. It has not come from anywhere, has not become anyone. Unborn, everlasting, eternal, primeval, it is not slain when the body is slain." (*Kaṭha Upaniṣad* 2.18. [17])

The Soul is not affected by the accumulated actions which shape the individuality of the living being. Yet, in contact with individual characteristics, it appears colored by them just as a crystal placed near a China rose appears red.

"He who sees this, who knows this, who understands this, who desires the Soul, who plays with the Soul, who makes love with the Soul, who attains volupty in the Soul, becomes his own master and wanders at will through the worlds. But they who know otherwise are dependent. They dwell in perishable worlds and cannot wander at their will." (*Chāndogya Upaniṣad* 7.25.2. [18])

The "I" and the Self

THERE IS a considerable difference between the notion of the Self or Soul and the entity known as the individuality. The Soul is a continuum which exists within and without all things. The "I" or individuality, on the other hand, is a temporary knot, a "tying together" of different universal faculties in a particular point of consciousness. It is a center within the Self just as any object is a group of energies tied together in a particular location within indefinite space. The Soul can exist independently of the notion of particularized existence, without thought, without individuality; not so the "I," which is the center of the vibrations of thought.

The Realization of the Soul

BEING THE substratum of man's own consciousness, the Soul is the universal substratum easiest for man to reach. The realization of the universal Soul is thus the highest realization accessible to man. The Soul is man's absolute. There is for him no other transcendent reality.

"That Soul is hidden in all things; it does not shine forth, but it can be perceived by the seers with the subtle eyes of the intellect." (*Kaṭha Upaniṣad* 3.12. [19])

The point where the identity of the individual soul and the universal Soul is realized, the point where all living beings unite, is called the "point-limit" (*bindu*). It is the point where space, time, and all the forms of manifestation begin and through which they are ultimately withdrawn. In the order of manifestation, the *bindu* is described as the limit between the universal Consciousness (*cit*), which is passive and extensionless, and the universal Intellect (*buddhi*), which is active and thus requires a sphere of activity, some form of extension.

The "experience of the Soul," identified with the *bindu*, is the point where the universal Being and the individual being unite.

"The Soul is a bridge that links together these worlds so that they may not part. Neither day nor night, nor old age, nor death, nor sorrow, nor good or evil deeds, can cross over that bridge.

"All evils turn back therefrom, for that immense world is free from evil. Therefore, upon crossing that bridge, the blind regain sight, the bound are liberated, those who suffer are freed from pain. Upon crossing that bridge, the night appears as the day; for that immense world is ever luminous." (*Chāndogya Upaniṣad* 8.4.1–2. [20])

"The Soul is not realized through teachings, nor by intellect, nor by learning. It can be reached only by the one who woos it. To him the Soul reveals its form. He who has not renounced action, who is not at peace, who cannot concentrate, who has not silenced his mind, cannot obtain it by mere intelligence." (*Kaṭha Upaniṣad* 2.23–24. [21])

"It cannot be grasped by sight nor by speech, nor by any of the sense organs, nor by penance or deeds. He who meditates and whose nature is purified by knowledge can behold it in its undivided entirety." (*Muṇḍaka Upaniṣad* 3.1.8. [22])

"Hence he who knows this, who is at peace, calm, quiet, patient, sees the Self in himself. He sees the Soul everywhere. Evil does not overcome him; he overcomes all evil. Evil does not burn him; he burns all evils. Free from evil, free from impurity, free from doubt, he becomes a knower of the Immensity." (*Bṛhad-āraṇyaka Upaniṣad* 4.4.23. [23])

Immensity (*brahman*), the Common Substratum

THAT THE three continua may be the different aspects of one further, still more subtle, causal substratum is a hypothesis which can never be verified, since all its elements are beyond the reach of perception and the methods of logical reasoning cannot apply to regions which are beyond the reach of natural laws. This potential, imaginary substratum is spoken of as "the Immensity," the Brahman. It is a prodigious generalization, a most inspiring idea, which became also a dangerous instrument in the development of Hindu thought, indeed of all later religions.

The Immensity, which can be described as the space-time-thought continuum, is the absolute and ultimate stage in which are united existence, the source of spatial form; consciousness or knowledge, the basis of thought; and limitless duration or eternity, the basis of experience or enjoyment. Thus, "the Brahman is indivisible existence, knowledge, and eternity" (*Taittirīya Upaniṣad* 2.1 [24]).

This ultimate principle is beyond the reach of form, of thought, of experience. It is beyond all categories of manifestation, beyond divisible time, beyond divisible space, beyond number, beyond name and shape, beyond the reach of mind and words. It is spoken of as the stage "whence mind and speech, having no hold, fall back" (*Taittirīya Upaniṣad* 2.9 [25]).

There sight cannot go, speech cannot go, nor the mind.
We cannot know, we cannot understand. How can one explain It?
It is other than all that is known. It is above the Unknown.
(*Kena Upaniṣad* 1.3. [26])

This ultimate stage cannot be called either non-Being or Being. It is neither one nor many. We can only define it negatively, saying that it is nothing of what man can know or conceive, neither god, nor man, nor thing. It is thus spoken of as nondual, unknowable, formless, changeless, limitless, etc. It cannot be positive or negative, male or female; hence it is spoken of in the neuter gender.

"Invisible, inactive, beyond grasp, without qualifications, inconceivable, indescribable, it is the essence aimed at through the notion of Self, ever aloof from manifestation. Calm, peaceful, auspicious (*śiva*), it is the nondual, unmanifest Fourth stage [beyond the three stages of existence, gross, subtle, and causal, beyond the three corresponding stages of experience, waking consciousness, dream consciousness, and deep sleep]." (*Māṇḍūkya Upaniṣad* 1.7. [27])

This Immensity, this Void, this Unknown, this nonexistent Absolute, is the innermost nature of everything.

It is the hearing of the ear, the thought of the thinking faculty,
the spoken word of speech, as also the breathing of the breath
and the sight of the eye.

(*Kena Upaniṣad* 1.2. [28])

That which speech cannot express but through which speech is expressed,
that indeed know as the Immensity and not what is here worshiped.
That which thought cannot conceive but through which thought is thought,
that indeed know as the Immensity and not what is here worshiped.
That which sight cannot see but through which sight sees,
that indeed know as the Immensity and not what is here worshiped.
That which hearing cannot hear but through which hearing is heard,
that indeed know as the Immensity and not what is here worshiped.
That which breath cannot breathe but through which breathing is breathed,
that indeed know as the Immensity and not what is here worshiped.

(*Kena Upaniṣad* 1.4–8. [29])

"The sun does not shine there, nor the moon, nor the stars; lightning does not shine there, nor the [earthly] fire. As he shines, everything is illumined after him. The whole world shines by his light." (*Muṇḍaka Upaniṣad* 2.2.10; *Kaṭha Upaniṣad* 5.15. [30])

"It has never begun; one cannot say that it exists nor that it does not exist. . . . All the perceptions of the senses rest upon it, yet it perceives nothing. It knows no connections, yet supports all things. It has no quality, yet it is the enjoyer of all merits.

"External to all things, it dwells in all things, animate or inanimate. It is so subtle that it cannot be grasped. Always near, it is ever beyond reach. Indivisible, it only appears in the fragmentation of life. It feeds all that lives, yet devours it and gives it birth again.

It is the light of lights beyond darkness.
It is both knowledge and the object of knowledge,
which knowledge [*alone*] *can reach,*
and it dwells in the hearts of all.
Thus the field [*of knowing* (*i.e., the mind*)], *knowledge, and the thing to be known*
are spoken of as one.

(*Bhagavadgītā* 13.12, 14–18. [31])

The Three Fundamental Qualities and the Trinity

WHEN—THROUGH the power of illusion, which is its own nature—the first tendency, the first movement, appears in the undifferentiated Immensity, this already implies the existence of three elements: two opposing forces and their opposition. Thus the first stage of manifestation from nonduality is, of necessity, a triad. We shall soon discover that this triad pervades all things and appears in all the aspects of the universe, physical as well as conceptual. These three basic forces or tendencies, known as the three fundamental-qualities (*guṇa*), cannot, in their essence, be directly grasped by the mind. We can only try to understand their nature through the observation of their operation in the different fields of the manifest universe.

In cosmology the three qualities are envisaged as the centripetal-attraction (*ādāna*), the centrifugal-force (*utkrānti*), and their equilibrium (*pratiṣṭhā*), from which originate the revolving impulse and movement of all the spheres.

The centripetal attraction, which creates cohesion, is known as existence (*sattva*), for existence is concentration of energy, a coming together, a power of agglomeration. On the mental plane the power of cohesion appears as the tendency that creates light, oneness. It can be pictured as the attraction toward the Sun of Consciousness, source of light and life. This tendency, which binds the world together, is the preserving tendency personified in Viṣṇu, the All-Pervader, the Preserver of the universe, the embodiment of *sattva.*

The centrifugal force, known as darkness or inertia (*tamas*), is the power that aims at preventing concentration. It is obscurity, since dispersion of energy leads to darkness just as concentration of energy is light. *Tamas,* the centrifugal tendency, the tendency toward dispersion, dissolution, annihilation of all individual, cohesive existence, can be taken as the symbol of dissolution into non-Being, into the unmanifest causal Immensity. It thus represents liberation from all that binds, all that is individual and limited. This tendency, which ever aims at dissociating, destroying the universe, is personified in Rudra, the lord of tears, the destroyer of the worlds, also called Śiva, the lord of sleep, who embodies the abysmal obscurity into which all activity in the end dissolves. "This Great-Lord (Maheśvara) is the innermost nature of all things"[4] (*Liṅga Purāṇa* 1.17.12).

"Ultimately everything arises from disintegration (*tamas*) and ends in disintegration. Because he rules over disintegration and controls it, the lord of sleep is the principle of the universe." (Karapātrī, "Liṅgopāsanā-rahasya," p. 155.)

The balance of *sattva* and *tamas*, of the centripetal and the centrifugal, of cohesion and dispersion, of light and darkness, gives birth to the third tendency, the revolving tendency, known as "activity" or "multiplicity" (*rajas*). It is the source of the endless variety of the forms of the manifest universe.

From *rajas*, from the revolving tendency, comes all motion, all rhythmic division of the continua of space and time, all cerebration or mental activity that is rhythmic division of the thought continuum. This third tendency is the process through which creation in its endless variety of forms takes place in the divine mind. It is personified as the Immense-Being (Brahmā),[5] the Creator, who builds the universe. Brahmā is the source of all rhythms, all forms; he is the thought-form from which the universe rises, the universal Intellect from which springs forth the Golden-Embryo (Hiraṇya-garbha), the world's egg.[6]

Though fundamentally distinct, the three qualities are inseparable and cannot exist without each other. If we stress their unity, we can consider them as the forms of the power of manifestation of the Immensity (*brahman*). We shall see that this manifestation is thought to be a mere appearance and that the three qualities thus constitute the power-of-illusion (*māyā*) of the Immensity.

When manifestation begins, when the whirlpool of illusion first appears, the two other tendencies arise from the state of absolute rest which is the lord of sleep, the *tamas* tendency.

"First there was only [absolute] darkness (*tamas*). Stimulated by quiddity, it became unbalanced, and the form of the revolving-tendency (*rajas*) appeared.

4 *Sarvātmatve maheśvaraḥ.*

5 Brahmā is the nominative singular masculine of Brahman, the personified form of Brahman, the nominative singular neuter of which is Brahma.

6 Cf. *Liṅga Purāṇa* 1.17.12: *Hiraṇyagarbho rajasā.*

Stimulated, this revolving tendency became unbalanced, and out of it the tendency toward disintegration, the centrifugal-tendency (*tamas*), appeared. Stimulated, in its turn it became unbalanced, and the tendency toward cohesion (*sattva*) appeared." (*Maitrāyaṇī Upaniṣad* 5.2. [32])

The conception of the three qualities appears to pertain to the ancient Śaivite tradition. The word *guṇa*, which means "quality," first appears in the particular acceptation of the three fundamental qualities in the *Maitrī Upaniṣad* and the *Śvetāśvatara Upaniṣad*, which are connected with Śaivite philosophy. The word *guṇa* itself seems to have meant originally "part of a whole" or, more concretely, one of the filaments constituting a rope. The word *tri-mūrti*, meaning "trinity" [7] and used to represent the personification of the three qualities as the three gods Brahmā, Viṣṇu, and Śiva, seems to be comparatively recent and never was widely employed.[8]

The Three States of Experience

THE REALIZATION of the three tendencies is linked with that of existence-consciousness-experience. We find again here the three substrata of space, thought, and time. This realization is said to take place, respectively, in the three states of awareness, dream, and deep sleep. Awareness is linked with *rajas*, dream with *sattva*, and deep sleep with *tamas*.

The revolving tendency, *rajas*, which depends on the substratum of space,

7 The symbols connected with the Hindu *trimūrti* are not altogether unconnected with the Christian conception of the Trinity.

Śiva as the ultimate cause is called the Progenitor, the Father. His symbol is the *liṅga*, the organ of procreation. In the notion of "God the Father" the person of the procreator has been substituted for the symbol of procreation.

Viṣṇu as the Protector always descends in the world as an avatar, an incarnation. It is he who ever redeems angels and men when they go astray from their destinies. As such he corresponds to the Son, the God incarnate. Many of the symbolic elements found in the stories relating to the birth of Christ have very near equivalents in the tales of the birth of Kṛṣṇa and other avatars.

The Holy Ghost is represented as the link between the Father and the Son, proceeding from both. A parallel can be made with the *rajas* tendency resulting from the equilibrium of *sattva* and *tamas* and personified as Brahmā.

It might not be difficult to find a historical link between the Trinity and the *trimūrti*. Hindu philosophical conceptions were known in Greece and the Middle East before and after the beginning of the Christian Era. It may, however, be noted that, whereas the Trinity is presented in Scholastic philosophy as a mystery, it is a fundamental definition of Hindu religious philosophy.

8 See L. Renou and J. Filliozat, *L'Inde classique*, I, 518. (Hereafter cited as: Louis Renou, *L'Inde classique*.)

is the origin of all the spheres of perceptible existence. In the state of wakefulness, man experiences existence as depending on relative space and time manifested in the principles-of-the-elements (*tattva*), which are the basis of perceptible forms. This state is thus associated with Brahmā, the Immense Being, the Creator. Action—and more particularly ritual action—is the corresponding way of realization.

In the state of dream, man experiences the centripetal tendency, the substratum of thought, which is the process of manifestation of the world's subtle scheme. The man who dreams behaves like the sleeping Viṣṇu resting on the causal ocean. The corresponding form of realization is through thought, or knowledge.

The sleeping man verily re-creates the world.

"When he goes to sleep, the worlds are his, . . . he becomes a great king, or a learned man; he enters the high and the low. As a great king, taking with him his people, moves around his country as he pleases, even so here, taking with him his senses, he moves around in his own body as he pleases." (*Bṛhad-āraṇyaka Upaniṣad* 2.1.18. [33])

"When a man goes to sleep, he takes along the material of this all-containing world, tears it apart, and builds it up again in his dream, illuminating this inner world with his own light.

"There are no chariots there, no yokes, no roads. But he projects out of himself chariots, yokes, roads. There are no joys there, no happiness, no pleasures. But he projects from himself joys, happiness, pleasures. There are no pools there, no lotus ponds, no streams. But he projects from himself pools, lotus ponds, and streams. For he is the Creator." (*Bṛhad-āraṇyaka Upaniṣad* 4.3.9–10. [34])

Deep sleep, that is, the unconscious state of consciousness, is the blissful causal stage of experience, just as the disintegrating-tendency (*tamas*) is the causal form of the three qualities. Thus wakefulness and dream are said to spring from the obscurity of deep sleep and to fall back into it.

The state of dreamless sleep is connected with Śiva, lord of sleep. It is in nonaction, in the complete silence of the mind, that we may realize the higher states of consciousness, the perfect joy of pure existence. From the standpoint of human realization, Śiva represents the final dissolution of the individuality—and toward this end the metaphysically inclined mind will tend—while the Pervader (Viṣṇu) represents supreme enlightenment, transcendent divine experience, to which all religion aims. Indeed, most religions speak and know of the Viṣṇu principle only.

The Three Qualities and Manifestation

THE SILENCE which is at the origin and the end of manifestation is found at both ends of consciousness, in the supraconscious and the subconscious states. Thus *tamas*, the disintegrating tendency, is said to be the nature of the transcendent faculties, beyond thought, as well as the nature of the unconscious inertia of matter. While dealing with the relative action of the three qualities within the manifest universe we shall meet mainly the inert, subconscious form of *tamas*, since its transcendent aspect is the Unmanifest.

The hierarchy of the three qualities therefore varies according to the standpoint from which they are envisaged. From the point of view of worldly action *tamas* is the lower aspect, *sattva* the higher one. *Tamas* is associated with death, evil, inaction where action alone seems to bring results. Yet from the point of view of spiritual achievement, where action is the main obstacle, *sattva* is the lower state, that which binds with the bonds of merit and virtue, *tamas* is the higher state, that of liberation through nonaction. Thus there are two main paths through which man can escape from the bonds of Nature (*prakṛti*). The lower path, which is the way of merit and its fruits, leads toward concentrated power, toward union with manifest divinity, that is, toward the concepts of Heaven and salvation. On the other hand, the higher path is the path of liberation and nonaction, through which man becomes free from the bonds of individual existence and dissolves into the immensity of Infinite Bliss.

In the process of manifestation more and more complex relations between the three qualities appear. These give rise to different types of existence, different beings, different entities.

"Among the energies of each universe, those energies in which the disintegrating tendency predominates are the source of the world of physical-forms (*bhautika prapañca*). In these lower aspects of existence, some elements of the cohesive and of the revolving tendencies are, however, found. From the cohesive element are formed the inner faculties [9] and the senses of perception; [10]

9 The inner faculties are four:

a. Mind (*manas*), the nature of which is discussion, deliberation.
b. Intellect (*buddhi*), the nature of which is choice or decision.
c. The mental-substance (*citta*), upon which is imprinted memory.
d. I-ness or notion-of-individual-existence (*ahaṁkāra*).

10 There are five senses of perception and five forces of action corresponding to the five elements (ether, air, fire, water, and earth), which are but the spheres of action of the senses.

The senses of perception have as their organs "ear, skin, eye, tongue, and the fifth, the nostril," while the corresponding forces of action have as organs "voice, hands, feet, genitals, and anus."

from the revolving element arise the life breath and the forces of action; from the disintegrating element physical-bodies (*sthūla bhūta*) are formed. Hence from the mainly descending aspect of the universal power the perceptible world springs forth." (Karapātrī, "Śrī Viṣṇu tattva," *Siddhānta*, V, 1944–45, 73.)

The various stages of existence are differentiated by the relative proportions of the three qualities.

Sattva in *sattva*, consciousness within consciousness, is the nature of the Self, the Ātman.

Rajas in *sattva*, existence within consciousness, is Divinity, Īśvara.

Tamas in *sattva*, experience within consciousness, is the nature of the living-being (*jīva*).

Sattva in *rajas*, consciousness within existence, forms the inner-faculties (*antaḥkaraṇa*).

Rajas in *rajas*, existence within existence, forms the life-energies (*prāṇa*).

Tamas in *rajas*, experience within existence, forms the senses (*indriya*).

Sattva in *tamas*, existence within experience, gives rise to the principles-of-the-elements (*mahābhūta*).

Tamas in *tamas*, experience within experience, forms the inanimate world.

One or the other of the three tendencies predominates in each sort of thing, in each kind of being. In angels, ever attracted by the divine light, consciousness predominates. Experience-enjoyment is the main constituent of the spirits of darkness; existence, being activity, predominates in the rulers of creation and in men, whose nature is action.

Hence from the *sattva* part of the Cosmic Being are born the hosts of the gods (*deva*); from the *rajas* part spring forth the lords-of-progeny (Prajāpatis); from the *tamas* part arise the lords-of-destruction (Rudras).

Human beings, according to their nature and their stage of development, are inclined toward these different aspects of the Cosmic Being. Those in whom consciousness is predominant worship the gods (*deva*); those in whom action or existence predominates worship genii (*yakṣa*) and antigods (*asura*); and those in whom enjoyment or sensation predominates worship ghosts and spirits (*bhūta* and *preta*).

In the microcosm, that is, in man, the three qualities are more particularly localized in certain subtle centers. Hence Brahmā (existence) dwells in the heart, the physical center, Viṣṇu (consciousness) in the navel, the subtle center, Śiva (experience) in the forehead, the abstract center, and in the sex center, the center of enjoyment. In the "daily meditation" (*sandhyā*) the three gods are worshiped through mental concentration on their respective centers.

In plants, the physical center is in the root; hence the formula of veneration of the sacred fig tree:

"I bow to the sacred fig tree, to Brahmā in the root, to Viṣṇu in the trunk, and to Śiva in the foliage." (*Aśvattha Stotra* 16. [35])

All moral, mental, and physical impulses in living beings belong to the sphere of Nature, and are the effect of the relative combinations of the three basic tendencies. Thus we can understand that moral values are essentially relative, true only on a certain plane, at a particular moment of our development. All that goes against the preservation of life, that is, all pleasure (self-destruction), passion, cruelty, but also all renunciation and detachment, is of the nature of disintegration (*tamas*). All that goes toward preservation, maintenance, devotion, purity has cohesion (*sattva*) for its nature. All creative impulses spring from the revolving-tendency (*rajas*). Hence those efforts, those qualities, those virtues which take us toward one form of realization take us away from another. Every virtue or vice gets its reward, every good or bad action brings a result,[11] but these results, these rewards, are themselves within the limits of the three qualities. They chain us further within the prison of existence. It is only in nonaction, in the liberation from virtue as well as vice, from good as well as evil, from pleasure as well as pain, that we may be freed from the bondage that carries us endlessly from one world to another, from earth to heavens or hells and again to earth once the fruit of our actions has been enjoyed.

"Having enjoyed these immense heavens, once their [accumulated] merits have been spent, they come back to the world of death and, following the triple path of merit, those seekers of enjoyment keep on coming and going [endlessly]." (*Bhagavadgītā* 9.21. [37])

The Power-of-Illusion (*māyā*)

THE SUBSTRATUM is, of itself, eternally motionless. Yet, if any form is to be, there must appear somewhere a motion, a wave, in the unmoving Immensity.

The power that creates the appearance of a polarization, of a localization of a rhythm—likened to the whirlpool that forms a star in the undifferentiated continuum of ether—is called illusion (*māyā*). This pure movement without substance is represented as the mysterious source of all that is.

The nonsubstantial character of this apparent motion, from which all forms

11 For the average human being, "the fruit of good action is pure and of *sattva*, that of *rajas* is pain, that of *tamas* is ignorance." (*Bhagavadgītā* 14.16. [36])

develop, explains the nature of the universe, which seems to exist though it has ultimately no substance.

The power of illusion may be compared to an introspective-deliberation (*vimarśa*) which would plan things. It may be represented as a "divine thought" of which the universe would be the materialization.

The energy, gross or subtle, by which an all-pervading seer thinks out, that is, creates, all things is named the power of illusion, "the entity that visualized the universe." [12] The conscious centers of energy—the gods and the living beings—and the unconscious ones—the spheres and the atoms of the universe—are all the display of this power.

From the point of view of man "the power of illusion appears to be of two kinds. It is a covering (*āvaraṇa*) which, like a veil, obstructs perception, and it is an evolving (*vikṣepa*) through which the illusion becomes an independent, self-propelling entity. During deep sleep we experience the covering aspect; a veil seems to be cast around the mind, shutting off all experience; there is no perception, and there is nothing that may be characterized as a development." (Upaniṣad Brahmayogin's commentary on *Nṛsiṁha-uttara-tāpinī Upaniṣad* 9.4.)

In the state of dream we experience an evolving which resembles the creative aspect of illusion.

When asked how an illusion can be the substance of the gods and of the cosmos, the Vedāntist replies:

"An illusion is a false appearance, but an appearance is of necessity based on a reality; for no illusory thing can exist without a support, and the reality of the support remains, pervading the illusion. In worshiping the illusion, or its manifestations, one worships the reality behind it, the unknowable Immensity on which it rests." (Karapātrī, "Śrī Bhagavatī tattva," *Siddhānta*, V, 1944–45, 246.)

"O lovely visage: I never said that an illusion is to be worshiped. It is the conscious support of the illusion which deserves worship. Illusion, energy, and other like words merely point to a particularized stage. It is the worship of the Immensity which is aimed at through such words as 'illusion.'" (A Tantra quoted in *Siddhānta*, V, 243. [39])

"An illusion is different from an error. In the Abysmal Immensity, there can be no room for error. The Immense Substratum, which is the only reality, forms the substance of the power of illusion and remains ever interwoven with it." (Karapātrī, "Śrī Bhagavatī tattva," p. 275.)

12 See [38] in the appendix.

Illusion and Ignorance

Māyā is equally the source of the cosmos and of the consciousnesses that perceive it. Both are interdependent. The nonperceived cosmos has no existence and the nonperceiving consciousness no reality.

Manifestation exists only in relation to perception. If none perceived the cosmos, one could not say that it exists. Hence the principles of the senses, like the principles of the elements, are considered the causes of manifestation, the forms of the Creator.

The perceiving consciousness is the necessary corollary of the manifesting power; the living being and the divine Being exist only in relation to one another. Hence the necessity of the individual consciousnesses of the living beings for the creating power, the dependence of the Creator on his creation.

In the microcosm, that is, the manifested individuality, the power-of-illusion (*māyā*) becomes the power-of-ignorance (*a-vidyā*) or un-knowing (*a-jñāna*), the perceiver of the forms of illusion.

"Whether through knowing or through unknowing, all things take their reality from that which perceives them." (Karapātrī, "Śrī Bhagavatī tattva," p. 242.)

The difference between the power-of-illusion (*māyā*) and the power-of-ignorance (*avidyā*) is that through *māyā*, through the cosmic illusion, the manifestation of the universe takes place, the Abysmal Immensity manifests itself in the immense cosmos, while through ignorance centers of perception are formed so that the illusion may be perceived and thus become a relative reality. It is through ignorance (*avidyā*) that individual beings come into existence as distinct entities.

Here unknowing (*ajñāna*) is not mere absence of knowledge but represents a state beyond knowledge, the nature of which is transcendent Being.

"Illusion is the experience of the form of darkness (or unknowing) [by which the substratum is veiled]." (*Nṛsiṁha-uttara-tāpinī Upaniṣad* 9.4. [40])

"Perception veiled by unknowing" [13] is the intrinsic nature of the universe. This is only possible because unknowing is the nature of existence; the non-existent cannot veil. Unknowing, like illusion, is a veil.

"Before creation, perception (*jñāna*) and its object (*artha*)—namely, all that may be perceived (*dṛśya*)—do not exist separately." (Quoted in *Siddhānta*, V, 1944–45, 263. [41])

So long as the power-of-being-seen (*dṛśya-śakti*), that is, the nature of

13 *Ajñānenāvṛtam jñānam* (*Bhagavadgītā* 5.15).

Nature, has not yet arisen, the universal Soul, the Self-of-consciousness (*cid-ātman*), can only think of itself as nonexistent (*asat*).

In such a statement as "None can see me surrounded by the illusion of identity," [14] "me" represents the "I," the first notion of individual-existence (*asmat*), which is the first manifest form of the Abysmal Immensity veiled by unknowing. Hence divinity depicts itself as:

> "I am the unknown" (*aham ajñaḥ*),
> "I do not know myself" (*mām ahaṁ na jānāmi*),
> "I do not know you" (*tvām ahaṁ na jānāmi*).

Unknowing is the source of experience. If unknowing were mere absence of perception, such experience could not take place, for all illusion is based on consciousness.

Nature

THE ESSENTIAL character of manifestation lies thus in the encounter of the perceived and the perceiver, of the power of illusion and that of ignorance, of the cosmos and the living being.

If we envisage Nature (*prakṛti*) as the source of the elaborate structure that constitutes the universe, we must at the same time realize that this structure becomes a "reality" only when perceived by an independent consciousness and that this consciousness becomes "real" only when there is something external to itself to be conscious of. Thus the cosmic Nature and our own nature are interdependent and the term *prakṛti* is used for both.

The word "Nature" (*prakṛti*) is said to mean "that which is transcendent" (*parama*).

"The prefix *pra* means 'higher'; *kṛti* (action) stands for creation. Hence she who in creation is transcendent is the transcendent goddess known under the name of Nature (*prakṛti*)." (*Brahma-vaivarta Purāṇa* 2.1.5. [43])

"Nature (*prakṛti*) is that from which [things] are born." [15] (*Pāṇini Sūtra* 1.4.30.)

"Nature is that which acts constantly. It is the first basis, the state of balance of *sattva*, *rajas*, and *tamas*." (*Sāṅkhya-tattva-kaumudī*, commentary on *Sāṅkhya Kārikā* 3. [44])

"Being the Nature (*prakṛti*) [of things] implies being the immanent cause

14 *Bhagavadgītā* 7.25 [42].
15 *Janikartuḥ prakṛtiḥ*.

[of all things] through the absolute hierarchy [of causes and effects]. It is defined as transcendent action, that is, action in the form of evolution. Nature (*prakṛti*) is often taken as the synonym of Energy (*śakti*), of the Unborn (*ajā*), of the First-Basis (*pradhāna*), of the Nonevolved (*avyakta*), of Disintegration (*tamas*), of Illusion (*māyā*), and of Ignorance (*avidyā*)." (Vijñāna Bhikṣu, *Sāṅkhya-sāra* 1.3. [45])

Creation is born of the power of knowing, more or less veiled by that of action. The veil is thickest in inanimate matter and gradually lighter in plants and mountains, insects, birds, wild and tame animals, in man, in angels and genii, and in gods.

The *Viṣṇu Purāṇa* (6.7.61 [46]) divides the veiling power of Nature (*prakṛti*) into three stages: (1) The transcendent (*parā*), all-pervading power, (2) the power of experiencing or knowing external forms (*kṣetra-jña*), which is the nontranscendent power, the cosmic Intellect, the world-planning process, and (3) a third power, action (*karma*), which is the manifestation of unknowing (*avidyā*).

Ultimately the source of knowledge is ever unknowing (*avidyā*), for this is the only name that can be given to the realization of the unknowable. We shall see that this ultimate power is pictured as a Supreme Goddess (p. 253), source of all that is.

"She whose shape even the Creator and the other gods cannot know is called 'the unknowable' (*ajñeyā*). She whose end cannot be found is called 'the endless' (*anantā*). She who alone is everywhere present is called 'the One' (*ekā*).

"In all knowledge she is the transcendent consciousness; in all voids she is the Void. She, beyond whom there is no beyond, is sung as Beyond-Reach (Durgā)." (*Devī Upaniṣad* 26–27. [47])

The Living Individuality as the Power That Can Oppose Nature

FOR BEINGS whose senses are different from ours the universe is different. It is ultimately within the centers of perception, that is, within the living individuality, that we must search for the reality of the otherwise illusory cosmos.

What we picture as the cosmic or elemental energies must be basically found also in our own beings, for we cannot know of something which is not in ourselves. The heavenly worlds and the lower worlds exist only in so far as they are found in a perceiving mind. It is there that they are experienced. Our effort toward knowing the outside world is limited to the knowledge we can have of ourselves. Our perception of an external world is but a projection of our inner world. Hence the whole pantheon is also a picture of man's inner life. "The Gods represent the inclinations of the senses enlightened by revelation." (Śaṅkarācārya on *Chāndogya Upaniṣad* 1.2.1. [48])

"Whoever departs from this world without having realized his own inner world, to him life has been of no service; it remains unlived, like the unrecited Vedas or any other undone deed." (*Bṛhad-āraṇyaka Upaniṣad* 1.4.15. [49])

The Power of Nature as the Obstacle to Knowledge

AT EVERY stage of manifestation, the causal power appears as the veil of unknowing, as an obstacle to knowledge which prevents the seer from piercing the secret of illusion, from defeating it and reducing the world to nothingness.

"Thus the transcendent-power-of-illusion (*mahāmāyā*) prevents the basis of all, the self-illumined Immensity, from being dis-covered. It forcibly deceives the minds of even the seers soaked in the secret knowledge of the Scripture. In the form of knowledge, it is the source of liberation, while, as ignorance, it is the principle that binds the world together. This power of illusion is represented as the sleep-of-reintegration (*yoga-nidrā*) or as the illusion of identity at the time when, at the end of ages, the power of cohesion goes to sleep upon the coils of the serpent, the remainder (*śeṣa*) of destroyed universes." (Karapātrī, "Śrī Bhagavatī tattva," p. 263.)

Everything in the work of manifestation is intended to create the illusion of multiplicity and to prevent the realization of the basic oneness of all beings, for this would lead to the destruction of the notion of I-ness, which is the power of cohesion that holds together the individual being, the witness that gives reality to the cosmos. Any weakening of the centripetal tendency characteristic of the individuality is contrary to the process of the world's creation. The aim of any creator is to prevent a realization which would destroy his creation. This is why "the Soul is not within the reach of the weak." [16] It has to be conquered by going against all the forces of Nature, all the laws of creation.

Nature is the expression of the Creator's thought; it is the power that creates forms. It is also the power that prevents escape from the world of forms. In his efforts toward liberation man has to overcome all the artifices of Nature, which ever delude him. All revealed knowledge is intended to keep man a manifest individuality. We can therefore understand why all the rules of social morality, all the forms of worldly and sacred knowledge, all the bonds of religion and its rites, seem basically intended to take man away from the path of liberation through the promise of heavenly bliss or pleasures or other advantages.

16 *Nāyam ātmā balahīnena labhyaḥ.* (*Muṇḍaka Upaniṣad* 3.2.4.)

All our means of perception are oriented outward. Like insects attracted by a flame, we are attracted by the sights and sounds of the external world that are intended to prevent us from looking inward.

"[The uncreated Creator], the Self-born (*svayambhū*), pierced the openings [of the senses] outward. Therefore man looks outward, not within.

"Once a wise man, seeking immortality, looked inwardly and beheld the Soul face to face." (*Kaṭha Upaniṣad* 4.1. [50])

When the yogi, the seeker of liberation, makes some headway in his attempt to free himself from all bonds, Nature offers him new abilities, new temptations, new achievements, to bring him back into her power. Each of the qualities of Nature, instead of being a way toward liberation, becomes an instrument of bondage.

"O sinless Arjuna! The power-of-cohesion (*sattva*), whose purity illumines all things, binds men through the attraction of joy, through the illusion of knowledge.

"O son of Kuntī! The power-of-action (*rajas*) is attachment, born with desire. It binds the living through the bonds of action.

"Know the power-of-disintegration (*tamas*) to spring from ignorance; it misguides all living beings and binds them, O scion of Bharata! through carelessness, laziness, and sleep." (*Bhagavadgītā* 14.6–8. [51])

All worship is intended to keep man within the bonds of manifestation, of which the gods are the basic energies.

"Whoever worships any divinity other than the Immensity, thinking 'He is one and I another,' he knows not. He is like cattle for the gods. Just as many animals would be of service to a man, so also each living being is of service to the gods. If even one animal is taken away it is not pleasant. What, then, if many? Therefore it is not pleasing to the gods that men should know this." (*Bṛhad-āraṇyaka Upaniṣad* 1.4.10. [52])

The Fundamental Duality

WHEN looked at from the point of view of manifestation, the substratum—that is, the Immensity—appears as one of the two elements of a duality. It is then called a Person (*puruṣa*) and is considered male. The manifestation of the Person is known as Nature (*prakṛti*), which is the second of these elements, and is considered female.[17]

17 "The word *puruṣa* (person) is defined as *puruṣaḥ sarvapūraṇāt puri śayanāc-ca*, 'that which fills' (*pūraṇa*) all, or 'that which dwells in a [bodily] city' (*pura*)." (Śaṅkarācārya's commentary on the *Chāndogya Upaniṣad* 3.12.6.)

The Person acts according to its nature.

"Limited by the power of my own power and compelled by my Nature, I create, again and again, these conglomerations of elements. Ruled by my law, the power of Nature gives birth to the animate and inanimate worlds." (*Bhagavadgītā* 9.8, 10. [53])

One cannot really distinguish a person from its nature or its power. Person and Nature, though distinct, remain ever inseparable as the two aspects of one thing. This dual unity appears in every form of their manifestation.

Every aspect of the cosmos or of the cosmic consciousness has thus to be represented in a dual form; hence every god is shown as having a consort or energy inseparable from himself.

The Immensity is coupled with illusion, the power-of-disintegration (Śiva) with energy (Śakti), the power-of-cohesion (Viṣṇu) with multiplicity (Lakṣmī), the power-of-creation (Brahmā) with knowledge (Sarasvatī).

When dealing with the Hindu trinity and with the forms of the Goddess we shall see the significance of these various entities.

Some systems of philosophy consider the manifesting energy as more fundamental than the underlying continuum. This leads to religious forms where Supreme Divinity is considered female. God is woman. Such systems are known as Śākta, cults of Energy.

"God" (Īśvara) and the Illusion of Divine Unity

THE NOTION of duality is applicable only to what is already multiple, since the first manifestation of the nondual implies a trinity. Unity appears merely as the global apprehension of seven concepts, which are the three aspects of the trinity and their respective natures or powers, all envisaged as one unit and again identified with the substratum of Immensity, itself beyond number. The notion of divine unity is therefore a fiction, a mental construction which is merely a projection of the living notion of individuality into the causal complex, a shaping of "god" to the image of man. Hence "God (Īśvara) becomes [likened to] a 'particular individual' (*puruṣa*) in whom would be found no trace of pain nor expectation and who would not be affected by his own deeds." (*Yoga Sūtra* 1.24. [54])

This imagined unity of "God," being a projection from the manifest stage, is an illusion, just as is the oneness of the human individuality—which is but the knot tying together the various faculties. The notion of God leads inevitably to a new duality, a distinction between a Divine Being and his creation. The oneness of "God" may be envisaged only in the sense in which a family can be spoken of as one unit. As soon as we want to have any dealing with the family we find that it cannot be done; we have to face the personality of each member separately or together. Thus in the field of manifestation, as in that of realization, it is the trinity and the multiplicity derived from it which can be experienced. In any form of ritual, of prayer, of mystical experience, man can approach only one of the manifest aspects, one of the several "gods"; never can he reach the vague Immensity, which, in any case, could bring him no comfort but that of nonexistence.

The oneness or interdependence of the three fundamental tendencies, considered as one entity, is known as Īśvara, "the Lord," and is the notion from which is derived the simplified monistic idea of God.

God is the state of balance of the three qualities and as such is the form attributed to illusion.

In later mythology, the Lord (Īśvara) is called Bhagavān, the All-Powerful. This term, which probably originally merely meant "the one who receives his share" and referred to one entitled to a full share in the tribal property, came to be a polite expression referring to any dignitary, to any god, but particularly to a ruler or a sovereign deity. It is used even today as a polite term of address for holy men.

According to the *Viṣṇu Purāṇa* (6.5.74–76 [55]): "The six powers, absolute-might (*aiśvarya*), righteousness (*dharma*), glory (*yaśas*), beauty (*śrī*), knowledge (*jñāna*), and nonattachment (*vairāgya*), are called *bhaga* (shares). The 'Changeless Being' represented by the syllable *va* is the name given to the embodiment of the notion that beings dwell in the universal Soul, which in its turn dwells in all beings.

"O Maitreyī! thus does this great word *bhagavān* properly represent the Being who is the supreme Immensity, the resplendent Indweller, and none other."

"He who understands the rise and dissolution, the coming and going, the wisdom and ignorance, of all beings should be called 'Bhagavān.' " (*Viṣṇu Purāṇa* 6.5.78. [56])

Life as the One Deity

IN THE *Bṛhad-āraṇyaka Upaniṣad* (3.4.1.), the principle of life, or life-breath (*prāṇa*), is spoken of as the inner Self of all deities. Without life, there can be no individual perceiver, no witness, hence no reality to the appearance of the cosmic manifestation. Life is the manifestation of "existence" envisaged as a "boundless form of reality (*satya*) and knowledge (*jñāna*)" and is the one Supreme Being.

All the verses of the Veda can be said to be directly or indirectly but the praise of life. All the gods are the sharers of existence. All the names of divinities are but the different names of life.

The Relationship of "God" and the Universe

IF WE accept the indefinite term "God" to represent the source of the subtle and supramental stages of the physical, mental, and intellectual spheres that we perceive or believe we perceive, we find that the relationship of this "God" with the world can be of six kinds; these are: "(*a*) 'God' is in the world; (*b*) the world is in 'God'; (*c*) the world is 'God'; (*d*) the world and 'God' are distinct; (*e*) 'God' is distinct from the world, but the world is not distinct from 'God'; (*f*) it cannot be said whether the world is distinct from 'God' or not." [57])

We can replace the word "God" by the word "cause" or any other word that suits our thinking habits, and then we see that these definitions cover the main possibilities of relationship. That these different relationships can coexist is illustrated in a traditional example in terms of thread and cloth.

a. There is thread in a cloth.

b. Cloth is in thread (within the sphere of thread).

c. Cloth is thread.

d. Yet cloth is different from thread.

e. Thread has an existence independent from that of cloth, but cloth has no existence independent from thread.

f. None can say whether cloth and thread are distinct things or not.

From these distinct conceptions are derived different forms of approach, all of which are valid, although they may appear contradictory. These different approaches are the basis of the different religious forms, as they are the subjects of the different theological and philosophical approaches.

The Causal Word

SPEECH HAS the power to evoke images and ideas. The process through which a thought, at first indistinct, gradually becomes definite and exteriorizes itself is similar to the process through which the divine thought becomes the universe. The difference is only one of degree. If our power of thought, our power of expression, was greater, things we speak of would actually appear. With our limited powers only their image is evoked. Speech can therefore be represented as the origin of all things. The cosmos is but the expression of an idea, a manifested utterance. Supreme Divinity can be represented as the causal word (*śabda-brahman*).

The process of the manifestation of speech, like that of the universe, takes place in four stages. First, in the undifferentiated substratum of thought, an intention appears. Gradually this intention takes a precise shape. We can visualize what the idea is, though it is not yet bound to a particular verbal form and we are still searching for words to express it. This is the second stage of the manifestation of the idea. Then we find words suitable to convey our thought. This transcription of the idea in terms of words in the silence of the mind is the third stage, the fourth being the manifestation of the idea in terms of perceptible sounds. These four stages are known as the four forms of the word.

"The place [where the idea originates], the instrument [which permits its manifestation], the first impulse [toward thought], the self-radiant consciousness wherein there is no differentiation into words, is the 'voice beyond' (*parā-vāc*).

"The first mental impulse, like a shoot springing from an invisible seed, is the 'voice that sees' (*paśyantī*) [literally, 'seeing'; this is the stage where the idea is visualized].

"The potential sound, which is the vehicle of the thought, is the 'intermediary voice' (*madhyamā*) [the stage where the idea takes a yet-silent verbal form].

"The exteriorized sound in the form of articulate syllables is the 'voice manifest' (*vaikharī*)." (Karapātrī, "Śrī Bhagavatī tattva.")

According to Mallinātha: "*Vaikharī* manifests the words, *madhyamā* is seen through the mind, *paśyantī* throws light on the idea; the subtle voice is [identical with] the undifferentiated causal Immensity." (Commentary on the *Kumārasaṁbhava* of Kālidāsa 2.17. [58])

"Through the voice manifest only the external form of knowledge can be transmitted. It is a valid form of knowledge but an approximate and perishable one." (Yogatrayānanda, *Śrī Rāmāvatāra kathā*, p. 34.)

Similarly the external world, the visible manifestation of the causal word, is the only perishable aspect of creation.

"The three lower stages of manifestation are symbolized as the three sides of a triangle which represents the divine thought, the source of existence. These three stages correspond to the power-of-will (*icchā-śakti*), the power-of-knowledge (*jñāna-śakti*), and the power-of-action (*kriyā-śakti*), also spoken of as intention, formulation, and expression. [We shall see that these are but the forms of the three fundamental qualities, *tamas*, *sattva*, and *rajas*, personified as Śiva, Viṣṇu, and Brahmā.]

"The center of the triangle, the undifferentiated notion, assimilated to *parā-vāc*, is the unmanifest Fourth stage. This triangle with its center becomes a complete symbol of divinity (*īśvara*) conceived as the principle-of-speech (*śabda-brahman*) or the word-principle (*vāc-tattva*)." (Rāmacandra Śankara Takkī, "Parā aur aparā Śakti," *Kalyāṇa*, Śakti aṅka, p. 477.)

The theory of the "creative word" and the "revealed word," the Veda, is derived from this conception of the manifestation of ideas.

The realization of the word principle by going back along the path of its manifestation is one of the essential practices of yoga.

The deeper we go in the search for the causal word, the more language becomes meaningful. At the end of the quest we find the first manifestation of articulate language, the monosyllable AUM,[18] which is said to include all language and all meaning. AUM is the seed from which speech is derived, the nutshell containing the whole of wisdom. The four Vedas are merely the commentaries on this infinitely meaningful syllable, which corresponds to the ultimate attainment, the Fourth stage, representing the cosmic law or unmanifest Veda.

"AUM is the one eternal syllable of which all that exists is but the development. The past, the present, and the future are all included in this one sound, and all that exists beyond the three forms of time is also implied in it." (*Māṇḍūkya Upaniṣad* 1.1. [59])

"AUM is the one indestructible [sound], the Immensity. He who, his mind intent upon me [Kṛṣṇa], abandons his body and leaves the world uttering this syllable attains the supreme purpose of his destiny." (*Bhagavadgītā* 8.13. [60])

"Through speech alone, O King, can relationship be known. The 'Knowledge of Meters' (*Ṛg Veda*), the 'Knowledge of Contents' (*Yajur Veda*), the 'Knowledge of Extension' (*Sāma Veda*),[19] and the 'Knowledge of Subtle

18 The sound AUM is made of the guttural *A*, the labial *U*, and the nasal *M*, forming the triangle which physically delimits all the possibilities of articulation.

19 *Sāmans* (or *Sāma* when used with the term *Veda*) represent the part of the Vedas that is sung. Depending on the co-ordinates of rhythm and scale, considered

Correspondences' (*Atharva*) [or 'Magic Lore'] of the Aṅgirases, history, myths, science, and the secret knowledge, the hymns of praise, the wise sayings, the additional commentaries and explanations, the rites of sacrifice and oblation, food and drink, this world and the other, and all the beings within them are known through speech." (*Bṛhad-āraṇyaka Upaniṣad* 4.1.2. [61])

We shall meet again the theory of the manifestation of the Word in the philosophy of Śaivism, and also when dealing with the aspects of Śiva, with the goddess of speech, and with the *mantras*.

Dangers of Applied Metaphysics

THOUGH some of the Upaniṣads use the names of the different continua as almost equivalent expressions, their unity remains a speculation, a cosmic projection of man's self-centered individuality. We imagine that, at the other end of the cosmic hierarchy, there might exist an all-inclusive entity who can say "I," who can consider all the gods and all the spheres as part of himself. This speculation, ever impossible to substantiate, has to be regarded as an abstraction without possible connection with the spheres of action. The theory of the substrata is therefore a forbidden subject, meant only for those who can play with ideas without trying to put them into practice.

"Verily, a father may explain this Immensity to his eldest son, or to a devoted pupil, but to no one else." (*Chāndogya Upaniṣad* 3.11. [62])

The idea of a substratum or that of divine unity as applied to religion and morals was considered as fraught with danger because its expression was of necessity inaccurate. Such notions should have no place in practical religion.

The application of the metaphysical notion of divine unity to the spheres of religion and human behavior would, according to Hindu ideas, form part of what is known as *anadhikāra vedānta*, "the end of knowledge as visualized by the nonqualified." A traditional example of the absurdity it may lead to is given in the following reasoning: "All beings are parts of the Self; their difference is purely illusory, hence there is no difference between a wife, a mother, a daughter; we can behave with all of them in the same way." In this case we easily notice the inadequacy of the argument, yet when it is applied to other categories of what we know we readily accept it. A great part of modern sects,

characteristics of time and space, they are taken as symbols of extension, giving dimension, because there is extension or prolongation of a syllable when it is sung.

The cosmological principle of extension is, however, represented by the term *rajas* since *rajas* is the dimension-creating movement resulting from the opposition of *sattva* (cohesion) and *tamas* (dispersion).

in India as elsewhere, base their doctrines on a similar confusion of planes. Many political and social theories of our age are based on this type of ill-adapted reasoning. Almost every time the modern man refers to "God" he is, from the Hindu point of view, confusing planes, and is thus both mistaken and sacrilegious.

The Cosmic Being

Macrocosm and Microcosm

When the universe is identified with the Cosmic Being, it is not the physical universe only that is meant but the entire universe with its mind, its guiding energies, the laws which rule its development, and the consciousness which pre-exists its appearance. The perceptible world of forms is no more the whole of the cosmos than his visible limbs and organs are the whole of a man.

"Those who consider the sun merely as a sphere and know nothing of the life that animates it, those who see the sky and the earth as two worlds but do not know their presiding consciousness, possess, indeed, a limited knowledge. A science which studies only the inanimate part of things and does not reach their inner life, their presiding consciousness, is incomplete and leads to no stable knowledge." (Vijayānanda Tripāṭhī, "Devatā tattva," *Sanmārga,* III, 1942, 682.)

There is an inner life, an inner consciousness, ruling every aspect of existence, every form of Nature (*prakṛti*). Different deities, which are aspects of the cosmic consciousness, govern the movements of the stars as well as the functioning of our bodies. The technique of introspection known as yoga appears to have been a remarkable instrument for the investigation of what we may call the cosmic world. Yet the yogi is not usually able to translate his vision in terms of words. The obstacle to any attempt at describing the cosmos is not merely a difficulty of experience but one of expression.

In the state of suprasensorial identification reached through the practice of yoga, the adept can passively witness worlds different from his own, but may not have the means of elaborating mentally or describing with word-symbols based on human experience things for which he has no terms of comparison. Imprisoned in his body, man has no other means of reference than comparison with the impressions his senses and his mind convey to him. Yet sensorial impressions are fragmentary and delusive. His inner universe alone is really within man's reach. Only by analogy with its own forms can the mind depict what lies beyond itself. The outward world is but an appearance, a reflected image; the only thing real is the mirror. This is why the formulation of knowledge can go only as far as the seeker possesses an articulate knowledge of his own self.

Because of this limitation of all knowledge to the limits of the knowledge the knower has of himself, there appears to be a strict equivalence at every stage between the structure of man himself and the structure of the universe as he can perceive or conceive it. It is therefore but logical to depict the universe as a greater man with a body, subtle faculties, and a guiding spirit. The Upaniṣads describe the Cosmic Being as a man with eyes and ears and a mind and a life breath. This may be a mere analogy, but we have no means of ever devising a more accurate one. On the other hand, we can picture our own being as a miniature universe, and find within our body the "sun," the "moon," the "earth," the "elements." Any conception we can have of man and of the universe is but a reciprocal reflection of one upon the other.

Man is the fragmentary-universe (*vyaṣṭi*) or microcosm (*kṣudra brahmāṇḍa*) (literally, the "small egg of the Immensity"), and the Cosmic Being is the universe-totality (*samaṣṭi*), the macrocosm or "Egg of the Immensity" (*brahmāṇḍa*).

Man and the universe appear as two parallel beings similar to one another. The Vedas, as interpreted by tradition, compare them to a pair of birds.

"Two birds, beautiful of wing, inseparable friends, dwell together on the same tree (the universe). One of them (the individual being) eats the fruit [of action], the other (the universal Being) looks on but does not eat." (*Ṛg Veda* 1.164.20; *Muṇḍaka Upaniṣad* 3.1.1; *Śvetāśvatara Upaniṣad* 4.6. [63])

Like the Total Being, the living being is eternal, "unborn, everlasting, abiding, ancient, not slain though the body be slain" (*Bhagavadgītā* 2.20 [64]).

Man's body is "a city with eleven doors, in which dwells the faultless Consciousness, the Unborn. He who rules over it is free from pain and, when he leaves it, attains liberation" (*Kaṭha Upaniṣad* 5.1 [65]).

Man, as seen by himself, occupies a central place in creation, for he is alleged to be the only being morally responsible for his actions, a responsibility which neither angels nor beasts have to bear. The state of man is thus called the "womb of action" (*karma-yoni*), and man's actions and thoughts have a creative power similar to that of the actions and thoughts of the Divine. In this respect also man is likened to the Cosmic Being. "That which is I is he, that which is he is I." [66]

The potentiality of the whole is contained in each fragment. Hence, "They are in me and I in them" (*Bhagavadgītā* 9.29 [67]).

All the higher stages of being can be reached through either of the two parallel orders of manifestation, the macrocosm or the microcosm.

"What is here is there, what is there is here; he wanders from death to death who sees a difference." (*Kaṭha Upaniṣad* 4.10. [68])

The Cosmic Being, totality of all beings, is itself a being. Its constituent elements, its intellect, its mind, work like those of individual beings. It dies and is reborn. It is the universe, and the universe is its form. The Cosmic Being is not a personal deity who creates out of nothingness. It creates and destroys because that is its nature, its life, just as man's blood creates new cells, his hair grows, or his stomach digests other forms of life.

As a spider emits and draws in its thread,
as plants grow upon the earth,
as the hairs of the head and body spring forth on a living being,
so from the Imperishable arises everything here.

(*Muṇḍaka Upaniṣad* 1.1.7. [69])

The manifestation of the Cosmic Being appears, from the point of view of man, to take place within three distinct yet correlated orders. One is a successive order implying some form of duration; the second is a matter of relative location implying some form of space; the third is an order of perception implying degrees of consciousness and therefore stages of manifestation.

Cosmic Duration

THE COSMIC-PERSON (*puruṣa*) is the inactive or male aspect of a duality. It is through his active or female counterpart, spoken of as his Nature (*prakṛti*), that he manifests himself. Person and Nature are inseparable complements of one another, and every form of creation will bear the sign of this duality.

A person is an entity which lasts through different stages of development. The person, *puruṣa*, is therefore dependent upon the substratum of duration.

From the point of view of duration, the Total Being, or Cosmic Whole, can be divided into three sections, called the "Impermanent," the "Enduring," and, further beyond time, the "Changeless."

The Impermanent includes the perceptible and the subtle worlds. The Enduring is the body of permanent laws which rule the appearance, existence, and

THE STRUCTURE OF THE COSMOS: DURATION

<table>
<tr><th>THE COSMIC BEING</th><th colspan="5">manifest as Duration</th></tr>
<tr><td>The Cosmic Whole (samaṣṭi)</td><td colspan="5">The Transcendent-Self (paramātman)</td></tr>
<tr><td>THE CHANGELESS-PERSON
(avyaya puruṣa)
is called
the lord-of-progeny (Prajāpati)
or the Driver (Paśupati)
and is the substratum of the universe</td><td colspan="5">Perception (jñāna); Timeless-Eternity (kālātīta)</td></tr>
<tr><td rowspan="5">THE INDESTRUCTIBLE-PERSON
(akṣara puruṣa)
or
the Enduring
represents
THE INDESTRUCTIBLE PERMANENT LAWS
of the universe
and is called

Manifest-Divinity or "God" (īśvara)
or the "reins" (pāśa)</td><td colspan="5">Transcendent-Nature (parā prakṛti)
(i.e., the life breath of the Changeless Person)
is
activity (kriyā), principle of limitless-undivided-Time (akaṇḍa-kāla),
manifest as</td></tr>
<tr><td>Action</td><td>Life</td><td colspan="3">Energy</td></tr>
<tr><td>inner-impulse
(antaścara)</td><td>indweller
(antaryāmin)</td><td>heart
(hṛdaya)</td><td>transmigrant-self
(sūtrātman)</td><td>outer-impulse
(bahiścara)</td></tr>
<tr><td>Brahmā</td><td>Viṣṇu</td><td>Indra</td><td>Soma</td><td>Agni</td></tr>
<tr><td>rajas</td><td>sattva</td><td colspan="3">Maheśvara; tamas</td></tr>
<tr><td rowspan="3">THE DESTRUCTIBLE-PERSON
(kṣara puruṣa)
or the Impermanent is
the Evolving (vikāra),
i.e., the apparent form of the universe,
and is twofold,
the "driven animal" (paśu)
and
the "moving one" (jagat)</td><td colspan="5">Nontranscendent-Nature (aparā prakṛti)
is
substance (artha), principle of divisible-time (kāla),
manifest as</td></tr>
<tr><td>life-breath
(prāṇa)</td><td>primeval-
waters (ap)</td><td>the word
(vāc)</td><td>the devouring
(annāda)</td><td>the devoured
(anna)</td></tr>
<tr><td>rajas</td><td>sattva</td><td colspan="3">tamas</td></tr>
</table>

end of the Impermanent. The Changeless is the substratum beyond manifestation, beyond change, beyond particularized existence.

The Impermanent aspect of the Cosmic Being is known as the Destructible-Person (*kṣara puruṣa*); the Enduring, or permanent, aspect is the Indestructible-Person (*akṣara puruṣa*); the substratum is the Changeless-Person (*avyaya puruṣa*).

To these three persons are related the three constituent elements of existence: substance (*artha*), activity (*kriyā*), and perception (*jñāna*).

"The Changeless Person is the shelter of all that exists but remains itself beyond activity and beyond substance. It is not the world nor its creator but the common origin of both, the source of both the efficient and the immanent causes of manifestation." (Giridhara Sarmā Caturvedi, "Siva mahimā," *Kalyāṇa*, Siva aṅka, p. 46.)

"Do not think of me as the creator [of this and other worlds]. I am changeless and create nothing." (*Bhagavadgītā* 4.13. [70]) "In me all beings stand; I am not within them and they are not in me." (Ibid. 9.4–5. [71])

"He is not their cause nor their effect." (*Svetāśvatara Upaniṣad* 6.8. [72])

The permanent body of universal laws by which all the forms of manifestation are ruled is called the Indestructible Person. It is the permanent frame within which the universe develops. This power that plans the future course of the planets as well as the growth of a blade of grass before their coming into existence can be identified with the primordial energy, the universal motor, or with manifest Divinity (*īśvara*). This power is the Transcendent-Nature (*parā prakṛti*) of the Changeless Person and is represented as its life-breath (*prāṇa*).

Each attempt at understanding the nature of the universe is a search for the Indestructible Person. The mere observation of changing forms cannot constitute knowledge. Knowledge is the perception of the changeless, permanent laws which rule the forms' evolution.

"He who looks for that which evolves cannot see the higher nature of things. Like a child, he does not understand. The man of [higher] vision understands easily." (*Mahābhārata* 12.215.26. [73])

The Indestructible Person is the power (*bala*) that appears when the latent energies of the Changeless Person bind themselves together. As such, it is the first individuality, for an individuality is a point where different forms of energy are tied together. From the point of view of perception this relationship appears to be inverted and we have the notion of a "Self endowed with power" (*ātma-śakti*) rather than a "power endowed with individuality."

This power of the Indestructible Person is the efficient cause of the universe.

It appears under three forms, energy, life, and action. Potential power, that is, power as it exists in the state of deep sleep, is energy; active power, power ready to act, as it exists in thought or dream, is life (*prāṇa*); applied power, that is, power as used in the state of being awake, is action (*kriyā*). Thus, we live in dream but do not act, we exist in dreamless sleep but do not live.

The Indestructible Person can further be divided into five main constituent aspects, known as the inner impulse, the indweller, the heart, the outer impulse, and the transmigrant self.

The inner-impulse (*antaścara*) is a tendency toward self-expression, toward manifestation. It corresponds to the revolving tendency and is thus a form of Brahmā, the Immense Being.

The indweller (*antaryāmin*) represents the cosmic power latent in all forms of existence. It corresponds to the cohesive or centripetal tendency and is thus a form of Viṣṇu, the Pervader.

The heart (*hṛdaya*) is the center from which emanate the natural laws that rule all things. It corresponds to Indra, the heavenly ruler.

The outer-impulse (*bahiścara*), the perceptible activity found in all individual-bodies (*piṇḍa*), takes the form of a combustion identified with Agni (Fire).

The transmigrant-self (*sūtrātman*) is the substance consumed by activity. It is identified with Soma, the offering, the seed.

The three last aspects of the Indestructible Person, when envisaged together, are called Maheśvara (the transcendent Lord) or Siva, the lord of sleep. They are the forms of the disintegrating or centrifugal tendency (*tamas*).

The transient outward form of the universe is the Destructible-Person (*kṣara puruṣa*). This aspect of the Cosmic Being is also known as "that which evolves" (*vikāra*) or as the "moving universe" (*jagat*). This is the nontranscendent-Nature (*aparā prakṛti*) of the Changeless Person. It is fivefold: the life-breath (*prāṇa*), the primeval-waters (*ap*), the word (*vāc*), the devouring (*annāda*), and the devoured (*anna*). These five aspects of the Destructible Person are the outer expression of the five entities constituting the Indestructible Person.

Thus the life breath is the manifestation of the inner impulse, that is, of the Creator, Brahmā.

The primeval waters pervading all substance are the manifestation of the indweller, of the all-pervading Viṣṇu.

The word is the manifestation of the heart, where lies the Law or its personification, the ruler Indra.

The devouring is the manifestation of the outer impulse, that is, Fire (Agni).

The devoured is the manifestation of the transmigrant self or life-monad, which is Soma, the offering, the victim, the seed of life.

Cosmic Location

FROM THE point of view of location, the Cosmic Being appears to manifest itself on three planes, in three orders of things, corresponding to the different channels through which it is perceived. These three planes are called the celestial or angelic (*ādhidaivika*), the individual or subtle (*ādhyātmika*), and the elemental or sensorial (*ādhibhautika*) planes.

These three planes coexist and interpenetrate one another. Each is divided into five concentric spheres (*maṇḍala*).

On the spiritual plane the five spheres are known as:

1. The Self-born (*svayambhū*), which is the creative aspect of the Changeless Person.
2. The Supreme-Ruler (*parameṣṭhin*), that is, the Nature (*prakṛti*) of the Self-born.

Taken together, the Self-born and the Supreme Ruler constitute the lord-of-progeny (Prajāpati), who is equivalent to the Driver or Herdsman (Paśupati) of Śaivism.

3. The sun (*sūrya*), the origin of all evolution, source of all that exists in a given universe, is the fiery principle.
4. The moon (*candra*), the end of all evolution, is the offering (*soma*). It is the devoured, the substance on which the fiery solar principle lives.

Taken together, the sun and the moon constitute the cosmic sacrifice; their relationship is the nature of all the forms of life. They are considered the spatial equivalent of the Indestructible Person and are spoken of as the "reins" (*pāśa*) in Śaivite philosophy.

5. The earth (*pṛthivī*) is the substance, the driven-animal (*paśu*), the spatial aspect, of the Destructible Person.

The cosmic spheres are alternately of the nature of Agni and Soma, devouring and being devoured, consuming and being consumed. The Self-born is fiery, hence the Supreme Ruler is fuel, the sun is fiery, the moon is fuel, the earth is fiery.

In each of the spheres one of the five components of the Indestructible Person is predominant and the sphere is called the "dwelling place" of that particular aspect.

In the sphere of the Self-born dwells Brahmā, the Creator. In the sphere of the Supreme Ruler dwells Viṣṇu, the Pervader. In the solar sphere dwells Indra, the celestial ruler. In the earthly sphere rules Agni, the lord of fire. In the lunar sphere is Soma, the offering.

Each of the spheres is an emanation from the previous one. In the order of creation the moon is the last born, although from the point of view of reintegration, the point of view of man, the lunar sphere is between the earth and the sun.

On the individual (*ādhyātmika*) plane, the five spheres are:

1. The nonevolved (*avyakta*), that is, consciousness.
2. The transcendent-principle (*mahat*), that is, intellect.

These two form the Herdsman (Paśupati), who controls the herd of manifest beings, and are aspects of the Changeless Person.

3. Mental-knowledge (*vijñāna*).
4. Intuitive-knowledge (*prajñāna*).

These two form the "reins" (*pāśa*) which control all life, and are aspects of the Indestructible Person.

5. The body (*śarīra*) is the driven-animal (*paśu*), the individual form of the Destructible Person.

On the elemental (*ādhibhautika*) plane the five spheres are related to the five elements:

1. The cave (*guhā*) is the space within which a given universe develops. Because space is a quality of ether (*ākāśa*), and wherever there is ether there is space and the possibility of physical location, ether-space is the first condition for the manifestation of existence. Only within ether are things called "real" (*satya*). The cave, the space that is inside the heart, is the dwelling place of consciousness. Ether is the sphere-of-perception of the sense of hearing. The cave is thus the center of hearing and consequently of knowledge revealed.
2. The primeval-waters (*ap*) form the causal substance, the nature of which is intellect. This is the realm of Varuṇa, the sphere of the gods, associated with the element air. Air is the sphere-of-perception of the sense of touch. Earthly waters are fundamentally distinct from the primeval waters, sphere of the sense of touch.

The cave and the primeval waters are the forms of the Changeless, the Herdsman.

THE STRUCTURE OF THE COSMOS: LOCATION

THE COSMIC BEING		*manifest as Location*		
The Cosmic Whole (*samaṣṭi*)		The Transcendent-Immensity (*para brahman*) and illusion (*māyā*), the dormant seed, manifest on the celestial-plane (*ādhidaivika*)	individual-plane (*ādhyātmika*)	elemental-plane (*ādhibhautika*)
		Germinating-Potentiality (*ucchūnāvasthā*)		
THE CHANGELESS-PERSON (*avyaya puruṣa*) is called the lord-of-progeny (Prajāpati) or the Driver (Paśupati) and is the substratum of the universe	*RAJAS*	1. The Self-born (*svayambhū*) is Brahmā (Extension personified), the creative aspect of the Changeless	1. The Nonevolved (*avyakta*) is universal Consciousness, inclination to awaken	1. The cave (*guhā*) is the source of hearing (i.e., knowledge revealed) and the element ether
		The Point-Limit (*bindu*) or Self (*ātman*)		
		The Resulting-Stage (*kāryāvasthā*)		
THE INDESTRUCTIBLE-PERSON (*akṣara puruṣa*) or the Enduring represents THE INDESTRUCTIBLE PERMANENT LAWS of the universe and is called Manifest-Divinity or "God" (*īśvara*) or the "reins" (*pāśa*)	*SATTVA* The lord-of-progeny (Prajāpati) or the Driver (Paśupati)	2. The Supreme-Ruler (*parameṣṭhin*) is Viṣṇu (Pervasiveness) or the Nature (*prakṛti*) of the Self-born	2. The universal-principle (*mahat*) of manifestation is Intellect (*buddhi*) or analytical consciousness	2. The primeval-waters (*ap*) are the source of touch and the element air

		Individuality (*aham-tattva*)			
THE DESTRUCTIBLE-PERSON (*kṣara puruṣa*) or the Impermanent is the Evolving (*vikāra*) i.e., the apparent form of the universe, and is twofold, the "driven animal" (*paśu*) and the "moving one" (*jagat*)	*TAMAS* Abode of Maheśvara (the Arch-Sovereign), i.e., Power personified	3. The sun (*sūrya*), abode of Indra (the celestial fire)	The Cosmic Sacrifice	3. Mental-knowledge (*vijñānātman*) Mind (*manas*)	3. Light (*jyotis*), source of sight, of mental perception, and of the element fire
		4. The moon (*candra*), abode of Soma (the sacrificial elixir)		4. Intuitive-knowledge (*prajñānātman*) The senses (*indriya*)	4. Feeling (*rasa*), source of taste, of emotional perception, and of the element water
		5. The earth (*pṛthivi*), abode of Agni (the earthly fire)		5. The body (*śarīra*)	5. The seed-of-life (*amṛta*), source of smell, of physical sensation, and of the element earth

3. Light (*jyotis*) is the principle of sight, that is, of mental perception, associated with fire, the third element.
4. Feeling (*rasa*), that is, emotional perception, is the prototype of the sense of taste and as such is connected with water, the fourth element.

Mental perception and feeling are the "reins" which control all physical life.

5. The seed-of-life (*amṛta*), that is, perpetuation of life or physical immortality, is the physical manifestation of the Destructible Person, ever dying and ever reborn. It is connected with the element earth, with the sense of smell, and with physical sensation.

The Nature of Manifestation

THE FIRST plan of a universe is built within a consciousness, within a sphere of pure thought. It remains unmanifest, a mere idea, so long as no independent center of perception has been evolved to grasp it as a reality. Manifestation thus implies the existence of an individual independent perceiver. Being the meeting point of two forms of consciousness, it has of necessity the character of a limit. Manifestation can appear only in a definite location, at the junction between two forms of thought, between two orders of things. There must be a moment when a thing is going to exist and yet has not begun to exist; the point where it will appear must exist before it appears. It must thus have a position, though as yet it may have no extension. The place where manifestation will appear is determined by the first contact of the macrocosm and the microcosm, but even then the manifest form has as yet no extension. This first moment of contact is known as the point-limit, the *bindu*. To one such point-limit can be traced the origin of all the forms of manifest existence. This point, in which all future developments are potentially implied, is sometimes identified with the Self, the Ātman.

From the point-limit is issued the transcendent-principle-of-manifestation (*mahat-tattva*), which is universal Intellect (*buddhi*). After the principle of manifestation we meet another limit, that is, the principle-of-individuality (*aham-tattva*), the first form of differentiated existence. Only then can the mind exist and work within an individualized consciousness. From the mind arise, gradually, in order of subtlety, all the elements or spheres of perception.

Thus,

> *Beyond the senses are their objects.*
> *Beyond the objects of the senses is the mind* (manas).
> *Beyond the mind is intellect* (buddhi).
> *Beyond intellect is the transcendent Self, the Soul* (*or point-limit*).

Beyond the Transcendent is the Unmanifest (avyakta).
Beyond the Unmanifest is the Person.
There is nothing beyond the Person.
That is the limit, the highest that may be reached.
(*Kaṭha Upaniṣad* 3.10–11. [74])

The Appearance of the Universe

IN ACCORDANCE with this hierarchy, the birth of the universe can be compared to the growing of a plant.

"The first dormant stage of the seed is the theoretical potentiality known as *māyā*, the power of illusion. The Nonevolved (*avyakta*) is the stage of germinating-potentiality (*ucchūnāvasthā*), intermediary between that of the seed and that of the sprout, when the seed gets ready to develop at the first contact with warmth and moisture. The sprouting of the seed is the resulting-stage (*kāryāvasthā*), which includes all the developments from the point-limit onward.

"In man we may take the state of sleep as the seed stage; consciousness, yet devoid of analytical faculty, as the universal principle of manifestation. It is from this first principle, and from the principle of individuality which springs from it, that the multiplicity of the perceptible resulting world arises." (Karapātrī, "Ahamartha aur ātmā," *Siddhānta*, II, 1941–42, 67.)

The Nonevolved, the universal principle of manifestation, and the principle of individuality, taken together, form the subtle body of the universal Man.

When these all-pervading entities happen to be tied together at a particular point, just as different strings happen to form a knot, this constitutes an individuality. If all of the causal entities are involved in this knot, the individuality is called a universe. If only fractions of these entities are tied together, the individuality is an individual being. The individual being is thus a smaller replica of the universal Being. The individual *ātman* is a fragment of the universal Ātman, the individual intellect a part of the universal Intellect, and so on. The body and the mind, also, are but parts of the universal Substance and Mind. Each of these elements will return to its own store of substance once the individual knot is undone and the individual being ceases to exist. Matter returns to matter, the mind to the universal Mind, the faculties to universal Faculties, etc., from which they were never really separated.

The undoing of the knot of individuality may, however, be progressive, that is, accomplished by stages; when the outer envelopes are first released, some of the more subtle elements may remain tied together. Thus is formed the transmigrant body, the part of the individual being which remains united and in existence as a distinct unit after death. These transmigrant bodies can again become involved in a new knot with physical substance, an occurrence known as rebirth; or they may, on the contrary, further dissociate, and this is the final liberation, in which the individual being completely ceases to exist and dissolves into universal Being and, ultimately, into non-Being.

"As the rivers that flow toward the sea, on reaching the sea, disappear, their name and form destroyed, and are just called the sea, so, too, this individual spectator, made of sixteen components, on reaching the Cosmic Person disappears. His name and form are destroyed, and he is called simply 'the Person.' Having attained knowledge and being without parts, he becomes immortal. Hence the Scripture says:

> *Know that he in whom all components are firmly set,*
> *like the spokes on the hub of a wheel,*
> *is the Person to be known.*
> *Knowing this, you will not fear death."*
> (*Praśna Upaniṣad 6.5–6.* [75])

Cosmic Consciousness

FROM THE point of view of consciousness the Cosmic Being has a triple form, causal, subtle, and gross. These forms correspond to the manifestation of the three fundamental qualities (see pp. 22 ff.) and are as such the cosmic equivalent of the trinity. In any form of manifestation there are of necessity a causal, a subtle, and a physical aspect. The causal body is unmanifest, undistinguishable from the substratum. It is spoken of as the being-of-consciousness or of knowledge, made of *tamas*, the centrifugal tendency, and realized in the state of deep sleep.

The subtle body is activity, that is, intellect (*buddhi*). It originates from *sattva*, the cohesive or centripetal tendency, and is realized in the state of dream.

The gross body, which includes the mental and whose nature is substance, originates from *rajas*, the revolving tendency, realized in the state of wakefulness.

In the Cosmic Being, the gross body, totality of all gross bodies, is called "the Glorious" (*virāṭ*) and forms the perceptible universe. It is ruled by Brahmā, the lord of vastness.

The subtle body, totality of all subtle bodies, is called "the Golden Embryo" (*hiraṇya-garbha*). It is ruled by the Pervader, Viṣṇu.

The causal body is known as "the All-knowing" (*sarvajña*) and is ruled by Śiva, the lord of sleep.

These divisions of the macrocosm correspond to those of the microcosm. The individual living-being (*jīva*) as an individual (*vyaṣṭi*) gross body experienced in the state of wakefulness (*jāgrat*) is called "the Envelope" (*viśva*). As an individual subtle body experienced in the state of dream (*svapna*), it is called "the Fiery" (*taijasa*). As an individual causal body, the living being is known as "the Conscious" (*prājña*) or "the Unmanifest" (*avyākṛta*), an aspect of existence experienced in dreamless sleep.

THE STRUCTURE OF THE COSMOS: CONSCIOUSNESS

THE COSMIC BEING	*manifest as Consciousness*	
The Cosmic Whole (*samaṣṭi*)	The Transcendent-Lord-of-Sleep (*parama śiva*) The Fourth-Stage (*turīya*), Pure-Joy (*ānanda*)	
	Macrocosm	*Microcosm*
	TAMAS (disintegration)	
THE CHANGELESS-PERSON (*avyaya puruṣa*) is called the lord-of-progeny (Prajāpati) or the Driver (Paśupati) and is the substratum of the universe	The All-knowing (*sarvajña*), unmanifest consciousness, or the universal causal body, corresponds to Śiva, the lord of sleep	The Conscious (*prājña*), unmanifest-Self (*avyākṛta*), or the individual causal body, the state of deep sleep
	SATTVA (cohesion)	
THE INDESTRUCTIBLE-PERSON (*akṣara puruṣa*) or the Enduring represents THE INDESTRUCTIBLE PERMANENT LAWS of the universe and is called Manifest-Divinity or "God" (*īśvara*) or the "reins" (*pāśa*)	The Golden-Embryo (*hiraṇya-garbha*), the universal subtle body, corresponds to Viṣṇu, the Pervader	The Fiery (*taijasa*), the individual subtle body, the state of dream
	RAJAS (circular movement)	
THE DESTRUCTIBLE-PERSON (*kṣara puruṣa*) or the Impermanent is the Evolving (*vikāra*), i.e., the apparent form of the universe, and is twofold, the "driven animal" (*paśu*) and the "moving one" (*jagat*)	The Glorious (*virāṭ*), the Universe-Totality (*samaṣṭi*) or universal physical body, corresponds to Brahmā, the lord of vastness, the source of creation	The Envelope (*viśva*), the individual (*vyaṣṭi*) gross body, the living-being (*jīva*); the state of wakefulness

In the state of dreamless sleep the universal Being and the individual being are not really distinct. They appear to dissolve in the unmanifest substratum, in the experience of pure joy. There is therefore no real difference between the All-knowing (*sarvajña*) and the Conscious (*prājña*). The macrocosm and microcosm have here become one. This state can be realized, with the help of the practice of yoga, through the absolute silencing of all mental activity. A distinction is, however, sometimes made between the individual-consciousness (*prājña*) and the universal Consciousness (*sarvajña*). The universal Consciousness is then spoken of as the Fourth stage, the unmanifest stage, of consciousness.

THE THREE QUALITIES OF NATURE AND THE ORDERS OF BEING

DURATION *(Basis of Existence)*	LOCATION *(Basis of Manifestation)*	CONSCIOUSNESS *(Basis of Liberation)*
→	↓	↑
	rajas	*tamas*
rajas sattva tamas	*sattva*	*sattva*
	tamas	*rajas*

All existence is conditioned by the three fundamental qualities of Nature (*prakṛti*) and the three deities which are their personifications. From the point of view of location, that is, of manifestation or creation, *rajas* (Brahmā) is the causal or the more abstract stage, and *tamas* (Siva) appears as the lower or physical stage. From the point of view of consciousness (which is that of liberation), *tamas*, that is, Śiva, is the highest stage and *rajas*, that is, Brahmā, appears as the most manifest one. *Sattva* (Viṣṇu) is in every case the middle stage. Duration, that is, the basis of existence, corresponds to another dimension and operates across location and consciousness (see accompanying diagram). Thus we can see that creation and liberation are two contrary processes dependent at all stages on duration.

The co-ordinates of duration and location are not always at the same stage of manifestation. Hence *prāṇa* (life), a form of the Impermanent from the point of view of duration, is related to the Self-born, the Nonevolved, the cave, which are forms of the Changeless from the point of view of location.

Through this ambivalence of the nature of everything, contacts are made possible between different orders of being. We can reach the principle of duration through ritual, the principle of consciousness through introspection, the principle of location through the evolution of life. But at all stages we can, through a more manifest, perceptible aspect of the world of forms, experience a more subtle, less manifest one.

The Personification and the Description of the Cosmic Being

"THE GLORIOUS" (*virāṭ*), the perceptible form of the Cosmic Being, is the entity pictured in all attempts at representing divinity. There are numerous descriptions of the Cosmic Being either in its totality or in its manifestations. The Upaniṣads depict him as a gigantic microcosm.

"He has, verily, eyes on all sides, mouths on all sides, arms on all sides, and feet on all sides. He is the Progenitor, the only Lord, and upholds with his arms the falling heaven and earth." (*Śvetāśvatara Upaniṣad* 3.3; *Mahānārāyaṇa Upaniṣad* 1.14. [76])

"Within this universal Man the three worlds [earth, space, and sky] appear. The earthly world, supporting all, is called his feet; because it is highest, the sky-world (*dyu-loka*) is his head; the sphere of space, because of its depth, is his navel; the sun, the giver of vision, is his eye, air his nostril, the directions his ears; the lord-of-progeny (Prajāpati) is his organ of generation, and the lord-of-death (Yama) his brow, Destruction his anus. The world's-guardians (Loka-pālas), who are the regents of the eight directions, are his arms. The moon is his mind; shame is his upper lip and greed his lower lip; moonlight is his teeth, illusion his smile, all that grows upon the earth his body hairs." (Karapātrī, "Śrī Viṣṇu tattva," *Siddhānta*, V, 1944–45, 73.)

The main Vedic deities rule over the various regions of the cosmic body and over the corresponding parts of the human body:

> *Mitra, the spirit that personifies the day, is his inward breath* (prāṇa),
> *Varuṇa, the spirit personifying the night, is his outward breath* (apāna),
> *Aryaman, embodiment of the sun, is his eye,*
> *Indra is his power [his arms],*
> *Bṛhaspati [the teacher of the gods] is his intellect and his speech,*
> *Viṣṇu, the Pervader, whose stride is great, is [the directions and] his feet.*
> (Śaṅkarācārya, Commentary on the *Taittirīya Upaniṣad* 1.1. [77])

"[From] his outward breath [spring forth] the Vedas, [from] his sight the five elements, [from] his smile all the moving and unmoving universe, [from] his sleep the great destruction." (*Bhāmatī*, Commentary on Śaṅkara's ***Brahma Sūtra Bhāṣya*** 1.1.1. [78])

In the *Bhagavadgītā*, Arjuna has a vision of Viṣṇu as the personified Cosmic Being, the sum of all existence, of all life and death.

He had countless visages and countless eyes,
countless astonishing forms decked with divine ornaments,
countless arms with weapons ready to strike.

He was garlanded with celestial flowers,
anointed with exquisite perfumes; he wore splendid garments.

This divine, eternal form of the Cosmic Man
was the sum of all wonder.
A thousand divine suns, suddenly risen together,
could perhaps equal the splendor of this great spirit.

Struck with wonder, his hair raised on end,
the conqueror of wealth
bowed before this divine being,
and spoke to him with folded hands.

"O Resplendent! Within Thee I behold
all the gods and all the beings assembled.
I see the Creator on his lotus throne
and the King of Heaven
and the sages and celestial serpents.

"Thou hast no beginning, no middle, no end.
Thy strength is unrivaled, and Thine arms countless.

"The sun and moon are as Thine eyes,
and I can see Thy glorious visage
burning the worlds with its shining rays
as the sacred fire devours the victims.

"O powerful arm! Thy form appears immense
with all these limbs and all these eyes,
all these faces and all these forms,
all these bellies and all these fearful teeth.
Seeing Thee, the worlds shudder,
and I tremble myself.

"O Pervader!
Seeing Thee touching the sky,
resplendent, many-hued,
with open jaws, vast shining eyes,
my soul is perturbed.
I lose courage and all peace of mind.

"I can see Thy jaws with their teeth sharpened,
shining like the flames of Time.
I know not where I am, I cannot be calm.
Have pity on me. Lord of gods!
Thou art the refuge of the worlds!

"I see among other kings
the sons of King Dhṛtarāṣṭra
and Bhīṣma and Droṇa, [Karṇa] the son of the Charioteer,
and the great warriors of our side

"running into Thy mouth,
awesome with its fearful teeth.
I see the heads being crushed,
remaining stuck between Thy jaws.

"I can see these great heroes running toward Thy flaming mouths
as rivers run to the sea with all the thrust of their flow.

"Like insects that fly with all their strength
toward the flames of lamps but to find their death,
the worlds roll toward Thy mouth
as if seeking their end.

"All-Pervader! Thou dost seize with thy burning teeth and devour
all the assembled spheres.
Thy spreading flames cover the world
and burn it to ashes.

"All-Powerful, O Fearful Form!
Tell me who Thou art.
I lie prostrate at thy feet.
Be pacified. Best of gods!
I have wanted to know Thy true form,
but Thy deeds are beyond my understanding."

(*Bhagavadgītā* 11.10–31 passim. [79])

TWO

The Gods of the Vedas

The Cosmic Sacrifice

Fire and Offering, Agni and Soma

THE UNIVERSE appeared to the Vedic Aryan as a constant ritual of sacrifice. The strange destiny which compels every living thing to kill, to devour other things so as to exist, struck him with awe and wonder. The transformation of life into life seemed the very nature of the universe. "To live is to devour life" [80]. All existence could be brought back to the fundamental dualism of two factors: food (*anna*) and the devourer (*annāda*). Every creature is the devourer of another and is the food of some other. Existing means devouring and being devoured.

The "devouring" is the only permanent entity, the nature of creation and its creator. It is a function in which the devoured and the devourer are engaged as transient beings. This function is particularly apparent in one of the elements, fire, which grows at once when fed and dies as soon as it starves. The nature of fire appears to be the nature of existence, as well as its source and its symbol. At each moment innumerable forms of destruction, of fire, devour some form of life, of fuel. The sun shines, devouring its own substance. All the aspects of combustion, of digestion, are subtle forms of fire. The relation of food and eater, of fire and offering (*soma*), or fuel, is the visible form of an all-pervading divinity.

"I am food, I am food, I am food! I am the eater, I am the eater, I am the eater, . . . the first born," claims the divinity of the *Taittirīya Upaniṣad* (3.10.6. [81]). The same teaching appears in other Scriptures. "This whole world, verily, is just food and the eater of food." (*Bṛhad-āraṇyaka Upaniṣad* 1.4.6. [82]) "All this universe, conscious and unconscious, is made of fire (*agni*) and offering (*soma*)." (*Mahābhārata*, Śānti parvan, 338.52. [83])

Agni is all that burns, or devours, or digests: sun, heat, stomach, lust, and passion. Soma is all offering, all fuel, the cold, the moon, the food, the victim, the sperm, the wine. Agni is the warm outward breath of the Indestructible-Person (*akṣara puruṣa*) [the permanent Law of things]; Soma is his cool inward breath. Fire is the life, Soma the activity; Fire is the enjoyer and Soma all that is enjoyed. Fire is red, Soma is the color of night. "The fiery form is golden red, the offering dark blue." (*Chāndogya Upaniṣad* 6.4. [84])

Fire had been captured and domesticated. Legendary men of great wisdom and skill had been able to bring this divinity to their home and keep it alive through careful feeding. This deity had now become friendly and was the center of the household. It had to be maintained with constant care and attention. It had to be propitiated with offerings. Its likes and dislikes could easily be observed. In the patriarchal home of the noble-ones (*ārya*) could constantly be heard this invocation: "Come! Agni! O God! accept this offering" (*Ṛg Veda* 7.11.5. [85]). Should the god of fire be neglected and die, untold hardships were likely to arise in communities living widely separated in the unfriendliness of the primeval forest.

This powerful deity became the ally of human progress, the power through which man could improve his condition and master the forces of Nature (*prakṛti*). Hence Agni is the wealth-giver (Draviṇodas). "Because he gives wealth, Agni is called wealth-giver." (*Bṛhad-devatā* 3.65. [86])

It is through fire that man could communicate with higher states of being, with the gods and the heavenly spheres. Through fire he could take part in the cosmic life, co-operate with the gods. He could feed them through the mouth of fire. "Agni is the mouth of the gods; through this mouth they take their breath." (*Kapiṣṭhala-kaṭha Saṁhitā* 31.20 and *Śatapatha Brāhmaṇa* 3.7. [87]) "Agni, the mouth of the gods, is first among them." (*Aitareya Brāhmaṇa* 1.9.2. [88])

"Actually, the gods do not eat nor do they drink, but seeing the offering they are pleased." (*Chāndogya Upaniṣad* 3.6.3. [89]) Only through Fire can the gods be reached, hence "Agni must be worshiped before all other deities" (*Taittirīya Brāhmaṇa* 3.7.1. [90]). He appears as the most ancient and most sacred object of worship.

The counterpart of Agni, the fiery or devouring principle, is Soma, the gentle devoured substance. The substance of the universe is spoken of as "food." "Food is the principle of all, for, truly, beings here are born from food, when born they live by food, when dead they themselves become food." (*Taittirīya Upaniṣad* 3.2. [91])

In the *Maitrī Upaniṣad* 6.11–12 [92] it is said:

"Food is the form of the Soul, the Ātman, for life consists of food. The

Scripture says that if a man does not eat he can no longer think, no longer hear, no longer touch, no longer see, nor speak, nor smell, nor taste, and his vital energies abandon him.[1] But it is said [2] that, if he eats, he becomes full of life. He can think and hear and feel. He can speak and taste and smell and see. Thus it has been said: [3]

All creatures are born from food;
whatever dwells on the earth
lives by food and shall turn into food in the end.

"All beings here move about day by day in search of food. The sun draws its food to itself through its rays, and gives back heat. Food causes fire to burn. This world was fashioned by the hunger of the Immensity. Hence one should worship food as the Self of the universe. The Scripture declares: [4]

From food all things are born.
By food, when born, they grow up.
All are eaten and eat.
Hence everything is food."

It is not possible to say whether food is more important than the eater, fuel more important than fire, substance more important than action. There can be no sacrifice without a victim. Both fire and offering are necessary to one another. Both arise from the same root and are the two aspects of one divinity, that is, the sacrifice.

The food of the ritual fire is *soma*, the ritual offering. Every substance thrown in the sacramental fire is a form of *soma*, but the name is more particularly that of the sacrificial liquor through which the flames can be kindled. This is the "elixir of life," the ambrosia which stimulates the fire and intoxicates its priests. Under its influence man discovers mysterious worlds, enters into a magic frenzy, and becomes capable of deeds beyond his natural power. He who drinks this ambrosia partakes of divinity. Hence the *soma* plant is the king of plants, the process of preparing the *soma* wine is a holy sacrifice, and the instruments used are sacred.

The ritual *soma* used in the Vedic sacrifices was prepared from a creeper thought to be the *Sarcostemma viminale* or *Asclepias acida*. The stalks were

1 Cf. *Chāndogya Upaniṣad* 7.9.1.
2 Cf. *Taittirīya Upaniṣad* 2.2.1.
3 In *Taittirīya Upaniṣad* 2.2.1.
4 In *Taittirīya Upaniṣad* 2.2.1.

pressed between two stones (*adri*) by priests, then strained, mixed with clarified butter, and fermented.

Soma is identified with the beverage-of-immortality (*amṛta*), the beverage of the gods, first produced at the time of the churning of the ocean (see p. 167). *Soma* is also semen, the essence of life. "Whatever is moist, that he created from semen and that is *soma*." (*Bṛhad-āraṇyaka Upaniṣad* 1.4.6. [93]) There are references to sacrifices of semen as an alternative to human sacrifices.

Soma is personified as a deity and is one of the most important gods of the Vedas. All of the 114 hymns of the ninth book of the *Ṛg Veda* are in praise of Soma. There are six more hymns addressed to him in other books of the *Ṛg Veda*. The whole of the *Sāma Veda* is dedicated to Soma. Soma is represented as an all-powerful god, healer of all diseases, bestower of riches, lord of all the other gods, and is sometimes identified with the Supreme Being.

Like Agni, Soma is pictured as a priestly sage, beneficial to men and gods. He is the Son-of-Heaven (Gagana-ātmaja), and was kept in a bronze castle. A celestial-musician (*gandharva*) and the archer Kṛśānu, who causes the moon to wane,[5] were his wardens. *Soma* was brought to earth by a large hawk or by the thunderbolt (Indra). The symbolism of the number 3 plays an important part in the descriptions of *soma*. In the Brāhmaṇas, the triple-song or solar-hymn (Gāyatrī) is said to have seized this beverage, giver of immortality.

The nature of Agni is to spread, that of Soma to contract and vanish. "When a thing has spread to its limit it has to contract again. Hence fire becomes *soma* at each change of plane and *soma*, falling into the fire, itself becomes fire. The acts of devouring and being devoured are successive states of everything. This alternation of Agni and Soma gives rise to the division of the spheres considered as alternately fiery and oblational. Such are the spheres of the earth and the sun, and of all the celestial bodies which perform a constant cosmic ritual of sacrifice." (Giridhara Śarmā Caturvedi, "Siva mahimā," *Kalyāṇa*, Veda aṅka, p. 40.)

The Relation of the Spheres

THE RELATION between different spheres can be expressed as an exchange of radiations. Thus there is an emanation from the sun which feeds the earth's fire. This is known as *śyeta*, the white-light. But there is also an emanation from the earth which feeds the sun. This is known as *naudhasa*, the "exultation."

5 The moon is the cup of *soma*.

(Motilāl Śarmā Gauḍ, "Veda-kā svarūpa vicāra," *Kalyāṇa*, Vedānta aṅka, 1937, 384.)

The inner fire which pervades the body of the earth (*pṛthivī-piṇḍa*) is called the fire-of-immortality (*amṛta agni*). It radiates from the earth till it reaches the sun. This expanding radiation can be divided into concentric regions, each of which is called a "completed ritual" (*stoma*). The *stomas* are divided into sections called the "parts of a sacrifice" (*ahargaṇa*). From the center of the earth to its surface three sections are envisaged. Beyond this, every further division of six sections constitutes a region.

The earthly-world (*pṛthivī-loka*), which is the world of Agni, expands up to the ninth section; the intermediary-world (*antarikṣa*), the sphere of wind (Vāyu), up to the fifteenth section; the heavenly sphere, ruled by the sun, up to the twenty-first section. Hence, "the sun is called 'the twenty-first' " (*Chāndogya Upaniṣad* 2.10.5 [94]).

Beyond the solar sphere the immortal fire is changed into offering. It expands twelve sections further. Up to the twenty-seventh section it is called the "triple region" (*trivṛt-stoma*). This is the "sphere of the Supreme Ruler" (*parameṣṭhi-maṇḍala*), also known as the "transcendent world" (*mahar-loka*) or paradise (*jana-loka*). It is also the "world of the waters" (*ab-loka*).

Beyond this world, up to the thirty-third section, is the "sphere of the Self-born" (*svayambhū-maṇḍala*), the world of the higher gods. These two last spheres, beyond the three worlds, are the celestial spheres; they are made of two kinds of offering, the offering-of-space (*dik-soma*) and the offering-of-radiance (*bhāsvara-soma*).

The Ritual of Sacrifice (*yajña*)

EXISTENCE implies action. None can remain for a moment without breathing, thinking, dreaming. Even inaction is a form of action. Actions can be neutral, having no moral value, or they can be positive or negative. Actions, such as the *yajñas*, the rituals of sacrifice, that bring man into contact with the higher states of being, the deities, are the most important functions of man. We cannot live without taking part in the cosmic ritual either as instruments or as victims. Yet that part is positive only when we do it consciously and with the proper knowledge of forms and utterances. Through the voluntary ritual of sacrifice man takes his place in the cosmic symphony as an equal. The main purpose of his existence is the performance of this ritual.

"The Creator, the lord-of-progeny (Prajāpati), created at the same time the sacrificial ritual and man. And he said to man: Through this ritual shalt thou progress; it will fulfill thy desires. Thou shalt please the gods with its help, and in return the gods will protect thee. Thus, helping one another, thou shalt gain true happiness. Pleased with thy worship, the gods will grant thee all enjoyments. He who enjoys their gifts without giving them their due is a thief. He who eats but the remains of the offerings is freed from sin. He who prepares food for himself alone eats but sin. All beings live on the fruits of the earth; these fruits depend on the rain from the sky, and the rain is the result of the sacrifice, and this sacrifice is the fruit of right action. The value of action is determined by the knowledge of the permanent values found in the Eternal Law, the Veda, and this Law is the expression of the principle of indestructibility (*akṣara*) which manifests itself in the perpetual rite of sacrifice that is the universe. O son of Kuntī (Arjuna)! He who does not take [a willing] part in this endless sacrifice is made of sin. Prisoner of his senses, his existence is without a purpose." (*Bhagavadgītā* 3.10–16. [95])

It is through the development of the fire ritual that the all-pervasiveness of fire could be experienced. The fire sacrifice became the essential instrument of man's participation in the cosmic sacrifice. Through great sacrifices, which became more and more elaborate and developed into gigantic rituals, man took his place among the forces of Nature.

The Vedic ritual aimed at resembling more and more perfectly the very ritual through which the universe exists. The household fire was the image of the cosmic fire. The universe in turn was but a vast sacrifice in which Fire, the great, fearful, and violent god, constantly devoured the gigantic oblation of all that was gentle and soft.

Most of the Vedic texts that have come to us are related to the ritual of sacrifice. Around the large Vedic altar on which were the hollow pits in which the offerings and victims were thrown into the mouth of Fire, a most complex ceremonial was evolved in which the deities of the eight corners of space and the gods of the elements were given their place and honored. Different classes of priests, representing different cosmic forces, performed an elaborate ceremonial with gestures and invocations and hymns and songs which were intended to react upon the cosmic order and to bring the gods into the power of man.

In an attempt to establish the supremacy of man over the cosmic forces, the ritual of sacrifice took on fantastic proportions. There were sacrifices the rituals of which lasted for years, employing thousands of priests and draining the whole revenue of large kingdoms.

The succession of rituals, once started, had to be completed following the cycles of months and season. An incomplete or faulty ritual was sure to bring evils. "If one Agnihotra sacrifice is not followed by the sacrifices of the new moon and the full moon, by the four-months sacrifice, by the harvest sacrifice; if one of these is unattended by guests, or not offered at all, or performed without giving a proper share to the ancestral gods, or not according to the rules, it may destroy the seven worlds."[6] (*Muṇḍaka Upaniṣad* 1.2.3. [96])

"If, after the morning litany has commenced, the chief-officiant (*brahmā*) interrupts himself before the concluding verse, like a chariot with a broken wheel he forms only one track on the path; the other is irregular.

"As a one-legged man or a chariot proceeding on one wheel suffers injury when moving, so this sacrifice suffers injury. The instituter of the sacrifice suffers when the sacrifice is injured. He becomes worse for having sacrificed.

"But if, after the morning litany has commenced, the chief officiant never stops until the concluding verse has been uttered, both tracks are formed; the second one is not irregular.

"Like a two-legged man or a chariot supported on two wheels, this sacrifice is well supported. The sacrificer is on strong ground when well supported. He becomes better off by having sacrificed." (*Chāndogya Upaniṣad* 4.16.2–5. [97])

The officiants at ritual sacrifices become qualified through their good deeds, and are thus able to grasp the meaning of the Scripture. Having visualized the Eternal Law and the essence of all things and seen what exists beyond the reach of the senses, they enter into the hearts of the seers and obtain the true wisdom, the real Veda, which dwells there in a subtle form, even at the time of universal destruction. Having grasped the Law, they spread it in the world." (Yogatrayānanda, commenting on *Ṛg Veda* 10.71.3a, *Siva-rātrī*, p. 132.)

The Forms of the Sacrifice

THERE are many forms of sacrifice, whether cosmic or human; each human form is the image of a cosmic one. The universe was created through sacrifice, and every form of creation, divine or human, has the character of this ritual. "Any action which may promote the betterment of man has of necessity the nature of a ritual sacrifice." (Yogatrayānanda, *Śiva-rātrī*, p. 171.)

Fire is the all-purifier; hence all that has been purified by fire is worthy of the gods, and "all that purifies is a ritual sacrifice" (*Chāndogya Upaniṣad*

6 The seven worlds are the concentric spheres of Earth (Pṛthivī), Wind (Antarikṣa), Moon (Candra), Sun (Sūrya), Stars (Nakṣatra), the Supreme-Ruler (Parameṣṭhin), and the Self-born (Svayambhū).

4.16.1 [98]). Since the digestive acids are considered forms of fire, the offering may be eaten, though such a sacrifice is incomplete (see *brahma-odana*, p. 71). The fire of anger, the fire of lust, open the possibility of other forms of ritual. War is one of the great sacrifices.

In the *Rāma-carita-mānasa*, the epic of Tulsī Dās, the hero Paraśu-Rāma says:

> *The offering of arrows was performed by the bow.*
> *The fire of my anger was kindled.*
> *The army of four arms was my fuel,*
> *the great kings were the sacrificed animals whom I killed with my ax.*
> *In this way I performed millions of war sacrifices.*
> (*Rāma-carita-mānasa*, Bāla kāṇḍa, 287.8.2–4. [99])

Mankind unconsciously performs a constant ritual. "Those who are hungry and thirsty and know no pleasure are keeping the vigil. Those who eat and drink and enjoy life are the offering. Those who laugh and eat well and make love are the song of praise. Those who do penance, perform charities, and practice humility and nonviolence and who speak the truth are the wealth distributed. . . . Death is the ablution after the ceremony." (*Chāndogya Upaniṣad* 3.17.1–4. [100])

The life of each individual is an offering. "Verily, a human life is a sacrifice. The first twenty-four years are the morning *soma* libation, with which are connected the spheres of the elements, the Vasus. . . . The next forty-four years are the midday *soma* libation, connected with the deities of space and life, the Rudras. . . . The next and last forty-eight years of life are the evening offering, connected with the sovereign principles, the divinities of the sky, the Ādityas." (*Chāndogya Upaniṣad* 3.16.1–4. [101]) Thus are completed the 116 years which are the life span of man.

The Technique of the Sacrifice

WHEN an edible substance is offered to a deity and then thrown into the fire with the accompaniment of prescribed gestures and utterances, this constitutes a ritual sacrifice. There are therefore four essential elements in a sacrifice: the offering, the fire, the utterances, and the gestures.

A sacrifice is a technical process, yet its form and its purpose are essential elements of its efficacy. "The sacrifice performed without ritual, without distribution of food, without offerings of wealth to the priests, and without piety is a black sacrifice." (*Bhagavadgītā* 17.13. [102]) "One should not offer sacrifices merely to fulfill a wish." (*Bṛhad-āraṇyaka Upaniṣad* 1.5.2. [103])

In sacrifices the offering may vary according to the nature and purpose of the ritual, the deity to be placated, and the place of the offering in the universal sacrifice. Thus there are offerings of wheat or rice, of oil or butter, of seed or wine, of goats, horses, or buffaloes, or even of men.

Blood sacrifices involving the killing of a victim or several victims are still commonly performed in India. Now, however, they follow mainly the Tantric ritual, which is less elaborate than the Vedic and can be witnessed by anyone. This ritual is considered a substitute for the Vedic form, and is better suited to the conditions of the present age. Human sacrifices are not uncommon in Tantric rituals, though prohibited by modern law. The Vedic form was abolished in very ancient times. The horse sacrifice, performed by a king at the height of his power after he had subdued all the neighboring kingdoms, was one of the important events in the life of ancient India. The preparations for such sacrifices lasted several years and could drain all the resources of large countries. Political circumstances have prevented their performance for almost ten centuries.

In the Vedic sacrifices, as they are performed today, the offering is usually clarified butter, oil, and food grains poured with the hand or with a sacrificial ladle into fires burning in square pits dug in the altar or in the floor of the sacrificial hall. There can be dozens of such pits, each attended by several priests reciting distinct *mantras*. The ceremonial is directed by a high priest. He is assisted by group leaders who see that no technical mistake creeps into any part of the ritual. "The leader of the sacrifice enacts the whole ceremony mentally, while the other officiants, the sacrificer, the chanter, and the others, perform the actual utterance." (*Chāndogya Upaniṣad* 4.16.2. [104])

There is a different ritual for each type of sacrifice. These are explained in sacred texts which are not to be read by anyone except the sacrificing priests.

"The food offered to a deity is of two kinds, that eaten by the priests (*brahma-odana*) and that thrown into the fire (*pravargya*). The deity of the sacrifice is fed by that which the priests eat, and the creation of the universe takes place from that which is thrown into the fire. The 'part left over' (*ucchiṣṭa*) in the cosmic ritual is considered the immanent cause of all that exists. Hence, 'The whole world is called a remnant of food.' " (Motilāl Śarmā Gauḍ, *Īśopaniṣad Vijñāna Bhāṣya*, p. 61.)

The various rituals of sacrifice should each be performed in a special fire. All the rituals of offering carried on before an image form an incomplete sacrifice since the offering-to-be-consumed-by-fire (*pravargya*) is absent and only the offering-consecrated-and-afterward-eaten (*brahma-odana*) is there.

Sacrificial halls are specially constructed for the great sacrifices. The common rituals of sacrifice are performed in the home, never in temples. The plan of the house is conceived as having the form of a man lying down and is called the *vastu-puruṣa.* When rituals are performed in the home, "offerings to the goddess-of-fortune (Śrī) should be made on the head of the *vastu-puruṣa* [i.e., in the northeast direction], those to the fearful divinity of time should be made on the feet [the southeast]. Offerings to the Creator and the god of architecture should be made on the middle part of the image, those to the universal principles should be thrown in the air; offerings to the spirits of the day should be made in the daytime, those to the spirits of darkness in the night. The offerings to the universal Soul should be made on the back of the *vastu-puruṣa*, and if something is left it may be given to the Ancestors on the right." (*Manu Smṛti* 3.89–91. [105])

The Creation of Man

MAN IS SAID to have been born of a ritual having five stages; hence in every ritual the fifth offering is called "man."

In the first offering:

The world is the hearth, the sun is the spark,
its rays are the smoke, day is the flame,
the moon is the ember, the constellations are the sparks.
In this fire the gods offer their devotion,
and Soma, the royal offering, is born.

In the second offering:

The god-of-rain (*Parjanya*) *is the hearth, wind the fire,*
the clouds the smoke, lightning the flame,
the thunderbolt (vajra), *the ember, and the roar of thunder*
the sparks.
In this fire the gods offer the Soma,
and rain is born.

In the third offering:

The earth is the hearth, the year the fire,
space is the smoke, night the flame,

the four directions the embers, and the subdirections the sparks.
In this fire the gods offer rain,
and the food grains are born.

In the fourth offering:

Man is the hearth, his speech is the fire,
his breath the smoke, his tongue the flame,
his eyes the embers, his ears the sparks.
In this fire the gods offer the food grains,
and semen is born.

In the fifth offering:

Woman is the hearth, the male organ is the fire,
courtship is the smoke, the vulva the flame,
the penetration the ember, pleasure the spark.
In this fire the gods sacrifice semen,
and the child is born.
(*Chāndogya Upaniṣad* 5.4–8 [106]; for similar verses, see *Bṛhad-āraṇyaka Upaniṣad* 6.2.9–13.)

The Last Sacrifice

This man lives as long as he lives.
Then, when he dies, he is carried to the fire.
His fire returns to fire, fuel to fuel,
smoke to smoke, flame to flame,
coals to coals, sparks to sparks.
Into fire do the gods offer the body of man.
From this oblation a new being arises
who has the color of light.
(*Bṛhad-āraṇyaka Upaniṣad* 6.2.13–14. [107a])

The Way of the Gods

Those who know this and, in the forest, piously worship,
pass into the flame [of the funeral pyre],
from the flame into the day, from the day
into the fortnight of the waxing noon,
from the fortnight of the waxing moon
into the half year when the sun moves northward,

from these months into the world-of-the-gods (deva-loka),
from the world of the gods into the sun,
from the sun into lightning.
A pure spirit comes to these regions where lightning dwells
and leads them to the causal world.
In this Immense World they remain forever.
From there, there is no return.
(*Bṛhad-āraṇyaka Upaniṣad* 6.2.15. [107b])

The Way of the Fathers

They who through sacrifices, charity, and penance
have conquered the worlds
pass into the smoke [of the funeral pyre],
from the smoke into the half month of the waning moon,
from the half month of the waning moon into the
half year when the sun moves southward,
from these months into the world-of-the-Fathers (pitṛ-loka),
from the world of the Fathers into the moon.
Reaching the moon, they become food themselves
and the gods feed upon them,
just as if ordering King Soma (the moon) to increase and decrease.
And once the fruit of their acquired merits is exhausted
they again enter into space, from space into air,
from air into the rain, from the rain into the earth;
reaching the earth, they become food, are offered
into the fire of man
and the fire of woman.
Once born, they grow up in this world
and again start the cycles of existence.
But those who do not follow either of these ways
become the crawling and flying insects
and whatever there is here that bites.
(*Bṛhad-āraṇyaka Upaniṣad* 6.2.16 [107c]; for a similar passage to texts 107 a–c, see *Chāndogya Upaniṣad* 5.9–10.)

Divinity as the Embodiment of the Sacrifice

WE HAVE SEEN that the principle from which the universe arises has a triple aspect, the devourer, the devoured, and their relationship, the devouring or sacrifice. It is through this relationship that the universe exists and endures; thus the sacrifice can be identified with the all-pervading Preserver. "The Sacrifice is Viṣṇu." (*Taittirīya Saṁhitā* 1.7.8 and *Kṛṣṇa Yajur Veda* 3.5.2. [108])

"Because he is the intrinsic shape of all sacrifices, or because under the form of the sacrifice he satisfies all the gods, the Pervader himself is called 'the Sacrifice.' " (Śaṅkarācārya, *Viṣṇu-sahasra-nāma Bhāṣya* 20. [109])

The Sacrifice is personified as a deity:

"A great god with four horns, three feet, two heads, seven hands. He has the form of a bull, bound in three places, who, bellowing, descends among mortals." (*Ṛg Veda* 4.58.3; *Mahānārāyaṇa Upaniṣad* 10.1. [110])

"His four horns represent the four Vedas, the three feet the three ablutions of morning, midday, and evening. With these three feet he stands in the three worlds. The two heads are the food eaten by the priests and that offered in the fire. The seven hands are the seven horses which represent the meters used in the sacred hymns." (Motilāl Śarmā Gauḍ, *Īśopaniṣad Vijñāna Bhāṣya*, p. 61.)

The sacrificial animal is pictured as the embodiment of the cosmos.

Dawn is the head of the horse to be sacrificed,
the sun his eye, wind his breath.
The devouring fire is his open mouth,
the year his soul. The heavenly vault is his back,
the sphere of space his belly,
the earth the place of his flanks,
his ribs the intermediary points of space.

The seasons are his limbs,
the lunar months and fortnights his joints;
the days and the nights are his legs,
the constellations his bones, ether his flesh;
sand is the undigested food in his stomach.
The rivers are his anus.
The mountains are the place between his liver and his heart.

Herbs and plants are his mane.
The rising sun is his forepart,
the setting sun the hind part below his navel.
When it yawns there is lightning.
When it moves there is thunder.
His urine is rain. All speech is his voice.

(*Bṛhad-āraṇyaka Upaniṣad* 1.1 [111])

In the *Harivaṁśa*, the boar, that is, Viṣṇu, is depicted as the embodiment of the sacrifice.

The Vedas are his feet, the sacrificial post his teeth,
the offering his hand, the pyre his mouth.
Fire is his tongue, the sacred grass his hair,
his head the priestly order; his austerity is great.
He is of divine appearance, with day and night for his eyes.
The [six] Vedic-sciences (Vedāṅga) are his ornaments.
Clarified butter is his nose, the sacrificial ladle his snout;
the powerful sound of the Sāma Veda *is his loud cry.*
Made of righteousness and truth, he is rich.
His virtues are hierarchy and order.
His hooves are penance. He is fearful.
His knees are those of an animal. His arm is long.
The reciter is his entrails, the oblation his penis;
seeds and herbs are his large testicles. Air is his inner self.
Magic utterances are his buttocks, the sacrificial beverage (soma) *his blood.*
Great is his stride.
The altar is his shoulder, offerings his smell.
Oblations to gods and Ancestors are his speed.
The steps mounting to the altar on the east are his body.
He is honored in many initiatory ceremonies.
He is the great yogi whose heart is the wealth given,
whose substance is the sacrificial session.
His lips and teeth are the preliminaries to the spring sacrifices.
He is adorned with curly hairs
which are the preliminaries to the Soma sacrifice.
The many Vedic meters are his way in and out.
The most secret teachings of the Upaniṣads are his seat.
He is enthroned with Shadow (Chāyā), his wife.

(*Harivaṁśa* 3.34–41. [112])

The Image of the Sacrifice

THE SACRIFICE has its image in every temple.

"Placed in the southwest corner of the temple, the divinity who is the embodiment of the ritual sacrifice faces west. His color is that of heated gold. He has four horns, two heads, seven arms. He holds a discus, clarified butter, and [the four kinds] of ladles (*darvī, sruc, sruva, juhū*). He has three legs and wears a red garment and is adorned with all his ornaments. On his right and left are the two wives of the lord of fire, who are the Ritual-Utterance-at-offerings-to-Gods (Svāhā) and the Ritual-Utterance-at-offerings-to-Ancestors (Svadhā). Hence the lord of the ritual sacrifice is the source of merit. All the gods are his substance. He is greatest in all rituals." (*Vaikhānasāgama.* [113])

The Inner *Yajña* of the Yogi

"IN THE Soma sacrifice the liquid *soma* is drunk by the priests. This is the exoteric ritual, corresponding to the inner sacrifice (*yajña*), in which the vessel of divine liquor is man's own body and the essence of life which fills the vessel is reabsorbed inwardly and becomes the elixir of immortality. The senses are the cups from which the divine beverage is drunk. The procreative energy is produced in the lower region, called 'the southern direction,' in which the Ancestors dwell. The purified seed rises into the head in the center called [in the Tantras] *mūjavān* and flows from there into the nerve centers. Hence, 'Soma becomes the deity of the north (i.e., the head).' [7]

"The head is like an inverted urn; its contents flow down into the whole body. The inner reabsorption of the seed is represented as the drinking of the elixir of immortality. This process requires complete mental control and can only be achieved through the perfected practice of yoga. Thus the yogi alone drinks the ambrosia which the man of the world spills. Śiva is shown ever intoxicated with this beverage, and his cup shines like the moon on his forehead. In the symbolism of the physical body, the life-energy (*prāṇa*) is represented as a serpent (*nāga*) and the king-of-birds (Garuḍa), the eater of serpents, is semen. All beings try to capture the beverage of immortality without which there is no enjoyment, but only the gods can seize it. The gods here are the deities of the senses, strengthened by Soma, the essence of life, and shining around Indra, the king of heaven, who is the Self, the Ātman.

"Semen is the basis of lust; on it depends the energy of man, his power to know and act. It can be used either as a deadly substance or as a giver of immortality. Semen poisons the man of pride but pacifies and illumines the man who controls his passions. Should a mere trace of poison remain in the beverage the whole is poisoned, and the yogi cannot drink it. Misused by the antigods, this elixir of immortality becomes for them an intoxicant which renders their conduct disorderly and decreases the length of their life. It is Śiva who drinks

7 *Udīcī dik somo 'dhipatiḥ.*

the poisonous part of this energy and calms its burning flames so that the gods may drink the ambrosia. Śiva is the Yogi who has pierced through the five centers where are found the different forms of the life energy which bar the way toward reintegration. Only after having, through the practice of yoga, passed these five gates can the yogi conquer lust and acquire the power to drink the poison and purify the ambrosia. Hence the poison is said to stop in the throat of Śiva, where is situated the fifth center of the subtle body, and beyond which Nature has no longer any hold on the realized yogi." (Abridged translation from Vāsudeva Śaraṇa Agravāla, "Śiva-svarūpa," *Kalyāṇa*, Śiva aṅka, pp. 497–98.)

The yogi who can drink the poison and purify the ambrosia becomes himself the embodiment of the ritual sacrifice, that is, becomes identified with Viṣṇu.

{ 5 }

The Thirty-Three Gods

IN THE *Bṛhad-āraṇyaka Upaniṣad* (3.9.1) we are told that, when Śākalya asked the sage Yājñavalkya what was the number of the gods, the sage gave a cryptic answer.

"The gods are as many as are mentioned in the sacred books. They number three hundred and three, and three thousand and three (=3306)." Questioned again, he said: "The gods are six, the gods are three, the gods are two, the gods are one and a half, and the gods are one."

Explaining this, Yājñavalkya enumerated some of the main divisions of the natural and the subtle worlds to which these divisions of the divine power correspond.

Śākalya asked: "Which are the three hundred and three and the three thousand and three?" Yājñavalkya answered: "Those are only their spheres-of-expansion (*mahiman*). There are just thirty-three gods."

"Which are the thirty-three?"

"The eight spheres-of-existence (Vasus), the eleven divinities-of-life (Rudras), the twelve sovereign-principles (Ādityas), make thirty-one. The ruler-of-heaven (Indra) and the lord-of-progeny (Prajāpati) complete the thirty-three."

"Which are the spheres of existence?"

"Fire, Earth, Wind, Atmosphere, Sun, Sky, Moon, and Stars. These are called 'dwellings' [1] (Vasus), for the world dwells in them and they dwell in the world."

"Which are the divinities of life?"

"The ten forms of the life energy found in a living being and the mind as the eleven.

1 Vasu can mean both "dwelling" and "dweller."

"When they go out of this mortal body they make us lament, thus they are called the 'causes of tears' (Rudras)."

"Which are the sovereign principles?"

"Verily, the twelve months of the year. They move carrying along this whole world, hence they are called 'leaders' (Ādityas)."

"Who are this lord of heaven and this lord of progeny?"

"Thunder, verily, is the lord-of-heaven (Indra); the sacrifice is the lord-of-progeny (Prajāpati)."

"What is thunder?"

"The thunderbolt."

"What is the sacrifice?"

"The sacrificial animals."

"Who, then, are the six gods?"

"Fire and Earth, Wind and Space (*antarikṣa*), Sun and Sky. These are the six, for the whole world is within these six."

"Who are the three gods?"

"Verily, they are the three worlds, for in them dwell all the gods."

"Who are the two gods?"

"Food (*anna*) and Breath (*prāṇa*)."

"Which is the one and a half?"

"The Wind (the subtle world) that purifies."

Then someone asked: "Since the purifier need only be one, why should he be one and a half?"

"Because the world develops within him, he is one and a half."

"Who is the one God?"

"The Life Breath," said he, "which they call the Immensity (*brahman*)." (*Bṛhad-āraṇyaka Upaniṣad* 3.9.1–9. [114])

The Three Spheres of Agni

THE WORLD perceptible to man appears divided into three spheres, Earth, Space, and Sky. These three spheres are taken as the visible symbols of the "three worlds" in which all beings dwell: the earthly world of men, the spatial world of spirits, and the celestial world of deities. In the first world dwell the principles of the elements; in the second world are found the subtle principles of life, the laws that rule mankind and the cosmos; in the higher world are found the luminous principles of intellect.

The nature of all existence and the origin of all things being Fire (Agni, and Offering (Soma), a form of fire is, of necessity, found in each region of the perceptible world.

"The lord of fire, having divided himself into three, abides in these worlds, causing all the gods in due order to rest on his rays.

"The seers worship with chants under three names this Being who, under the three forms of fire, dwells in the worlds that have come into being. For he dwells resplendent in the hearts of all beings.

"His names are Fire (Agni) in this world, Thunderbolt (Indra) or Wind (Vāyu) in the intermediary sphere, and Sun (Sūrya) in the sky. These are to be known as the three deities." (*Bṛhad-devatā* 1.63–69. [115])

When envisaged together as one universal fiery principle, the three forms of fire are known as the lord-of-progeny (Prajāpati). Hence, "the divinity of all the sacred utterances taken collectively is the lord of progeny, while the deities of each individually may be Agni (Fire), Vāyu (Wind), and Sūrya (Sun), respectively" (*Bṛhad-devatā* 2.124 [116]). The spheres of the three worlds and all they contain seem to come forth from this lord of progeny, that is, from the totality of the three forms of fire.

"The lord of progeny, for the sake of the world, entered into meditation (*dhyāna*). From the heat [born of his thought] the essence of the three worlds sprang forth. From Earth came Fire, from Space Wind, from the Sky came the Sun." (*Chāndogya Upaniṣad* 4.17.1–3. [117])

The Three Aspects of Deities

WHENEVER we envisage one of the fundamental energies of the universe we can approach it from the point of view of the unconscious, as a power ruling the elements, or we can envisage it as a conscious subtle being or deity presiding over and guiding the forms of manifestation. These two viewpoints correspond to the elemental (*ādhibhautika*) and the celestial (*ādhidaivika*) approaches.

But, as we have seen, all knowledge of the outward world reflects the structure of the individuality which perceives it. And all the powers and forms of the cosmic world can be imagined by man only in terms of his inner world. The forces and powers which rule the universe appear to us as faculties of the Cosmic Being which have equivalents in the inner structure of the individual being. This conception of the universe as made of the component parts of a personified universal Being is known as the individual (*ādhyātmika*) approach.

Every universal principle can thus be represented as a natural force governing the elements, as a subtle mental or heavenly spirit dwelling in the world of thought or in a celestial abode, and as one of the inner faculties by which man, like the universal Being, exists as an individuality. These faculties express themselves in the laws that rule the universe as well as human society.

Though a particular deity can be envisaged in any one of these three aspects, one approach need not exclude the others. The symbolism of the deities applies simultaneously to the three spheres. Every sacred text has therefore three distinct, though related, meanings.

The story of the *Mahābhārata*, for example, has been explained as representing the inner conflict of the higher instincts against the lower instincts of man; that Arjuna is Truth personified, that Bhīma is Strength, Bhīṣma Wisdom, and that their adversaries are Greed, Lust, Ambition, etc. This interpretation may have been intended by the writers of this immense epic, whose purpose was not merely to write a historical chronicle. Yet it does not exclude the view that the inner conflict of man corresponds to the eternal conflict of cosmic forces, the physical battles of the powers of Truth against the powers of Darkness, the celestial conflict of angels and demons. The story deals also with a historical war, in which history itself is seen as a symbol, as the expression of the inner laws that rule mankind. The tale is therefore the expression of a dual reality, and the historical reality is the symbol of its causal permanent law. The *Mahābhārata* depicts an actual battle as well as an eternal cosmic conflict and the inner struggle within every man.

The Number of the Gods

ALL EXISTING beings, subtle or gross, live within the three spheres of Agni, within the three worlds. The gods are the powers that rule these three worlds. There are therefore three kinds of gods, and the gods are said to be ruled by the number 3. This is why they are symbolically represented by multiples of the number 3. Their main epithet is the "thirty" (*tridaśa*), though their number is often given as thirty-three or its multiples.

The Iranians also thought thirty-three to be the "number of the gods." The Brāhmaṇas divide this number into eight deities ruling the spheres and the elements, eleven deities of life or the subtle world, and twelve divinities of knowledge or aspects of consciousness. These last deities are the Ādityas (sovereign principles), embodiments of the laws that rule the universe as well as human society. To these are added two deities which are given different names in different works but which always represent the transcendent and the co-ordinating element of the other gods.

The number thirty-three is taken as a symbolic expression representing a particular aspect of the pantheon. Actually there can be no limit to the number

THE THIRTY-THREE GODS

The Spheres, the Eight Vasus		*Manifest Energies*		*Ruling Deities*	*Caste and Corresponding Qualities*	*Veda and Corresponding Ritual and* Mantra
Sphere	Active Principle					
1. EARTH (*pṛthivī*)	2. FIRE (Agni) Food	Elemental-manifestation (*ādhibhautika*), the natural forces	The five elements	The AŚVINS, the gods of agriculture	*viśaḥ* working-class (youth, skill)	*Ṛk* (meters), morning libation, BHŪR
3. SPACE (*antarikṣa*)	4. WIND (Vāyu) Life breath	Celestial-manifestation (*ādhidaivika*), the subtle beings, deities	9–19. The eleven RUDRAS, the life energies	32. INDRA, Might, the thunderbolt	*kṣatra* warrior-class (maturity, strength, courage)	*Yajus* (contents), midday libation, BHUVAS
5. SKY (*dyaus*)	6. SUN (Sūrya) Intellect	Individual-manifestation (*ādhyātmika*), the moral forces	20–31. The twelve ĀDITYAS, the sovereign principles	MITRA-VARUNA, the cosmic law, relation of man with man and man with gods	*brāhman* priestly-class (old age, wisdom)	*Sāman* (extension), evening libation, SVAR
7. CONSTELLATIONS (*nakṣatra*)	8. MOON (Soma) Seed, offering, ambrosia, immortality	The Unmanifest, the Fourth stage	The Unmanifest, the Ancestors	SVAYAMBHŪ, the Self-born PARAMEṢṬHIN, the Supreme Will	*sannyāsa* asceticism, eternity, timelessness	AUM

33. The LORD-OF-PROGENY (Prajāpati) is formed from the union of the three forms of Fire: Agni, Vāyu, and Sūrya.

of the gods. Each aspect of manifestation is a channel through which man can reach the Divine. The number of the Hindu gods is therefore the same as that of the possible aspects of manifestation, created or potential. It is, in later Hinduism, represented by the symbolic number of thirty-three *crores* (330,-000,000).[2]

2 According to Vedic tradition, offerings may be given only to the thirty-three main gods. There are numerous other inhabitants of heaven who deserve praise and veneration but, as they have not the full status of gods, may not be offered sacrifices.

The Spheres and Their Deities

The Eight Spheres of Existence, the Vasus

THE SPHERES of existence and the powers which dwell in them are the principles from which the physical or elemental (*ādhibhautika*) world develops. They are thus for man the most immediate aspects of divinity, the most easily perceptible deities. As the elemental stages of manifestation, they represent the youth of the world. The *Chāndogya Upaniṣad* (3.16.1) links them with the first twenty-four years of life or the morning *soma* libation.

The word *vasu,* according to the *Uṇādi Sūtra* (1.11 [118]), means "that which surrounds." According to Śaṅkarācārya's commentary on the *Chāndogya Upaniṣad* 3.16.1 [119], "the Vasus are so called because they 'dwell' or 'cause to dwell.' "

That in which something dwells or that which dwells in something is called *vasu,* meaning both "dwelling" and "dweller." Thus all the spheres of extension, that is, space and the elements, and the powers that rule over them are the Vasus (the dwellings), the deities of the spheres.

There can be no substance, no form, no being, without a place, a dwelling, in which it can exist and expand. The Vasus are thus the forms of Brahmā, the Immense Being, the lord of extension, the manifestations of the revolving tendency, *rajas,* origin of space. Like *rajas,* the Vasus are said to be red in color.

The word *vasu* can also be derived from the root *vas,* "to shine." The word then refers to the splendor of Agni and of the spheres over which he rules. The Vasus are sometimes shown as the attendants of Indra, the thunderbolt, the heavenly form of Agni.

The eight Vasus include the earthly-sphere (*pṛthivī*) and the fiery energy which dwells in it, Agni; the sphere-of-space (*antarikṣa*) and the fiery energy which dwells in it, Vāyu, the Wind; the heavenly-sphere (*dyaus*) and the fiery energy which dwells in it, the Sun (Sūrya); then come the sphere-of-the-constellations (*nakṣatra*) and the gentle energy which dwells in it, the Moon or Offering (Soma).

Thus the Vasus are the three forms of fire—Fire, Wind, and the Sun—and the worlds in which they are found—Earth, Space, and Sky—to which are added the Moon or Offering (Soma), and its dwelling place, the constellations.

From the relation of these different spheres and their ruling energies are evolved the bodies and the senses of living beings. The whole of the moving universe shelters in them.

THE VASUS, OR SPHERES OF EXISTENCE

The earth (*pṛthivī*)	in which dwells	Fire (Agni), the principle of Food (digestion).
Space (*antarikṣa*)	in which dwells	the Wind (Vāyu), the principle of Life.
The sky (*dyaus*)	in which dwells	the Sun (Sūrya), the principle of Intellect.
The constellations (*nakṣatra*)	in which dwells	the Moon (Soma), the principle of Immortality.

The *Mālatī-mādhava*, the *Kirātārjunīya*, and many other works mention the eight Vasus. In the Purāṇas and the *Mahābhārata* the names given the Vasus vary slightly, although the principles aimed at are the same.[1]

1. Dhava (the flowing) or Dharā (the support) represents the earth.
2. Aha or Āha (the pervading) or Ap (the waters) or Sāvitra (descended from the sun) stands for the sphere-of-space (*antarikṣa*).
3. Prabhāsa (shining dawn) is the sky.
4. Anala (the living) or Pāvaka (the purifier) is fire (*agni*).
5. Anila (the one by whom one lives) represents the wind (*vāyu*).
6. Pratyūṣa (the scorching or luminous) is the sun.
7. Soma (the offering) is the moon.
8. Dhruva (the motionless or the Polestar) stands for the constellations.

As the spheres of the elements, the Vasus are the visible form of the laws of the universe. They are therefore said to be the sons of the lawgiver (Manu) or of the Law (*dharma*) itself (*Mahābhārata* 12.7587 and 7540).

1 "The names of the Vasus are: Āpa, Dhruva, Soma, Dharma, Anila, Anala, Pratyūṣa, Prabhāsa." (*Viṣṇu Purāṇa* 1.15.111. [120])

"The eight Vasus are: Dhara, Dhruva, Soma, Aha, Anila, Anala, Pratyūṣa, Prabhāsa." (*Mahābhārata* 1.66.19. [121])

Personified as the laws of righteousness, the spheres of the elements appeared upon the earth as the sons of the river Gaṅgā, the all-purifier. Later they returned to the heavens. (*Mahābhārata* 1.3887.)

The Earth

THE FIRST sphere is the earth, the support (*dharā*) of all creatures, the "nourisher" of all physical life.

The earth is also represented as a goddess, or as a cow that feeds everyone with her milk. She is the mother of life, the substance of all things.

Pṛthu, the "first king" and inventor of agriculture, forced the reluctant earth to yield her treasures and feed men, hence she is called Pṛthivī, the "domain of Pṛthu."

The Earth is associated with the Sky to form the couple Sky-Earth (Dyāvā-Pṛthivī), also spoken of as the two "laments" (*rodasī*), abodes of the lord-of-tears (Rudra).

When invoked alone the Earth is often identified with Aditi, the primordial vastness, "the Inexhaustible, the source of abundance," the most ancient of all goddesses and the mother of the gods.

All the forms of the earth and of life on it are the forms, the children, of this goddess, Earth.

Mountains, trees, rivers, animals, have in them a common yet multiple life and are guided by conscious beings who are the attendants of the earth goddess.

"Rivers and mountains have a dual nature. A river is but a form of water, yet it has a distinct body. Mountains appear a motionless mass, yet their true form is not such. We cannot know when looking at a lifeless shell that it contains a living being. Similarly within the apparently inanimate rivers and mountains there dwells hidden a genie. Rivers and mountains take the forms they wish." (*Kālikā Purāṇa* 22.10–13. [122])

Agni (Fire)

THE EARTH is the dwelling place of fire. Fire captured and tamed by man has been the greatest assistant in his progress, the instrument of his power. Every form of fire is worshiped as a deity, but the divinity of fire is more directly experienced in the ritual fire, born of two pieces of wood rubbed together to the accompaniment of ritual utterances and ceremonies.

Agni is one of the most important deities of the Vedas. He is the mediator between men and gods, the protector of men and their homes, the witness of their actions, invoked on all solemn occasions. He presides over all sacraments, all the great events of life.

The shining quality in anything is the quality of Agni, hence, worshiping him, man gains the brilliance of intelligence, of strength, health, and beauty.

As a cosmic principle, Agni is the chief deity among the spheres-of-the-elements (Vasus), but when he is envisaged merely as the earthly fire, the leading role may be attributed to two of his aspects, Indra, the thunderbolt, the form of fire dwelling in the intermediary sphere of space, and the solar Viṣṇu, the All-Pervader, who is the ruler of the heavenly sphere, as well as the inner fire hidden within all things, within all beings, as their power of devouring and digesting.

Agni is thus called the "all-pervader" (Vaiśvānara). The understanding of the nature of fire leads to the understanding of the universe. The science of fire is the key to all knowledge. Agni is the power of inner as well as outer illumination, the power of knowledge as well as of perception. He is the lord of knowledge. The "Ancient Lore of Agni" (*Agni Purāṇa*) is the encyclopedia of all the traditional sciences.

In the *Viṣṇu Purāṇa* Agni is called the Proud (Abhimānī) and is represented as the eldest son of the Creator, Brahmā. He sprang from the mouth of the Cosmic-Man (*virāṭ puruṣa*). In the world of man, Agni was born as the ritual fire from the Daughter-of-Light (Vasubhāryā), wife of Eternal-Law (Dharma). Intelligence (Medhā) is his sister.

His own wife is the Invocation-at-Offering (Svāhā). By her he had three sons, named the Purifier (Pāvaka), the Purifying (Pāvamāna), and Purity (Śuci). These sons in their turn had forty-five children, all of whom are various aspects of fire. They bring the forms of fire to a total of forty-nine.

Agni is described in the *Harivaṁśa* as one of the eight regents of space. He rules over the southeastern direction, called the forward-light (*puro-jyotis*).

Red in color, with yellow eyes and two heads, he carries to the gods the offerings of the sacrifice. His image is of gold with red attributes. He has four arms, which carry an ax, a torch, a fan, and a spoon, and sometimes also a rosary and a flaming spear (*śakti*).

Adorned with flames, he is dressed in black. His standard is smoke. He is accompanied by a ram and sometimes rides it. At times he sits in a chariot drawn by red horses. The seven winds are the wheels of his car. Agni also has seven tongues, each of which has a distinct name, and he uses them to lick the butter poured as an offering.

"Strongly built, with a large belly, Agni is red, with golden brown mustaches, hair, and eyes. Seated on a ram, he holds a rosary and a sphere. He has seven tongues of fire." (Quoted in *Śabda-kalpa-druma* at the word *agni*. [123])

As the god of sacrifices, Agni is called Oblation-eater (Hutāśa or Hutabhuj), Oblation-bearer (Havyavāhana), the Conveyer (Vahni).

Among the names of Agni the most common are: All-Possessor (Jātavedas), Purifier (Pāvaka), Burning (Jvalana), Rich-in-Light (Vibhāvasu), Multicolored (Citrabhānu), Resplendent (Bhūritejas), Flaming (Śikhin), Yellow-hued (Piṅgeśa), Gold-maker (Hiraṇyakṛt), Flickering (Plavaṅga), He-who-Develops-within-his-Mother (i.e., within the fire stick) (Mātariśvan).

He is the All-Pervader (Vaiśvānara). His-standard-is-smoke (Dhūmaketu). He is a javelin-bearer (Tomara-dhara). Lotus-in-hand (Abja-hasta), he is the bright-one (Śukra), the pure (Śuci). Having-red-horses (Rohitāśva), he rides on a ram (Chāgaratha). Seven-tongued (Sapta-jihva), he is the giver-of-wealth (Draviṇodas).

In a well-known hymn of the *Ṛg Veda*, Indra and other gods are called upon to destroy the flesh-eaters (*kravyāda*), or demons (*rakṣas*), enemies of the gods. Agni himself is a flesh eater. As such he is represented under a fearful form. He sharpens his iron tusks, and devours his enemies.

The Ten Forms of Fire

THERE ARE ten main forms of fire, five natural forms and five ritual forms. The five natural forms are these:

1. Agni is the earthly or common fire, either visible or potential, that is, hidden in fuel.
2. Indra (or Vāyu), the power of the thunderbolt which dwells in the clouds, is the fire of space, of the intermediary world. It is the source of conflagrations and of the dreaded forest-fires (*dāva-agni*).
3. Sūrya (the Sun), the fire of the heavenly sphere which illumines the world, is known as the celestial-fire (*divya-agni*).
4. Vaiśvānara (the all-pervader) is the power of digesting, found in all things, all beings. It is the support of life.
5. The fire of destruction, Agni's most fearful form, was born of the primeval waters and remains hidden under the sea, ever ready to destroy the world. Spoken of as the Stallion's fire or submarine-fire (*vāḍava-agni*) from the root *vāḍ* or *bāḍ*, "to dive," this fire, which will destroy the world, lies dormant in

a volcano called the Stallion's Mouth (*vāḍava-mukha*) below the austral sea at the antipodes of the polar mountain Meru.

The five forms of ritual fire are: the fire-of-the-Immensity (*brahma-agni*), the fire-of-the-lord-of-progeny (*prājāpatya-agni*), the householder's-fire (*gārhapatya-agni*), the Ancestors'-fire (*dakṣiṇa-agni*), and the funeral-fire (*kravyāda-agni*).[2]

"The *fire of the Immensity* is said to appear spontaneously during the ritual of sacrifice at the sound of the magic formula (the *Anaṇi-manthana Mantra*) that is uttered while the fire stick is revolving. This is the fire born of the world.

"The *fire of the lord of progeny* is handed over to the unmarried student when he is invested with his sacred thread. In this fire he is to perform the ritual offering known as Agnihotra. He is pledged to preserve this fire, worship it, and feed it with offerings, till the day when, at the approach of old age, he abandons his home to retire into the forest.

"The *householder's fire* is brought into the house after the marriage ceremony and is the center of family rituals. It is to be kept ever alive and all the offerings of the married man should be offered into its flames.

"The *Ancestors' fire* or '*Southern fire*' is that in which offerings are made to Ancestors. The rituals of exorcism (*abhicāra yajña*) are to be performed in this fire. During the great ritual sacrifices a fire lighted from a 'Southern fire' has to be maintained outside the southern gate of the sacrificial-hall (*yajña-maṇḍapa*). This fire is expected to burn away the obstacles which would otherwise arise to prevent the completion of the ritual.

"The *funeral fire* is the fire of the funeral pyre into which the body of man is thrown as a last offering. It should never be approached by the living." (Vijayānanda Tripāṭhī, "Devatā tattva," *Sanmārga*, III, 1942, 687.)

The Sphere of Space and the Lord-of-Wind (Vāyu)

BETWEEN THE earth and the sky, abode of the sun, is the intermediary-sphere (*antarikṣa*) or sphere of space, the dwelling place of subtle beings whose king is the lord of wind, Vāyu.

2 Elsewhere the ritual fire is shown under six forms:
the fire of the householder, *gārhapatya-agni*,
the fire of Vedic rituals, *āhavanīya-agni*,
the fire of the Ancestors, *dakṣiṇa-agni*,
the fire of the assembly, *sabhya-agni*,
the fire of the Sacrifice (Agnihotra), *āvasathya-agni*,
the fire of divine service, *aupāsana-agni*.
(Quoted in Vijayānanda Tripāṭhī's "Devatā tattva," *Sanmārga*, III, 1942.)

Just as fire, the devourer, was the mouth of the gods, wind is their breath. In the Upaniṣads, Vāyu appears as the cosmic life breath. The *Mahābhārata* (12.328.35 [124]) calls him the life breath of the world, the universal "spirit," the impeller of life and of the living. Vāyu is also the substance and the essence of speech (*vāc*). A few Vedic hymns are addressed to him. The name Vāyu comes from the root *vā*, "to blow."

Vāyu is the purifier, the first to have drunk the ambrosia, the *soma*. He is an explorer, the messenger of the gods, the leader of sacrifices.

Vāyu is also called the "wanderer" (Vāta) (*Mahābhārata* 1.5908; 3.11914), "the one without whom one dies" (Marut) [125], "the one by whom one lives" (Anila) [126], the "cleanser" (Pāvana).

The first three names (including Vāyu) refer to the wind's destructive aspect, the two last to its gentle, beneficial forms. Vāyu is the friend of Agni, whom he strengthens and helps. "Vāyu, the friend of Fire, fragrant, caressing, wanders through the homes of the gods, arousing all the senses." (*Mahābhārata* 12.8418. [127])

Vāyu also means "pervader." "Subtle, he abides in space, pervading (*vyāpya*) the three worlds; the seers worship him, calling him Vāyu." (*Bṛhad-devatā* 2.32. [128]) He is the son of the four directions of space; he is also the regent of the northwest quarter where he dwells. In the *Puruṣa Sūkta* 13 [129],[3] Vāyu is said to have sprung from the breath of the Cosmic-Man (*puruṣa*). In another hymn he is the son of Tvaṣṭṛ, the divine craftsman. In the Vedas Vāyu is the friend of Indra, the thunderbolt, and rides with him in a chariot of gold which is drawn by a thousand horses and which can reach the sky. The *Viṣṇu Purāṇa*, however, makes Vāyu a servant of Indra.

Vāyu is pictured as a strong and powerful white man riding a deer. He holds a bow and arrows. All his attributes are white.

"When the powerful Vāyu came, I stopped him with all my strength, for he easily breaks trees, mountains, and everything else. There is no being whose strength can be compared to that of Vāyu. The wielder-of-the-thunderbolt (Indra) and the ruler-of-death (Yama), the lord-of-wealth (Kubera), and the lord-of-the-waters (Varuṇa) cannot stand before him; much less can you, O tree!" (*Mahābhārata* 12.528. [130])

The *Bhāgavata Purāṇa* relates that the sage Nārada once incited the wind to break the summit of the polar mountain, Meru. Vāyu blew in a terrible storm which lasted for a year, but Viṣṇu's mount, the bird Wings-of-Speech (Garuḍa), shielded the mountain with his wings and the efforts of the wind god were in

3 The *Puruṣa Sūkta* is *Ṛg Veda* 10.90.

vain. Nārada then suggested that he should attack the mountain in Garuḍa's absence. He did so, and broke off the summit, which he threw into the sea, where it became the island of Ceylon.

Vāyu is the father of the hero Bhīma and of the monkey Hanuman. He is king of the celestial musicians. (*Viṣṇu Purāṇa.*)

The Sky (Dyaus)

THE SKY (Dyaus), the supreme firmament, is one of the oldest divinities of the Indo-Europeans. The Sky is the Father and, with the Earth, the origin of everything. All the gods, Sun, Moon, Wind, Rain, Lightning, Dawn, and the rest, are children of the Sky. Dyaus covers the Earth and fertilizes her with his seed, that is, with rain.

The word *dyaus* represents "the place where the gods shine" [131] and is often taken as an equivalent of ether (*ākāśa*), which means "where the sun and other [luminaries] shine" [132].

A tale in the *Mahābhārata* (1.99) relates that, because of a curse, Dyaus had to become a man. He was incarnated as Bhīṣma, the father of heroes.

Among the names of Dyaus the main ones are: home-of-the-clouds (Abhra), abode-of-the-clouds (Meghaveśman), the veil (Ambara), without-parts (Anaṅga), the covering (Vyoman), the great-veil (Mahā-vila), the reservoir-of-water (Puṣkara), the abode-of-the-three-worlds (Triviṣṭapa), space (Antarikṣa), the path-of-the-winds (Marudvartman), the endless (Ananta), the path-of-the-clouds (Meghavartman), the divider (Viyat), the path-of-birds (Vihāyas), the moving-one (Gagana).

The Sun (Sūrya)

THE SUN (Sūrya) is one of the three chief deities of the Vedas. It is envisaged under two aspects. As one of the spheres, one of the Vasus, the physical sun is the celestial form of fire, of Agni. As the source of light, of warmth, of life, of knowledge, the solar energy is the source of all life, represented in the twelve sons-of-the-Primordial-Vastness (Ādityas), the twelve sovereign principles.

The sun is at the center of creation, at the center of the spheres. Above it are the unmanifest spheres, those of the Self-born (*svayambhū*) and the Supreme-Ruler (*parameṣṭhin*). Below are the manifest spheres, those of the moon and the earth. The sun represents the limit, the point, where the manifest and the unmanifest worlds unite. "The sun thus represents the supreme Principle, first nonmanifest, then manifest." (*Chāndogya Upaniṣad* 3.19.1. [133])

It is for us the gate toward the unmanifest aspects of divinity, the *Ostentorium* through which the divine reality can be perceived. "The sun is the gateway to the path of the gods." (*Mahābhārata* 13.1681. [134])

As the source of light, physical, mental, spiritual, the sun is the nearest image we can have of divinity. "The sun is visible divinity, the eye of the world, the maker of the day. Eternal, no other deity can be compared to him. He is the source of time. The planets, the stars, the spheres-of-the-elements (Vasus), the divinities-of-life (Rudras), the lord of wind and the lord of fire, and all the other gods are but parts of him." (*Bhaviṣya Purāṇa.*)

The sun is the visible source of the world in which we live. "All that exists was born from the sun." [135] "Of what is and has been and is to be, and what moves or remains still, the sun alone is the source and the end." (*Bṛhad-devatā* 1.61. [136])

The solar spirit, the divinity that dwells in the solar sphere (*sūrya-maṇḍala*), is the source of development and thus is known as the Evolver (Bharga). "This Evolver is the Soul of all that exists in the three worlds, whether animate or inanimate. There is nothing apart from it." (*Brāhmaṇa-sarvasva.*)

At the time of creation, "the world's egg divided itself into two parts, the one of silver, the other of gold. The silver part became the earth, the golden part the sky. The outer cover of the egg became the mountains; the inner cover, the clouds and the snow; the inside veins became the rivers, the liquid in the egg became the ocean. When the sun appeared there was a great cry from which all the beings and all their pleasures were born. Hence at his rising and setting, cries and songs are heard; all beings and desires rise toward it. Those who worship the sun as the Absolute ever hear beautiful sounds and are filled with joy." (*Chāndogya Upaniṣad* 3.19.1–4. [137])

Made of a fire that consumes its own substance, the sun is identified with the cosmic sacrifice. It is said that the "lord of progeny who is the ritual sacrifice" (Yajña-Prajāpati), becoming the sun, procreates all living things. As the lord of procreation he is represented in the form of a bull. In the self-born solar fire the "seed of the Supreme Ruler" (*pārameṣṭhya-soma*) is ceaselessly poured as fuel.[4]

"Through his rays he puts life into food grains and living beings. He is the father of all." (*Mahābhārata* 3.135. [138]) The Sun is thus called the Nourisher (Savitṛ).

4 See Motilāl Śarmā Gauḍ, *Īśopaniṣad Vijñāna Bhāṣya*, p. 61.

"When the sun rises, it enters the eastern quarter and sustains with its rays the beings of the east. It illumines the south and the west, the north, the upper and lower directions, and all that lies between them, and it sustains all beings with its rays.

"It rises as the universe, as the Cosmic Being, as life, as fire. Hence the Scripture describes it as the resplendent sun, embodiment of the universe, all-knowing, support of all, luminous, and warm, with a thousand rays and hundreds of whirlpools. Ever-present, it rises giving life to all creatures." (*Praśna Upaniṣad* 1.6–8. [139])

As the devourer, the Sun is also the destroyer. "At the end of time the Sun dries up the whole world." (*Mahābhārata* 12.11057. [140])

The Sun, envisaged as perpetually creating, supporting, and destroying life, pleasing all by its multifold brilliance, is the visible form of *māyā*, the power of enchantment of the Supreme Being. He is "deserving of adoration" (*vareṇya*). "When the Sun rises, all turn toward him." (*Mahābhārata* 3.11847; 7.8459. [141])

"I bow to that which is the substance of all, which is all, the embodiment of the universe, the light on which the yogis meditate." (*Mārkaṇḍeya Purāṇa* 105.5. [142])

"He is the cause of all, supremely worthy of praise, the Supreme Light, distinct from fire, that was in the beginning.

"I bow to you who are matter and of whom the gods are the Soul. Resplendent, you existed first, transcendent." (*Mārkaṇḍeya Purāṇa* 105.7. [143])

"He is the Self of the yogis who seek the dissolution of intellect. He is the knower of the conscious for those who seek knowledge, and the lord of sacrifice to the sacrificer." (*Mārkaṇḍeya Purāṇa* 3.2. [144])

"The Sun is the Soul of the world." (*Ṛg Veda*, 1.115.1. [145])

This sun god is the very spirit who dwells in our inner soul. "He who dwells in man and who dwells in the Sun is one." (*Taittirīya Upaniṣad* 2.8. [146])

As our inner self, the solar deity is ever directing our inner faculties just as it directs all our vital cycles.

This inner Sun is realized within his heart by the yogi as a prodigious source of light, which he compares to a smokeless fire.

The Image of the Sun

"THE GOLDEN being who dwells in the sun has a golden beard and golden hair. All in him is shining, even the tips of his fingernails.

"His eyes are brown like the *kapyāsa* flower. His fame is great. He is above evil. Verily, he who knows this rises above evil.

"His two voices are the *Ṛk* and the *Sāman*. Therefore he is called the 'high-chant' (*udgītha*) and the singer is the high-chanter (Udgātṛ). He is the Lord of the high worlds which are beyond and where the gods' desires are fulfilled." (*Chāndogya Upaniṣad* 1.6.6–8. [147])

There are temples of the Sun where he is the main object of worship. His image is "copper colored, red, and brown. He is auspicious, fearless, surrounded by the thousand powers of life, the Rudras, sheltering in all the directions." (*Nīlarudra Upaniṣad* 1.9. [148])

According to the *Viṣṇu Purāṇa*, the Sun is of dwarfish stature, with a body like burnished copper and slightly reddish eyes. He dwells in the Resplendent-City (Vivasvatī or Bhāsvatī).

He has a neck like a tortoise shell, he wears bracelets and a diadem which illumine all the quarters of heaven (*Mahābhārata* 3.17077). His earrings are the gift of the mother goddess Aditi (ibid. 3.17118).

The Sun has two long arms or four short arms. He is clad from feet to chest in the "northern fashion" [5] (*Bṛhat Saṁhitā*) or wears high boots and a belt. "The sun god, watching the worlds, wanders in a car of gold, moving round with darkness, establishing the immortals and the mortals [in their proper places]." (*Taittirīya Saṁhitā* 3.4.11.2. [149])

The horses of the Sun are mentioned in the *Ṛg Veda* (5.45.9 [150]). "May the Sun with its seven horses arrive." His chariot has but one wheel. "The Resplendent-One (Vivasvat) moves in his orbit in a one-wheeled car" (*Mahābhārata* 12.362.1 [151]). The Sun sits on a lotus in his chariot. The golden horses, or mares, can be four or seven. Sometimes the chariot has only one horse with seven heads surrounded with rays. Elsewhere it is said to be drawn by a dragon (*nāga*).

The Sun's charioteer is the Red-One (Aruṇa), the wise elder brother of the bird Wings-of-Speech (Garuḍa). Aruṇa, like the resplendent Vivasvat, also a son of Kaśyapa, is the deity of dawn. He stands on the chariot in front of the Sun, and his strong body shelters the world from the Sun's fury. Aruṇa is said to be more beautiful even than the Moon.

In the Purāṇas the Sun is the son of Vision (Kaśyapa) [6] and of the Primor-

5 The northern fashion seems to refer to the dress of Central Asia.

6 According to the *Mahābhāṣya*, the word *kaśyapa* is the inverted form of *paśyaka* (seer). The inversion is an element of the symbolism of the name. In the *Mārkaṇḍeya Purāṇa*, Kaśyapa is said to mean "wine-drinker."

dial-Vastness (Aditi), the progenitors of all the gods. In the *Rāmāyaṇa* the Sun is referred to as a son of the Immense-Being (Brahmā), though Brahmā is usually pictured as the grandfather of Kaśyapa.

According to the *Kūrma Purāṇa* (adhyāya 20), Sūrya has four wives: Knowledge (Saṁjñā), the Queen (Rājñī), Light (Prabhā), and Shade (Chāyā). The *Mārkaṇḍeya Purāṇa* speaks only of Saṁjñā and Chāyā. Elsewhere his wives are given as Colored (Savarṇā), Self-Existence (Svāti), and Great-Courage (Mahā-vīryā). The Sun is sometimes made the husband of Dawn (Uṣas), though he is also spoken of as the child of Dawn. In the *Mahābhārata* (1.2599), Knowledge (Saṁjñā) is said to be the daughter of the world's architect, Viśvakarman. She is called the Resplendent (Suvarcalā) (ibid., 12.6751).

The Sun has several sons. The lawgiver (Manu), the lord-of-death (Yama), and the river Yamunā were born to Saṁjñā, according to the *Kūrma* and *Mārkaṇḍeya Purāṇas*. The *Mahābhārata* replaces Yamunā by Yamī, twin sister of Yama.

According to the *Kūrma Purāṇa*, Revanta was born to Rājñī, Dawn (Prabhāta) to Light (Prabhā), and Sāvarṇi (one of the lawgivers) to Chāyā. The *Mārkaṇḍeya Purāṇa* gives Sāvarṇi, Revanta, and Saturn (Sani) as the sons of Chāyā.

According to the *Mahābhārata*, the hero Karṇa was the Sun's illegitimate son by Kuntī. The Sun is also the father of the monkey chief Sugrīva. Vaivasvata Manu, the lawgiver, son of Saṁjñā and the Sun, was the father of Ikṣvāku. The solar race of kings, the *sūrya-vaṁśa*, takes its origin from this grandson of the Sun.

The Sun's brightness was so great, the *Mahābhārata* records, that Knowledge (Saṁjñā), unable to bear it, left Shadow (Chāyā) by his side and retired into the forest to devote herself to religion. To hide, she took the form of a mare. The Sun discovered her and approached her, taking the form of a horse. She bore him two sons who are the horse-headed gods of agriculture, the Aśvins.

After the birth of the Aśvins, the Sun brought his wife back home. To relieve her plight, her father, the cosmic architect, Viśvakarman, placed the Sun on his lathe and cut away one-eighth of his rays, trimming him in every part except the feet. The fragments fell upon the earth; from them Viśvakarman formed the discus of Viṣṇu, the trident of Śiva, the mace of Kubera, the lance of Kārttikeya, and the weapons of the other gods.

Sūrya (the luminous) and Āditya (son of the primordial vastness) are the two most common names of the Sun. The word *sūrya* comes from the root *sur* or *svar*, "to shine." From the same root also comes *svarga* (heaven). "When the

Eternal, the one Self, the power of knowledge, wished for a second, light was born and was called Sūrya." (*Varāha Purāṇa* 26.1–2. [152])

Āditya means "son of the primordial vastness," but it can also mean "the source." "Since the Sun is the source of the world, it is called Āditya" (*Varāha Purāṇa* 26.7 [153]). The Sun is also called the One-legged-Goat (Aja-ekapāda), the goat being the representation of the three qualities of Nature (*prakṛti*). He is the Purifier (Pāvaka), the Source-of-Life (Jīvana), the Victorious (Jayanta), the Divider (Ravi). (Ibid. 26.5.) Born from *mṛtāṇḍa*, a lifeless egg, he is called Mārtāṇḍa.

He is the Procreator or Nourisher (Savitṛ or Savitā), the Lord-of-the-Day (Aharpati), the Eye-of-the-World (Jagat-cakṣus or Loka-cakṣus), the Witness-of-Deeds (Karma-sākṣin), the King-of-Planets (Graha-rājan), Having-a-Thousand-Beams (Sahasra-kiraṇa), Having-a-Thousand-Rays (Sahasrāṁśu) or Shorn-of-his-Beams (Vikartana), Made-of-Twelve-Parts (Dvādaśātman), Having-Seven-Horses (Saptāśva), Gem-of-the-Sky (Dyu-maṇi), Lord-of-the-Planets (Graha-pati), the Pervader (Heli), the Wanderer-of-Space (Khaga), the Friend-of-the-Lotus (Padma-bandhu), Lotus-in-Hand (Padma-pāṇi), Enemy-of-Snow (Himārāti), Effacer-of-Darkness (Tamopaha).

The other names of the Sun merely refer to his brilliance (see the *Mahābhārata*, Hymn to the Sun, 2.166, and *Varāha Purāṇa* 26). Arka comes from *arc*, "to radiate, to shine," Tamisra-han means "killer of darkness"; Tamo-nuda is "dispeller of darkness"; Divā-kara, "maker of the day"; Dīptāṁśu, "having blazing rays"; Prabhā-kara, "source of extreme light"; Citra-bhānu, "with colored rays"; Bhānu, "shining"; Bhāskara, "maker of light"; Vibhā-vasu, "abode of light"; Vivasvat, "resplendent"; Sahasrāṁśu, "thousand-rayed"; Rohita, "the red one"; Gopati, "lord of beings"; Bradhna, "tied by his rays."

Dawn (Uṣas)

IN THE *Ṛg Veda* the Dawn (Uṣas) is shown as a young woman who uncovers her breast for men to admire. Always young, she pushes back darkness and awakens all beings. She moves about in a splendid chariot. She is the sister of Night, the wife or mistress of the Sun, the daughter of the Sky. According to the the Brāhmaṇas, she has incestuous relations with her father, the lord-of-progeny (Prajāpati).

The Constellations (*nakṣatra*)

BEYOND THE solar sphere are immense spheres which no longer belong to the world of man and where all the relative aspects of space and time which condition human existence are no longer valid. These spheres represent the transcendent aspects of the Cosmic Being, the boundless powers from which universes are born. They are the abode of the Unknowable, spoken of as the Self-born (*svayambhū*). Beyond them is the sphere of Supreme-Will (*parameṣṭhin*). Situated beyond the sun, the limit of our universe, these faraway spheres are spoken of as the spheres of the constellations.

Thus the sun truly appears to be the center of the world, being the limit between the manifest earthly world and the sphere of space on one side and the transcendent spheres of the Self-born and Supreme Will on the other. The symbols we may use to describe these unknown spheres are, to say the least, inadequate, but the symbols are the only means we have of pointing at their reality.

The higher principles, the higher gods, dwell in these suprasolar worlds known as the spheres of the stars, and so do the spirits of the Ancestors. Contact with these worlds is possible only through the rites of sacrifice, hence the constellations, the Nakṣatras, are represented as the daughters of Ritual-Skill (Dakṣa). They are the wives of the Moon, which is the chalice of ambrosia and the ruler of the mind.

The Moon, the Cup-of-Offerings (Soma)

IN THE later hymns of the *Ṛg Veda*, as well as in the *Atharva Veda* and in the Brāhmaṇas, the Offering (Soma) is identified with the moon and with the god of the moon. Soma is the most frequently occurring name for the moon in the *Mahābhārata*. The moon is the vessel of divine ambrosia drunk by Ancestors and gods yet ever refilled again. The substance of the moon is all that is gentle: the offering, the victim, the fuel of the cosmic sacrifice, the sperm, the seed of life.

As the ambrosia, the chalice of immortality, Soma does not belong to the world of death. Its nature is that of the suprasolar spheres. The Moon is the ruler of the world of the stars and the symbol of the world beyond death, the world of immortality, the sphere where the Ancestors dwell.

In Yoga, "ambrosia" is the name given to sexual energy. Semen is of the same substance as the mind. By sublimating his seed, the yogi acquires prodigious mental powers. The moon is the chalice of semen, the substance of the mind. The moon is the mind of the Cosmic Man, Virāṭ Puruṣa, the presiding deity of the mind.

As the sublimated essence of lust, the moon is made of the bones of Kāma, the god of lust, whose body was destroyed by a glance of Śiva, the great Yogi.

The moon is divided into sixteen digits. Each day the gods drink one digit. During solar eclipses the last digit is drawn by the neighboring sun. In an attempt to have at last a share of ambrosia the demon Rāhu tries to devour the sun.

"When the gods were receiving the ambrosia of immortality, the Moon detected the antigod Rāhu disguised as a god. Because of the Moon Rāhu had to die, but although his head was severed from his body, he could not truly die, for he had tasted the ambrosia. His head remained alive. As a revenge, whenever the moon is full, Rāhu tries to devour it. This is the tale of the eclipses." (Vijayānanda Tripāṭhī, "Devatā tattva," p. 682.)

The world is a divine thought, a vibration in the causal substratum; hence the moon, the cosmic mind, is assimilated to the causal-waters (*ap*), from the waves of which all tangible forms develop.

"For the sun is the principle of life and the primeval waters are the moon. And these waters are the source of all that is visible or invisible. Hence the waters are the image of all things." (*Praśna Upaniṣad* 1.5. [154])

The Moon, as the presiding deity of the watery element, rules over the tides of the sea. The sphere of the Moon is the reservoir of rain water. As the reservoir of rain water, the Moon is the lord of plants, the deity protecting all vegetable life. Medicinal herbs are said to increase their activity during eclipses. The moon brings rain; its light makes the lotus blossom. Its soft rays soothe the earth burnt by the solar ardors.

The subtle beings, coming from the heavenly worlds, have to cross the sphere of the moon, and they come down to the earth with rain water. This is how the wandering souls seeking incarnation enter first into plant life and then into animals and men. Being the place whence the wandering souls come to earth, the moon is considered the dwelling place of the migrating souls and of the Ancestors.

"Though, from the point of view of creation, the moon is the last born, the lowest world, yet it surrounds the earth and, from the point of view of reintegration, its sphere, which is the sphere of the mind, the sphere that separates the physical world, the earth, from the solar world of light or intellect, has to be crossed to reach the sun, the world of truth, the door to transcendent worlds." (Vijayānanda Tripāṭhī, "Devatā tattva," p. 691.)

The Moon is represented as a god, a crescent on his forehead, accompanied by the Sun or by two queens. All his attributes are white. His vehicle is the antelope.

"The moon god is white, clad in white, with golden ornaments. He sits in a chariot drawn by ten horses. He has two hands; one holds a mace, the other shows the gesture of removing fear." (*Kālikā Purāṇa* 81. [155])

"Two spans tall, he is seated on a lotus. Belonging to the merchant class, he is born of Detachment (Atri), the son of the Ocean." (*Grahayāga-tattva*. [156])

According to the Purāṇas, the chariot of the Moon has three wheels, and is drawn by ten horses as white as the jasmine, five on the right of the yoke, and five on the left. It has two drivers.

The Moon has many names and epithets. It is the Luminous (Candra), the Drop [of Soma] (Indu), Marked-with-a-Hare (Śaśin), the Maker-of-Night (Niśā-kara), Lord-of-Constellations (Nakṣatra-nātha), Having-Cool-Rays (Śītamarīci), Having-White-Rays (Śītāṁśu), Marked-like-a-Deer (Mṛgāṅka), the Crown-of-Śiva (Śiva-śekhara), the Lord-of-the-Lotus (Kumuda-pati), Drawn-by-White-Horses (Śveta-vājin). According to the *Bṛhad-devatā* (7.129 [157] commenting on *Ṛg Veda* 10.85), the Moon's principal name, Candramas, is derived from the following expressions: "The Moon 'runs beautifully,' or '[runs] observing,' or 'runs as one worthy to be observed'; or 'the first [two syllables are] from the verb *cam*' (to drink [*soma*]); or 'he fashions the aggregate of beings.' " [7]

"The Moon is not commonly worshiped at present, but the phases of the moon regulate the ordinance of all festivals and fasts. By worshiping the Moon a man is said to become free from physical and mental weakness. He gains the ability to concentrate his mind. The Moon is also worshiped to gain physical beauty. Moreover, by concentrating on the lunar disk the yogis are able to see all events, present, past, and future." [8] The influence of the Moon destroys unhappy lovers.

The Story of the Moon

IN THE *Viṣṇu Dharmottara* (1.106) and *Skanda Purāṇa* (4.1.14), Soma, the Moon, is the son of Detachment (Atri) and his wife Benevolence (Anasūyā). Elsewhere he is described as the son of Eternal-Law (Dharma) or of the Resplendent (Prabhākara), a descendant of Atri. He is also said to have sprung forth during the churning of the ocean (*Bhāgavata Purāṇa* 11.13; *Mahābhārata* 12.208). The *Viṣṇu Purāṇa* makes him a *brāhmaṇa* and calls him king of priests,

7 From the *Bṛhad-devatā* (tr. Macdonell), p. 284 (with slight changes), q. v., for the Sanskrit terms and etymology based on Yāska's *Nirukta*.

8 Vijayānanda Tripāṭhī, "Devatā tattva."

but the *Bṛhad-āraṇyaka Upaniṣad* considers him a *kṣatriya* and makes him a princely knight.

"When the ocean was churned (see p. 167), the Moon sprang forth joyfully, just after the goddess-of-fortune (Lakṣmī), spreading a cool light with its thousands of rays." (*Mahābhārata* 1.18.34. [158])

"Detachment (Atri), born from the mind of the Immense-Being (Brahmā), was a great ascetic. Wishing to have issue, he practiced severe penance for three thousand celestial years. So we are told. His semen, drawn upward, was changed into ambrosia, and sprang forth from his eyes. It broke into ten parts, which illuminated the ten corners of space. Instructed by the Immense Being, the goddesses of the ten corners received it in their wombs. But, O King! they were unable to bear it. These [goddesses of the] corners of space, unable to hold the embryos, fell with them on the earth. Seeing [the divine seed], the *soma*, fall, the Immense Being, the Patriarch, considering the welfare of the world, took the Moon in his car and with him went thrice seven times round the earth that the ocean surrounds. Some drops of lunar ambrosia fell upon the earth and became the useful plants on which the world lives. The Moon was reared by the Immense Being, who married him to the twenty-seven daughters of Ritual-Skill (Dakṣa), [the lunar mansions] named Aśvinī, etc. But the Moon was in love with Rohiṇī alone. . . . [Ritual Skill] then cursed him, saying: 'Since you failed in your promise, you shall be seized by consumption, and your seed shall be wasted. You will recover during the second fortnight of each month, that consumption may again devour you during the next fifteen days.' Having thus received a curse and a boon, Soma [the cup of Ambrosia] shines in the sky, increasing and decreasing alternately." (*Padma Purāṇa*, Sarga khaṇḍa, and *Mahābhārata*, Śalya parvan, ch. 36 [159]; see also *Bhāgavata Purāṇa* 6.7.23–24.)

The moon god was at first pious and performed the great Rājasūya sacrifice. Afterward he became arrogant and licentious. He carried away as a concubine the Star (Tārā or Tārakā), wife of Bṛhaspati, the teacher of the gods, and refused to send her back. A quarrel ensued in which the sage Uṣanas, supported by the antigods and the genii (*dānava, daitya*, etc.), sided with Soma. The king-of-heaven (Indra) and most of the gods sided with Bṛhaspati. In the fierce battle the earth was shaken to her center. The body of Soma was cut in two by Siva's trident. Brahmā in the end stopped the fight and compelled the Moon to send back the Star to her husband. But to the Star was born a child of the Moon who is [the planet] Mercury (Budha). The lunar race springs from him." (*Viṣṇu Purāṇa* 4.6; *Bhāgavata Purāṇa* 9.14; *Harivaṁśa* 1.25; *Padma Purāṇa* 12; *Brahma Purāṇa* 23; *Devī Bhāgavata Purāṇa* 1.11; *Vāyu Purāṇa* 90–91.)

The Divinities of the Sphere of Space

The Divinities of Space and of Life, the Maruts and Rudras

THE MARUTS and the Rudras are the divinities of the subtle world, the middle sphere, or sphere of space, situated between the earth and the sky (*Ṛg Veda* 5.5). They are sometimes considered to be the same entities, sometimes considered to be distinct. As the divinities of the winds, said to represent the life-breath (*vāyu-prāṇa*) of the cosmos, both are called Maruts (immortals).

These genii of the air enter the ten vital centers of all living bodies as the life-energies (*rudra-prāṇa*). They are then called Rudras (the howling ones).

"These vital-energies (*prāṇa*) of man are ten, with the mind (*ātman*) as the eleventh." (*Bṛhad-āraṇyaka Upaniṣad* 3.9.4. [160])

The Rudras are thus the principles of life, intermediary between unconscious physical elements and intellect, between the earthly sphere and the sphere of the sun.

Akin to the deities ruling the sphere of space, the Rudras belong to the second stage of cosmic evolution, the second stage of creation, where the principle of life appears hovering above inanimate matter. The Rudras are therefore the deities of all intermediary stages. They preside over the second ritual of sacrifice, the midday offering, over maturity, the second period of man's life (from his twenty-fourth to his sixty-eighth year). During that period "should any sickness overtake [a man] . . . let him say: 'You vital breaths, you Rudras, let this midday libation of mine continue till the third libation. Let not the ritual which is my life be broken off in the midst of the vital breaths, the Rudras.' " (*Chāndogya Upaniṣad* 3.16.2. [161])

The name Rudra, which can be translated as the "howler" or the "red one," is also said to mean the "cause of tears." "Verily, the vital breaths are the cause of tears, for [on departing] they cause everyone to lament." (*Chāndogya Upaniṣad* 3.16.3. [162])

"When they leave this mortal body of ours they make us cry. And because they cause tears (*rud*) they are called Rudras." (*Bṛhad-āraṇyaka Upaniṣad* 3.9.4. [163])

In the *Viṣṇu Purāṇa*, Rudra, the lord of tears, is said to have sprung from the forehead of the Immense-Being (Brahmā) and, at the command of that god, to have divided himself into a male form and a female form, of which the male form multiplied into eleven beings, some of which were white and gentle, others black and furious. Elsewhere it is said that the eleven Rudras were sons of Vision (Kaśyapa) and Fragrant-Earth (Surabhi), who represents the cow of plenty.

The number of the Rudras is usually given as eleven, being the same as that of the vital-energies (*prāṇa*). The *Mahābhārata* (13.984), however, mentions eleven hundred.

The Rudras everywhere appear as the faithful companions of Rudra-Śiva. They are his friends, his messengers, whom everyone fears. Some of them are identified with aspects of Rudra himself. We shall meet them again among the attendants of Śiva.

Eight of the Rudras are equivalents to eight of the auspicious manifestations of Śiva (*aṣṭa-mūrti*); the others represent the fearful forms of fire. The first can be propitiated through worship; man should keep aloof from the others.

The Rudras are not celestial aristocrats but the working class of heaven. The *Śatapatha Brāhmaṇa* explains that Rudra the prince is one but that countless craftsmen, the Rudras, are his subjects.

The symbols of the eleven Rudras are the letters: *ḍ, ḍh, ṇ, t, th, d, dh, n, p, ph, b.*

The Maruts (Immortals)

IN THE Purāṇas the name Marut is said to mean "weep not." "Each one wept seven times. They were told, 'Weep not' (*mā rodīḥ*)." (*Bhāgavata Purāṇa* 6.18.62. [164]) " 'Do not cry (*mā rud*)! O powerful ones who move in the sky! Your name will be Marut (cry not).' " (*Vāmana Purāṇa*, ch. 69. [165]) Otherwise the etymology of the name Marut appears uncertain. It may mean "flashing or shining ones" or it may mean "immortal" and come from the root *mṛ*, "to die." "That by the lack of which beings die (*mṛ* + *ut*) is immortal (*marut*)." (*Uṇādi Sūtra* 9.14. [166]) This etymology identifies them with the vital energies and the Rudras.

The Maruts (immortals) are a restless, warlike troupe of flashy young men, transposition in space of the hordes of young warriors called the *marya* (mortals). They have been compared to a society of war-minded men with esoteric practices and formulae. They are the embodiment of moral and heroic deeds and of the exuberance of youth. Closely united, "they have iron teeth. Roaring like lions, they roam on their golden chariots drawn by tawny stallions. They dwell in the north." (*Ṛg Veda* 1.133.6.) They also hold bows and arrows and round projectiles (ibid. 5.52.13). Riding on the whirlwind, they direct the storm, and move with great noise, singing. Often brutal, though usually good humored, they are feared by everyone. Clad in rain, their duty is to spread rain (ibid. 1.38.9), to create or push away storms. Mountains tremble and trees fall when they move (ibid. 1.39.5; 5.53–54).

The Maruts are the friends of Indra, the wielder of the thunderbolt (*Ṛg Veda* 8.7.31), and also of his wife Indrāṇī (ibid. 10.86.9). In the *Mahābhārata* their leader is Indra. From him come their ornaments and their shining weapons. They help Indra in his wars, hence Indra is called the chief-of-the-Maruts (Marutvat).

In the Vedas the Maruts are said to be the sons of the bull-shaped Rudra, the giver of life, and the cow Pṛśni which represents the ocean or the earth (*Ṛg Veda* 5.452.16–17), hence they are also called sons-of-Rudra (Rudriyas). The *Vāmana Purāṇa* makes them (like the Rudras) the sons of Vision (Kaśyapa) and the Primordial-Vastness (Aditi).[1] Indra raised them to the status of gods (*Vāmana Purāṇa* 68–69). In the *Mahābhārata* (12.7540) and the *Bhāgavata Purāṇa* (6.6.17–18) they are the sons of the Law (Dharma), identified with the ruler-of-the-dead (Yama), himself an aspect of the Destroyer (Śiva). Īśāna, the Ruler, the All-Enjoyer (i.e., Śiva), is their protector (*goptṛ*). (*Mahābhārata* 12.4498.) They are also spoken of as the sons and brothers of Indra, the sons of the Ocean, the sons of Heaven, the sons of Earth.

Like the Rudras, the Maruts are pictured in the Brāhmaṇas as the chiefs of the working class, the agriculturists-herdsmen.

The world of the Maruts is the sphere of space, or the intermediary world. It is called Māruta, and is the heaven of the intermediary caste, that of the traders (*vaiśya*).

The Maruts are worshiped to gain supernatural powers and for the fulfillment of ambitious projects.

The number of Maruts varies. The *Ṛg Veda* speaks of them as twenty-one (1.133.6), twenty-seven, or forty-nine (seven groups of seven each in

1 The same origin is attributed to them in the *Rāmāyaṇa* 1.47, *Mahābhārata* 1.132.53 and 12.207.2, *Bhāgavata Purāṇa* 6.18, and *Matsya Purāṇa* 146.

5.52.16–17)[2] or (in 8.96.8) even as one hundred and eighty (three times sixty). The *Harivaṁśa* gives twenty-four distinct names for the Maruts. The *Brahmāṇḍa Purāṇa* (3.5.91–95) gives the names of forty-nine. In the *Mahābhārata* (1.67.2–4; 1.132.51, Kumbakonam ed. [167]), "the Maruts are eleven" (like the Rudras) and are called: Mṛgavyādha (hunter), Sarpa (snake), Nirṛti (misfortune), Ajaikapāda (herdsman), Ahirbudhnya (sea snake), Pinākin (archer), Dahana (burning), Īśvara (Lord), Kapālin (bearer of skulls), Sthāṇu (pillar), Bhaga (fortunate).

Other lists, slightly different, are found in *Mahābhārata* 12.207.19–20 [168][3] and 13.255.12 [169].[4] In the *Devī Purāṇa* the Maruts are seven, called Pravāha, Nivaha, Udvaha, Saṁvaha, Vivaha, Pravaha, Parivaha. The *Agni Purāṇa* (Gaṇabheda adhyāya) speaks of forty-nine and calls them Ekajyotis (one light), Dvijyotis (two lights), Trijyotis (three lights), etc.

The *Bhāgavata Purāṇa* (6.6.17–18 [170]) gives their names as: Raivata, Aja, Bhava, Bhīma, Vāma, Ugra, Vṛṣākapi, Ajaikapāda, Ahirbudhnya, Bahurūpa, Mahān.

The *Brahmāṇḍa Purāṇa* (3.5.79–88) explains that the seven groups of seven Maruts dwell respectively in seven spheres known as the earth, the sun, the moon, the stars, the planets, the Seven Seers (Great Bear), and the Changeless star (Polestar) and gives their names as:

GROUP I (Earth). Citra-jyotis (colored light), Caitya (funeral pyre), Jyotiṣman (resplendent), Śakra-jyotis (lightning), Satya (truth), Satya-jyotis (light of truth), Sutapas (burning penance).

GROUP II (Sun). Amitra (friendless), Ṛta-jit (conqueror of absolute truth), Satya-jit (conqueror of truth), Sūta-mitra (friend of the charioteer), Sura-mitra (friend of angels), Suṣeṇa (he who has a good missile), Sena-jit (conqueror of armies).

GROUP III (Moon). Ugra (fearful), Dhanada (giver of wealth), Dhātu (root), Bhīma (terrible), Varuṇa (lord of water), Abhiyutākṣika (watchful-eyed), Sāhūya (having a name).

GROUP IV (The Stars). (Names not found in the printed edition of the *Brahmāṇḍa Purāṇa*.)

2 They are also forty-nine in the *Rāmāyaṇa* 1.47, *Mahābhārata* 1.132.53 and 12.207.2, *Bhāgavata Purāṇa* 6.18, and *Matsya Purāṇa* 146.

3 "Ajaikapāda, Ahirbudhnya, Virūpākṣa, Raivata, Hara, Bahurūpa, Tryambaka, Sureśvara, Sāvitra, Jayanta, Pinākin, Aparājita."

4 "Ajaikapāda, Ahirbudhnya, Pinākin, Aparājita, Ṛta, Pitṛ-rūpa, Tryambaka, Maheśvara, Vṛṣākapi, Śambhu, Havana, Īśvara."

GROUP V (The Planets). Anyādṛś (otherwise), Īdṛś (such), Dru (moving), Mita (brief), Vṛkṣa (tree), Samit (equal), Sarit (fluent).

GROUP VI (The Seven Seers). Īdṛś (such), Nānyādṛś (not otherwise), Puruṣa (man), Pratihartṛ (doorkeeper), Sama-cetana (even mind), Sama-vṛtti (even tendencies), Saṁmita (equal).

GROUP VII (The Changeless Star). (Names not given in the printed edition of the *Brahmāṇḍa Purāṇa.*)

A Legend of the Maruts

IN THE *Rāmāyaṇa* (1.46), the Maruts spring forth from an unborn son of Diti, the mother of the antigods.

The mother of the antigods was in great distress. Viṣṇu had destroyed her two sons, Golden-Eye (Hiraṇyākṣa) and Golden-Fleece (Hiraṇya-kaśipu). In her desire for revenge, Diti, with womanly patience and cleverness, endeavored to please her husband Vision (Kaśyapa) and obtain from him a son who would destroy Indra, himself a son of Kaśyapa.

Vision would not co-operate directly, but he advised Diti to perform the son-giving (*puṁsavana*) penance. As the penance approached its completion, Indra felt anxious. He descended upon the earth and began to serve Diti like a disciple. Should she succumb to pride but for one instant this would give him a chance to frustrate her aim. For a long time Diti was cautious in her austerities, but one day, at sunset, she fell asleep. Indra took advantage of this. Entering the womb of Diti, he tore the fetus into forty-nine fragments with his thunderbolt. These fragments became the Maruts. Indra made them guardians of the chalice of Soma.

Indra, the Ruler of Heaven

"INDRA represents the power of the thunderbolt (*stanayitnu*), the all-pervading electric energy (*taḍit-śakti* or *vidyut-śakti*) which is the nature of cosmic as well as animal life. This power is brought to the earth by the rain water. It is stored as the semen (*vīrya*) of all beings." (Vijayānanda Tripāṭhī, "Devatā tattva," *Sanmārga*, III, 1942, 689.)

In the Vedas, Indra appears as the deity of the sphere of space, the dispenser of rain who dwells in the clouds. Feared as the ruler of the storm, the thrower of the thunderbolt, he is also the cause of fertility. As the ruler of the sky world he is the companion of Vāyu, the wind, which is the life breath of the cosmos. In several hymns of the *Ṛg Veda* the highest divine functions and attributes are ascribed to him. In the triad of gods, Agni, Vāyu, and Sūrya, who hold pre-eminence above the others, Indra frequently takes the place of Vāyu as the ruler of the sphere of space. Agni, Indra, and Sūrya then represent the three forms of fire: the fire of the earthly world, the thunderbolt or fire of the sphere of space, and the sun, the fire of the sky.

As the king of the gods, Indra is a prominent deity. In the Vedas, more hymns are addressed to Indra than to any other deity.[5] "Just as the Earth is pregnant with Fire, the Sky (Dyaus) is pregnant with Indra." (*Bṛhad-āraṇyaka Upaniṣad* 6.4.22. [171]) He embodies the qualities of all the gods. "Indra was made of all the other gods, hence he became the greatest." (*Avyakta Upaniṣad* 5.1. [172]) His forms are endless, and he assumes all the shapes he wills.

Indra represents "might" and is the chief of the Maruts, the genii of the storm. His comrade Viṣṇu is the embodiment of the cosmic law and of wisdom. Ever young, Indra embodies all the virtues of youth: heroism, generosity, exuberance. He stands for action and service but also for the need of force which leads to power, to victory, and booty. He leads the warriors and protects them with his thunderbolt and his bow, the rainbow.

In the later mythology, Indra is considered an aspect of Śiva and is a minor deity when compared to the three main gods. He remains, however, the chief of all the other gods. He is the ruler of the sacrifice. His name is always mentioned in the Soma rites. He is also a dancer and a magician.

Indra's enemies are the sons of Diti, the antigods, and also Namuci, the genie who prevents the heavenly waters from flowing, and Puloman, with whose daughter Divine-Grace (Śacī) he eloped.[6] Indra destroys the powerful cities of the enemy, defeats the antigods (*asura*) and the savages (*dasyu*). He overcomes with his thunderbolt Vṛtra or Ahi, the demon-magician who creates drought. In the Purāṇas, Vṛtra is made into a *brāhmaṇa* (priest) and Indra, to expiate his murder, has to give up his throne in heaven. He hides in the stem of a lotus, from where he comes back only at the request of Agni and the gods' teacher, Bṛhaspati. The *Bhāgavata Purāṇa* (6.10–13) represents him as haunted by his crime in the form of a woman of low birth.

5 In the *Ṛg Veda* the main references to the myth of Indra are in 1.11; 1.33; 2.12; 2.14; 2.15; 4.18; 7.18.16; 8.100; 10.86.

6 The names of some of Indra's enemies are given in the *Ṛg Veda* (1.84.13).

Indra loves intoxicants and pleasure. He drinks the *soma* which he stole from his father, Kaśyapa, and which gives him strength. He then goes forth against his foes and performs fabulous deeds.

In the *Mahābhārata* he is shown as being compelled by the sage Activity (Cyavana) to allow the low-born twin gods of agriculture, the Aśvins, to partake of the sacred *soma* libations.

Indra has numerous love affairs. Many instances are recorded of his lasciviousness, and his example is often referred to as an excuse for adultery. He sends celestial nymphs to disturb holy men and bring an end to the penances that give them a power which he fears (*Bhāgavata Purāṇa* 11.4.7).

He took the disguise of King Rukmāṅgada to seduce Mukundā, the wife of the sage Vācaknavī, who felt attracted toward the king (*Gaṇeśa Purāṇa* 1.36.40). He seduced the wife of the sage Utathya and had to suffer grave consequences for this (*Skanda Purāṇa* 2.7.23). He also seduced Ahalyā, the wife of the sage Gautama. She was rejected by her husband and made invisible, while the sage's curse impressed upon Indra a thousand marks resembling the female organ as signs of his lewdness. Later these were ennobled into eyes; hence he is called Sayoni (with pudenda), pudenda-eyed (Netra-yoni), thousand-eyed (Sahasrākṣa).

As the embodiment of virility, Indra is represented in the bull, the perfect male. He took the form of a bull to become the mount of King Purañjaya, who went to help the gods in their fight against the antigods (*Bhāgavata Purāṇa* 9.6).

Indra is the regent of the eastern direction, the chief of the regents of space. He is sometimes considered the ruler of the spheres of the elements, the Vasus. His name is also given to the sun during the month of Śrāvaṇa (*Bhāgavata Purāṇa* 1.10.30).

The etymology of the name Indra is uncertain. The grammarian Vopadeva derives it from the root *ind*, which means "equipping with great power." Originally, however, the name Indra may have come from *indu*, a drop, since Indra is "the giver of rain." The *Aitareya Upaniṣad* gives a symbolic etymology of the name. "Once born, he [Indra] looked at all existing-things (*bhūta*), thinking, 'Of what can one speak as different from oneself?' He saw the one Immensity, the Brahman, as the only self-sufficient entity and said cryptically, for the gods are fond of the cryptic, 'I have seen It' (*idam ādarśam*). Therefore his name is Idaṁ-dra (It seeing)." (*Aitareya Upaniṣad* 1.3.13, 14. [173])

Śakra (the mighty) is a common name of Indra, although Śakra is sometimes considered a distinct deity (an Āditya; see p. 126). Some of his other names are: Indra-the-Great (Mahendra), the Magnificent (Maghavan), Lord-of-Heavenly-Craftsmen (Ṛbhukṣa), Lord-of-the-Spheres (Vāsava), Worthy-of-Praise (Arhat), Thunderbolt-bearer (Vajrapāṇi), Riding-upon-the-Clouds (Megha-vāhana), Glorified-in-a-hundred-Sacrifices (Śata-kratu), Lord-of-the-Gods (Deva-pati), King-of-the-Gods (Surādhipa), Regent-of-Space (Divas-pati), Lord-of-the-Winds (Marutvan), Lord-of-Paradise (Svarga-pati), Leader-of-the-Celestial-Host (Jiṣṇu), Destroyer-of-Cities (Puraṁdara), the Owl (Ulūka), the Fearful-Archer (Ugra-dhanvan), etc.

Indra's appearance and behavior are described in the Vedas. He has a body, long arms, a belly. He drinks the *soma*. He has lips, teeth, a beard. His size is prodigious. His color is golden or tawny like that of the horses drawing his car. In the Purāṇas he is shown as a fair young man riding a white horse or an elephant and bearing the thunderbolt in his right hand.

Indra is not uncreated: "a vigorous god begot him; a heroic female brought him forth." His father is Vision (Kaśyapa), his mother the Primordial-Vastness (Aditi). Indra's wife, Indrāṇī or Aindrī, is also called Divine-Grace (Śacī) and is invoked among the goddesses (*Ṛg Veda* 10.159). The *Śatapatha Brāhmaṇa* calls her Indra's beloved. The *Taittirīya Brāhmaṇa* states that Indra chose Indrāṇī to be his wife in preference to other goddesses because of her sensuousness. He ravished her, and slew her father, the *daitya* Puloman, to escape his curse. Bharadvāja's daughter, the beautiful Knower-of-the-Scripture (Śruta-vatī), practiced great austerities to become the wife of Indra (*Mahābhārata* 4.49).

Indra had three sons by Divine Grace. Their names are Victorious (Jayanta), the Bull (Ṛṣabha), and Liberality (Mīḍhuṣa). (*Bhāgavata Purāṇa* 6.18.7.) Indra is the father of the mighty monkey-king Vālin, who is also considered his partial incarnation (*Brahmāṇḍa Purāṇa* 3.7.114). Vālin was killed by Rāma to help Sugrīva.

The hero Arjuna is also a son or a partial incarnation of Indra (*Mārkaṇḍeya Purāṇa* 5.22). For Arjuna, Indra robbed Karṇa of his magic coat of mail and gave Karṇa in recompense a deadly javelin.

Indra's mount is the white elephant Airāvata (or Airāvaṇa) who stands at the entrance of the heavens. It has four tusks and resembles the pleasure mountain Kailāsa. It is said to have been an ancient serpent-king reborn at the time of the churning of the ocean.

Indra's white horse is Loud-Neigh (Uccaiḥśravas), which also came forth at the time of the churning of the ocean.

The golden-chariot (*vimāna*) of Indra is called Victorious (Jaitra). It is drawn by two or by ten thousand tawny horses, or by one thousand white horses as speedy as the wind (*Mahābhārata* 13.173). Crossing the sky, it scatters the clouds and fills all the quarters of heaven with the crash of thunder. Thunderbolts, swords, and spears, as well as serpents, are stored in this chariot. Its flagstaff, Emblem-of-Victory (Vaijayanta), is gold and dark blue. This staff is the object of a separate cult. With it Indra destroys the antigods.

Mātali, Indra's charioteer and friend, is his equal in bravery. Mātali's wife is called Virtuous (Sudharmā); his daughter Lovely-Hair (Guṇakeśī) is famous for her beauty. When Mātali could not find among gods or men a bridegroom suitable for her, he went to the underworld and brought back the beautiful serpent Lovely-Face (Sumukha), who became Lovely Hair's husband (*Mahābhārata* 5.3672).

Indra's thunderbolt was made by the celestial smith Tvaṣṭṛ from the bones of the seer Dadhīci (*Brahmāṇḍa Purāṇa* 3.1.85). Shaped like a mace, it surpassed all weapons. With it Indra could cleave mountains, and struck off Vṛtra's head (*Mahābhārata* 5.10.41; 12.288). In the epic the thunderbolt is equated with the penis and in the Tantras with sexual power envisaged as the basic energy.

Indra also carries a hook, a noose, the bow Victory (Vijaya), which is the rain-bow (Indra-dhanus), the sword Conquest (Parañjaya), and the conch Gift-of-God (Deva-datta), but his main weapon is magic.

Indra's kingdom is a region of great magnificence and splendor. His city is the Immortal-City (Amarāvatī), situated near the axial mountain Meru. His palace is the Palace-of-Victory (Vaijayanta). Its park is the Abode-of-Delight (Nandana) or the Garden-of-Bulbous-Plants (Kandasāra), or the Disheveled (Pāruṣya). His court is a model one, affording all pleasures.

In the *Rāmāyaṇa* (7.29–30) Rāvaṇa, the demon-king of Laṅkā, attacked Indra in his own heaven. Indra was defeated and carried off to Laṅkā by Rāvaṇa's son Roar-of-the-Cloud (Meghanāda), who, for this exploit, received the title of Conqueror-of-Indra (Indrajit). Brahmā and the gods had to purchase Indra's release with a conditional boon of immortality. Brahmā then told the humiliated god that his defeat was a punishment for the seduction of Ahalyā.

The Purāṇas contain many tales of Indra. He appears several times in rivalry with Kṛṣṇa. He roused the anger of Durvāsas by slighting a garland the sage presented to him. As a result of the curse of Durvāsas, he was defeated by the *daityas* and was reduced to such poverty that he had to beg for a little sacrificial butter. His conquerors, however, neglected their duties and became easy prey, so that Indra recovered his possessions (*Padma Purāṇa* 3.8; *Brahmavaivarta Purāṇa*, Prakṛti khaṇḍa, 36).

Indra had been the deity worshiped among the pastoral people of Vraja. Kṛṣṇa persuaded them to cease their worship. Indra, enraged, sent a deluge of rain to overwhelm them. But Kṛṣṇa lifted up the mountain Govardhana and held it for seven days as a shelter till Indra came to render homage to him. (*Bhāgavata Purāṇa* 10.24–25.) When Kṛṣṇa went to heaven to carry off the Pārijāta tree, Indra was defeated and Kṛṣṇa took the tree away (ibid. 10.59). Indra is connected with the birth of the Maruts (ibid. 6.18). He also cut the wings of troublesome mountains with his thunderbolt (*Rāmāyaṇa*, Sundara kāṇḍa, 1.121–23).

He discovered and rescued the cows of the gods which had been stolen by an *asura* named Paṇi or Vala, whom he killed (*Ṛg Veda* 10.108).

"Observing for a long time the chaste life of the student, Indra obtained from the Immense Being himself the lesson of supreme-knowledge (*brahma-jñāna*), and it is through him that spiritual knowledge entered the world of men. He is the first teacher of the 'Knowledge of Contents,' the *Yajur Veda*. He also taught medical science to the sage Dhanvantari. He is the inspirer of many forms of knowledge." (Vijayānanda Tripāṭhī, "Devatā tattva," p. 690.)

In later mythology an independent god, Parjanya, replaces Indra as the god of rain. Today Indra is not the object of direct veneration, but he receives incidental worship and there is a festival in his honor called the "Raising of the Standard of Indra" (Śakra-dhvajotthāna).

Strabo describes the Indians as worshiping Jupiter Pluvius, probably meaning Indra.

The Ādityas, the Sovereign Principles

THE ĀDITYAS, or sovereign principles, are the personification of the laws that rule the universe and human society. They dwell in the sky, the higher sphere, and dominate life and the elements. They pre-exist all forms, being the principles according to which the universe is built.

From the point of view of man, these universal laws refer to two main aspects of existence. They regulate the relation of man with man and the relation of man with the forces of Nature (*prakṛti*), that is, with the cosmic laws or deities perceptible through the elements. Thus there are two kinds of sovereign principles, referring to "this" or to "that" world.

Because of the similarity between the human world and the cosmic world, there is always a universal principle corresponding to each of the basic principles or laws that rule human society. The Ādityas, therefore, always go in pairs and are of even number. They are six in the *Ṛg Veda* (2.27.1); they are eight in most of the Brāhmaṇas (*Taittirīya Brāhmaṇa* 1.1.91); they become twelve in the *Śatapatha Brāhmaṇa* (11.6.3, 8) and, henceforth, are linked with the solar months, the "cycle of the law" being identified with the "cycle of destiny" whose unit is the year. They are represented as the spokes of the wheel of Time. Their solar character is still further accentuated in the Purāṇas, where "Āditya" is taken as the name of the Sun. The *Mahābhārata* (2.1119) calls them the "supreme sovereigns."

Aditi (the Primordial Vastness), Source of the Ādityas

THE ĀDITYAS (sovereign principles) are the sons of the Primordial-Vastness (Aditi), which is the primeval power, the unbroken totality, the eternal, inexhaustible, unimpaired First Goddess, who is also the devourer, that is, death, the Destitute who has nothing to give. She is the boundless heaven, the endless night, the essence of divinity, the mother of all the gods (*deva-mātṛ*). The gods are born from Vastness (Aditi), Water, and Earth (*Ṛg Veda* 10.63.2). This primordial vastness has the form of the sky (*dyaus*) and the earth (*Ṛg Veda* 1.72.9; *Atharva Veda* 13.1.38). She is the support of the gods and is sustained

THE ĀDITYAS, THE SOVEREIGN PRINCIPLES

ADITI (*the primordial vastness*)

The Six Major Sovereign Principles
or
Ādityas (sons of the primordial vastness)

	In "this" world		*In "the other" world*
MITRA	(friendship) Solidarity, the sacredness of the word given, the link of man with man.	VARUṆA	(the coverer or binder) The mysterious laws of fate, the unexpected, the favor of the gods, the link of man with the gods.
ARYAMAN	(chivalry) Honor, nobility, the rules of society.	DAKṢA	(skill) The rules of the sacrifice, ritual skill, and ability.
BHAGA	(the inherited share)	AṀŚA	(the gods' given share)

The Six Minor Sovereign Principles

TVAṢṬṚ	(the shaper) Craftsmanship, the weapons.	SAVITṚ	(the vivifier) The magic weapons, the magic power of words.
PŪṢAN	(the nourisher) Inner security, prosperity.	ŚAKRA	(the mighty) Courage, outer security, heroism.
VIVASVAT	(the resplendent) Ancestral custom, morality, the Ancestor, the law of righteousness or law of man, traditional order.	VIṢṆU	(the Pervader) Knowledge, i.e., the perception of the all-pervading cosmic law.

by them. She is "the visible infinite, the endless expanse beyond the earth, beyond the clouds, beyond the sky." [1] In the Purāṇas, Aditi is sometimes identified with the earth goddess.

Dawn is the visage of the Primordial-Vastness (Aditi) (*Ṛg Veda* 1.15.3; 8.90.16; 10.11.1).

"The Primordial Vastness is the mother of Ritual-Skill (Dakṣa) and the Primordial Vastness is the daughter of Ritual Skill." (*Ṛg Veda* 10.72.4. [174])

Yāska remarks in the *Nirukta* (11.3.23 [175]) that "It is in the nature of the gods that they may be considered as born of each other, as the nature of one another."

"The Primordial Vastness is the sky, the Primordial Vastness is the sphere of space; the Primordial Vastness is the mother, the father, the son; the Primordial Vastness is all the gods, the five sorts of men, all that was born and shall be born." (*Ṛg Veda* 1.89.10; *Vājasaneya Saṁhitā* 25.23.[176]) "Auspicious (*śivā*), she contains the world. Hence we, who wish for our welfare, worship the Primordial Vastness." (*Taittirīya Saṁhitā* 4.4.12.5; *Kāṭhaka Saṁhitā* 22.14. [177])

In the *Mahābhārata* and the *Rāmāyaṇa*, Aditi, daughter of Ritual-Skill (Dakṣa), is the wife of Vision (Kaśyapa), by whom she became the mother of Cosmic-Law (Viṣṇu) and of Might (Indra or Śakra). Viṣṇu was incarnated as the Dwarf (Vāmana), and as Trivikrama or Urukrama he encompasses the three worlds. Kṛṣṇa being an incarnation of Viṣṇu, his mother, Devakī, is a manifestation of Aditi.

According to the *Taittirīya Saṁhitā*, the Primordial-Vastness (Aditi) had eight sons; seven were normally born, but the eighth appeared as a lifeless egg, Mārtāṇḍa. From this egg the Sun was born. These eight sons are identified with the eight spheres of existence, the Vasus. In the *Taittirīya Āraṇyaka* (1.13), as in most other texts, Aditi has twelve sons, the Ādityas. In the *Ṛg Veda*, where she is frequently implored for blessings on children and cattle, for protection, and for forgiveness, she is praised as the mother of the Ādityas (4.25.3; 10.36.3).

In the *Viṣṇu Purāṇa* the father of the twelve sovereign principles is Vision (Kaśyapa). When their mother, the Primordial-Vastness (Aditi), daughter of Ritual-Skill (Dakṣa), was unable to bear the radiance of her offspring, the father divided the fetus into twelve parts. Each of these gave rise to one of the sovereign principles, which are identified with the months of the year.

The *Ṛg Veda* (8.25.3; 8.10.3, 83; 8.4.79) mentions Aditi as the mother of

1 Max Müller.

Mitra (solidarity), Varuṇa (fate), and Aryaman (chivalry) in particular. The *Taittirīya Āraṇyaka* mentions the twelve sons of Aditi.

The twelve sovereign principles are generally given as Mitra (solidarity), Varuṇa (fate), Aryaman (chivalry), Dakṣa (ritual skill), Bhaga (the inherited share), Aṁśa (the gods' given share), Tvaṣṭṛ (craftsmanship), Savitṛ (the magic power of words), Pūṣan (prosperity), Śakra (courage), Vivasvat (social laws), and Viṣṇu (cosmic law).

There are, however, a few variants. In the *Mahābhārata* (1.2523 and 1.65) and *Viṣṇu Purāṇa* (180), Order (Dhātṛ) replaces Ritual-Skill (Dakṣa). The *Bhāgavata Purāṇa* (6.7.40) replaces Aṁśa by Vidhātṛ (the bestower). Sometimes it is Bhaga (the inherited share) which is called the "bestower." In the *Mahābhārata* some of the names occasionally differ, though the notions represented remain the same. In the *Mahābhārata* (19.11548), Might (Indra) replaces Courage (Śakra), the Sun (Ravi) replaces Magic-Power (Savitṛ), the Lawgiver (Manu) stands for Social-Laws (Vivasvat), the god-of-rain (Parjanya), who is an aspect of Indra, replaces Ritual-Skill (Dakṣa).

The sovereign principles, which are the law of men and gods, reveal themselves as the expanded spheres of knowledge, the part of the cosmic wisdom said to find its expression in the *Sāma Veda*. These are the principles sought by mature men during the wiser part of their life, the last forty-eight years (from sixty-eight to one hundred and sixteen). They are also related to the concluding part of the ritual sacrifice.

"The Ādityas live upon the third essence (the *Sāma Veda*). Varuṇa is their chief." (*Chāndogya Upaniṣad* 3.8.1. [178])

Mitra (Friendship), Solidarity

AMONG the sovereign principles of "this" world, the first is human solidarity, the respect for laws and treaties, the sacredness given to all that links man to man. Friendship (Mitra) appears to have been the most important divinized virtue of the early Aryans, although, at the time of the *Ṛg Veda*, its role had already paled before the expectation of divine grace represented as Varuṇa. Only one hymn of the *Ṛg Veda* is addressed to Mitra. This could mean that, during the period of the composition of the available Vedic hymns, ritual, that is, magical values, had already taken precedence over social morality, over the rules of association and companionship of an earlier tribal society.

The comradeship of men and the favor of gods, Mitra and Varuṇa, are the complements of each other. The clear rules of human association and the mysterious laws of fate govern "this" known world and "that" unknown world, symbolized as the day and the night, between which man's life is divided.

Mitra and Varuṇa are therefore always associated. Solidarity is the rule of the day when man's law is sovereign, while the mysterious law of the gods rules over the night. Together Mitra and Varuṇa rule the earth and the sky, encourage the virtuous and pious, and punish the sinful.

Mitra's main influence is to make men abide by their promises and associate together. He shows all the virtues of comradeship, truthfulness, and honesty, the sacredness of the word given, the code of honor which renders possible the association of men in tribal groups and nations.

Mitra is the divinity of contracts, of pledges. Comforting and benevolent, he protects the honest and orderly relations which render social life possible. He is the enemy of quarrels, of violence, the guide toward right action.

Mitra and Varuṇa placed their semen in an urn in front of the Dawn (Urvaśī), represented as a nymph. From their seed were born the Mover-of-Mountains (Agasti) and the Owner-of-Wealth (Vasiṣṭha), the two seers who defined the human code of behavior.

Mitra had, further, three sons born of Prosperity (Revatī), his wife. They are named Impulse (Utsarga), Ill-Omen (Ariṣṭa), and Pleasure (Pippala) (*Bhāgavata Purāṇa* 6.18.5–6).

Mitra's Iranian equivalent is Mithra, the god of light. From Iran his name returned to India as Mihira (Miiro, on early coins).

Aryaman (Chivalry)

THE SECOND sovereign principle of "this" world is Chivalry (Aryaman), that is, the quality of being a gentleman, an Ārya, and the virtues it implies. The main function of Aryaman is the maintenance of an aristocratic society and its high code of honor. Aryaman governs marriage contracts and the laws of hospitality, the rules of chivalry, the maintenance of tradition, custom, religion.

Aryaman protects the freedom of the roads. He presides over matrimonial alliances, bringing men together as fathers-in-law, sons-in-law, brothers-in-law.

Master of the Aryan rites, Aryaman regulates the performance of rituals from the outward, the social, point of view, while Dakṣa sees to their technical, magical efficacy.

Wealth forms part of the aristocratic prerogatives. Aryaman protects the family and tribal heirlooms and possessions and maintains the standards of dignified living.

Representing the principle of the aristocratic clan, Aryaman came to be considered as the Great Ancestor, the source of blue blood. Later he was made king-of-the-Ancestors (*pitṛ-rāja*). Offerings are made to him in the rituals (*śrāddha*) through which the Ancestors are fed. He shares with Mitra and Varuṇa the offerings made with the word *svāhā* in sacrifices to gods and the offerings made in the Ancestors' rituals with the word *svadhā*.

Aryaman's royal path is the Milky Way (*Taittirīya Brāhmaṇa, Bṛhat Saṁhitā*).

Bhaga (the Inherited Share)

BHAGA, "the share" of tribal possessions, stands for democratic institutions: It is the personification of an ancient Aryan custom, the annual division of tribal property between grown-up men. The receiving of a share meant admission into full status, full membership, in the manhood of the tribe; hence the title "shareholder" (*bhagavant*) is a title of honor. The younger people were not entitled to a share, hence the *Ṛg Veda* (1.91.7) opposes *bhaga*, the prerogative of the elders to a share in property, to *dakṣa*, technical ability, which belongs to the young.

The share concerns wealth (*rayi, rai, dhana, vasu, apnas*, etc.) exclusively. It is a regular previsible amount distributed to each one according to his due, whether he be strong or weak; it is a secure share, kept calmly, without passion.

It appears that originally, in the Aryan clan, the share was distributed without competition, irrespective of individual strength or influence. This implies a system of repartition which may give to one man the better land, the better cattle; hence the *Ṛg Veda* calls Bhaga "the bestower" (Vidhātṛ).

"In the morning we invoke Bhaga, the strong, the conqueror, the son of the primordial vastness, the bestower, of whom the poor and the mighty, even the king, say, 'Give me my share.' Be our guide, Bhaga! whose gifts are recurrent. Hear our hymn, Bhaga, and give us wealth. Increase our stock of cows and horses. May we be rich in sons and men." (*Ṛg Veda* 7.41.2–3. [179])

All the affinities of Bhaga are with Mitra, with the laws of "this" world. He is also connected with Pūṣan, the god of herds and fecundity, the giver of inward security and prosperity.[2]

2 See G. Dumézil, *Les Dieux des Indo-Européens*, p. 52.

Bhaga is also the name of one of the eleven Rudras. Since he makes no difference between individuals great or small, rich or poor, Bhaga is said to be blind. This blindness has given rise to various myths. According to the *Śatapatha Brāhmaṇa* (1.7.4), Rudra fought the lord-of-progeny (Prajāpati) who wished to commit incest with his own daughter. The gods then gathered the semen dropped by Prajāpati and used it as an oblation. Bhaga, standing south of the altar, saw the oblation and became blind.

In the sacrifice offered by Dakṣa, Vīrabhadra, an emanation of Śiva, pulled out the eyes of Bhaga, who was acting as one of the priests (*Bhāgavata Purāṇa* 4.5.17–20). According to the *Mahābhārata* (13.265.18), Rudra himself blinded him.

Bhaga's wife is Realization (Siddhi). By her he had three sons, Power (Vibhu), Sovereignty (Prabhu), and Greatness (Mahimān). His daughter is Hope (Āśis). (*Bhāgavata Purāṇa* 6.18.2.)

Varuṇa (the Coverer or Binder), the Mysterious Law of the Gods

VARUṆA presides over the relationship of man with the gods. He is the ruler of the "other side," of the invisible world. The sudden favor of the gods and the elements, their unaccountable cruelty, cannot be understood. The behavior of Varuṇa, who rules over the invisible, cannot be foreseen; hence he appears a dangerous lord, a despot. "He is the owner of the magic-power (*māyā*)" (*Ṛg Veda* 6.48.14; 10.99.10 [180]) through which forms are created. He represents the inner reality of things, higher truth (*ṛta*), and order in their transcendent aspects, beyond the understanding of man. His absolute power is felt during the night and in all that is mysterious, while man-made laws, represented by Mitra, rule the day.

Varuṇa is said to be an antigod, a magician: "I am King Varuṇa; these magic (*asurya*) powers were first given to me" (*Ṛg Veda* 4.42.2 [181]). This may indicate that while the earlier Aryans stressed the human side of morality, that is, Mitra, who deals with "this" world, it was from the pre-Vedic Indians that the conception of propitiating supernatural beings through rites was borrowed. This might also explain the royal character of Varuṇa, if we accept the theory that the notion of kingship was originally foreign to the Aryan clan.

Although usually linked with Mitra, Varuṇa is occasionally invoked alone and is the uncontested ruler (*samrāj*) of the Ādityas. He is everywhere, in the universe and around it, pervading all things as the inner law and order of creation. "He bound together the hours of the day and established the morning with magic art. He is seen beyond all things." (*Ṛg Veda* 8.41.3. [182]) He is the creator and sustainer of the world, having inherited [3] the prehistoric function of the Sky (Dyaus). He established and maintains natural and moral laws, expressions of the cosmic order. His laws are unassailable and rest upon him as on a mountain.

As the king, Varuṇa is the justice-giver, whose duty is to punish the guilty. He catches the evildoers and binds them with his noose. "The Lord who punishes is Varuṇa. He is the king whose duty it is to punish." (*Manu Smṛti* 9.245. [183]) He is "the binder," whose envoys are watching over both worlds, whose spies are ever at work. He gives freedom to the sinner who repents.

Varuṇa is omniscient (*Ṛg Veda* 8.41.6–7). "He knows the track of the birds in the sky. Sovereign of the seas, he knows the paths of ships. Observing the days of fast, he knows the twelve months and their progeny [the days and nights]. He knows the moon and the course of far-traveling winds. He knows the gods who live in heaven. The wise, law-abiding Varuṇa is enthroned as a king, governing all and beholding all things that have been or shall be." (*Ṛg Veda* 1.25.7–9. [184])

Varuṇa is far-seeing (Urucakṣas) and pushes up the firmament far above the trees of the forest. He is the support of the spheres.

Varuṇa made the sun shine in the sky. The wind is his breath. He traced the path of the sun, and dug channels for the rivers which flow by his command and never fill the ocean. He made the moon walk in brightness, and the stars mysteriously vanish in daylight. Varuṇa initiated the seer Vasiṣṭha in his mysteries. His secrets and those of Mitra are not to be revealed to the unwise. Varuṇa knows a hundred thousand remedies. He is entreated not to steal life away but to prolong it and to spare his devotees.

In the later mythology Varuṇa came to be relegated to the position of a god of death. Indra, the ruler of the sphere of space, took precedence over him, the ruler of the sky. In the *Mahābhārata* (2.9) and all later texts Varuṇa appears as the lord of the waters, the ruler of the sea or the subterranean waters. He is the giver of rain, of hydropsy, and has been the owner of the *soma*. He rules over the rivers and their genii. The serpent gods, the *nāgas*, are his subjects. He also rules over the antigods. He is the regent of the western direction. His domain is the Western Ocean. He is rich and happy. He also rules over one of the lunar mansions (*nakṣatra*).

The name Varuṇa may come from the root *vṛ*, meaning "to surround,

3 Louis Renou, *L'Inde classique*.

envelop, cover." It refers to the sky, all that veils or covers, all that is mysterious, cryptic, hidden. Varuṇa is also the lord of the causal waters that surround the world. "Because with visible moisture he alone covers (*vṛṇoti*) the three worlds, the bards in their praise call him the Coverer (Varuṇa)." (*Bṛhad-devatā* 2.33. [185])

The name Varuṇa can also be derived from the root *vṛ*, "to restrain," "to check," referring to the god's character as the giver of punishment.

"He covers all things or binds, hence he is Varuṇa (*vṛ* + *unan*)." (*Uṇādi Sūtra* 3.53. [186])

According to the Vedas, Varuṇa has four faces, one of which is like the face of Agni (*Ṛg Veda* 7.88.2). He has a tongue; he eats and drinks. His eye, shared with Mitra, is the sun. Sometimes he has a thousand fierce eyes. (*Ṛg Veda* 7.34.10.) He winks; his breath is the wind. He has arms and beautiful hands, as well as a shining foot. He is splendidly dressed, wearing a golden mantle. (*Ṛg Veda* 5.48.5; 1.25.13.)

"Two-armed, he stands on the back of a swan. His right hand shows the gesture of removing fear. In his left hand he holds a noose made of a serpent. He carries all the things to be enjoyed. The virgin waters of whom he is the lord should be shown on his left. On the left should also be [his consort] Prosperity (Ṛddhi), on his right [his] auspicious [son] the Nourisher (Puṣkara). He is surrounded by serpents, rivers, the sons of Yadu, and the oceans." (*Hayaśīrṣa Pāñcarātra*. [187])

"Smiling, gentle, the color of snow, lotus, or moon, with all ornaments and all characteristics, he stands happily surrounded with an auspicious, cool radiance. People worship him with streams of salt water." (*Varuṇa-dhyāna*. [188])

Varuṇa's parasol, formed of the hood of a cobra, is called Enjoyment (Ābhoga). His emblem is a fish.

The chariot of Mitra and Varuṇa shines like the sun. It has an extended forepart (*Ṛg Veda* 1.122.15). The solar rays are its reins.

Varuṇa's favorite resort is the Flower-Mountain (Puṣpa-giri). His palace is of gold. Cool water drips from its roof (*Mahābhārata* 5.3544). His city, the most beautiful in the world, is called Starry-Night (Vibhāvarī), or Earthly-City (Vasudhā-nagara), or Joyful (Sukhā). Its palaces are peopled with celestial beauties and contain all the means of pleasure.

Varuṇa's assembly hall was built by the world's architect, Viśvakarman. Situated in the midst of the waters, it is adorned with precious trees bearing flowers of all colors and pearls for their fruits. There are bushes with singing birds. In this hall Varuṇa sits on a throne, his wife at his side, surrounded with serpents (*nāga*), genii (*daitya, dānava*), and many other beings.

According to the *Mahābhārata*, Varuṇa's father is Mud (Kardama). His wife, Varuṇānī or Vāruṇī, is the goddess of liquor. She is sometimes called Gauḍī or Gaurī, the Fair One (ibid. 2.9). Their son is sometimes said to be the Nourisher (Puṣkara) [4] and sometimes the sage Mover-of-Mountains (Agasti). Varuṇa is said to have eloped with Fortunate (Bhadrā), the wife of the *brāhmaṇa* Utathya. But Utathya compelled him to give her back.[5] Varuṇa is also in a way the father of the sage Vasiṣṭha (see p. 116).

According to the *Mahābhārata* 1.66.54–55), the sage Śukra's daughter Vāruṇī is Varuṇa's eldest wife. By her he had a son Strength (Bala) and a daughter Liquor (Surā). Another son, Wrong-Deed (A-dharma), married Misfortune (Nirṛti). Her sons are evil-omens (*nairṛta*) and demons (*rākṣasa*). Fear (Bhaya), Terror (Mahā-bhaya), and Death (Mṛtyu) are also her sons. Varuṇa had another son, Famous-Warrior (Śrutāyudha), by Cool-Water (Śītatoyā). (Ibid. 1.67; 5.98.) Another of his sons, the Bard (Bandi), defeated opponents in an argument in Janaka's assembly (ibid. 3.136).

Varuṇa is the Knower (Vidvas), the Wise (Medhira), the Intelligent (Dhīra), the Discriminating (Pracetas), the Clever (Gṛtsa), the Expert (Sukratu), the Inspired (Vipra), the Clairvoyant (Kavi), the Great-Poet (Kavitara), the Greatest-of-Poets (Kavitama), the Abode-of-Life (Viśvāyu), the Great (Mahān), the Vast (Bṛhat), the Mighty (Bhūri), the Immense (Prabhūti). Later he becomes Lord-of-the-Waters (Āpam-pati, Ambu-rāja, Jaleśvara, Jalādhipa, Vāripa, Udakapati), King-of-the-Watery-Animals (Yādas-pati [6]), "Watery Hair" (Vāriloman, Viloman), Lord-of-Rivers (Nadī-pati), Lord-of-All-that-Flows (Sarit-pati [7]), the Nourisher (Bhartṛ).

The correspondence of Varuṇa with Ouranos has been noted, but the parallel does not hold in all points. In Iran Varuṇa becomes the great *asura* Ahura Mazda.

Dakṣa (Ritual Skill)

SKILL (DAKṢA) represents the technical ability of the priest and the magician which makes ritual effective, renders contacts with the gods possible. It is

4 *Mahābhārata*, Udogya parvan, 98.12.
5 *Mahābhārata*, Anuśāsana parvan, 259–313.
6 From *yādasām patiḥ*.
7 From *sarvāsāṁ saritām patiḥ*.

composed of efficiency, intelligence, precision, imagination, and is thus mainly a privilege of able and young men. "We invoke you, O Ritual-Offering (Soma)! Bring us fortune. Make our youths truthful and give them skill (*dakṣa*)." (*Ṛg Veda* 1.91.7. [189])

The existence of all things is derived from *dakṣa*, from the technique of the ritual of sacrifice. Counterpart of Aryaman, who is the social ritual, the proper way of dealing with men, Dakṣa is the proper way of dealing with gods, a mysterious, complex, and creative art.

"O Dakṣa, the Primordial-Vastness (Aditi) was born thy daughter. She gave birth to the blessed gods, the sharers of the ambrosia." (*Ṛg Veda* 10.75.5. [190]) The gods themselves are created and fed through the ritual sacrifice. Dakṣa is said to have only daughters. They are the energies born of the power of ritual. He looks after them carefully and also guards the Offering, symbolized as the Moon (the chalice of *soma*), who was once cursed because he married the twenty-seven lunar mansions, Dakṣa's daughters, but showed more attachment to his favorite, Rohiṇī.

In the clan, Dakṣa represents the woman's father seeking alliances through the ritual of love from which new warriors are born, while Aryaman deals with the male side of society (see pp. 116–17).

In later mythology, Dakṣa, the art of the sacrifice, is personified as a sage, himself the performer of sacrifices. In the fourth book of the *Bhāgavata Purāṇa* we see Dakṣa's sacrifice disturbed by Śiva, the consort of Dakṣa's daughter Faithfulness (Satī), because Śiva had not been given his share, having disregarded the family protocol.

Aṁśa (the Share of the Gods)

AṀŚA, the gods' share, represents all that is gained through luck, or accident, or war, the unexpected profit, the discovered wealth or booty, as opposed to the inherited share, which is Bhaga.

"Increase our share [of booty] (*aṁśa*) in all battles." (*Ṛg Veda* 1.102.4. [191]) "His share (*aṁśa*) is exhausted like the wealth of the victorious." (*Ṛg Veda* 7.32.12. [192])

But the main acceptation of the word *aṁśa* is the "share of the gods," that share, mysterious in its destination and ways, that the gods receive during the sacrifice, and the share of food offered to the gods before partaking of a meal.

Aṁśa also represents the royal tax, the special share to be given to a king, as opposed to the normal distribution of wealth among the members of the clan.

Tvaṣṭṛ (the Shaper), Craftsmanship, the God of Industry

THE THREE minor sovereign principles of this world are Craftsmanship (Tvaṣṭṛ), Prosperity (Pūṣan), and Morality (Vivasvat).

Tvaṣṭṛ, the Shaper, represents the craftsmanship through which weapons are produced (*Atharva Veda* 12.3.33). The Shaper is therefore an essential aspect of security and progress. As a divinized power he is the craftsman who made the thunderbolt and the chalice of *soma*. Representing an art that originally belonged to pre-Aryan India, he appears as an antigod, an *asura*, but he is also one of the ancestors of the human race. He keeps in his house the ambrosia (*soma*) that the warrior Might (Indra) comes to drink. Might, to take away his cows, killed the Shaper's son Triple-Head (Triśiras), whose form was the universe (*viśvarūpa*). Angered, the Shaper forbade Might to enter his house but Might was able to take away forcibly the beverage of immortality.

The Shaper carries an iron ax. He forges the thunderbolts of Indra. He is a beautiful, skillful worker, and also the bestower of long life and prosperity. He imparts generative power. He shapes husband and wife for each other. He develops the seminal germ in the womb, and fashions all forms, human and animal. He has produced and nourished a great variety of creatures (*Śatapatha Brāhmaṇa*). The Shaper created the lord-of-the-great (Brahmaṇaspati) and the lord-of-fire (Agni), along with Heaven, Earth, the Waters, and the Cracks-of-the-Ritual-Fire (Bhṛgus). He is associated with the celestial craftsmen, the Ṛbhus, and is represented as sometimes envying and sometimes admiring their skill.

The Shaper has a daughter, Cloud (Saraṇyū), whom he married to Tribal-Law (Vivasvat). Their offspring were the gods of agriculture, the Aśvins. (*Ṛg Veda* 10.17.1–2.)

According to *Brahmāṇḍa Purāṇa* (3.1.86–87) he has three sons, Triple-Head (Triśiras), World-Shape (Viśva-rūpa), and World-Builder (Viśva-karman), the former two by Fame (Yaśodharā) and the last by Daughter-of-Brightness (Vairocanī). Triple Head and World Shape are sometimes considered one person. In the Purāṇas the Shaper is identified with the world's-builder or architect (Viśva-karman) and sometimes also with the lord-of-progeny (Prajāpati).

Pūṣan (the Nourisher), Security, the Protector of Cattle

SECURITY (Pūṣan) is connected with the Inherited-Share (Bhaga). Pūṣan is the guardian of the ways; he protects animals and men from the dangers of the road. He guides men and guides the dead, finds lost things and animals. He is the god of cattle, fecundity, and herds. Worshiped by magicians, he is the patron of conjurers, especially those who discover stolen goods.

As the source of fecundity Pūṣan is associated with semen, that is, the offering (*soma*), and its chalice, the moon. He is also connected with the marriage ceremonial. Pūṣan is frequently mentioned in the Vedas. Many hymns are addressed to him.

The name Pūṣan comes from the root *puṣ*, which means "nourisher." "Once the lord-of-progeny (Prajāpati) had shaped all the living creatures, it was Pūṣan who nourished them." (*Taittirīya Brāhmaṇa.*)

Pūṣan is the lover of his sister Sūryā (the solar one). He helps to perpetuate the cycle of day and night, and he shares with Soma the guardianship of living creatures. He is invoked, along with various deities, but most frequently with Indra and Bhaga. Pūṣan is said to be "splendid" (Āghṛṇi), "of wonderful appearance or power" (Dasra, Dasma, Dasmavarcas, and Kapardin).

In the *Nirukta*, and in works of later date, Pūṣan, like other Ādityas, is identified with the sun. He is the brother of Indra.

Pūṣan is toothless, and feeds upon a kind of gruel. All the oblations offered to him must be ground. He is called the gruel-eater (Karambhād). The cause of his toothlessness is variously explained. According to the *Taittirīya Saṁhitā*, Rudra, excluded from a sacrifice, pierced the offering with an arrow. A portion of this offering was presented to Pūṣan, and broke his teeth. According to the *Śatapatha Brāhmaṇa* (1.7.4), he lost his teeth while eating the offering in a sacrifice held when Rudra attacked Prajāpati to prevent him from committing incest with his daughter. In the *Mahābhārata*, Rudra ran up to the gods who were present at Dakṣa's sacrifice and, in his rage, knocked out Bhaga's eyes and with his foot broke the teeth of Pūṣan, who was eating the offering. In the Purāṇas, it is Vīrabhadra, a manifestation of Śiva, who disturbed the sacrifice of the gods and knocked out Pūṣan's teeth.

Only traces of Pūṣan's cult remain in later Hinduism.

Vivasvat, the Ancestor, the Embodiment of Morality or Ancestral Law

VIVASVAT IS the embodiment of morality, of the law of righteousness, the wise ruler of conduct handed down from the Ancestors. In the *Ṛg Veda* (10.14.1; 10.58.1) he appears as the father of Yama, king of the Ancestors. He was born, like all the Ādityas, from Vision (Kaśyapa) and the Primordial-Vastness

(Aditi). He was the father of Vaivasvata Manu, the lawgiver and first ancestor of present-day mankind (*Mahābhārata*).

Vivasvat was the father of the twin gods of agriculture, the Aśvins, the horse-headed physicians of the gods (*Ṛg Veda* 10.17.2). He is sometimes said to be the father of all the gods (ibid. 10.63.1). His wife is Tvaṣṭṛ's daughter, Cloud (Saraṇyū) (ibid. 10.17.1). Fire (ibid. 1.58.1, etc.) and Wind (ibid. 6.8.4) are mentioned as his messengers.

In the *Avesta* Vivasvat's name is Vīvahvant. A book of moral and political science (*Dharma Śāstra*) is attributed to him.

Savitṛ (the Vivifier), the Magic Power of Words

THE THREE minor sovereign principles of the other worlds are Magic (Savitṛ), Courage (Śakra), and Knowledge (Viṣṇu, i.e., perception of the cosmic law).

The seventh Āditya, Savitṛ, which is the magic power of words, is sometimes added to the six main sovereign principles (*Ṛg Veda* 9.114.3).

Savitṛ represents the magic power of utterances, also identified with the procreative power of the sun. The magic power of the word instigates men to act.

"The magic-power-of-the-word (Savitṛ) first took control of mind and thought. It seized the light of Agni and extracted it from the earth.

"With mind controlled we are inspired by the divine power of the word which leads to heaven and gives strength. Having controlled the powers that are conveyed through thought, the mind enters into bright heavens.

"May the power of the word inspire men, that great light may arise." (*Śvetāśvatara Upaniṣad* 2.1–3. [193])

Savitṛ is the mysterious word, the *mantra* uttered by priests, that causes the sun to rise. It is the very sound from which the sun itself was created. According to Sāyaṇa,[8] Savitṛ is the name given to the sun before it rises and it also applies to the setting sun.

The name Savitṛ is derived from the root *sū*, "to bring forth," and Savitṛ is thus a name of the sun considered as the source of creation.

Savitṛ has golden arms and hair. His wife is Ray-of-Light (Pṛśni). Eleven hymns of the *Ṛg Veda* are addressed to him as the progenitor. Yet he is more particularly connected with the celebrated verse of twelve syllables of the *Ṛg*

8 In his commentary on the Vedas, *Ṛg Veda Bhāṣya*.

Veda (3.62.10), also known as Gāyatrī, which is considered the most important of Vedic *mantras* and must be recited three times daily by all the twice-born.

Savitṛ also presides over the magic weapons which the gods give to the performers of sacrifices and which lead them to victory.

Śakra (the Mighty), the Divinity of Courage and Outer Security

ŚAKRA REPRESENTS courage, the necessity of brute force, of war, which brings victory, booty, power, outward security. He incarnates the victorious heroism of the warriors and the exuberance of youth. He wears the attributes of the conqueror, the attributes of a king. He destroys both natural and supernatural enemies and saves the city. He is drunk with the *soma* that gives him strength and fury.

The name Śakra comes from the root *śak*, "to be strong," and signifies "mighty."

Parjanya, a younger brother or an aspect of Indra, is sometimes substituted for Śakra as an Āditya. He is the benevolent god of rain. His name means "rain-giver."

Viṣṇu, the All-pervading Light of Knowledge, the Cosmic Law Pervading the Three Worlds

WE SHALL SEE, when describing the Hindu trinity (Part Three), the different etymologies of the name Viṣṇu. Its main meaning is, however, always derived from the root *viṣ*, "to pervade."

In Vedic mythology the Pervader is considered an Āditya and represents the perception of the cosmic law that pervades the three worlds. This law is revealed to man through the illumination called knowledge and is compared to the light of the sun striding in three steps across the seven regions of the universe. Some Vedic commentators explain the three steps as the three manifestations of light—fire, lightning, and sunlight—which are the respective luminaries of earth, space, and sky, and which render perceptible the three spheres encompassed by Viṣṇu's steps. Their symbols are the points where the sun rises, culminates, and sets. The three steps of Viṣṇu found their mythical illustration in the story of the Dwarf incarnation (see pp. 169–70).

In the Vedas, Viṣṇu is occasionally associated with Indra. Knowledge associates with Power. The priestly Viṣṇu helps the Sovereign, Indra, the embodiment of the Law, to kill the demon Vṛtra. With Indra he drinks the ambrosia.

He is called the secondary-Indra (Upendra) or the younger-brother-of-Indra (Indrānuja).

We shall see, in the chapters devoted to Viṣṇu, his importance as the embodiment of the power-of-cohesion (*sattva*) from which the sun is born.

In the *Ṛg Veda*, Viṣṇu does not appear in the first rank of gods. He does not have all the characteristics of the Viṣṇu of later times but he is already the unconquerable preserver.

In the Brāhmaṇas Viṣṇu acquires new attributes and is invested with legends unknown to the Vedas but still far distant from those of the Purāṇas. In the *Manu Smṛti*, the name is mentioned, but not as that of a major deity.

Other Vedic Deities

The Aśvins, the Twin Horse-headed Gods of Agriculture and Physicians of the Gods

Ancient commentators have given various interpretations of the significance of the Aśvins. According to the *Nirukta*, they were Heaven and Earth, Day and Night; Yāska mentions some old commentators who took them for "two king-performers of holy acts." The word *aśva* (horse) literally means "pervader." The horse is always a symbol of luminous deities. The Sun's car is drawn by horses.

In the celestial hierarchy, the Ādityas and Mitra-Varuṇa are the embodiments of the priestly function, the *brahma;* the Maruts belong to the warrior class, the *kṣatra;* the Aśvins represent the third social function, *viś*, the agriculturists-herdsmen. They are the givers of health, of youth, of fecundity, the source of abundance in food, men, and goods.

Knowing all the secrets of plant life, the Aśvins are the physicians of the gods. Healers, they help the sick, they bring honey to the gods and, with the help of the seer-magician Dadhīca (Aṅgiras), they find the *soma* hidden in Tvaṣṭṛ's house. They also taught gods and men the use of liquor (*surā*).

Marvelous legends surround the Aśvins. They help heroes, whom they save and heal. They rescued Enjoyment (Bhujyu), who was drowning, and Eater (Atri), whom a demon had put in a boiling cauldron.

Indra would not acknowledge the divinity of the Aśvins and their right to the *soma* offering since they belonged to the working class and thus were ritually impure (*Mahābhārata* 12.7590). But the sage Activity (Cyavana), who had received eternal youth from them, compelled Indra to receive them among the gods.

Often called Inseparables (Nāsatyas), the Aśvins are young, handsome youths, of bright golden complexion. They are agile, swift as falcons, and take any form they please. They have a wife in common. She is Sūryā, the daughter of the Sun. They are usually mentioned as one unit, rarely as one person. Their separate names are also names common to them. One is called Nāsatya (the inseparable), or "the one without untruth," and the other is Dasra (the miraculous). Other of their appellations are: ocean-born (*abdhi-jau*); wreathed-with-lotuses (*puṣkara-srajau*); sons-of-the-submarine-fire (*vāḍabeyau*). They are also the twin-undoers-of-illness (*gadāgadau*) and the twin-celestial-physicians (*svarga-vaidyau*). Their attributes are numerous but relate mostly to youth and beauty, light and speed, duality, curative power, and active benevolence.

Sons of the Sky (Dyaus), the Aśvins appear in the sky before dawn. They ride through space in a golden car drawn by birds or, sometimes, horses. The forerunners of the Dawn, they prepare the way for her. They are the parents of the Nourisher (Pūṣan). In the *Mahābhārata* they are the fathers of two of the Pāṇḍavas, Nakula and Sahadeva.

There are several versions of the birth of the Aśvins. The main one relates that Understanding (Saṁjñā), daughter of the Shaper (Tvaṣṭṛ), was married to Eternal-Law (Dharma), who is the embodiment of righteousness, Vivasvat, and whose visible form is the sun. Unable to stand the brightness of her husband, she left her shadow near him and, taking the shape of a mare (Aśvinī), that is, of the solar light, she began to practice austerities. Righteousness (Vivasvat), taking the shape of a horse, searched for Understanding and found her, and twins were born. (*Mahābhārata* 1.67.35; *Bhāgavata Purāṇa* 6.6.40.) Because their mother had the form of a mare, these twins are called "the mare's boys" (Aśvinī-kumāra).

A celebrated book on medical science is known as *Aśvinīkumāra Saṁhitā*. The number of Vedic hymns addressed to the Aśvins testifies to the importance of their worship. They are invoked during the marriage ceremony.

The Regents of the Directions

SPACE, the substratum of the cosmos, is the abode, the source, of all forms. Hence the directions, the determinants of space, have a special significance. Particular powers or deities are symbolically connected with the directions of space, the nature of which they reveal and express.

Orientation is an essential element of ritual. The east where the sun rises, the west where it sets, the north and the south toward which it travels during the cycle of the seasons represent complementary notions which express themselves in the personalities of some of the gods.

The regents of the directions are the Protectors-of-the-World (Lokapālas) and are shown with royal attributes. They are the rulers of the spheres, the kings of all the regions of the three worlds. In the Upaniṣads they are usually four, sometimes five. In the Purāṇas, the epics, and the *Manu Smṛti*, the Lokapālas are eight. In the Tantras they are ten, the zenith and the nadir being included.

It is on the division of the respective spheres of these divinities that all sacred architecture, the planning of cities, and some aspects of most ritual observances are based. We find some recognition of their importance in all countries and at all times. The southern gate has always been the Way of the Dead, the Way of Ancestors.[1] According to Manu (3.206), ritual offerings to the dead must always be performed facing south.

In the *Bṛhad-āraṇyaka Upaniṣad* we find the Sun as the regent of the east, Yama in the south, Varuṇa in the west, Soma in the north, and Agni in the zenith. But in the *Chāndogya Upaniṣad* we meet the common classification followed everywhere in the Purāṇas, the Tantras, the epics, and the works on architecture and astrology. This classification is as follows:

Indra, king of heaven and protector of heroes, dwells in the east.

Yama, king of Ancestors, lord of the dead, and keeper of the Law, dwells in the south.

Varuṇa, lord of the waters, lord of destiny, guardian of rites, dwells in the west.

Kubera, lord of riches, king of men and genii, dwells in the north.

In the ceremony in which the child is given a name, invocations are made to the four quarters. According to the *Chāndogya Upaniṣad* (3.15.2 [194]), "The eastern quarter is the sacrificial ladle [for one faces east when offering sacrifices or when starting for war].[2]

"The western quarter is royal [for it is the direction of the lord-of-destiny (Varuṇa) clad in the royal purple of twilight].

"Wealth dwells in the northern quarter [for there lives Kubera, lord of riches].

"The Wind is the child of the quarters of heaven. He who knows the secret of the wind never mourns for a son."

1 Cf. the Via Appia, lined with tombs, in Rome.

2 Explanations within brackets are those in Śaṅkarācārya's commentary.

The regents of the half directions are variously represented. In the northeast they can be the Offering or Moon (Soma), the Purifier (Īśāna), an aspect of Śiva, or the Earth, the Nourisher (Pṛthivī). Fire (Agni) dwells in the southeast, the Sun (Sūrya) or Misery (Nirṛti) in the southwest. The Lord-of-Wind (Vāyu or Marut) dwells in the northwest.

The two additional regents mentioned in the Tantras are: the Immense-Being (Brahmā), the giver of knowledge, in the zenith, and the Boundless (Ananta), that is, Viṣṇu, rescuer of the world, in the nadir.

These two last attributions are connected with the myth of the *liṅga* of light in which Śiva appears as the axis of the universe and Brahmā rises to the

THE REGENTS OF THE DIRECTIONS

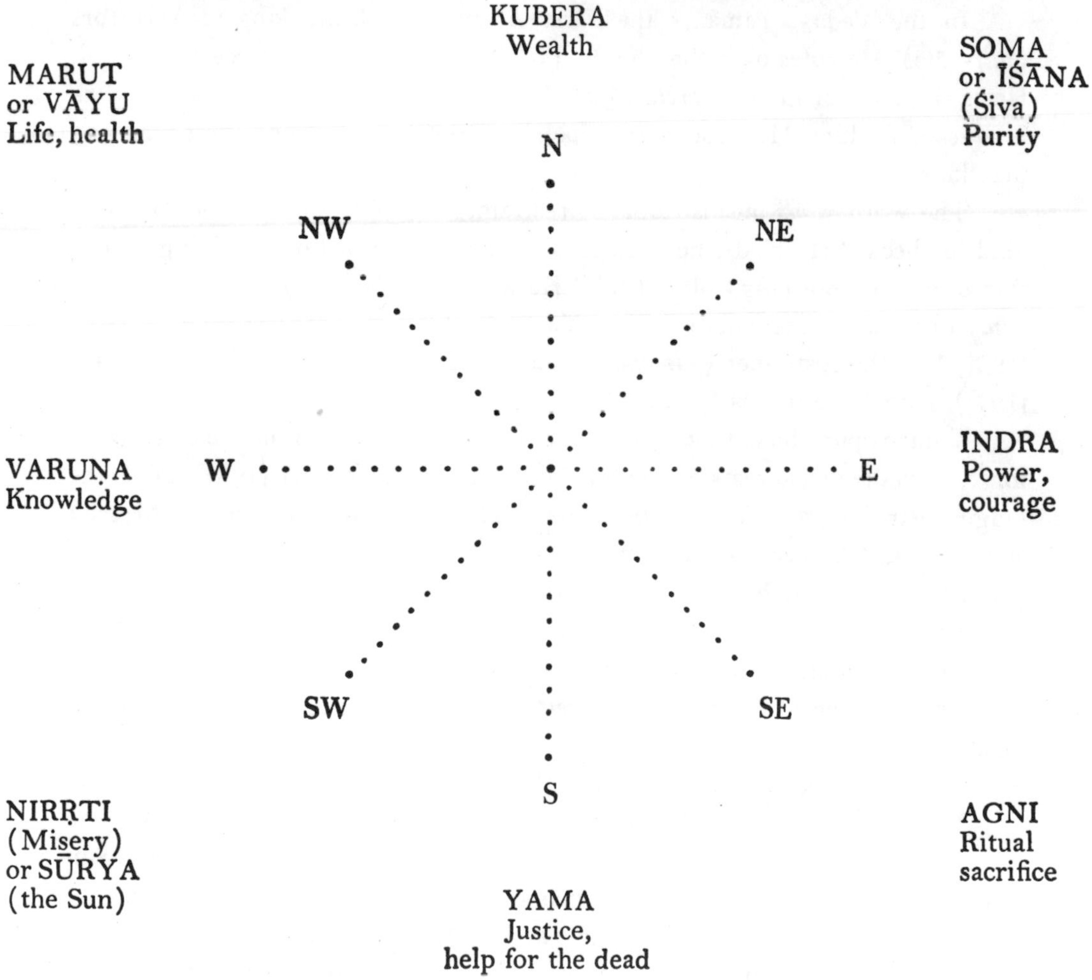

zenith in the form of the swan-of-knowledge (*haṁsa*) while Viṣṇu, as the boar, support of the earth, dives to the nadir.

We have already met most of the regents of the directions. We shall now envisage briefly the significance of Yama, Kubera, and Nirṛti. Īśāna will be described in Chapter 16 on the aspects of Śiva.

Yama (the Binder), the Lord of Death

YAMA IS the god of death, the sovereign of the infernal regions. Sinister and fearful, he judges the dead whom his messengers drag before his throne. He is the embodiment of righteousness (*dharma*) and the king-of-justice (*dharma-rāja*). He is, however, amenable to pity.

In the Vedas, Yama is the First Ancestor and the king-of-Ancestors (*pitṛ-rāja*). He rules over the kingdom of the dead where the Ancestors dwell. He is the king-of-ghosts (*preta-rāja*). He has the full rank of a god, for *soma* is pressed for him. He closely corresponds to the Iranian Yima, first man and first king.

The word *yama* means "binder, restrainer." It is Yama who keeps mankind in check. "He binds, he decides what are the actions of the living beings that bear or do not bear fruit" [195]. "He who controls (*yacchati;* from the root *yam*) all beings without distinction is Yama, the binder." (*Mahābhārata* 12.3446. [196]) "As the restrainer (*yamana*) of men he is called Yama." (Ibid. 3.16813. [197]) Yama also means "twin."

Yama is punishment (*daṇḍa*), the Eternal Law on which the universe rests, for "the whole world rests on the law" (*Mahābhārata* 12.4407 [198]). He is the judge, restrainer, and punisher of the dead. He is himself called Death (Mṛtyu) and the End (Antaka). He is Time (Kāla), the Finisher (Kṛtānta), the Settler (Śamana), the Rod-bearer (Daṇḍin or Daṇḍadhara). As Bhīma-śāsana, his decrees are dreaded. He is the noose-carrier (Pāśin), lord-of-Ancestors (Pitṛ-pati), lord-of-memorial-rites (Śrāddha-deva).

As the ruler of the southern direction, Yama is called lord of the south (Dakṣiṇa-pati).

There is a code of ethics (*Dharma Śāstra*) which bears the name of Yama.

Yama is the son of the resplendent Vivasvat (*Ṛg Veda* 10.14.5), the embodiment of social morality represented as one of the aspects of the Sun and envisaged as the progenitor of mankind. His mother is Cloud (Saraṇyū) (ibid. 10.17.2), daughter of the cosmic architect, Viśvakarman. Yama's brother is the Lawgiver, Manu, who shares with him the title of progenitor of mankind. Yama is closely connected with the Aśvins, who are the sons of Vivasvat. The Aśvins' mother, Understanding (Saṁjñā), is an exact likeness of Cloud (Saraṇyū), the mother of Yama. Yama's twin sister is Yamī, who loves him passionately, though he is sometimes said to have resisted physical union with her (ibid. 10.10). After his death she mourned him so bitterly that the gods created Night (Yāminī) to make her forget. Yamī later appeared on the earth as the river Yamunā. (*Mārkaṇḍeya Purāṇa* 77.7.)

Yama married ten of the daughters of Ritual-Skill (Dakṣa), who are the powers born of the ritual sacrifice (*Mahābhārata* 1.2577). Elsewhere his wife is said to be the shroud-of-smoke (Dhūmorṇā) that rises from the funeral pyre (ibid. 13.7637), or to be Fortune (Śrī). Yama is sometimes shown with three wives, called Golden-Garland (Hema-mālā), Good-Behavior (Suśīlā), and Victory (Vijayā).

Yama is of fearful and grim appearance. His body is ugly and ill-shaped. He is of dark green complexion with glowing red eyes. He dresses in blood red garments. His hair is tied on the top of his head and he wears a glittering crown. He holds a noose and a staff, and also carries an ax, a sword, and a dagger. He rides a black buffalo and sometimes appears himself in the form of a buffalo. When identified with Time (Kāla), he is shown as an old man with a sword and a shield. In many stories he is, however, described as a handsome man. "For a moment he saw a man clad in yellow, his tuft of hair bound. He was splendid like the Sun, of faultless blackness, beautiful, with red eyes. A noose in his hand, he inspired fear." (*Mahābhārata* 3.16754–16755. [199])

The virtuous and the sinners see Yama in different forms. To the virtuous he appears to be like Viṣṇu. "He has four arms, a dark complexion. His eyes resemble open lotuses; he holds a conch, a discus, a mace, and a lotus. He rides on Wings-of-Speech (Garuḍa). His sacred string is of gold. His face is charming, smiling. He wears a crown, earrings, and a garland of wild flowers." (*Padma Purāṇa*, Kriyāyogasāra: adhyāya 22. [200])

"To the sinner his limbs appear three hundred leagues long. His eyes are deep wells. His lips are thin, the color of smoke, fierce. He roars like the ocean of destruction. His hairs are gigantic reeds, his crown a burning flame. The breath from his wide nostrils blows off the forest fires. He has long teeth. His nails are like winnowing baskets. Stick in hand, clad in skins, he has a frowning brow." (*Padma Purāṇa*, ibid. [201])

"He rides the buffalo Fearful (Ugra). His hands are like claws." (Vijayānanda Tripāṭhī, "Devatā tattva," *Sanmārga*, III, 1942.)

Yama resides in the south, at the end of the earth under the earth, in darkness. His city has four gates and seven arches. Within the city flow two rivers: Stream-of-Flowers (Puṣpodaka) and the Roaring-One (Vaivasvatī). The judgment hall is the Hall-of-Destiny (Kālāci). There Yama sits upon the Throne-of-Deliberation (Vicāra-bhū).

"Yama's city is the City-of-Bondage (Samyaminī). Manifold-Secret (Citra-gupta) is his scribe. His ministers are Wrath (Caṇḍa) and Terror (Mahācaṇḍa). Shroud-of-Smoke (Dhūmorṇā) and Victory (Vijayā) are his beloveds. The place of judgment is below the earth. The messengers of death are his attendants." (*Jaṭādhara*. [202])

These messengers, dressed in black, have red eyes and bristling hair. Their legs, eyes, and noses are like those of crows. (*Mahābhārata* 13.3399). Yama's charioteer is Sickness (Roga). He is surrounded with demons who are the different diseases. (Ibid. 5.3779.) But there are also many sages and kings who assemble in his court to pay him homage. Musicians and heavenly dancers charm his visitors. At the door of the judgment hall is a guard called Legality (Vaidhyata).

Yama owns two four-eyed dogs with wide nostrils, who were born to the Fleet-One (Saramā), the bitch who guards the herds of Indra. They watch the path of the dead.

When the soul leaves the body, the messengers of Yama lead the tired being through a barren district without shade or water till he reaches the city of Yama. There the dead ones go alone without friends or family. Their deeds accompany them. After the record-keeper, Citragupta, has read an account of the dead man's actions, kept in a book called "Main Records" (*Agra-samdhānī*), the soul is brought to receive its sentence before the throne of Yama, who appears gracious to the just, fearful to the evildoers.

"The sinners, entering from the southern gate, have to pass a gate of red-hot iron and cross the fetid and boiling river Abandonment (Vaitaraṇī), filled with blood, hair, and bones and peopled with fearful monsters." (Vijayānanda Tripāṭhī, "Devatā tattva.")

Manifold-Secret (Citra-gupta), the Scribe of the Lord of Death

THE CREATOR, having completed his work, meditated upon the Supreme Immensity.

"Suddenly, while he sat in meditation, a man of divine appearance sprang forth from his body. This man held in his hand an account book and a pen. He came to be known as Manifold-Secret (Citra-gupta). Dwelling near the king-of-justice (Yama), he was instructed to write down an account of the good and bad deeds of all living beings. The Immense-Being (Brahmā) revealed to him all the subtle things and made him a sharer of the oblations offered in the fire sacrifices. Henceforth the twice-born forever feed him with offerings. Since he was born from the body (*kāya*) of Brahmā, his caste is that of scribes (*kāya-stha*)." (*Padma Purāṇa*, Sṛṣṭi khaṇḍa. [203])

"Citragupta has nine sons, named Panegyrist (Bhaṭṭa), City-Dweller (Nāgara), Dependent (Senaka), the Fair-One (Gauḍa), Servant-of-Fortune (Śri-vāstavya), Gambler (Māthura), Serpent-throned (Ahiṣṭhana), Tartar-Slave (Śakasena), Water-Dweller (Ambaṣṭha), all of whom are the ancestors of particular castes of scribes.

"Citragupta is worshiped on the second day of the clear fortnight of the month of Kārtika." [3] His image is of iron with black attributes.

Kubera, the Lord of Riches

THE REGENT of the northern direction is Kubera. His name first appears in the *Atharva Veda* (8.10.28), where he is the chief of the spirits of darkness and is known as the Son-of-Fame (Vaiśravaṇa). In the *Mahābhārata* Kubera is said to be a son of Smooth-Hair (Pulastya), who was the father of Fame (Viśravas) and is elsewhere mentioned as his grandfather. The name appears in a Bhārhut inscription of the second century B.C.

Kubera is the god of wealth, the chief of the genii, called the mysterious-ones (*yakṣa*) or the secret-ones (*guhyaka*), who guard the precious stones and metals stored inside the earth. They also own the "nine treasures." (*Harivaṁśa* 13131.)

Kubera's mother is Call-of-Praise (Iḍaviḍā). The *Viṣṇu Purāṇa* says that she was the daughter of a seer called Speed (Bharadvāja). According to the *Bhāgavata Purāṇa* (1.4.3), she was the daughter of the royal sage Speck-Drop (Tṛṇa-bindu). According to the *Rāmāyaṇa* and the *Viṣṇu Purāṇa*, she was the wife of the sage Smooth-Hair (Pulastya), and their son was Fame (Viśravas). Speed gave his daughter Extoller-of-the-Gods (Deva-varṇinī) as wife to Fame.

Kubera's half brothers were Roarer (Rāvaṇa), the powerful king of Ceylon, Jar's-Ear (Kumbhakarṇa), and Terrific (Vibhīṣaṇa), who became Rāma's ally. Their sister is Sharp-Nails (Śūrpaṇakhā). (*Rāmāyaṇa* 7.9.28–35.) Rāvaṇa drove Kubera away from Ceylon's capital, where he had previously ruled.

3 Vijayānanda Tripāṭhī, "Devatā tattva."

Kubera's wife, Auspicious (Bhadrā) (*Mahābhārata* 1.216.6), or Kauberī, is the daughter of the *dānava* Mura. She is called the Fairy (Yakṣī) or Splendor (Cārvī). Kubera's sons are Reed-Axle (Nalakūbera), who is also called "son of Mayu-rāja (the king of animals resembling men)," and Bejeweled-Neck (Maṇi-grīva), who is also called Colorful-Poet (Varṇa-kavi). His daughter is Fish-eyed (Mīnākṣī).

Kubera is the companion and friend of Śiva and, as such, is called God's-Friend (Īśa-sakhi). He is also called Yellow-Left-Eye (Ekākṣi-piṅgala). (*Rāmāyaṇa* 7.13.31.)

Kubera is shown as a white dwarf with a large belly. He has three legs, eight teeth, and one eye. His body is covered with ornaments. He holds a mace and sits in the immense assembly hall in the center of his domain, the Curl-City (Alakā-puri), north of the Himālaya near the Pleasure-Mountain (Kailāsa). This city is also called Splendid (Prabhā), Bejeweled (Vasudhārā), and Abode-of-Treasures (Vasu-sthalī). A poetic description of it is found in Kālidāsa's *Meghadūta*. The garden of Kubera is called Colorful-Chariot (Caitra-ratha) or the Fragrant (Saugandhika). (*Bhāgavata Purāṇa* 4.6.23.) It is located on the Mandara mountain where Kubera is waited upon by faun musicians, the *kinnaras*. His palace is sometimes said to have been built by the world's architect, Viśvakarman. Kubera's chariot is the Flowered-One (Puṣpaka). His ministers are called Seed (Śukra) and Stool-Foot (Proṣṭhapada) (*Rāmāyaṇa* 7.15.11). Blessed-Jewel (Maṇi-bhadra) is the chief of Kubera's army. The *Devī Bhāgavata Purāṇa* (12.10) mentions the names of six commanders of Kubera's army.

The name of Kubera seems to be of unknown origin, though it has been suggested that it may be derived from *ku-bera*, the "ill-shaped one," a word similar to *kim-puruṣa*, *ku-puruṣa*, etc. Kubera is called lord-of-riches (Dhana-pati), wealth-at-will (Icchā-vasu), chief-of-the-genii (Yakṣa-rāja), king-of-the-animals-resembling-men (Mayu-rāja), king-of-the-fauns (Kinnara-rāja), lord-of-the-demons (Rakṣasendra), womb-of-jewels (Ratna-garbha), king-of-kings (Rāja-rāja), and king-of-men (Nara-rāja).

Kubera's image should be made of gold with many multicolored attributes. An offering is made to him at the end of all ritual sacrifices, though he does not appear to have a separate cult. He is now worshiped mainly in Nepal, but is one of the seven divinities of wealth known all over Asia.

Kubera is the giver of jewels, the protector of travelers. He is associated with Gaṇeśa, the lord of categories.

"Whatever treasures are in the earth, they all belong to Kubera. Only through his kindness do men obtain precious metals and stones from the entrails of the earth. The 'science of treasures' (*nidhi-vidyā*) teaches that mineral wealth is alive and moves of itself from place to place. According to the merits of men, Kubera brings out his treasures or hides them. During the rule of a deserving king precious stones and jewels come near to the surface of the earth and are easily found." (Vijayānanda Tripāṭhī, "Devatā tattva.")

The *Yakṣas*, Guardians of the Earth's Treasures

THE *yakṣas*, with their king, Kubera, were originally antigods (*asura*), but they made friendly overtures to the gods and were accepted in their midst.

The term *yakṣa* comes from a Vedic word meaning "marvelous" or "mysterious." The mysterious-ones (*yakṣa*) are also the secret-ones (*guhyaka*). They are often mentioned with the night-wanderers (*rākṣasa*), or demons. The *yakṣas* are also connected with the serpents (*nāga*). With Kubera at their head they seceded from the *rākṣasas*.

The origin of the *yakṣas* is variously described. They are said to be the sons of Smooth-Hair (Pulastya) or of Bristling-Hair (Pulaha) or of Vision (Kaśyapa) and also to be born from the feet of the Immense-Being (Brahmā). Their function is to protect their prince, Kubera, lord of riches, and his treasures with their javelins, clubs, and swords, and to guard his fortresses and his garden. They are otherwise benevolent beings living upon the earth or on its borders. According to the *Bhāgavata Purāṇa* (5.24.5), Brahmā created a number of divine beings who all asked, "What is our duty?" Some said, "We shall perform sacrifices" (*yakṣāmaḥ*). They are known as *yakṣas*. Others replied, "We shall protect" (*rakṣāmaḥ*). They are called *rākṣasas*. Kubera is the lord of them all.

The *yakṣiṇīs* are female *yakṣas*, shown as genii of the air who seize or take possession of children.

Misery (Nirṛta)

IN THE Purāṇas the regent of the southwestern direction is Misery (Nirṛta). Misery is the son of Vision (Kaśyapa) and Fragrance (Surabhī). He is also one of the eleven Rudras (*Padma Purāṇa*, Sṛṣṭi khaṇḍa, ch. 40). He is the lord of elves (*nairṛta*), ghosts (*bhūta*), and night-wanderers (*rākṣasa*) and also the lord-of-the-directions (Dikpāla). People worship him to gain victory over their enemies. (*Bhāgavata Purāṇa* 2.3.9.)

A legend says that once there was a virtuous king of the criminal tribe of the Śabara named Brown-Eye (Piṅgākṣa). One day in the forest he heard people crying for help. He ran and found travelers being looted by a group of savages (*dasyu*). He fought them and was killed. As a reward he was made the regent of a direction. (Vijayānanda Tripāṭhī, "Devatā tattva.")

The *nairṛtas* are the descendants of Nirṛti and are represented as a kind of elf attached to Kubera.

Nirṛti, the Goddess of Misery

NIRṚTI IS a sinister goddess representing misery, disease, and death. Her images are painted on cloth and show red attributes. Her ceremonies are characterized by black garments and ornaments.

"Embodiment of all sins, she appeared at the time of the churning of the ocean before the goddess of fortune, Lakṣmī. Hence she is older than Lakṣmī. Her abode is the sacred fig tree, the *pippala*, where, every Saturday, Lakṣmī comes to visit her. To her realm belong dice, women, sleep, poverty, disease, and all the forms of trouble.

"She is the wife of Sin (Adharma), the son of Varuṇa. Her sons are Death (Mṛtyu), Fear (Bhaya), and Terror (Mahābhaya)." (*Mahābhārata* 1.67.52.)

In this world all those who are born under a handicap, in the families of thieves or evildoers, and yet are virtuous and kind are protected by Nirṛti.

Trita (the Third) or Āptya, the Water Deity

TRITA, in the *Ṛg Veda*, appears as a minor double of Indra. He associates with the gods of the atmosphere, the Maruts, and with Vāyu and Indra. With Agni he prepares the *soma*. In battle he defeats the antigods Obstruction (Vṛtra), Cloud (Vala), and the three-headed Shape-of-the-Universe (Viśva-rūpa), son of the Shaper (Tvaṣṭṛ). He dwells in the remotest region of the world. Trita is the bestower of long life.

Sāyaṇa, commenting on *Ṛg Veda* 1.105, relates that Trita (third), with two other seers called Ekata (first) and Dvita (second), suffering from thirst, found a well from which Trita began to draw water. The other two pushed him in and closed the well with a wheel. Trita composed a hymn to the gods and miraculously managed to prepare the sacrificial *soma* that he might drink it himself or offer it to the gods and so be extricated. This is alluded to in *Ṛg Veda* 9.34.4.

The name Āptya, which may come from *ap* (water), is said to refer to Trita's connection with rain, water, and *soma*.

{ 10 }

Gods and Antigods

WE HAVE SEEN that for each individual being the stages of development which are ahead of him appear luminous, angelic, and can be represented as divinities, while all contacts with the stages which he has left behind hamper his progress and seem obscure, lifeless, evil.

The difference between gods (*sura*) and anti-gods (*a-sura*) is therefore not one of kind but of degree. According to the path we follow, certain powers will be for us obstacles or helpers, demons or angels, drag us toward our lower instincts or liberate us from their grip.

"In contrast to the gods, the antigods are the inclinations of the senses which, by their nature, belong to the obscuring tendency, and which delight (*ra*) in life (*asu*), that is, in the activities of the life energies in all the fields of sensation." (Saṅkarācārya, commentary on *Chāndogya Upaniṣad* 1.2.1. [204])

The antigods are, thus, all that draws man away from the path of realization. They are those powerful instincts and attachments which keep man within the power of Nature (*prakṛti*), prevent his progress, and obscure his intellect.

The division of gods and antigods need not therefore be clearly drawn. In the general evolution of man, a few antigods will become gods, while some divinities may be reduced to the status of antigods. The principles that are gods on a particular path of spiritual development may be demons on another. This becomes particularly clear if we compare the Tantric and Vedic forms of ritual and the corresponding moral codes. At each stage the gods will represent the beneficial powers of Nature, the antigods those powers which are antagonistic to enlightenment, the dark forces which appear cruel and destructive on the physical plane. Vṛtra (obstruction personified), the withholder of rain, is opposed to Indra, the rain-giver.

The antigods are older than the gods. They are the gods of an age when the world was still in its infancy.

"The gods and the antigods are the twofold offspring of the lord-of-progeny (Prajāpati). Of these the gods are the younger, the antigods the older. They have been struggling with each other for the dominion of the worlds." (*Bṛhad-āraṇyaka Upaniṣad* 1.3.1. [205])

"The earth with its forests, oceans, and mountains was first ruled by powerful genii (*daitya*). But the gods, guided by Knowledge (Viṣṇu), killed them in battle and captured the three worlds with their inhabitants." (*Rāmāyaṇa* 7.2.16–17. [206])

The Antigods (*asura*)

THE TERM *asura*, used for the Supreme Spirit in the oldest parts of the *Ṛg Veda*, is the equivalent of the Ahura of the Zoroastrians. In the sense of "God" it was applied to several of the chief deities, to Indra, Agni, and Varuṇa. Later it acquired an opposite meaning and came to signify an antigod, a demon or enemy of the gods. The word is found with this signification in the last book of the *Ṛg Veda* and in the *Atharva Veda*.

The word *asura* is said to have come from the root *as*, which means "to be," and thus the *asuras* are the forms of existence, of life. The Brāhmaṇas and the Purāṇas derive the word from *asu*, meaning "breath." It can, however, have other meanings.

"Those who dislike their dwelling place or were driven away from it, or those whose breaths, that is, whose life energies, are strongly knit, are *asuras*.

"From the higher life energies he created the gods; that is why they are gods (*sura*). From the lower life energies he created the *asuras*; that is why they are antigods." (*Nirukta* 3.2.7. [207])

The *Rāmāyaṇa*, however, calls *asuras* those who abstain from wine, a prejudice common among pre-Aryan Indians.

"As they took to wine (*surā*) [which appeared when the ocean was churned], they are known as gods (*sura*), while the sons of Diti, who refused it, are considered anti-gods (*a-sura*)." (*Rāmāyaṇa* 1.45. [208])

According to the *Taittirīya Brāhmaṇa*, the breath (*asu*) of the lord-of-progeny (Prajāpati) became alive and "with that breath he created the *asuras*." The word *asura* could, however, also come from the other root *as*, meaning "to frighten away," and thus represent the fearful aspect of deities. The name is undoubtedly of Indo-Iranian origin.

The Gods of Pre-Vedic India

THE TERM *asura* came to be used to represent some of the gods of pre-Vedic India. Like other socioreligious groups, the peoples who fought for the domination of the Indian continent tended to represent their ideal of life, of morality, of goodness, the divine powers who protected their homes, their cattle, their society, as the true gods and the divinities protecting the other side as antigods or demons. Thus the Vedic poet saw mankind divided into the noble Āryas, worshipers of the gods and doers of sacrifices, and the unholy Dasyus (barbarians), builders of sinful cities, expert in magic. The heavens were similarly divided between the gods and the antigods.

It is significant that it was not for their sins that the antigods had to be destroyed but because of their power, their virtues, their knowledge, which threatened that of the gods—that is, the gods of the Āryas. The antigods are often depicted as good *brāhmaṇas* (Bali, Prahlāda). Defeated, they serve the gods faithfully (*Śiva Purāṇa*).

The later mythology tries to explain the change in the status of the *asuras*, saying that originally they were just, good, and charitable, respectful of divine law and performers of sacrifices, possessors of many virtues. Therefore Śrī, the goddess of fortune and beauty, dwelt with them during the early ages at the beginning of the world. "I used formerly to dwell with the virtuous *dānavas*." (*Mahābhārata* 12.8381. [209])

As they multiplied, the *asuras* became proud, vain, quarrelsome, shameless. They infringed the law, neglected the sacrifices, did not visit holy places to cleanse themselves from sin. They were envious of the happiness of the *devas*. They tortured living beings, created confusion in everything, and challenged the gods.

"In the course of time, on account of their change of heart, I saw that the Divine Law had disappeared from them, who were animated by passion and rage." (*Mahābhārata* 13.8360. [210])

For a time they succeeded in dethroning Indra and putting Bali in his place. But, as they had lost their virtues, Fortune (Śrī) forsook them.

With new political alignments and alliances, as well as with changes in moral conceptions and ritual, some of the gods changed side. The teachings of the wise *asuras* came to be incorporated into those of the Vedic sages and often, more or less openly, replaced them.

On the other hand, the *asuras* gradually assimilated the demons, spirits, and ghosts worshiped by the aboriginal tribes and also most of the gods of the other non-Vedic populations of India. In the later epics the term *asura* becomes a common name for all the opponents of the Aryan gods and includes all the genii, the *daityas,* and *dānavas* and other descendants of the seer Vision (Kaśyapa), although not usually the demons (*rākṣasa*) said to be descended from Smooth-Hair (Pulastya).

Some of the ancient heroes, later recognized as incarnations of Viṣṇu or connected with their legend, came down from the background of pre-Vedic culture and have carried with them the tales of the great *asuras* whose names and wisdom had remained untarnished.

Tales referring to the peoples and the aboriginal tribes with whom the Āryas were first in conflict when they settled in northern India came to be incorporated in the myths of the *asuras* and the *rākṣasas*. The allusions to the disastrous wars between the *asuras* and the *suras,* found everywhere in the Purāṇas and the epics, seem to include many episodes of the struggle of the Āryan tribes against earlier inhabitants of India. The *rākṣasas* appear as guerrillas who disturb the sacrifices. A *rākṣasa* carries off Bhṛgu's wife, who was originally betrothed to the *rākṣasa* Puloman. Many Āryas contracted alliances with *asuras*. Arjuna married King Vāsuki's sister. Mātali's daughter married the *nāga* Sumukha (*Mahābhārata* 5.3627). The *nāga* Takṣaka is an intimate friend of Indra (ibid. 1.18089). Ghaṭotkaca is a son of Bhīma by the *rākṣasī* woman Hiḍimbā. *Rākṣasas* and *yakṣas* are named occasionally as being in the army of the *devas*. In the war described in the *Mahābhārata* some *asuras* support the Kurus in battle (ibid. 7.4412). The *asuras* are often grouped with different Hindu tribes such as the Kaliṅga, the Magadha, the Nāgas. There are still today Nāga tribes in Assam, and the Asur are a primitive tribe of ironsmiths in central India.

Description of the Antigods

THE ANTIGODS were the sons of the earth goddess, the Bounded (Diti), and the non-Aryan sage Vision (Kaśyapa). Elsewhere they are represented as the offspring of the thirteen daughters of Ritual-Skill (Dakṣa). They are the elder brothers of the gods and the Ādityas. Manu says that the *asuras* were created by the lords-of-progeny (Prajāpatis). According to the *Viṣṇu Purāṇa,* they were born from the groin of Prajāpati. The *Taittirīya Brāhmaṇa* says that the lord of progeny created the *asuras* from his breath, the *Śatapatha Brāhmaṇa* that he created the *asuras* from his digestive breath. The *Taittirīya Āraṇyaka* explains that Prajāpati created gods, men, Ancestors, *gandharvas,* and *apsarases* from water and that the *asuras*, *rākṣasas*, and *piśācas* sprang from the drops which were spilled.

The *asuras* dwell in mountain caves, in the bowels of the earth, and in the infernal region, where they have large cities: Golden-City (Hiraṇya-pura), City-of-Ancient-Light (Prāg-jyotiṣa), City-of-Liberation (Nirmocana), all built by their magician-architect Maya. The *asuras* also live in the sea, where they are ruled by Varuṇa, and in the sky, where they have three splendid fortresses made of iron, silver, and gold from which they attack the three worlds.

The *asuras* are powerful in battle. They uproot trees and hurl the tops of mountains against their enemies. They are skilled in magic. They can transform themselves into all sorts of shapes and become invisible. They frighten people with their roar.

The preceptor of the *asuras* is the sage Śukra, who obtained from Śiva a method for protecting them against the gods. The marriage by purchase is known as the *āsura* form of marriage.

Different Kinds of *Asuras*

THE *Mahābhārata* gives a list of the different kinds of *asuras*. The main ones are the *daityas* (genii), the *dānavas* (giants) known to the Vedas, the *dasyus* (barbarians), the *kālakañjas* (stellar spirits), the *kālejas* (demons of Time), *khalins* (threshers), *nāgas* (serpents), *nivāta-kavacas* (wearers of impenetrable armor), *paulomas* (sons of the sage Smooth-Hair [Pulastya]), *piśācas* (eaters of raw flesh), and *rākṣasas* (night wanderers). Of these the most frequently mentioned are the *dānavas* and the *rākṣasas*.

All these beings are depicted as worshipers of Śiva and are therefore connected with the ancient Śiva cult, at first probably the strongest opponent of the establishment of the Vedic modes of worship throughout India.[1]

The Gods (*sura*) or the Resplendent-Ones (*deva*)

THE WORD *sura* (god) has been said to come from the root *svar*, "to shine." The word *deva* (deity) comes from the root *div*, also meaning "to shine." A traditional etymology gives for the word *sura* the meaning of "delighting in himself." The word *sura* meaning "god" may, however, have been coined from *a-sura*, the older name for gods, the initial *a* being mistaken for a negative prefix.

1 For a description of some of the different kinds of *asuras*, see Chapter 25.

Asura was then understood to mean "antigod" and to refer to the gods of the enemy.

The two main names of the gods (*sura* and *deva*) are said to have also a number of secondary meanings, all indicative of godly qualities. The main ones are: play (*krīḍā*), desire for supremacy (*vijigīṣā*), relation (*vyāpāra*), light (*dyuti*), praise (*stuti*), enjoyment (*moda*), intoxication (*mada*), dream (*svapna*), radiance (*kānti*), movement (*gati*). Thus, "The gods play. The rise, duration, and destruction of the world is their game.

"The gods conquer. They destroy the power of the antigods, as well as sorrow and sin.

"The gods are the source of all activity. In a world where all is relative, they are the links which unite the moving to the unmoving, the subtle to the gross world, spirit to substance.

"The gods are the inner light of knowledge and the outer light which reveals the world.

"The gods deserve praise; the whole universe sings their glory.

"[The gods enjoy all things. It is divinity hidden within ourselves that enjoys all our pleasures.

"[The gods intoxicate the mind, make us forget the agitation inherent in attachments.

"[The gods are subtle beings corresponding to the state of dream.

"[The gods ever shine. Their splendor illumines the worlds.] The gods are not bound by space and time. They are present everywhere at every moment. Their nature is movement, their substance is knowledge." (Vijayānanda Tripāṭhī, "Devatā tattva," *Sanmārga*, III, 1942.)

The gods move in the high spheres of space. They dwell in heaven (*svarga*), far above the earth, from where they descend upon the earth. When they appear before mortal eyes, the signs (*liṅga*) which distinguish them from men are that they do not sweat, their eyelids do not wink, their feet do not touch the ground, they always wear fresh wreaths and have no shadows.

The meeting place and pleasure ground of the gods is the highest of all mountains, the axial northern mountain sometimes identified with a mountain in the Himālaya, between Mālyavat and Gandhamādana. (*Mahābhārata* 1.1098; 1.1114; 12.12986.) According to the *Mahābhārata* (13.4862), this mountain, Meru, is round like the morning sun, and resembles a flame without smoke. It is 84,000 *yojanas* (350,000 miles) high and goes as far down in depth. It overshadows the worlds above and below and across. All the birds on this mountain have beautiful feathers. This is why the bird Beautiful-Face (Sumukha), a son of

Beautiful-Wing (Suparṇa, i.e., Garuḍa), left the mountain in protest, for there was no difference between good, average, and bad birds. The Sun, the Moon, and the lord-of-wind (Vāyu) move ceaselessly round this mountain. Its gardens are filled with flowers and fruit. Everywhere can be seen shining palaces of gold. Hosts of gods, celestial-musicians (*gandharva*), genii (*asura*), and demons (*rākṣasa*) play with heavenly nymphs (*apsaras*). The top of Mount Meru is covered with forests. Its fragrant flowering trees and huge *jambu* trees resound with the melodious voices of celestial singing girls, the *kinnarīs*.

The Age and the Felicity of the Gods

THE AGE of the gods is always sixteen. Sixteen represents the number of perfection, of plenitude. In man it is after the sixteenth year that the first elements of decay begin to appear, and when the moon reaches the sixteenth digit it begins to decrease.

"God, the death of death, ever remains an adolescent of sixteen years." (*Bhāgavata Purāṇa* 10. [211])

The sixteenth digit represents the fullness of existence-consciousness-experience. The nature of the Total Being and all his manifestations are parts of this immense store of joy, this immense existence. At each stage manifestation further fragments itself. Thus the lower forms of creation, although basically made up of existence, consciousness, and experience, have a smaller share of each and a graduation can be made between things and living beings in terms of relative consciousness, relative experience or enjoyment, and relative existence.

The *Taittirīya Upaniṣad* gives the relative scale of the happiness of the celestial beings in relation to man.

"This is the scale of happiness. The unit of happiness can be taken as that enjoyed by a man young and virtuous, learned and eager, healthy, powerful, rich, master of the whole earth.

"Those who, through their merit, have reached the heaven of the *gandharvas* know a happiness a hundredfold greater.

"So does the sage who has reached the stage that is beyond desire.

"The happiness of the celestial musicians, the *deva-gandharvas*, is again a hundred times greater.

"Such is also the happiness of the sage who has reached the stage that is beyond desire.

"The happiness of the Ancestors (*pitṛ*) in their immortal world is again a hundred times greater.

"So can be the happiness of the sage who has reached the stage that is beyond desire.

"A hundred times greater is the happiness of the saints who through ritual observances have become gods.

"Such is also the happiness of the sage who has reached the stage that is beyond desire.

"A hundred times greater is the happiness of the gods also known to the sage who has reached the stage that is beyond desire.

"A hundred times greater than that of the other gods is the happiness of Indra, king of heaven, a happiness equal to that of the sage who has reached the stage that is beyond desire.

"A hundred times greater than that of Indra is the happiness of the teacher of the gods, Bṛhaspati, a happiness attained also by the sage who has reached the stage that is beyond desire.

"A hundred times greater than that of the teacher of the gods is the happiness of the lord of progeny, Prajāpati, also known to the sage who has reached the stage that is beyond desire.

"And the happiness enjoyed by the Immense-Being (Brahmā) is one hundred times greater, yet equaled by that of the sage who has reached the stage that is beyond desire." (*Taittirīya Upaniṣad* 2.8.1–4. [212])

THREE

The Trinity

Viṣṇu, the Pervader

Sattva, the Cohesive Tendency

IN THE COSMOLOGICAL TRINITY, Viṣṇu is the name given to the cohesive, or centripetal, tendency known as the *sattva* quality. All that in the universe tends toward a center, toward more concentration, more cohesion, more existence, more reality, all that tends toward light, toward truth, is the Viṣṇu tendency, while Śiva, the centrifugal principle, means dispersion, annihilation, nonexistence, darkness.

The Name Viṣṇu

IT IS the centripetal tendency which holds the universe together, which is the cause of all concentration, hence of light, of matter, of life. It pervades all existence, hence it is known as the Pervader. The name Viṣṇu comes from the root *viṣlṛ*, which means "to spread in all directions," "to pervade."

According to the *Bṛhad-devatā* (2.69 [213]) the name Viṣṇu may come from the root *viṣ* (*viṣṇāti*, to spread), or *viś* (*viśati*, to enter), or from *viṣli* (*viveṣṭi*, to surround), all expressing pervasion.

As the inner cohesion through which everything exists Viṣṇu dwells in everything, owns everything, defeats the power of destruction. "He is Viṣṇu because he overcomes all." (*Mahābhārata*, 5.70.13. [214]) [1]

1 Louis Renou (*L'Inde classique*, p. 323) considers the origin of the name Viṣṇu as obscure and possibly non-Āryan. He mentions among the etymologies suggested by different scholars *vi* + *sānu*, "crossing the heights" and *vis*, "active," and mentions the epithet *śipi-viṣṭa*, "realized through the penis," as indicating a possible phallic origin.

The Nature of Viṣṇu

VIṢṆU IS the inner cause, the power by which things exist. He has no concern with their outward form, which comes within the realm of the Creator Brahmā, the Immense Being. There is no state of existence which does not depend on destruction as well as duration. There can be no life without death. Hence Viṣṇu and Śiva are interdependent. But while Śiva is the lord of destruction, Viṣṇu is the principle of duration and can be considered a symbol of perpetual (i.e., eternal) life. He is the power that holds the universe together. He is therefore the aim toward which all temporary beings tend. He is the hope of all that must die, the goal pointed out by all religions.

The State of Dream

THE PURE Viṣṇu principle is the source, the plan, of life. It is identified with the world of dream, where things are conceived as prototypes yet to be realized. The real, lasting creation is this mental creation. We create a machine when we conceive it. Once the plans are made in the abstract, realization in perishable materials is a secondary matter which the inventor may leave to technicians. World planning is the work of Viṣṇu, who is the universal Intellect.

On the plane of creation, the three states of the mind—sleep, dream, and awareness—are the relative conditions corresponding to the three qualities, the three deities. Thus Śiva is experienced in the emptiness of dreamless sleep, Viṣṇu in the vision of dream, and Brahmā in the state of awareness.

Knowledge of outward forms is obtained in the state of awareness, knowledge of inner principles in the state of mental vision which is dream, while perception of the formless transcendent reality is gained only through the absolute stillness, the complete silence, of the mind.

All Religion Is of Viṣṇu

EVERY RELIGION includes a theology and a moral code. The first aims at defining the principles which rule all existence and the destiny of our subtle individuality, the other proposes rules of action that may prepare the transmigrant self for its journey toward light, toward perfection, toward illumination or divine reality. Both are therefore concerned exclusively with Viṣṇu. All religion is a form of Vaiṣṇavism, while all science refers to Brahmā, and all attempts at transcendental knowledge, at apprehending that which *is*—or is not—beyond existence, beyond individuality, refer to the Śiva aspect of divinity. Science bases itself on sensorial perception. Religion makes use of mental and intellectual faculties, of faith and knowledge. Transcendent knowledge can be attained only through the methods of yoga and the control of the mind.

The Names of Viṣṇu

ACCORDING TO the aspect envisaged, Viṣṇu is known under many names. Saṅkarācārya's commentary on the *Viṣṇu-sahasra-nāma* explains the meaning of a thousand names of Viṣṇu.

From the religious point of view, Viṣṇu is Hari, "the Remover." In his commentary on the *Kali-santaraṇa Upaniṣad* 2.1 [215], Upaniṣad Brahmayogin explains this name, saying: "That which takes away ignorance and its effect is Hari, the Remover, who destroys [the belief that] things [can exist in themselves] apart from him." Hari, the Remover, is also the remover of sorrow, the giver of consolation.

When Viṣṇu sleeps, the universe dissolves into its formless state, represented as the causal ocean. The remnants of manifestation are represented as the serpent Remainder (Śeṣa) coiled upon itself and floating upon the abysmal waters. It is on this serpent that the sleeping Viṣṇu rests. Viṣṇu is then called Nārāyaṇa (moving on the waters). The name Nārāyaṇa can also mean the "abode of man."

The Image of Viṣṇu

All the qualities and attributes which are inherent in the nature of the Pervader and which are found in his manifestations are symbolized by the different qualities and attributes of his image. The image of a deity is merely a group of symbols, and no element of its form should be the fruit of the inventiveness of an image maker. Every peculiarity of the attitude, of the expression, or of the ornaments is of significance and is intended as a fit object for meditation.

The significance of the icon of Viṣṇu is explained in the Purāṇas and several minor Upaniṣads. The two most common representations show him sleeping above the causal ocean on the coils of the serpent Remainder (Śeṣa-nāga) or standing with four arms and a number of attributes as the ruler of *sattva*, the cohesive or centripetal tendency.

The *Gopāla-uttara-tāpinī Upaniṣad* (46–48 [216]) describes the main features of the image of Viṣṇu.

Viṣṇu speaks: "My feet have lines forming a celestial standard, a royal parasol. On my chest are the lock of hair Beloved-of-Fortune (Śrī-vatsa) and the shining jewel Treasure-of-the-Ocean (Kaustubha). In my four hands are a conch, a discus, a mace, and a bow (or a lotus). My arms are adorned with armlets. I wear a garland, a shining diadem, and earrings shaped like sea monsters."

The Four Arms

Four, the number of the earth, represents the fulfillment of manifestations in all the spheres of existence, the four stages that may be found in every form of development, of life. In the images of all deities the four hands express dominion over the four directions of space and thus absolute power, but they also represent the four stages of human development and the four aims of life, which are pleasure, success, righteousness, and liberation. The relative predominance of these aims results in the division of human life into four periods, of human society into four castes, of human history into four ages. These four stages are also connected with the orientation of images in temples. The aspects of knowledge pertinent to these four aspects of human destiny are represented by the four Vedas.

In the case of Viṣṇu more particularly "the four arms [can be said to] represent the three fundamental qualities and the notion of individuality [from which all existence arises]." (*Gopāla-uttara-tāpinī Upaniṣad* 55. [217])

In each of his hands Viṣṇu holds one of his four attributes. In the usual image these are in a given order.

"In my [lower right] hand, which represents the revolving or creative tendency, I hold the conch, symbol of the five elements.

"In the [upper right] hand [which represents the cohesive tendency], I hold the discus, [shining like an] infant [Sun [1]], symbol of the mind.

"In the [upper left] hand [which represents the tendency toward dispersion and liberation], I hold the bow, symbol of the causal power of illusion [from which the universe rises], and the lotus, symbol of the moving universe.

"In my [lower left] hand [which represents the notion of individual existence] is the mace, symbol of primeval-knowledge (*ādyā vidyā*)." (*Gopāla-uttara-tāpinī Upaniṣad* 55–57. [218])

The Twenty-Four Icons of Viṣṇu

THE RELATION of the three fundamental qualities and I-ness, or of the spheres of perception of the senses, to the elements, the mind, the power of illusion, and the power of knowledge or intellect can, however, vary for different kinds of beings, different forms of creation, different ages. The aspects of divinity ruling these various spheres of manifestation are represented in twenty-four images of Viṣṇu holding their attributes in different hands. These are described in the *Padma Purāṇa* (Pātāla khaṇḍa). The *Rūpa-maṇḍana*, a technical work on architecture, gives a similar list but with a slightly different distribution of the attributes. In accordance with these different possible relations between the basic elements of existence, Viṣṇu, the all-pervading form of divinity, in each of the important ages of the world's history, descends as an incarnation, an avatar, to establish the law of righteousness and the ways of knowledge suited to the conditions of the world. (The icons of Viṣṇu listed in the Sanskrit texts mentioned above [220 and 219, respectively] are tabulated on page 154.)

1 The text is here corrupt.

THE TWENTY-FOUR ICONS OF VIṢṆU

	LOWER RIGHT	UPPER RIGHT	UPPER LEFT	LOWER LEFT
1. Keśava, the Long-haired One	lotus	conch	discus	mace
	conch	*discus*	*mace*	*lotus*
2. Nārāyaṇa, the Universal Abode	conch	lotus	mace	discus
	lotus	*mace*	*discus*	*conch*
3. Mādhava, the Lord of Knowledge	mace	discus	conch	lotus
	discus	*conch*	*lotus*	*mace*
4. Govinda, Rescuer of the Earth	discus	mace	lotus	conch
	mace	*lotus*	*conch*	*discus*
5. Viṣṇu, the Pervader	mace	lotus	conch	discus
	conch	*discus*	*lotus*	*mace*
6. Madhusūdana, Destroyer of Madhu	discus	conch	lotus	mace
	conch	*lotus*	*mace*	*discus*
7. Trivikrama, Conqueror of the Three Worlds	lotus	mace	discus	conch
	mace	*discus*	*conch*	*lotus*
8. Vāmana, the Dwarf (literally, "deserving of praise")	conch	discus	mace	lotus
	discus	*mace*	*lotus*	*conch*
9. Śrī-dhara, Bearer of Fortune	lotus	discus	mace	conch
	discus	*mace*	*conch*	*mace*
10. Hṛṣīkeśa, Lord of the Senses	mace	discus	lotus	conch
	discus	*mace*	*conch*	*lotus*
11. Padma-nābha, He whose Navel is the World's Lotus	conch	lotus	discus	mace
	lotus	*conch*	*mace*	*discus*
12. Dāmodara, the Self-restrained	lotus	conch	mace	discus
	conch	*mace*	*discus*	*lotus*
13. Saṅkarṣaṇa, the Resorber	mace	conch	lotus	discus
	conch	*lotus*	*discus*	*mace*
14. Vāsudeva, the Indweller	mace	conch	discus	lotus
	discus	*conch*	*mace*	*lotus*
15. Pradyumna, the Wealthiest	discus	conch	mace	lotus
	conch	*mace*	*lotus*	*discus*
16. Aniruddha, the Unopposed	discus	mace	conch	lotus
	mace	*conch*	*lotus*	*discus*
17. Puruṣottama, Best of Men	discus	lotus	conch	mace
	mace	*discus*	*lotus*	*conch*
18. Adhokṣaja, the Universe's Sphere	lotus	mace	conch	discus
	mace	*conch*	*discus*	*lotus*
19. Nṛsiṁha, the Man-Lion	discus	lotus	mace	conch
	lotus	*mace*	*conch*	*discus*
20. Acyuta, the Never-falling	mace	lotus	discus	conch
	lotus	*conch*	*discus*	*mace*
21. Janārdana,* Giver of Rewards	lotus	discus	conch	mace
	mace	*lotus*	*discus*	*mace*
22. Upendra,* Indra's brother	conch	mace	discus	lotus
	discus	*lotus*	*mace*	*conch*
23. Hari,* the Remover of Sorrow	conch	discus	lotus	mace
	lotus	*discus*	*conch*	*mace*
24. Kṛṣṇa, the Dark One	conch	mace	lotus	discus
	lotus	*discus*	*mace*	*conch*

NOTE. The arrangement according to the *Rūpa-maṇḍana* [219] is shown in roman type; according to the *Padma Purāṇa*, pt. 4, ch. 79 [220], in italics. The asterisks (*) on items 21–23 indicate icons not mentioned in text 220.

"The attributes should always be mentioned starting from the lower right and going upward round the image." (*Padma Purāṇa*, pt. 4, ch. 79. [221])

The Conch

THE CONCH is the symbol of the origin of existence. It has the form of a multiple spiral evolving from one point into ever-increasing spheres. It is associated with the element water, the first compact element, and thus is spoken of as born of the causal waters. When blown, it produces a sound associated with the primeval sound from which creation developed.

The conch is taken as the representation of the pure-notion-of-individual-existence (*sāttvika ahaṁkāra*) from which are evolved the principles of the five elements (*bhūta*).

"He holds the conch named Born-of-Five (Pāñcajanya), which represents the [*sattva*, cohesive] part of I-ness, origin of the elements." [222]

The Discus

"THE DISCUS [or wheel] of Viṣṇu is [called] Beauteous-Sight (Sudarśana). It has six spokes [and is the symbolic] equivalent of a six-petaled lotus." (*Nṛsiṁha-pūrva-tāpinī Upaniṣad* 5.2. [223]) "It represents the [universal] Mind" (*Viṣṇu Purāṇa* 1.22.68 [224]), the limitless power which invents and destroys all the spheres and forms of the universe, the nature of which is to revolve. According to the *Ahirbudhnya Saṁhitā* (2.62 [225]), Sudarśana is the "will to multiply."

"The six spokes in the year's cycle represent the six seasons; in the center is the nave in which the spokes are set [within this center is the magic syllable *hṝṁ*, which represents the changeless, motionless center, the supreme causal continuum]. The circle around the wheel is *māyā*, the divine power of illusion." (*Nṛsiṁha-pūrva-tāpinī Upaniṣad* 5.2. [226])

The universal Mind corresponds in the microcosm to the active-notion-of-individual-existence (*rajas-ahaṁkāra*) that is associated with the fiery principle. "The prodigious power of the mind can destroy all forms of ignorance, hence the discus is the fearful weapon that cuts off the heads of all demons, of all errors." (Karapātrī, "Śrī Viṣṇu tattva," *Siddhānta*, V, 1944–45.)

The Lotus

THE LOTUS represents the universe, the flower that unfolds in all its glory from the formless endlessness of the causal waters.

"From the Ocean of Creation rises the universe which appears in my mind; the regents of the eight directions are its eight opened petals." (*Gopāla-uttara-tāpinī Upaniṣad* 51. [227])

"The immaculate lotus rising from the depth of the water and ever remote from the shore is associated with the notion of purity and with the cohesive-tendency (*sattva*) from which spring the law-of-conduct (*dharma*) and knowledge (*jñāna*). It is sometimes taken as the emblem of the six transcendent powers (*bhaga*) which characterize divinity (*bhaga-vān*).

"As the representation of the unfolding of creation the lotus is a symbolic equivalent of the egg of nescience, seed of endless millions of universes." (Karapātrī, "Śrī Viṣṇu tattva.")

The Bow, Arrows, and Quiver

THE BOW is the destructive-aspect-of-the-notion-of-individual-existence (*tāmasa-ahaṁkāra*), the aspect that is associated with the disintegrating tendency and is the origin of the senses (*Viṣṇu Purāṇa* 1.22.70. [228]). It is the instrument through which we send feelers into the unknown spheres of a purely illusory creation.

"He [Viṣṇu] has a bow called Śārṅga, which represents the [*tamas*] part of I-ness, origin of sensorial perception." [229] The bow therefore "corresponds to the divine power of illusion." (*Kṛṣṇa Upaniṣad* 23. [230])

"The numerous arrows of Viṣṇu are the senses, the fields of activity of the intellect." (*Viṣṇu Purāṇa* 1.22.73. [231]).

The quiver is the storehouse of actions.

The Mace

"THE MACE is the power of knowledge" (*Viṣṇu Purāṇa* 1.22.69 [232]) which dazzles and intoxicates the mind, hence it is called the stupefier-of-the-mind (Kaumodakī). "Kaumodakī is that which inebriates the mind." [233]

The power of knowledge is the essence-of-life (*prāṇa tattva*), from which all physical and mental powers are derived. Nothing else can conquer time and itself become the power of time. As such the mace is identified with the goddess Kālī, who is the power of time.

"The mace is Kālī, the power of time. It destroys all that opposes it." (*Kṛṣṇa Upaniṣad* 23. [234])

The Jewel Treasure of the Ocean

ON THE chest of Viṣṇu shines a brilliant gem, Treasure-of-the-Ocean (Kaustubha [2]). "This jewel represents consciousness, which manifests itself in all that shines: the sun, the moon, fire, and speech." (*Gopala-uttara-tāpinī Upaniṣad* 54. [236])

[This total consciousness, which is] "the Soul of the world, unsoiled, subtle, pure, is the jewel" (*Viṣṇu Purāṇa* 1.22.68 [237]), made of the total of the living consciousness of all living beings. It is the enjoyer of all creation.

To the mystic, the living consciousness appears as if clinging to the breast of the divine beloved. In the myth of Kṛṣṇa we read:

"When the flowers and pearls and precious stones [which are the angels and the saints and the sages] ever cling to the Remover-of-Sorrow (Hari) once they have reached his breast, how could cowherd-women possessed by love ever abandon him?" (*Bhāgavata Purāṇa* 10. [238])

The Lock of Hair Beloved of Fortune

ON THE left breast of Viṣṇu is a lock of golden hair called the Beloved-of-Fortune (Śrī-vatsa). It represents the source of the natural world, Basic-Nature (*pradhāna*) (*Viṣṇu Purāṇa* 1.22.69 [239]). The jewel is the enjoyer; the curl stands for all that is enjoyed, for the multifold beings and forms of the perceptible world.

"The curl Beloved of Fortune is my own form. Those who know the essence of things describe it as the mark of Fortune." (*Gopāla-uttara-tāpinī Upaniṣad* 53. [240])

The Garland of the Forest

ACCORDING TO the theory of Yoga, the center of extreme purity, *viśuddha cakra*, is situated in the throat. It is in this center that the Principle without

2 Kaustubha means "born from the waters that surround the earth" (*Śabda-cintāmaṇi* [235]).

quality can be experienced. The garland around the throat of Viṣṇu is the display of manifestation surrounding the qualityless Immensity. "Called the Garland-of-Victory (Vaijayantī), the garland of Viṣṇu, made of five rows [of fragrant flowers or of five rows of jewels] representing the [five] spheres of the senses, is the garland-of-the-elements" (*bhūta-mālā*) (*Viṣṇu Purāṇa* 1.22.72 [241]). It is also called the Garland-of-the-Forest (Vana-mālā) and is spoken of as *māyā*, the power of illusion of the Pervader.

"The throat is the qualityless [Immensity]. The garland that surrounds it is the primeval unborn energy [that creates all the forms of Nature (*prakṛti*)]." (*Gopāla-uttara-tāpinī Upaniṣad* 59. [242])

The Earrings, the Armlets, and the Crown

SHAPED LIKE sea-monsters (*makara*), the earrings of Viṣṇu represent the two methods of knowledge, intellectual-knowledge (Sāṅkhya) and intuitive-perception (Yoga).

The armlets, said to be made of divine substance, are "the three aims of worldly life: righteousness, success, and pleasure" (*Gopāla-uttara-tāpinī Upaniṣad* 57 [243]).

"The crown is the Unknowable reality." (*Gopāla-uttara-tāpinī Upaniṣad* 59. [244])

The Yellow Veil and the Sacred Thread

VIṢṆU AND especially his incarnations are always shown wearing a thin yellow scarf around the hips.

This veil, called Pītāmbara, is said to represent the Vedas. "The dark body shines through the thin golden veil just as divine reality shines through the sacred utterances of the Veda." (Karapātrī, "Śrī Viṣṇu tattva," p. 144.)

The sacred thread shown across the chest of Viṣṇu is made of three threads, said to represent the three letters of the sacred syllable AUM.

The Chariot

"THE CHARIOT of Viṣṇu represents the mind with its power of action. From the mind are evolved the five spheres of perception, object of the five senses. Divinity, riding on the mind in which dwells the power of action, fits the arrows which are the senses to the bow of Time and aims at their objects." (Karapātrī, "Śrī Viṣṇu tattva," p. 146.)

"The chariot moves at will, like the swift mind." (*Mahābhārata* 13. [245])

The Dark Color

VIṢṆU IS always represented as black or dark blue. Darkness is the color of ether, the formless, pervasive substance of the spatial universe, and thus a symbol of the Pervader.

Black is, however, a color associated with disintegration, the *tamas* quality which is Śiva, while white is the color of cohesion, the *sattva* quality which is Viṣṇu. Why, therefore, should Śiva be represented as white and Viṣṇu as black? The answer given to this is that "both qualities, being interdependent, are the selves of each other, and each degree of manifestation being inverted in relation to the previous one, all outward manifestations of Viṣṇu, whose nature is the pure white, cohesive tendency, must be black and all outward manifestations of Śiva, whose inner self is the abysmal darkness, appear white." (Karapātrī, "Śrī Viṣṇu tattva," pp. 142–43.)

Though Viṣṇu himself is black, his incarnations appear in different colors according to the ages of the world and the predominant qualities of each age. "In the first age [the golden age, the cohesive-tendency (*sattva*) predominates, and] Viṣṇu appears white. In the second age, he is red [like the revolving-tendency (*rajas*)]. In the third age, he is yellow [the mixture of *rajas* and *tamas*]. In the fourth age [the dark age], he is black." (*Brahma Purāṇa*. [246]) This also refers to his incarnations in the four human races. "White, then red, then yellow, he has now become black." (*Bhāgavata Purāṇa* 10.8.13. [247])

The attributes and attendants of Viṣṇu are of different colors.

"The color of the bird Garuḍa is [white] like the lotus; the mace is black. The earth goddess is like the acacia flower, Lakṣmī is golden, the conch is the color of the full moon, the jewel is the color of dawn, the discus is like the sun, the lock of hair is like the jasmine flower, the garland is of five colors, the serpent is like a cloud, the arrows are like lightning, and so are all the attributes not here mentioned." (*Garuḍa Purāṇa* 1.11. [248])

The Whisk, the Fan, the Flag, and the Parasol

"THE WHISK of Viṣṇu is eternal-law (*dharma*), the life breath [of the universe] which arises at the moment of manifestation." (*Kṛṣṇa Upaniṣad* 20. [249])

The fan of Viṣṇu is the ritual-sacrifice (*yajña*).

"The glory of the sun and the moon is his flag." (*Gopāla-uttara-tāpinī Upaniṣad* 53. [250])

The parasol, emblem of the royalty of Viṣṇu, represents the Land-of-No-Hindrance (Vaikuṇṭha), the heaven of Viṣṇu, the land where there is no fear. (Karapātrī, "Śrī Viṣṇu tattva," p. 146.)

"To know no hindrance (*kuṇṭha*) to one's motion is to be unhindered (*vikuṇṭha*). That which is unhindered is the Land-of-No-Hindrance (Vaikuṇṭha)." [251]

"The mountain Meru [axis of the world] is the parasol's golden pole, which represents the transcendent world." (*Gopāla-uttara-tāpinī Upaniṣad* 53. [252])

The Sword and Sheath

"THE PURE sword [Nandaka (source of joy)] which the Never-falling holds in his hand represents pure knowledge (*jñāna*), whose substance is wisdom (*vidyā*)." (*Viṣṇu Purāṇa* 1.22.74. [253]) This knowledge of the Immensity is associated with the causal ether and with Śiva as the embodiment of knowledge. (Karapātrī, "Śrī Viṣṇu tattva," p. 145.)

The flaming sword of knowledge is the powerful weapon which destroys ignorance. "Maheśvara, the Great God [embodiment of knowledge], takes the form of a burning sword." (*Kṛṣṇa Upaniṣad* 20. [254])

The sheath which hides the sword of knowledge is Nescience (Avidyā) (*Viṣṇu Purāṇa* 1.22.74 [255]). "It represents the darkness which is also the form of divinity." (Karapātrī, "Śrī Viṣṇu tattva," p. 145.)

The Bird Wings of Speech

WHEN VIṢṆU is awake he rides upon a bird, half vulture, half man, named "Wings of Speech" (Garuḍa [3]). His Vedic name is Garutman, also mentioned in the *Mahābhārata* 1.33.24, 5.112.1, etc.

Garuḍa is said to represent the hermetic utterances of the Vedas, the magic words on whose wings man can be transported from one world into another with the rapidity of light, the strength of lightning.

"The triple Veda, said to be a bird, carries Viṣṇu, the lord of the sacrifice." (*Matsya Purāṇa*. [256])

3 The name Garuḍa comes from the root *gṛ*, "to speak" (*Uṇādi Sūtra*, "Gira Uḍac," 4.155).

"The sound of the *Sāma Veda* is his body. He is the vehicle of the Supreme Ruler." (*Matsya Purāṇa.* [257])

As the embodiment of the sacrifice Viṣṇu has for his vehicle the rhythms (*Ṛk*), sounds (*Sāman*), and substance (*Yajus*) which are the instruments of ritual.

The different branches of the Vedic lore are represented as the parts of the body of Wings of Speech.

"The triple hermetic utterance is your head, the hymns of the *Sāma Veda* are your eyes, your heart is made of the other hymns. The *Vāmadevya* hymns are your body. The *Bṛhad* and *Rathantara* hymns are your wings. The ritual songs form your tail. Other utterances are your limbs and resting place. The verses of the *Yajur Veda* are your heels, those of the *Atharva Veda* your other parts.

"You are possessed of mighty wings, O Garutman! and soaring toward heaven, you cross beyond the sky." (*Garuḍa Purāṇa* 11. [258])

Garuḍa is also taken as the personification of courage. "This bird, beautiful of wing, is courage itself made into a bird." (*Śatapatha Brāhmaṇa* 6.7.2.6. [259])

In the Purāṇic lore Garuḍa is a son of Vision (Kaśyapa) and She-before-whom-Knowledge-Bows (Vinatā), one of the daughters of Ritual-Skill (Dakṣa) (*Mahābhārata* 1.32). Wings of Speech's brother Aruṇa (the red one) is the charioteer of the Sun.

She-before-whom-Knowledge-Bows quarreled with her co-wife, Chalice-of-Immortality (Kadru),[4] the mother of the "ever-moving," the *nāgas* or serpents who are the cycles of time. From her Garuḍa inherited his hatred of serpents. With the help of Indra he later became their master. (*Mahābhārata* 1.20–35.)

Garuḍa's wife is Progress (Unnati), also called the queen-of-knowledge (Vināyikā). According to the *Mahābhārata* (5.10.2–8 [260]), Garuḍa had by her six sons, called Beautiful-Face (Su-mukha), Beautiful-Name (Su-nāma), Beautiful-Eyes (Su-netra), Beautiful-Vigor (Su-varcas), Beautiful-Brightness (Su-ruk), Beautiful-Strength (Su-bala). From them are descended all the serpent-eating birds — the possessors of true knowledge, who can defeat Time — and who worship Viṣṇu as their protector.

Garuḍa lives south of the Niṣada country near a gold-producing river in the Land-of-Gold (Hiraṇmaya) (*Mahābhārata* 6.8.5–6 [261]). He is depicted as "a bird immensely big and strong, equal in splendor to the god of fire." He was so brilliant that at his birth the gods worshiped him, taking him for

4 For Kadru as the *soma* vessel, see *Ṛg Veda* 8.45.26.

Agni. Virile and lustful, he takes all the shapes he pleases. He goes where he pleases. Terrifying as the sacrificial poker, his eyes are red and brilliant as lightning. He shines like the fire of destruction at the end of the ages." (Ibid. 1.23.6–9. [262])

"This bird can stop the rotation of the three worlds with the wind of his wings." (*Mahābhārata* 5.105.2. [263])

"His speed is such that the earth, its mountains, waters, and forests seem dragged after him." (*Mahābhārata* 5.112.6–7 and 1.28.19. [264])

"[He is] huge and fierce-looking; his color is that of molten gold. He has the head of an eagle, a red beak, and feathered wings, together with a large belly and two arms like a man." (*Parameśvara Saṁhitā* 6.269.276–77. [265])

Once Garuḍa stole the ambrosia from the gods so as to purchase the freedom of his mother, who had been imprisoned by Chalice-of-Immortality (Kadru), the mother of serpents. Indra, who discovered the theft, recovered the ambrosia from Garuḍa, deluding him through friendly overtures when he saw that the thunderbolt could not kill him and battle would not lead to success. (*Mahābhārata* 1.32–34.)

Garuḍa has many names. He is beautiful-of-wing (Suparṇa),[5] king-of-birds or lord-of-knowledge (Vināyaka), lord-of-birds (Khageśvara), chief-of-birds (Pakṣi-rāṭ),[6] lord-of-the-sky (Gaganeśvara). He is the son-of-Ritual-Skill (Dākṣya), the son-of-Vision (Kāśyapa), and the son-of-Motion (Tārkṣya).[7] He dwells in the *śālmali* tree as Śālmalin. He is white-faced (Sitānana), red-winged (Raktapakṣa), the white-and-red-one (Śveta-rohita), golden-bodied (Suvarṇa-kāyā), destroyer-of-serpents (Nāgāntaka and Pannaga-nāśana), enemy-of-serpents (Sarpārāti), the swift-one (Tarasvin), he-who-moves-like-quicksilver (Rasāyaṇa), he-who-goes-where-he-will (Kāma-cārin), one-who-lives-as-long-as-he-pleases (Kāmāyus), one-who-eats-long (Cirād), the vehicle-of-Viṣṇu (Viṣṇu-ratha), the stealer-of-ambrosia (Amṛtaharaṇa and Sudhā-hara), vanquisher-of-Indra (Surendra-jit), subduer-of-the-thunderbolt (Vajra-jit), etc.

The Serpent Remainder

WHEN HE is asleep, that is, when creation is withdrawn, Viṣṇu is represented resting upon a thousand-headed gigantic serpent called the Endless (Ananta) or the Remainder (Śeṣa). (*Bhāgavata Purāṇa* 3.8.10–11.)

5 *Suparṇo'si garutman.* (*Vājasaneya Saṁhitā* 17.52; *Taittirīya Saṁhitā* 4.1.10; *Mahābhārata* 1.34.25.)

6 *Mahābhārata* 1.31.38.

7 *Ṛg Veda* 1.89.6; *Vājasaneya Saṁhitā* 25.19. [266]

"Then the whole universe is like an ocean. The Supreme God, having devoured all beings, sleeps on the lap of the serpent." (*Viṣṇu Purāṇa* 1.2.64–65. [267]) This serpent represents the nonevolved form of Nature (*prakṛti*), the totality of the causal stage of consciousness, the eternity of time's endless revolutions. Sometimes he is shown with "his head upholding the earth. He wears as a garland the world with its gods, men, and demons." (*Viṣṇu Purāṇa* 2.5.27. [268])

When creation is withdrawn it cannot entirely cease to be; there must remain in a subtle form the germ of all that has been and will be so that the world may rise again. It is this remainder of destroyed universes which is embodied in the serpent floating on the limitless ocean of the causal waters and forming the couch on which the sleeping Viṣṇu rests.

Remainder (Śeṣa) is depicted as the king of the serpent race or the ever-moving *nāgas*, who represent the cycles of time. He is the ruler of the infernal worlds, or Pātāla. "Below the earth dwells this serpent, endless, fierce, ruling over the serpent world." (*Mahābhārata* 1.36.24–26. [269]) "When the Endless (Ananta), his eyes dull with intoxication, yawns, he causes the earth to tremble with its oceans and its forests." (*Viṣṇu Purāṇa* 2.5.23. [270]) "At the end of each cosmic period he vomits the blazing fire of destruction, which devours all creation." (Ibid. 2.5.19. [271]) He was used as the rope twisted round the mountain Meru when the gods churned the ocean.

"Dressed in dark blue, intoxicated with pride, he wears a white necklace. In one hand he holds a plow, in the other a pestle." (*Viṣṇu Purāṇa* 2.5.17–18. [272])

In the Purāṇas, Remainder (Śeṣa) is said to be the son of Vision (Kaśyapa) and Chalice-of-Immortality (Kadru), hence he is the half brother of Garuḍa. His wife is the Head-of-Eternity (Ananta-śīrṣā). His hood is the Jewel-Island (Maṇi-dvīpa); his abode is the Jewel-Palace (Maṇi-maṇḍapa).

The Attendants of Viṣṇu

THE CHIEF attendant of Viṣṇu is All-Conqueror (Viṣvaksena), representing the "Scriptures of Earthly Wisdom," the *Āgamas*, on the techniques of worship.

"Wearing the flowers fallen from the altar of Viṣṇu, four-handed, he holds a conch, a discus, a mace. He wears long, matted hair and a beard and stands on a white lotus. His color is red and tawny." (*Kālikā Purāṇa*, ch. 12. [273])

The other attendants are the eight superhuman-powers (*vibhūti*) experienced by the yogis.

The Avatars, or Incarnations, of Viṣṇu

VIṢṆU, the Pervader, supreme cause of all, Self of all, is everywhere, pervading all things, limitless. His qualities, his actions, the manifestations of his power, are endless. Having manifested the world, he enters it again as its guide and ruler. "Having created it, he entered it." (*Taittirīya Upaniṣad* 1.2.6. [274])

At all the crucial moments of the world's history the Pervader appears as a particular individuality who guides the evolution and destiny of the different orders of creation, of species and forms of life. Hence "the story of his 'descents,' of his 'incarnations,' of his 'manifestations,' is endless. It would ever be impossible to give a full account of the descents of the limitless Pervader into the world of form.

"Fire, the Sun, the Wind, the Creator, the Pervader, the lord of destruction, the cosmic Intellect, the principle of existence, the principle of individuality, the five principles of the elements, the living soul, all are embodiments of divinity manifested through its power of illusion." (Yogatrayānanda, *Śrī Rāmāvatāra kathā*, p. 116.)

"Just as from an inexhaustible lake thousands of streams flow on all sides, so also from the Remover-of-Sorrow (Hari), sum of all reality, come forth countless incarnations. The seers, the lawgivers, the gods, the human races, the lords of progeny, all are parts of him." (*Bhāgavata Purāṇa* 1.3.26–27. [275])

Whenever, for a group of men or even for a single individual, those forms of knowledge that are essential for man's fulfillment of his spiritual destiny happen to be beyond reach, and thus human life fails in its purpose, which is realization, Viṣṇu is bound to make this knowledge available again, and thus a new revelation has to take place. There is, therefore, a new incarnation for each cycle, to adapt the revelation to the new conditions of the world.

"With the purpose of protecting the earth, priests, gods, saints, and the

Scripture, and righteousness and prosperity, the Lord takes a body." (*Bhāgavata Purāṇa* 8.24.5. [276])

The history of the present creation is spanned by ten main cyclic incarnations, the Yuga avatars. "These ten are the Fish, the Tortoise, the Boar, the Man-Lion, the Dwarf, Rāma of the ax and the other Rāma [i.e., the Charming], Kṛṣṇa, Buddha, and Kalki." (*Matsya Purāṇa* 285.67. [277]) Kalki is yet to come. Among these, Kṛṣṇa alone is considered a total incarnation (*pūrṇāvatāra*) by Vaiṣṇavite sects.

There are further partial incarnations, said to maintain, complete, and interpret the revelation. These are mainly seers and sages who embody certain virtues which they practice to a heroic degree.

The *Varāha Purāṇa* (15.9–18) mentions ten avatars, the *Bhāgavata Purāṇa* (1.3.6–25) twenty-two, the *Ahirbudhnya Saṁhitā* (5.50–57) thirty-nine.

According to the *Bhāgavata Purāṇa*, the twenty-two incarnations of Viṣṇu are: (1) Kumāra or Sanatkumāra, the Eternal Youth; (2) Varāha, the Boar; (3) the sage Nārada; (4) the saints Nara and Nārāyaṇa; (5) the sage Kapila; (6) Dattātreya, the magician; (7) Yajña, the Sacrifice; (8) Ṛṣabha, the righteous king; (9) Pṛthu, the First Ruler; (10) Matsya, the Fish; (11) Kūrma, the Tortoise; (12) Dhanvantari, the Physician; (13) Mohinī, the Enchantress; (14) Nṛ-siṁha, the Man-Lion; (15) Vāmana, the Dwarf; (16) Paraśu-Rāma, the destroyer of the *kṣatriyas;* (17) Veda Vyāsa, the compiler of the Vedas; (18) Rāma, the embodiment of righteousness; (19) Bala-Rāma, the embodiment of princely virtues; (20) Kṛṣṇa, the embodiment of love; (21) Buddha, the embodiment of delusion; (22) Kalki, the Fulfiller.

The incarnations of the Boar, the Tortoise, and the Fish are, in the earlier writings, sometimes represented as manifestations of the lord-of-progeny (Prajāpati) or the Creator (Brahmā). The "three steps" of Viṣṇu are linked with the myth of the Dwarf incarnation, but they have also an astronomical and a cosmic significance. In the *Mahābhārata* Viṣṇu is the most prominent of the gods, and some of his incarnations are referred to, but it is only in the Purāṇas that they are described in full.

The Planets

IN THE order of creation the existence of the planets must precede that of the beings who live upon them. They determine the background of the three worlds in which individual existence develops. They are the causal stages of life nearest to divinity and, from the point of view of man, can be considered the forms of divinity. The planets are thus connected with the incarnations of Viṣṇu.

"The Giver of Rewards [Viṣṇu as Janārdana], taking the shape of the planets, gives to the living beings the fruits of their actions. So that ritual action, through which the strength of demons is destroyed and the power of the gods increased, may be established, the auspicious planets rise one after another. Rāma is the incarnation of the Sun, Kṛṣṇa is the incarnation of the Moon, the Man-Lion is [Mars,] the son of Earth. Budha is [Mercury,] son of the Moon. The Dwarf is the learned teacher [of the gods, Bṛhaspati, i.e., Jupiter], Paraśu-Rāma is Venus, born of the Crack-of-the-Ritual-Fire (Bhṛgu), the Tortoise is [Saturn,] a son of the Sun, the Boar is Rāhu [who causes eclipses], the Fish is Ketu [the comet]. Whatever other incarnations may exist, they also are born of the wanderers of space. The beings in whom the spiritual element is predominant are the celestial wanderers, the planets, while those in whom the life element predominates are the living beings." (*Bṛhat Parāśara Horā* 1.26.31. [278])

"Thus the planets possess a consciousness, have power to act. They have presiding deities whom they obey. They give to the living beings the fruits of their good and bad deeds." (Karapātrī, "Śrī Viṣṇu tattva," *Siddhānta*, V, 1944–45.)

The Incarnations of the First Age, the Satya Yuga (Age of Truth)

The Fish-Incarnation (Matsya-avatāra)

The story of the Fish [1] is that of the deluge, from which the Fish saved the seventh lawgiver, Manu Satyavrata, founder of present-day humanity.

In the water brought to him for ablutions, Manu found a small fish which came into his hand and asked for protection. The fish said, "I shall save you from a flood which will sweep away all creatures." This fish grew to a large size and had to be kept in larger and larger vessels until nothing but the ocean

1 The story of the Fish incarnation is told in the Purāṇas (*Matsya Purāṇa*, ch. 1; *Bhāgavata Purāṇa* 8.24; *Agni Purāṇa*, ch. 2; *Varāha Purāṇa*, ch. 9, etc.). It appears to be an appropriation by Viṣṇu of an ancient legend, possibly of Babylonian origin (Louis Renou). The story varies slightly from one Purāṇa to another.

The first mention of the Fish incarnation occurs in the *Śatapatha Brāhmaṇa* (1.8.1–6). The *Śatapatha* version is repeated in the *Mahābhārata* (3.190.2–56) with some variants.

could hold it. Manu then recognized it as the incarnation of Viṣṇu. The god informed Manu of the approaching deluge and ordered him to prepare for it. He directed Manu to build a ship, and when the deluge came, he ordered him to embark on the ship with all the sages, plants, and animals. The fish, which was of a prodigious size, then swam to Manu, who fastened the vessel to the fish's horn, using the great serpent Remainder (Śeṣa-nāga) as a rope; and he was conducted to safety when the waters had subsided. The *Bhāgavata Purāṇa* (8.24) further relates that the fish fought in the ocean the demon Hayagrīva who had stolen the Vedas from the sleeping Brahmā. He gave the Vedas back to Manu Satyavrata and taught him the principles of the knowledge which should guide the human race during the present cycle of the four yugas, "the true doctrine of the Self, of the Immensity."

The Tortoise-Incarnation (*Kūrma-avatāra*)

Viṣṇu appeared again in the form of a tortoise [2] to recover some of the things of value lost in the deluge.

Gods and genii churned the ocean of milk, using the great serpent as a rope and the Slow-Mountain (Mandara) as a churning rod. They could succeed only when Viṣṇu, taking the shape of a tortoise, went to the bottom of the sea to serve as support for the mountain. (*Bhāgavata Purāṇa* 8.7.)

From the churning of the ocean came forth the ambrosia, the essence of life, and Dhanvantari, the physician of the gods, who is the bearer of the cup of ambrosia. Later appeared the goddess-of-fortune (Lakṣmī), the wine-goddess (Vāruṇī), the sacrificial-elixir (*soma*), the celestial-nymphs (*apsaras*), the divine horse Uccaiḥśravas, the celestial jewel Kaustubha, the celestial tree Pārijāta, the wish-cow Surabhi, the royal elephant Airāvata, the conch Pāñcajanya, the bow Śārṅga, and the poison (*hālāhala*). (*Mahābhārata* 1.18.48–53; *Bhāgavata Purāṇa* 8.8; *Rāmāyaṇa* 1.45.)

"The lord of progeny, having assumed the form of a tortoise, created offspring. He made (*akarot*) the whole creation, hence the name Deed (Kūrma) [given to the tortoise]." (*Śatapatha Brāhmaṇa* 7.5.1.5. [279])

The *Mārkaṇḍeya Purāṇa* (58.47) describes the Indian continent as resting permanently upon the back of this giant tortoise, which is Viṣṇu.

2 The first mention of this incarnation is found in the *Śatapatha Brāhmaṇa;* it is also mentioned in the *Mahābhārata* (1.18), the *Rāmāyaṇa* (1.45), and the Purāṇas (*Agni Purāṇa*, ch. 3; *Kūrma Purāṇa*, ch. 259; *Viṣṇu Purāṇa* 1.9; *Padma Purāṇa* 6.259; as well as in the *Bhāgavata Purāṇa*).

The Boar-Incarnation (*Varāha-avatāra*)

At the beginning of the age known by the name of the boar, the whole earth was submerged under the ocean. Viṣṇu, taking the shape of a boar,[3] dived into the waters and killed the demon Golden-eyed (Hiraṇyākṣa) who had thrown the earth to the bottom of the sea. "He then rescued the earth and re-established it floating over the ocean like a large ship. After planing the earth, he adorned it with mountains and then divided it into seven continents. After this, the god Remover-of-Sorrow (Hari), taking the shape and the four faces of the Immense-Being (Brahmā) and, in accordance with the revolving-tendency (*rajas*), created life." (*Viṣṇu Purāṇa* 1.4.45–50. [280])

In the *Taittirīya Saṁhitā* (7.1.5) the lord-of-progeny (Prajāpati) is said to have taken the form of a boar to raise the earth from the boundless waters. "This [universe] was formerly fluid. All was water. Over it the lord of progeny moved in the form of wind. He saw [the earth]. Becoming a boar, he lifted her. Becoming the world's-architect (Viśva-karman), he planed her. She extended. Hence the earth is called the Extended-One (Pṛthivī)." (Ibid. [281])

According to the *Taittirīya Brāhmaṇa* (1.1.3.6 [282]), "the lord of creation practiced austerities, [wondering]: 'How should this [universe] be?' He saw a lotus leaf standing and thought: 'This lotus must rest on something.' Assuming the shape of a boar, he dived beneath and found the earth. Breaking off a fragment, he rose to the surface and spread it on the lotus leaf. As he spread it, it became (*abhūt*) something that is spread. Hence is the earth called 'that-which-became' (Bhūmi)."

The *Taittirīya Āraṇyaka* (10.1.8 [283]) says that the earth "was raised by a black boar with a hundred arms." In the *Śatapatha Brāhmaṇa* (14.1.2.11 [284]), the earth "was only one span in breadth. A boar named Emūṣa raised her up."

The Man-Lion–Incarnation (*Nṛ-siṁha-avatāra*)

Prahlāda, son of the evil and powerful king of the genii Golden-Vesture (Hiraṇya-kaśipu), was a pious boy devoted to Viṣṇu. His father tried to discourage his pious inclinations and inflicted on him cruel punishments. Even-

3 In addition to the *Taittirīya Āraṇyaka*, the *Taittirīya Saṁhitā*, the *Taittirīya Brāhmaṇa*, and the *Śatapatha Brāhmaṇa* mention this myth. It is also found in the *Mahābhārata* (2.45; 3.144.1–29; 12.208), the *Viṣṇu-dharmottara Purāṇa* (1.3.1–12), the *Padma Purāṇa* (6.264), the *Vāyu Purāṇa* (ch. 6), the *Agni Purāṇa* (ch. 4), the *Brahmā Purāṇa* (ch. 213), the *Liṅga Purāṇa* (pt. 1, ch. 94), the *Kūrma Purāṇa* (1.6), as well as in the *Viṣṇu Purāṇa*.

tually the king decided to kill the child, who was ever lost in contemplation. But first several forms of torture were tried without effect, the boy being always miraculously protected.

Hiraṇyakaśipu was himself invulnerable. A boon he had received from Brahmā stated that he could not be killed by day or by night, by god, man or beast, inside or outside his palace. To save Prahlāda and destroy the evil king, Viṣṇu appeared at twilight (neither day or night) as a lion-headed man (neither man nor beast) within a pillar (neither inside nor outside the palace). Then with his claws he tore out the entrails of the genie.[4]

The cult of the man-lion is an ancient one. In the man-lion, valiance is worshiped as an aspect of divinity. This is a cult meant for kings and warriors (*kṣatriya*). It also has an esoteric significance.

"Why should the Divine Being be spoken of as a man-lion? For the reason that, among all creatures, man is the most powerful and excellent and [among the lower creatures] the lion is the most powerful and excellent. For the welfare of the worlds the imperishable Supreme-Ruler (*parameśvara*) took the form of a man-lion. He is extolled as Viṣṇu, the Pervader, for his valor [which destroys ignorance]. This fearful man-beast is the greatest being wandering on the earth." (*Nṛsiṁha-pūrva-tāpinī Upaniṣad* 2.13. [285])

"He is called fierce because he assumed the form of the fiercest beasts. He is called valiant because he is the embodiment of valor." (*Avyakta Upaniṣad* 2.3. [286])

Strength and courage are the qualities said to spring forth from the verses of the *Yajur Veda*. The man-lion is thus considered to be the embodiment of these verses. "This man-lion is the very Yajus." (*Avyakta Upaniṣad* 2.3. [287])

The Incarnations of the Second Age, the Tretā Yuga

The Dwarf-Incarnation (*Vāmana-avatāra*)

Bali, king of the genii (*asura*), had, through penance and valor, gained dominion over the three worlds. The gods, deprived of their abode and of the fumes of sacrifices, came to Viṣṇu for help. To help the gods, Viṣṇu was born

4 The story of the man-lion is told in many ancient works (*Bhāgavata Purāṇa*, pt. 7, ch. 8–10; *Agni Purāṇa*, ch. 4; *Matsya Purāṇa*, ch. 161–63; *Brahma Purāṇa*, ch. 189; *Viṣṇu Purāṇa*, pt. 1, ch. 17–22; *Padma Purāṇa*, pt. 6, ch. 265; *Liṅga Purāṇa*, pt. 1, ch. 95–96; *Mahābhārata* 3.273.57–61; *Harivaṁśa* 3.42; *Devī Bhāgavata Purāṇa* 4.16). It is also mentioned in the *Taittirīya Āraṇyaka* (10.1.7, 16) and the Upaniṣads.

as a priestly dwarf, son of the sage Vision (Kaśyapa) and his consort, the Primordial-Vastness (Aditi). One day the dwarf appeared before the virtuous Bali. He begged for as much land as he could encompass with three steps. Once this had been granted, the dwarf with one step covered the earthly world, with a second step the heavens and then, no space being left for a third step, rested his foot on Bali's head and pushed him down to the nether world. Bali, bound by his kingly promise, had to acknowledge his defeat, but in recognition of his virtues, Viṣṇu left him the dominion of the infernal regions.

The *Ṛg Veda* says that the dwarf's two first strides were visible but that the third led "beyond the flight of birds" to the abode of gods.

"Viṣṇu strode over this [universe]" and "in three places planted his step." (*Ṛg Veda* 1.2.22. [288]) "It is he who, in three victorious strides, encompasses the whole universe." (*Nṛsiṁha-pūrva-tāpinī Upaniṣad* 2.13. [289])

The Vedic commentators understood that on the earth Viṣṇu was fire, in the atmosphere lightning, and in the sky the solar light (see Sāyaṇa's commentary on *Ṛg Veda* 2.2.24). Viṣṇu is therefore here another name of Agni.[5]

This myth [6] has an Iranian parallel: the three steps of Ameša-Spenta.

Rāma-with-the-Ax (Paraśu-Rāma)

The sixth incarnation is Rāma-with-the-Ax (Paraśu-Rāma),[7] who reestablished the social order that had been disturbed by what has been called the "revolt of the *kṣatriyas*," the effort of kings to wrest spiritual leadership from the priestly order. One of the dangers that ever menaces human society, this revolt, if successful, is the first step in the unfolding of the four forms of tyranny: the uncontrolled rule of kings, the uncontrolled rule of merchants, the uncontrolled rule of the working class, and the uncontrolled rule of priests.

5 Aurṇavābha interprets the three steps as being "the different positions of the sun at the times when it rises, reaches the zenith, and sets." (Aurṇavābha is a commentator on the *Ṛg Veda* cited by Yāska in the *Nirukta*.)

6 The full myth of the Dwarf incarnation is told in the Purāṇas and the epics, namely, the *Vāmana Purāṇa* (ch. 23–31 and 89–94); *Bhāgavata Purāṇa* (pt. 8, ch. 17–22); *Agni Purāṇa* (ch. 5); *Matsya Purāṇa* (ch. 161–67, 244–48); *Brahma Purāṇa* (ch. 73 and 213); *Padma Purāṇa* (ch. 266–67); *Viṣṇu-dharmottara* (pt. 1, ch. 121.6–7); *Devī Bhāgavata Purāṇa* (pt. 4, ch. 16); *Mahābhārata* (2.47.1–30; 3.273.62–71); and *Rāmāyaṇa* (1.29.2–21). References to it also occur in the *Ṛg Veda* and the *Nṛsiṁha-pūrva-tāpinī Upaniṣad*.

7 Aside from the *Mahābhārata*, the main sources for the story of Paraśu-Rāma are *Vāyu Purāṇa*, ch. 91–93; *Bhāgavata Purāṇa*, pt. 9, ch. 15–16; *Agni Purāṇa*, ch. 6; *Brahma Purāṇa*, ch. 10; *Padma Purāṇa*, pt. 6, ch. 268; *Matsya Purāṇa*, ch. 47; *Devī Bhāgavata*, pt. 4, ch. 16. He also appears in the *Rāmāyaṇa*, but chiefly as an opponent of Rāmacandra (1.74–76).

Paraśu-Rāma is said to have defeated and destroyed the chivalrous aristocracy which thought itself the master of mankind, and he re-established the principle of a monarchy controlled by a priestly class. Another interpretation of this story is that it represents the final defeat of the non-Aryan kingdoms and of their kings, who had been invested with priestly functions by the Aryan theocracy. Paraśu-Rāma's hostility to the *kṣatriyas* evidently indicates a severe struggle between them and the *brāhmaṇas* for supremacy.

The scene of Paraśu-Rāma's exploits is said to have been the southwest coast of India (though some of the Purāṇas place it near the river Narmadā) whose nonbrahman inhabitants still claim to be descendants of the *kṣatriyas* defeated by Paraśu-Rāma and still give their daughters as concubines to the *brāhmaṇas*.

In the Purāṇic story, Paraśu-Rāma was the fifth son of the *brāhmaṇa* Jamadagni, who was deceived and killed by King Kārtavīrya and his sons who ruled over the Narmadā region. Single-handed, Paraśu-Rāma destroyed all the males of royal blood. He cleared the earth of the *kṣatriyas* twenty-one times, and gave the earth to the *brāhmaṇas*. "Thrice seven times did this lord clear the earth of *kṣatriyas*. He filled with their blood the five lakes of Samanta." (*Mahābhārata* 3.118.9. [290])

The present warrior class is said to have been born of the *kṣatriya* widows fecundated by the *brāhmaṇas*, although according to the *Mahābhārata* (12.48) the sage Vision (Kaśyapa) re-established as rulers the sons of ancient kings hidden by the sages during the war. Paraśu-Rāma later wrested some land from the sea, after which "he left the earth under the care of the great sage Vision (Kaśyapa) and, his conquests still unchallenged, retired to the Mahendra mountain" (ibid. 3.118.13–14 [291]) to lead the life of an ascetic. He was there visited by the Pāṇḍavas.

By his father Paraśu-Rāma descended from Bhṛgu and was, therefore, a Bhārgava; his mother belonged to the royal race of the Kuśikas. (*Mahābhārata* 3.116.) Paraśu-Rāma was present at the great war council of the Kaurava princes. (Ibid. 5.96.) He lived at the same time as Rāmacandra (see p. 172), but was by many years his elder, and he showed some jealousy of the younger incarnation.

Paraśu-Rāma was under the protection of Śiva, who, in his youth, had taught him the use of weapons and had given him the ax (*paraśu*) after which he is named. (*Mahābhārata* 8.28.) Angered when Rāmacandra broke Śiva's bow (*Rāmāyaṇa* 1.75–76), Paraśu-Rāma challenged him to fight, but was defeated and "excluded from a seat in the celestial world."

Paraśu-Rāma instructed Karṇa in the use of arms (*Mahābhārata* 8.36.4–6) and fought Bhīṣma in a battle in which both suffered equally (ibid. 5.178–85).

According to the *Brahmāṇḍa Purāṇa* (3.42), Paraśu-Rāma once fought Gaṇapati. During the fight his ax was broken. In his anger he broke the tusk of Gaṇapati.

A Tantric work, the *Kalpa Sūtra*, is ascribed to Paraśu-Rāma. The calendar of the Paraśu-Rāma era, also called Kollam aṇḍu,[8] is still followed in the Malabar country. There the year is the solar year, beginning in September.

THE TALE OF REṆUKĀ

Paraśu-Rāma's mother was Reṇukā, the wife of Jamadagni. Once, on the shore of a lake, she saw the king of the celestial musicians, Citraratha, in lustful enjoyment with heavenly *apsarases*, and she felt a desire to try such games with her husband. This thought was enough to destroy the brilliance of her virtue. Jamadagni noticed that his wife had lost her brilliance and, in meditation, saw what had come to pass. He instructed his elder sons to put their mother to death, but they dared not do so. The fifth son, Paraśu-Rāma, accepted the order, but made a request that she might be born again purified. She came back to life pure and resplendent, having forgotten all that had come to pass. (*Mahābhārata* 3.117.5–19.)

In Yoga, this story is given a particular meaning: Reṇu or Reṇukā means "semen." Her five sons are the five centers of the body. The smallest is the center of extreme-purity (*viśuddha cakra*), behind the forehead, here represented by Paraśu-Rāma. The mind is the abode of lust, symbolized by the forest where Citraratha and his heavenly damsels dwell. Once the mind has stimulated the power of sex, the yogi cannot recover his mastery over himself, the brilliance of his inner light, until he has burned up lust by bringing the power of his seed up to the fifth center.[9]

Rāma (Rāma-candra), the Charming, the Embodiment of Righteousness

The two next incarnations occupy a considerable place in the religious life of India and in the religious history of the world. Rāma, the embodiment of righteousness, is said to be the incarnation of the solar aspect of Viṣṇu.

8 Kollam is the name of an ancient country submerged under the sea beyond the Malabar coast; *aṇḍu* means "string," "chain." The era begins in A. D. 824.

9 See Vāsudeva Śaraṇa Agravāla, "Śiva kā svarūpa," *Kalyāṇa*, Śiva aṅka, p. 499.

The story of Rāma is told in the Purāṇas,[10] the *Mahābhārata*,[11] and several other works. The most ancient and most striking of the tales of Rāma is the *Rāmāyaṇa*, written by the sage Vālmīki, who is said to have been the creator of epic poetry.

Rāma was king of Ayodhyā. In the second age of mankind, he re-established a golden age of justice and happiness. The expression "Rāma-rājya" (the kingdom of Rāma) is still synonymous with peace and prosperity. As a prince Rāma was exiled in the forest and led an expedition to Ceylon to rescue his wife Sītā, who had been captured by the demon-king Rāvaṇa.[12] We are told that the merciful killing of Rāvaṇa was the main purpose of this incarnation.

"Rāma and his brother Lakṣmaṇa roamed the surface of the earth, ostensibly in search of Sītā." (*Rāma-pūrva-tāpinī Upaniṣad* 4.18–19. [292]) But the real reason was "to reclaim and release a foremost member of Viṣṇu's celestial retinue from the fearful fate of having been born a demon as a result of the curse of a *brāhmaṇa*, and to restore him to his original status." (Upaniṣad Brahmayogin's commentary on *Rāma-pūrva-tāpinī Upaniṣad* 4.18–19. [293])

Devotion to Rāma is one of the most prevalent cults in all classes of Indian society. The monkey-headed demigod Hanuman, the selfless helper and devotee of Rāma, is one of the main deities in most villages of northern India. Hanuman's image is also found in almost every one of the ancient forts of South India.

The symbolic value of the myth of Rāma does not exclude its historic reality, since a divinity incarnate would of necessity appear surrounded with the whole cosmic hierarchy. This is stressed in some of the texts relating to the meaning of Rāma's incarnation.

Sītā, consort of Rāma, is Nature (see p. 175; cf. also p. 253). She is primordial power, the embodiment of divine splendor. She is the heaven attained through penance, the nature of the universe, conscious and unconscious, "that which knows and that which does not know." (*Devī Upaniṣad* 2. [294])

"Sītā is the mother, Rāma the father, of the world. I bow to her who is the manifest-world (*prapañca*), to him the unmanifest (*niṣprapañca*). I bow to her who is contemplation, to him the object of contemplation. With offerings I bow to the evolved (*pariṇāma*) and the nonevolved (*apariṇāma*), to Sītā and the seed, and to Rāma the changeless. Sītā is Fortune (Lakṣmī) and you the Per-

10 Especially *Padma Purāṇa*, pt. 4, ch. 1–68, and pt. 6, ch. 269–71; *Agni Purāṇa*, ch. 5–11; *Brahma Purāṇa*, ch. 213; *Devī Bhāgavata*, pt. 3, ch. 28; *Kūrma Purāṇa*, pt. 1, ch. 21. It is mentioned in *Liṅga Purāṇa*, pt. 2, ch. 5.

11 2.50; 3.98, 149, 150, 274–93; 7.59; 12.28.

12 The story of Rāma was presumably the origin of the Prince Charming of Western legend, who goes through difficult ordeals to rescue his beloved.

vader; Sītā is the fair Pārvatī and you the lord-of-sleep (Śiva)." (*Padma Purāṇa* 6.270.29–31. [295])

THE MANTRA "RĀMA"

Rāma means "charming." Rāma is "that which on earth charms or shines." (*Rāma-pūrva-tāpinī Upaniṣad* 1.1. [296])

"The *mantra* 'Rāma,' true to its meaning, represents [the universe, conscious and unconscious] from the causal Immensity [to animate matter]. It stands for the ritual action, for the rites and the performer of rites. It is an object of meditation (*man*) and it protects (*trā*), hence it is called a *mantra* (a magic utterance), through which can be expressed all that words can express." (*Rāma-pūrva-tāpinī Upaniṣad* 1.11–13. [297])

"Just as the whole nature of the large banyan tree is contained in its tiny seed, so also the whole universe, moving and unmoving, is contained in the word-seed 'Rāma.'" (*Rāma-pūrva-tāpinī Upaniṣad* 2.2–3. [298])

The name Rāma is thus considered one of the basic *mantras* and its repetition is an important exercise of Yoga. "*Rāṁ*" is sometimes considered the basic sound, the causal word from which all language is issued.

"All the words of the sacred or the profane language are issued from the sacred name of Rāma and age after age dissolves into it." (*Lomaśa Saṁhitā* of the *Padma Purāṇa*. [299])

The *Tāra-sāra Upaniṣad* explains the myth of Rāma as the manifestation of the cosmic syllable AUM.

"From *A* came forth Brahmā, the Creator, who became Jāmbavat, king of monkeys. From *U* came Viṣṇu (Upendra), who became Sugrīva, king of the monkeys. From *M* sprang forth Śiva, who became the hero Hanuman. The nasal resonance (*bindu*) becomes the wielder of the discus, Śatrughna, the third brother of Rāma. The sound (*nāda*) of the sacred word became the great king Bharata, Rāma's first brother. It is this very sound which is symbolized by the conch of Viṣṇu. The quantity of the syllable (*kalā*) became Lakṣmaṇa, the younger brother of Rāma, the guardian of the earth. Its resonance (*kālātīta*) represents the great goddess of fortune, Lakṣmī, who became Sītā. Beyond this [the magic repercussion of the syllable] is the Supreme Self, the Cosmic Man, who is Rāma himself." (*Tāra-sāra Upaniṣad* 2.2–5. [300])

"That Supreme Immensity, in which the mind of the yogi delights, whose only desire is to obtain everlasting joy, is known as Rāma." (Yogatrayānanda, *Śrī Rāmāvatāra kathā*, p. 54. [301])

THE IMAGE OF RĀMA

"Rāma is pictured with Nature [Sītā] at his side. He is dark in color, and clad in a yellow veil; his hair is tied in a knot. He has two arms and large earrings, and wears a precious necklace. He looks proud, holding a bow, smiling.

"Ever victorious, the eight powers gained through the practice of Yoga add to his glory.

"On his left knee is seated the cause of the universe, the primordial energy called Sītā. She shines like pale gold. She has two arms and is adorned with heavenly jewels. In her hand she holds a lotus.

"Near Sītā, the joy of consciousness, Rāma appears, handsome and strong. Behind him his brother Lakṣmaṇa is seen. His color is that of pale gold. He holds a bow and some arrows. The three form a triangle." (*Rāma-pūrva-tāpinī Upaniṣad* 4.7–10. [302])

Kṛṣṇa, the Incarnation of the Third Age

THE EIGHTH incarnation belongs to the third age, the Dvāpara Yuga. Viṣṇu then manifests himself as the Dark-One (Kṛṣṇa),[13] the embodiment of love, of the divine joy that destroys all pain. "The root *kṛṣ* means 'to drag,' 'to give pain,' and stands for the Age-of-Conflicts (Kali Yuga). Should the name Kṛṣṇa but once come across the mind of his devotee, it takes away, devours, eliminates [the sufferings inherent to] this age of conflicts." (Upaniṣad Brahmayogin's commentary on *Kali-santaraṇa Upaniṣad* 2. [303])

"He (Kṛṣṇa) it is who destroys sin, he who is realized through the Vedas. He is the protector of all sacred utterances [symbolized as cows], the instigator of all the forms of knowledge (represented as cowherdesses)." (*Gopāla-pūrva-tāpinī Upaniṣad* 1.5. [304])

Each of the incarnations of Viṣṇu continues and fulfills the work of the previous ones.

"Once Rāma the Charming, the moonlight of the world, went into the deep forest to rescue some sages from the attacks of the demons. His beauty

13 The story of Kṛṣṇa is the main subject of the *Bhāgavata Purāṇa*, but it is also connected with the *Mahābhārata* and mentioned in the *Agni Purāṇa*, ch. 12–15; *Viṣṇu Purāṇa* pt. 5, ch. 1–33; *Brahma Purāṇa*, ch. 180–212; *Padma Purāṇa*, pt. 4, ch. 69–83, and pt. 6, ch. 272–79; *Devī Bhāgavata Purāṇa*, pt. 4, ch. 23–24; *Liṅga Purāṇa*, pt. 1, ch. 68–69, etc. The inner significance of Kṛṣṇa's worship is given in the *Gopāla-tāpinī* and *Kṛṣṇa Upaniṣads*.

was such that the sages arose seduced. Birds, beasts, animals, insects, trees, and creepers grew sick with longing to draw near and touch him. Even the fierce demons seeing him were spellbound. They said, in the words of Tulsī Dās (*Rāma-carita-mānasa*, Araṇya kāṇḍa 13 [305]):

" 'Although he disfigured our sister, he must not be killed, having no peer among men.

" 'O friend! Who is there with a physical body that would not feel attracted at the sight of his form.'

"Yet, while it was natural for women to be seduced, all of whose instincts incline toward manly beauty, how came it to be that men too, and not common men but sages of great penance who dwell in the forest, having renounced all desires, were so entranced that they could not veil their excitement and prayed to be permitted to touch the god?" (Karapātrī, "Bhagavān Kṛṣṇa aur unke parivāra," *Siddhānta*, V, 1944–45, 134.)

Rāma said to the sages: "Even if you should, through the power of Yoga, assume the form of females, I cannot gratify your desire during this incarnation in which, faithful to my word and my vow, I am wedded to but one wife." (Upaniṣad Brahmayogin's commentary on *Kṛṣṇa Upaniṣad* 1–2. [306])

" 'When, in another cycle, I shall be incarnated as Kṛṣṇa you will be cowherdesses and then can make love to me.' Filled with joy, they said: 'When you will be thus incarnate, other parts of your being will appear as cowherds. Let us be females that our bodies, well adapted to each other, may be in contact.' Having heard this prayer of Rudra and all [the gods and sages], Rāma said: 'Verily shall I then embrace you. I have acceded to your request.' " (*Kṛṣṇa Upaniṣad* 1–2. [307])

Born to establish the religion of love at the beginning of the Age-of-Strife (Kali Yuga), Kṛṣṇa was the son of Devakī, sister of the cruel king Kaṁsa. The sage Nārada had predicted that Kaṁsa would be killed by his nephew. So the king kept Devakī captive and killed her first six children. The seventh, Bala-Rāma, escaped, and the eighth, Kṛṣṇa, was secretly exchanged for the daughter of a cowherd. Kṛṣṇa was brought up as a cowherd. He played the flute and seduced the village maidens. Of great valor, he defeated a number of monsters and demons. Having killed Kaṁsa, he became master of the kingdom. Kṛṣṇa plays an important part in the war described in the *Mahābhārata*, being the cousin and ally of the Pāṇḍavas.

Kṛṣṇa has been taken by the Vaiṣṇavite schools of later times as a total incarnation of the Supreme Being and is given all the attributes of absolute divinity.

Rāma and Kṛṣṇa are both *kṣatriyas;* they belong to the warrior caste and not to the priestly class. Both are represented as dark in color. There is little doubt that, in their historical aspects, they represent ancient heroes of the non-Āryan tradition incorporated into the Āryan pantheon at a comparatively late period.

Kṛṣṇa, "around whom a vast mass of legend and fable has been gathered, probably lived in the Epic age, when the Hindus had not advanced far beyond their early settlements in the north-west. He appears prominently in the *Mahābhārata,* where his character is invested with a certain degree of mysticism. Additions and interpolations have raised him to divinity, and it is in the character of the 'Divine One' that he delivered the celebrated song, the *Bhagavadgītā,* a production of comparatively late date, now held to be part of the great epic. In this work he distinctly declares himself to be . . . 'the supreme universal spirit, the supreme dwelling, the eternal person, divine, prior to the gods, unborn, omnipresent.' The divine character of Kṛishṇa . . . was still further developed in the *Harivaṁśa,* a later addition to the *Mahābhārata;* in the Purāṇas, especially in the *Bhāgavata Purāṇa,* it attained full expansion. There the story of the life of Kṛishṇa, from his earliest days, is related with minute details, and it is upon this portion of his life that the popular mind delights to dwell. The mischievous pranks of the child, the follies of the boy, and the amours of the youth, are the subjects of boundless wonder and delight. . . . Much of the story of the early days of Kṛishṇa is thus of comparatively modern invention, while the incidents of his relations with the Pāṇḍava princes are among the most ancient." (Dowson, *Dictionary of Hindu Mythology,* pp. 160–61, with slight changes.)

The favorite of Kṛṣṇa is Rādhā (success), the lovely daughter of his adoptive father, Nanda. Rādhā and Kṛṣṇa are the theme of much of the medieval and later mystico-erotic poetry and cults in India.

"In the seventh heaven, the shepherds' heaven (*go-loka*), the one absolute supreme Self, Kṛṣṇa, unable to enjoy the pleasure of love because he was alone, manifested himself in dual form, a black light and a white light. From Rādhikā, the white light, impregnated by Kṛṣṇa, the black light, were born Universal-Intellect (Mahat-tattva), Basic-Nature (Pradhāna), and the Embryo-of-Splendor (Hiraṇya-garbha), which is the principle and totality of all subtle bodies. The love [of Kṛṣṇa and Rādhā] is an allegory of the union of Supreme-Man (*puruṣa*) and Nature (*prakṛti*), from which the universe gradually arose." (Karapātrī, "Kṛṣṇa tattva," *Siddhānta,* V, 1944–45.)

Since Kṛṣṇa is the incarnation of the Supreme Pervader, all the circumstances of his birth and his surroundings form an expression of cosmic harmony. All the gods have to be born with him.

"Supreme Joy became the chief Nanda (delight); Transcendent Knowledge was his adoptive mother, Yaśodā. . . . The [syllable AUM] was his mother, Devakī. The Vedic Scripture was Vasudeva [his father]. The meaning of the Vedas appeared as Kṛṣṇa and [his brother] Bala-Rāma. . . . The sacred verses of the Scriptures were the cows and cowherdesses. Brahmā, the Creator, became his club. The god Rudra was his flute. Indra was the conch, sin the antigod [he killed]. The garden of paradise appeared as Cow Land (Go-vana). The ascetics were its trees. . . . The serpent Remainder (Śeṣa) became [Bala-] Rāma . . . the 16,108 maidens [who played the game of love with him] are the verses of the Scripture which describe the nature of the Immensity.

"Hatred was the fighter Cāṇūra, spite the wrestlers Jaya and Muṣṭika, arrogance the elephant-king Torture of the Earth, vanity the bird-shaped demon Baka. Kindness became Rohiṇī, the mother [of Bala-Rāma]; the earth goddess was Satyabhāmā [the consort of Kṛṣṇa]. Black leprosy was the demon Agha. The Age of Strife was King Kaṁsa. Peace of mind was the friend Sudāma. Truth was Akrūra, and self-control Uddhava. The conch is the divinity of fortune, Lakṣmī, who is but the form of Viṣṇu himself. The milk jugs broken while he was stealing curds were the ocean of milk. As a child he [Kṛṣṇa] played [in this milk] as he did in the great ocean of milk. . . . Vision (Kaśyapa) [the father of the gods] is the mortar [to which the child Kṛṣṇa was once bound, and] the Primordial-Vastness (Aditi) is the rope [that bound him]. The power of attainment and the point-limit (*bindu*) of manifestation are the conch and the discus. The mace is the Power-of-Time (Kālī) that destroys all enemies. *Māyā* is his bow (Śārṅga), the cool season is the good food, the lotus stalk held in his hand as if for play is the world seed, the bird Wings-of-Speech (Garuḍa) is the *pippala* tree; the friend Sudāma is the sage Nārada; devotion is Rādhā. . . . Action is his intellect, which enlightens all beings, for this visible world is neither distinct nor nondistinct from him. With him the entire heavenly world, with its inhabitants, manifests itself on the earth." (*Kṛṣṇa Upaniṣad* 1.3–26. [308])

Mathurā, the sacred city of Kṛṣṇa, is described as the abode of wisdom. As the transcendental Being Kṛṣṇa dwells in absolute knowledge, of which his earthly abode is the symbol.

"When the whole universe is churned with the help of absolute knowledge, the essence obtained is called Mathurā." (*Gopāla-uttara-tāpinī Upaniṣad* 50. [309])

Rāma-the-Strong (Bala-Rāma)

Rāma-the-Strong (Bala-Rāma),[14] the elder brother of Kṛṣṇa, is considered the seventh avatar when Kṛṣṇa himself is taken as the full manifestation of Viṣṇu. Both are otherwise considered as partial incarnations.

The *Viṣṇu Purāṇa* (5.1.59–63) relates that Viṣṇu took two of his hairs, one white and one black, and these became Bala-Rāma and Kṛṣṇa, the two sons of Devakī.

Bala-Rāma was transferred secretly, shortly before his birth, from the womb of Devakī to that of Rohiṇī, so as to save him from the wrath of King Kaṁsa, and he was brought up with Kṛṣṇa by cowherds as a child of Rohiṇī (*Bhāgavata Purāṇa* 10.2). He and Kṛṣṇa grew up together. He took part in many of Kṛṣṇa's adventures and performed many heroic deeds.

Bala-Rāma's earliest exploit was the killing of the antigod Dhenuka, who appeared in the form of an ass. Bala-Rāma seized the demon, whirled him round his head, and threw his body into a tree. (*Bhāgavata Purāṇa* 10.15.) Another *asura* attempted to carry Bala-Rāma off on his shoulders, but the boy broke the demon's skull with his fists. (Ibid. 10.18.) Bala-Rāma accompanied Kṛṣṇa to Mathurā, and supported him till Kaṁsa was killed. (Ibid. 10.43–44.) When Sāmba, the son of Kṛṣṇa, was taken prisoner by Duryodhana at Hastināpura, Bala-Rāma asked for his release; throwing his plowshare under the ramparts, he drew the city walls toward him, and compelled the Kauravas to surrender their prisoner. (Ibid. 10.68.) Lastly, he killed the great ape Dvivida, who had stolen his weapons. (Ibid. 10.67.)

Bala-Rāma was addicted to wine (*madhu-priya*) (*Viṣṇu Purāṇa* 5.25) as Kṛṣṇa was to women. He was irascible and fought even with Kṛṣṇa; they had a serious quarrel about the jewel Syamantaka (ibid. 4.13.99–101). Once, when intoxicated, Bala-Rāma ordered the river Yamunā to draw near that he might bathe; when his command was not obeyed, he threw his plowshare into the river and drew it after him until the river, taking a human shape, asked for forgiveness. (Ibid. 5.25.8–24.)

Bala-Rāma's wife was Revatī, daughter of King Raivata, and he was faithful to her (*Brahma Purāṇa* 7.33–34). He had two sons by her, Niśaṭha and Ulmuka (*Kūrma Purāṇa* 1.25.79).

14 The story of Bala-Rāma is found mainly in the *Bhāgavata Purāṇa* (skandhas 10 and 11), the *Mahābhārata*, the *Viṣṇu Purāṇa* (Aṁśa 5). It is mentioned in the *Brahma Purāṇa* (ch. 182–210), *Agni Purāṇa* (ch. 12), *Brahmāṇḍa Purāṇa* (pt. 2, ch. 101–07), *Kūrma Purāṇa* (pt. 1, ch. 24), *Varāha Purāṇa* (ch. 15), etc., as well as in the *Brahma-vaivarta* and other Purāṇas.

Though inclining to the side of the Pāṇḍavas, Bala-Rāma refused to take an active part in their fight with the Kauravas. He taught Duryodhana, a Kaurava, and Bhīma, a Pāṇḍava, the use of the mace. (*Mahābhārata* 5.7.31.) He witnessed the combat between them, and Bhīma's unfair tactics made him so indignant that he seized Bhīma's weapons. Thereupon Kṛṣṇa prevented him with some difficulty from falling upon the Pāṇḍavas. (Ibid. 9.61.3–12.) He died shortly before Kṛṣṇa, as he sat under a banyan tree on the outskirts of Dvārakā. (*Bhāgavata Purāna* 11.30.26.)

Bala-Rāma was an incarnation of the serpent Remainder (Śeṣa). When he died the serpent issued from his mouth. (*Viṣṇu Purāṇa* 5.37.54–56.)

Bala-Rāma is represented as of fair complexion and clad in blue. His weapons are a club, a plow, and a pestle. He is called plower (Phāla), and plow-bearer (Hala), armed-with-a-plow (Halāyudha), plow-holder (Hala-bhṛt), plowman (Lāṅgalin). He has a palm on his banner. Other of his appellations are: moving-secretly (Gupta-cara), protector-of-desires (Kāma-pāla), and instigator-of-cycles (Saṁvartaka). "Because he changed wombs, he is called drawn-out (Saṅkarṣaṇa). Because he has no end, the Vedas call him the Endless (Ananta). Because of the strength of his arm, he is the divinity of strength, Bala-deva. He is the plow-bearer (Halin), because of his plow. Because of his blue garment, he is the Blue-clad–One (Sitivāsa). He is the enjoyer-of-Revatī (Revatī-ramaṇa). Because he dwelt in Rohiṇī's womb, he is the son of Rohiṇī." (*Brahma-vaivarta Purāṇa*, Kṛṣṇa-janma khaṇḍa, ch. 13. [310])

"He is Rāma (charming), because he charms the world." (*Bhāgavata Purāṇa* 10.2.13. [311])

The Incarnations of the Fourth or Present Age, the Kali Yuga (Age of Strife)

Buddha

Buddhism has left but few traces in the mythology and the religion of India. A certain number of philosophical and theological refutations of Buddhism are all that has remained in the Hindu scriptures to remind us of the importance that this reformation once had in the land of its birth.

It has been denied that the Buddha avatar represents Gautama Buddha, the founder of Buddhism. It seems, however, most probable that he does. His teachings are described as heterodox. "The great success of Buddha as a religious teacher seems to have induced the Brāhmans to adopt him as their own, rather than to recognize him as an adversary." (Dowson, *Dictionary of Hindu Mythology*, p. 38.)

According to Hindu tradition, the Buddha avatar [15] came to the world during the Age of Strife as the embodiment of illusion (*māyā*) and delusion (*moha*) in order to mislead men of low birth and genii who had become too proficient in sacred knowledge and were a threat to the supremacy of the gods. His preaching left aside the search for the understanding of the cosmos and the technique of ritual which enable man to participate in the process of creation and control his own destiny. It replaced ritual by moral values, in which the righteousness of the individual takes precedence over ritual observances. This, according to the Hindus, led people away from the Vedic rules, made them disregard the hierarchy of society, and replaced intellectual and ritual values by a theory of morality. Buddha's teachings led to contempt for the traditional wisdom and instigated men and genii to believe in the importance of the individual. This was intended to hasten the ruin which must mark the end of the present cycle.

Kalki

The tenth avatar, Kalki,[16] is yet to come. At the end of the Age of Strife, he will appear riding a white horse and holding a sword blazing like a comet. He will re-establish a golden age, punish the evildoers, comfort the virtuous, and then destroy the world. Later, from the ruins of the earth a new mankind will arise.

The *Bhāgavata Purāṇa* (1.3.26 [312]) says: "In the twilight of this age, when all kings will be thieves, the Lord of the Universe will be born as Kalki from [a priest named] Viṣṇu's-Fame (Viṣṇu Yaśas)."

15 The story of the Buddha avatar is found mainly in the *Matsya Purāṇa* (47.247), *Agni Purāṇa* (ch. 16), *Bhāgavata Purāṇa* (1.3.24), and *Bhaviṣya Purāṇa* (3.1.6).

16 The Kalki incarnation is mainly described in the *Kalki Purāṇa*, but is also mentioned in the *Mahābhārata* (2.50, 3.192), the *Bhāgavata Purāṇa* (1.3, 10.11.2), *Brahma Purāṇa* (ch. 213), *Agni Purāṇa* (ch. 16), *Vāyu Purāṇa* (ch. 98 and 104), *Liṅga Purāṇa* (pt. 1, ch. 40), *Varāha Purāṇa* (ch. 15), *Bhaviṣya Purāṇa* (3.4.26), etc.

The Minor Incarnations of Viṣṇu[1]

Nara and Nārāyaṇa, Devotion

NARA AND NĀRĀYAṆA[2] are two saints who brought to the world the message of divine love and devotion envisaged as an instrument of spiritual realization. (*Nārāyaṇīya* 732.) The *Mārkaṇḍeya Purāṇa* calls them "best among men." They were the sons of Righteousness (Dharma) and his wife Nonviolence (Ahiṁsā). Their austerities were such that the gods, frightened, sent the most beautiful *apsarases* to tempt them. Nārāyaṇa struck his thigh, and from it arose a nymph far more lovely than the celestial ones. This new *apsaras* was called Born-of-a-Thigh (Urvaśī) and became one of the prominent nymphs of paradise. (*Bhāgavata Purāṇa* 10.1.4; and *Devī Bhāgavata Purāṇa* 4.5–6.)

Kapila, Philosophy

KAPILA IS a celebrated sage who studied the ancient wisdom of the antigods. He taught the ancient cosmological philosophy, Sāṅkhya. We can recognize in him one of the chief sages and philosophers to introduce into the Sanskrit Āryan civilization the ancient knowledge inherited from the earlier inhabitants of India.

1 A number of minor incarnations are described in the *Bhāgavata Purāṇa* (pt. 1, ch. 3) and in other Purāṇas (*Mārkaṇḍeya, Brahma-vaivarta, Viṣṇu, Matsya,* etc.).

Two may be briefly mentioned here. Sanaka, who was born in the priestly caste, practiced difficult austerities and observed absolute chastity as a means of spiritual progress. (*Bhāgavata Purāṇa* 1.3, 6; *Brahma-vaivarta Purāṇa* 1.18, 13.) Several books of astrology mention a foreign (*mleccha*) avatar among the Western barbarians. This has sometimes been thought to refer to Jesus.

2 Nara and Nārāyaṇa are mentioned in the *Vāmana Purāṇa*, ch. 2, *Viṣṇu Purāṇa* 5.37.34–37, and *Mahābhārata* 3.147 and 157, as well as in most of the Purāṇas.

In the *Bhāgavata Purāṇa* (3.24) Kapila is said to be the son of Shadow (Kardama Prajāpati), one of the lords of progeny, and of a daughter of the Lawgiver Son-of-the-Self-born (Svāyambhuva Manu). According to the *Harivaṁśa*, he was the son of Inaccuracy (Vitatha).

Kapila is sometimes identified with Agni, the lord of fire (*Mahābhārata* 3.223.21). He destroyed with a glance of his flaming eye the sixty thousand sons of King Sagara who had come to disturb his meditation when they visited the underworld in search of a stolen sacrificial horse. (*Rāmāyaṇa* 1.40; *Mahābhārata* 3.106 and 107.)

Dattātreya, Magic

DATTĀTREYA [3] WAS another teacher of the antigods. He was the originator of the Tantras and the Tantric rites. He also restored Vedic rites (*Mahābhārata* 2.48.2–4). He is said to have been born of an emanation of Viṣṇu which fecundated the wife of the sage Devourer (Atri).

Dattātreya protects men from evil influences. He created the plant from which the sacrificial liquor, the *soma*, can be prepared. He enjoyed all the objects of the senses, was addicted to women and drink. His love for songs and musical instruments as well as his association with people of low birth made him ritually impure. Yet he was greatly praised by the gods whom he saved from the demons. (*Mārkaṇḍeya Purāṇa*, ch. 17–18.) They said of him: "No stain can soil the heart purified by the ablution of learning and into which the light of knowledge has entered." (Ibid. 18.29. [313])

Dattātreya was the patron of King Kārtavīrya, to whom he gave a thousand arms. (*Mahābhārata* 2.48; *Mārkaṇḍeya Purāṇa* 18.)

Yajña (Ritual Sacrifice)

VIṢṆU IS identified with the sacrifice (*yajña*) and the constant ritual of destruction through which the universe exists. Many mythical features link him to the sacrifice, and all his incarnations are connected with some form of sacrifice.

"Once in ancient times the lord of progeny named Desire (Ruci) married Will (Ākūti). This happened in the age when the Son-of-the-Self-born (Svā-

3 Dattātreya is mentioned in the *Vāyu Purāṇa*, ch. 70 and 98; *Brahma Purāṇa*, ch. 213; *Mārkaṇḍeya Purāṇa*, ch. 17–18; *Bhāgavata Purāṇa*, pt. 1, ch. 3; *Matsya Purāṇa*, ch. 47 and 243; *Viṣṇu-dharmottara Purāṇa*, pt. 1, ch. 25; *Mahābhārata* 2.48.

yambhuva) [4] was the Lawgiver (Manu). From Ruci and Ākūti were born Ritual-Sacrifice (Yajña) and his sister Sacrificial-Fee (Dakṣiṇā). They united as husband and wife and had twelve sons who were the deities called the Invocations (Yāmas)." (*Viṣṇu Purāṇa* 1.7.19–21 [314]; see also the *Bhāgavata Purāṇa* 1.3.12 and 2.7.2.)

Yajña had the head of a deer and was killed by Vīrabhadra at Dakṣa's sacrifice. He then rose to the heavenly sphere and became the constellation called the Deer's-Head (Mṛga-śiras). (*Harivaṁśa.*)

Ṛṣabha (the Bull), Morality

ṚṢABHA WAS the original founder of the pre-Āryan Jain philosophy and religion which considers morality an end in itself independent of theological notions.

According to the *Bhāgavata Purāṇa* (5.4–6) and the *Viṣṇu Purāṇa* (2.1), Ṛṣabha was one of the hundred sons of Nābhi (the wheel's hub) and his wife Meru, the axial mountain. Their eldest son was Bharata, after whom the Indian continent is called Bharatavarṣa.

Ṛṣabha taught his sons the path of wisdom, and to show the world the greatness of this path, he gave his kingdom to his eldest sons and retired to a hermitage. He practiced austerities so fearful that he became a mere "agglomeration of skin and fibers." He later visited the western and southern parts of India, teaching the path of wisdom.

Dhanvantari, Medical Science

DHANVANTARI (moving in a circle) [5] is a solar divinity personified as the physician of the gods. He arose at the time of the churning of the ocean, holding the cup of ambrosia (*Mahābhārata* 1.18.53). According to the *Vāyu Purāṇa* (93.9–22), Dhanvantari, after arising from the ocean, requested Viṣṇu to grant him a place among the gods. Viṣṇu assigned him a place in the sacrifice along with the sacrificial deities. Viṣṇu also gave him a boon by which he was born as a king of Benares, where he brought medical science to the earth. (See *Matsya Purāṇa*, ch. 251.)

As a Vedic deity Dhanvantari is a god to whom offerings are made at

4 Ākūti was Svāyambhuva's daughter.

5 Dhanvantari is mentioned in the *Brahma Purāṇa*, ch. 11, the *Vāyu Purāṇa*, ch. 92, the *Brahma-vaivarta Purāṇa*, pt. 4, ch. 51, the *Matsya Purāṇa*, ch. 251, the *Mahābhārata* 1.18, the *Bhāgavata Purāṇa* 8.8, etc.

twilight in the northeastern quarter. He is said to have had several existences and in each one to have been a master of universal knowledge.

Hayaśīrṣa (the Horse-headed), Protector of the Scripture

HAYAŚĪRṢA IS a horse-headed incarnation of Viṣṇu. He is sometimes identified with Hayaśiras and with Hayagrīva, two other horse-headed aspects of Viṣṇu. At the request of Brahmā, he dove to the bottom of the ocean to rescue the Vedas stolen by the two genii (*dānava*) Madhu and Kaiṭabha, whom he killed. (*Mahābhārata* 12.357.)

"In the cosmic sacrifice the All-Powerful himself was Hayaśīrṣa, the male of the sacrifice whose color is that of gold, of whom the Vedas and the sacrifices are the substance and the gods the Soul." (*Bhāgavata Purāṇa* 2.7.11. [315])

Vyāsa, the Compiler of the Scripture

VYĀSA,[6] the Compiler, "understood the weakness of the human mind [in the third age]. He divided the traditional knowledge, the Veda, into several branches." (*Bhāgavata Purāṇa* 1.3.21. [316]) He is also said to be "the arranger of the eighteen Purāṇas, the compiler of the *Mahābhārata* and its promulgator." (*Devī Bhāgavata Purāṇa* 1.3.17. [317]) He is also considered the first founder of the Vedānta philosophy.

Vyāsa is a cosmic entity born again and again to arrange and promulgate the Scripture. "Appearing age after age with the True-One (Satyavatī), he divides the tree-of-knowledge (*veda-druma*) into parts." (*Bhāgavata Purāṇa* 2.7.36. [318]) "Born on an island, [Vyāsa], incarnation of Viṣṇu, was the [illegitimate] and only son of Satyavatī and the seer Crusher (Parāśara)." (*Mahābhārata* 12.395.4–5. [319])

Pṛthu, the First King – Agriculture and Social Order

PṚTHU[7] IS mentioned in the *Atharva Veda* (8.10.22–23 [320]) as "having milked from the earth the art of agriculture and the food grains." The *Śatapatha*

6 Vyāsa is mentioned not only in the *Mahābhārata* and the *Bhāgavata Purāṇa* but in the *Viṣṇu Purāṇa* 3.3–4, the *Devī Bhāgavata Purāṇa* 12.4, the *Vāyu Purāṇa*, ch. 60, the *Brahmāṇḍa Purāṇa* 2.34, etc.

7 Pṛthu is mentioned in the *Mahābhārata* 12.107, the *Bhāgavata Purāṇa* 4.13–15, the *Vāyu Purāṇa* (ch. 62), the *Matsya Purāṇa* (ch. 10), the *Padma Purāṇa* 1.17, the *Harivaṁśa* 1.2, the *Brahma Purāṇa* (ch. 4), as well as in the *Atharva Veda*, the *Śatapatha Brāhmaṇa*, the *Viṣṇu Purāṇa*, and the *Viṣṇu-dharmottara Purāṇa*.

Brāhmaṇa (5.3.5.4 [321]) speaks of him as the "first man to be installed as a king." He is alleged to have established the main divisions of human society, to have dug the first well, invented agriculture, and thus forced the earth to yield her treasures. (*Viṣṇu Purāṇa* 1.13.) Pṛthu also discovered the properties of medicinal plants.

His father was opposed to all forms of worship and sacrifice. A group of pious sages beat him to death with blades of sacred grass. The priests then rubbed the right arm of the corpse and from it arose a majestic child, resplendent with beauty, who was Pṛthu. (*Viṣṇu-dharmottara Purāṇa* 1.109–10.)

Dhruva (the Immovable), Will Power

DHRUVA (the immovable, or the polestar) [8] was the son of King Uttānapāda (the constellation Ursa Minor), himself born of the Lawgiver Son-of-the-Self-born (Svāyambhuva Manu), the progenitor of present-day mankind. Dhruva and his mother, Good-Behavior (Sunīti), were insulted by Uttānapāda's favorite wife, Good-Looks (Suruci). Dhruva, indignant, left the palace at the age of five and, living in the forest among the sages, started practicing austerities on the bank of the river Yamunā. He later became the ruler of the earth and, rising to heaven, has now become the polestar. He is said to be the embodiment of will power.

Viṣṇu as Rescuer of the Elephant-King in Response to His Faith

GAJENDRA [9] WAS a king whom a curse changed into an elephant. While he was bathing in a lake a crocodile seized him and tried to drag him under water. The fight lasted for ages. When he began to lose strength the elephant invoked the protection of Viṣṇu, who helped him to free himself. Gajendra represents the power of faith.

Mohinī (the Enchantress), Lust

MOHINĪ [10] was an incarnation of Viṣṇu as a woman, who was meant to deceive the antigods and deprive them of the ambrosia that gives immortality. Mohinī appeared at the time of the churning of the ocean and was able to dupe

8 *Bhāgavata Purāṇa*, pt. 1, ch. 8–12, *Matsya Purāṇa*, ch. 4, *Viṣṇu Purāṇa*, pt. 1, ch. 11–12, *Mahābhārata* 13.6–15, *Liṅga Purāṇa* 1.62, *Brahma Purāṇa* 2.9–12, etc.

9 The story of Gajendra is found in the *Bhāgavata Purāṇa* (pt. 8, ch. 2–3), the *Vāmana Purāṇa* (ch. 85), the *Viṣṇu-dharmottara Purāṇa* (ch. 1.194), the *Viṣṇu Purāṇa* (pt. 1, ch. 11–12).

10 The story of Mohinī is found in the *Mahābhārata* (1.18–19), the *Bhāgavata Purāṇa* (8.9–10, 12), the *Rāmāyaṇa* (1.45), the *Padma Purāṇa* (3.10), etc.

the antigods. She also seduced Śiva and made him realize the power of Viṣṇu's magic.

Nārada, Music

NĀRADA IS one of the seven great seers. He is considered one of the exponents of the Tantric doctrine and the author of the *Nāradīya Dharma Śāstra*, a great work on law and behavior. The authorship of several hymns of the *Ṛg Veda* is ascribed to him. Several works on musical theory are also attributed to him. He invented the *vīṇā*, the principal stringed instrument of India, and is the leader of the celestial musicians. He is a wandering minstrel and also a mischief-maker. He is mentioned constantly in the Purāṇic literature.

According to the *Mahābhārata* (1.66.44), Nārada was the son of Vision (Kaśyapa) and one of the daughters of Ritual-Skill (Dakṣa). The Purāṇas make him a son of Brahmā.

"He was born from the throat of the Creator who is the giver-of-knowledge (*nara-da*), hence this lord of sages is called Nārada (son of the giver of knowledge)." (*Brahma-vaivarta Purāṇa* 1.22.2. [322])

The *Brahma-vaivarta Purāṇa* (1.12–30) and the *Bhāgavata Purāṇa* (1.5–6) give different versions of Nārada's birth.

Nārada is connected with a great number of mythological stories. He was condemned by a curse of Brahmā's to lead a life of sensuality and subjection to women (*Nārada Pāñcarātra* and *Brahma-vaivarta Purāṇa* 1.8.41–48). Another curse made him an eternal wanderer (*Bhāgavata Purāṇa* 6.5.38–43).

According to the *Mahābhārata* (12.29), Nārada married the daughter of King Conqueror-of-the-Flow (Sṛñjaya). He and his nephew, the sage Mountain (Parvata), cursed each other, and for a time Nārada had the face of a monkey and Parvata was not able to enter the heavenly world. Later they made a compromise and withdrew the curses. According to the *Brahma Purāṇa* (ch. 3), Nārada, as the son of Brahmā, advised the sons of Ritual-Skill (Dakṣa), one of the lords of progeny, to choose the path of asceticism. Ritual Skill, who desired them to help in the work of creation, became angry when he heard of this and wanted to curse the sage. Brahmā, however, together with the other divine sages, pacified Ritual Skill and agreed with him that Nārada would be born as a son to one of his daughters, one married to the sage Vision (Kaśyapa).

According to the *Devī Bhāgavata Purāṇa* (pt. 6, ch. 28–29), Nārada desired to know from Viṣṇu the greatness of his power of illusion (*māyā*). Viṣṇu led him to a lake, in which Nārada took a bath. He then found himself transformed into a female. He married King Tāladhvaja and took pride in his kingdom and his sons. Later Viṣṇu dispelled this illusion and brought him back to his original form.

Śiva, the Lord of Sleep

The Origin of Śaivism

SOME OF THE MOST profound aspects of Hindu thought have been linked in the past, as they are still now, with the philosophy of Saivism. This philosophy, originally distinct from that of the Vedas, belongs to another and earlier stratum of Indian civilization, which was gradually assimilated by the conquering Aryans. Rudra, the Vedic equivalent of Śiva,[1] begins to take his place clearly as the deity of transcendent darkness, embodiment of the disintegrating-tendency (*tamas*), only in the Upaniṣads, which are the expression of an age when Vedic thought had abandoned much of its primeval naturalistic vision to become impregnated with other conceptions borrowed from the ancient culture of the land. The Purāṇas and Āgamas, in which the myths and rituals of the Śiva cult are expounded, form a vast literature which contains, mixed with later material, some of the oldest documents on Indian religion. These works and the myths and rites they depict gradually found again, among the sacred books of India, a place that was for a long time contested by the three first Vedas and their appendages. (The fourth Veda, the *Atharva*, is of a different inspiration and is more akin to the Āgamas than to the *Ṛg Veda.*) Śaivism had always been the religion of the common people, for whom there was little place in the aristocratic Aryan fold, but it had also remained the basis of secret doctrines, transmitted by the initiative orders, whose mission it was and still is to carry the higher forms of metaphysical speculation through the periods of conflict and decadence, such as that which followed the Aryan conquest of India, when conquerors proclaimed the superiority of comparatively crude religious forms and conceptions over the age-old wisdom of the land, gradually, however, to be themselves deeply affected by Indian religious philosophy.

1 In the Vedas the word *śiva*, meaning "auspicious," is used only as an epithet of Rudra. This epithet later, in common usage, replaced the name of Rudra.

The more important documents which remain today on the symbolism, the myths, the philosophy of early Śaivism are found in the Śaiva Āgamas, the Śaiva Upaniṣads, and the six Śaivite Purāṇas: the *Liṅga Purāṇa*, the *Śiva Purāṇa*, the *Skanda Purāṇa*, the *Matsya Purāṇa*, the *Kūrma Purāṇa*, and the *Brahmāṇḍa Purāṇa*. Most of the other Purāṇas, as well as the great epics, are, however, also based on ancient Indian tradition, particularly the *Agni Purāṇa*. They all mention some of the tales of Śiva.

Several of the Purāṇas appear to be the summary in Sanskrit of a traditional lore which may have originated in some ancient, possibly Dravidian, tongue and of which much can still be found in the form of oral tradition and in the sacred literature of several Śaivite sects. The Sanskrit versions are abbreviated. This is obvious from the style of the *Śiva Purāṇa*, for example, which relates the mere skeletons of stories the detail of which is supposed to be known by all. The Purāṇas in their present form were written at a time when Vedism had so thoroughly conquered India that it could afford to make room for the ancient cults and philosophies without altering them except outwardly. Śaivism had been for centuries a persecuted religion, represented as the religion of antigods and demons. In the *Rāmāyaṇa*, Rāvaṇa, the demon-king of Ceylon, is a devotee of Śiva. After centuries of Aryan rule, the Vedic ritual and philosophy had, however, been so deeply penetrated by the older forms of Indian thought that they had changed almost beyond recognition. The difference between the non-Aryan and the Aryan mode of thinking had been narrowed down to such an extent that the Vedic religion could now easily make room openly for some aspects of the ancient Śiva cult upon which the earlier Aryans had looked down with awe and horror. It is then that the ancient sacred books of the non-Aryans began to be translated into Sanskrit, and this explains why they are written in a comparatively modern and often unscholarly Sanskrit while they contain, mixed with later additions, a great deal of material of great antiquity.

The sage Kapila is said to have studied the almost forgotten wisdom of the ancient *asuras* and taught it to the followers of the Vedas. The early Sangam literature of the Tamils, in many cases older than the available version of the Purāṇas, refers to a number of Śiva myths.

The complex Śaivite cosmology differs in its form and expression from the Vedic, although it has had an obvious influence on some of the later Vedic texts and Upaniṣads. Most of the terms of the two systems can be and have been equated with one another in later Hinduism, so that Hindus today can hardly believe that there may have been originally two distinct systems.

Today the Śaivite philosophy still represents the more abstract aspects of

Indian religious thinking. It brings to us the strange and profound teachings of the most ancient cosmology, as well as some of the methods of yoga which remain the cornerstone of all the conceptions of spiritual progress and realization in later Hinduism as they were of pre-Aryan India.

The Tendency toward Disintegration (*tamas*)

ALL THAT has a beginning must of necessity have an end. All that is born must die, all that comes into existence must cease to exist. Thus every existing thing unfailingly aims toward disintegration. The power of destruction is the nearest thing to nonexistence, to the "Qualityless Immensity" into which all must return. The universal power of destruction in which all existence ends and from which it rises again is known as Śiva, the lord of sleep, "whence all these elements came forth, by which once born they exist, into which they enter and dissolve." (*Taittirīya Upaniṣad* 3.1. [323])

Śiva is the embodiment of *tamas*, the centrifugal inertia, the tendency toward dispersion, toward disintegration and annihilation.

When the universe expands indefinitely it dissolves and gradually ceases to exist. That dispersion in the obscurity of the causal insubstantiality is the end of all differentiation, of all place and time.

Nothing that has existence can escape this process of destruction. Existence is only a stage of an expanding—that is, disintegrating—universe. It is from destruction that creation again rises; hence destruction is the ultimate cause, the unmanifest origin, of creation. Śiva, the power of disintegration, alone remains in the beginning and the end. He is pictured as a boundless void, substratum of existence, and is compared to the silence and obscurity that we experience in deep dreamless sleep, when all mental activity ceases.

"This being-of-darkness spreads everywhere like unconscious sleep, shapeless, ineffable, undefinable." (*Manu Smṛti* 1.5. [324])

From one point of view Śiva is thus identified with the substratum of Immensity; from another he is related to the origin and the end of existence. He is therefore the link between the impersonal-substratum (*brahman*) and the causal-divinity (*īśvara*). He is the supreme state of reality, since beyond him there is only nonexistence. The Upaniṣads describe him as a fathomless abyss.

"Beyond this darkness there is neither day nor night, neither existence nor nonexistence, but Śiva alone, the indestructible. Even the sun lies prostrate before him. From him springs forth the ageless wisdom." (*Śvetāśvatara Upaniṣad* 4.18. [325])

"There the sun does not shine, nor the moon, nor the stars. There lightning does not glitter, to say nothing of the earthly fire, for all that shines is but a reflection of the radiance of him whose splendor illumines the universe." (*Svetāś-vatara Upaniṣad* 6.14 and *Kaṭha Upaniṣad* 2.15. [326])

"He has no body, no senses; none like him or greater than him can be seen. We merely hear of the thousand forms of his inherent transcendent powers of knowledge, will, and action." (*Śvetāśvatara Upaniṣad* 6.8. [327])

The Many Aspects of Śiva

ŚIVA IS everything. According to the aspect of his divinity envisaged, he appears as one or three or five or eight or many. All these aspects are represented by his various names.

One thousand and eight names of Śiva are given in the *Śiva Purāṇa* (ch. 69) and Chapter 17 of the Anuśāsana parvan of the *Mahābhārata*.[2] The *Liṅga Purāṇa* (1.65, 98) also gives a thousand names of Śiva.

While studying the significance of the different aspects of Śiva represented by these names we need not usually refer to their historic or prehistoric origin. Some of these names may have belonged originally to the deities of various pre-Aryan peoples. But they were so completely assimilated that we can envisage them only in the sense in which they have been used and are used in the traditional theology of Śaivism.

Most of the more common names of Śiva are descriptive epithets such as Three-eyed (Tri-locana or Try-ambaka),[3] Blue-throated (Nīla-kaṇṭha), Five-faced (Pañca-ānana), Moon-crested (Candra-śekhara), Bearer-of-the-Ganges (Gaṅgā-dhara), Mountain-Lord (Girīśa), Wearing-Matted-Hair (Jaṭā-dhara), Whose-Form-is-Water (Jala-mūrti), Wearing-a-Garland-of-Skulls (Kapāla-mālin), Immutable (Sthāṇu), Of-Misinformed-Eyes (Virūpa-akṣa), Lord-of-the-Universe (Viśva-nātha).

The Fearful and Auspicious God

FROM THE point of view of the manifest world, destruction appears in two stages: the first is death, the second, dissolution of the subtle individuality; the one is the end of physical existence, the other liberation from its subtle bonds.

2 Ch. 45 of the Kumbakonam ed.
3 See [328] in the appendix.

Thus there are two aspects of Śiva, the one fearful, the other desirable, the one immediate, the other transcendent.

Ultimately Śiva is the death of death, that is, eternal life. On the other hand, it is from destruction that life arises. Life exists only by devouring life. Life is the image of the giver of death.

As the end of all things Śiva is the lord of death; as the origin of all creation he is the fount of life. Hence Śiva is represented as a fearful divinity who destroys, but also as a mysterious, lustful being who wanders through the forests and mountains giving birth to all the forms of life, creating new worlds and new beings through the rhythm of his dance, the sound of his drum, the postures of his yoga, the drops of his scattered seed.

Śiva's image, arising in the depth of prehistory, appears to be that of the most ancient of all the gods.

Rudra, the Lord of Tears, the Destroyer

IN THE later Hindu philosophy Śiva is the name given to the transcendent peaceful aspect of the disintegrating tendency, while Rudra represents the fierce, active, manifest personification of destruction. It is therefore Rudra who is the centrifugal dispersion or darkness (*tamas*), associated in the basic trinity with the two other tendencies, the centripetal, ascending illumination, *sattva*, and the dynamic revolving, expanding *rajas*, respectively symbolized by the Pervader (Viṣṇu) and the lord-of-the-Immensity (Brahmā).

In the Vedas Rudra appears as a powerful but dangerous god. He is the howling god of storms, the father of the divinities of the winds, and sometimes identified with the god of fire.[4] (*Taittirīya Saṁhitā* 3.2.4; *Taittirīya Brāhmaṇa* 3.2.8.33.) He has to be reckoned with, his name may not be uttered, his magic formulae are prohibitions. In rituals, his place is kept separate from that of other gods; his share is with that of antigods and evil spirits.

In the *Ṛg Veda* (1.114; 2.33) Rudra is spoken of as the lord of songs, the lord of sacrifices, the healer, brilliant as the sun, the best and most bountiful of gods who grants prosperity and welfare to horses and sheep, to men, women, and cows; he is the lord of nourishment who drives away sin; he is the wielder of the thunderbolt (2.33.3), the bearer of bow and arrows (2.33.10; 5.42.11; 10.126.6). Mounted on his chariot, he is terrible as a wild beast, destructive and fierce. In the *Yajur Veda* a long prayer, addressed to him, calls him "auspicious,

4 As Fire, Rudra is called Makhaghna (destroyer of offerings). This may be the origin of the story in which he destroys Dakṣa's sacrifice.

1

Śiva manifested in the trinity and in the dualism of Person and Nature
Brahmeśvara temple, Bhuvaneśvara (Orissa province), 11th century

2

The yogi fighting the power of Nature represented as a lion

Khajuraho, 10th century

The yogi master of the power of Nature
Rājarānī temple, Bhuvaneśvara, 12th century

4

A sacrifice in Bengal

5

A ritual sacrifice, or *yajña*, at Benares

The yajña hall during an interruption of the rites

6

Agni, or Fire

Rājarānī temple, Bhuvaneśvara, 12th century

7

Sūrya, or the Sun
Rāmgaṛh (Rajputana), 12th century

8

Yama, god of death

Brahmeśvara temple, Bhuvaneśvara, 12th century

Varuṇa, the mysterious law of the gods
Brahmeśvara temple, Bhuvaneśvara, 12th century

10

The man-lion, or Nṛsiṁha—an incarnation of Viṣṇu as courage—fighting Hiraṇya-kaśipu, king of the genii
Paṭṭadkal, 7th century

11

The triumph of Viṣṇu

Udayagiri cave, near Bhuvaneśvara, 5th century

12

Nara and Nārāyaṇa, incarnations of Viṣṇu as saints
Daśāvatāra temple, Deogaṛh (Central India), 7th century

13

An apparition of Viṣṇu to the elephant-king Gajendra in response to his faith

Daśāvatāra temple, Deogaṛh, 7th century. Upper left; Viṣṇu riding on the bird-man Garuḍa. Lower left; the elephant-king. Right; the serpent-king and his queen submitting to Viṣṇu

14

Mohinī, the Enchantress, an incarnation of Viṣṇu as a woman

Khandarya Mahādeva temple, Khajuraho, 10th century

Hanuman, the monkey-headed demigod, helper and devotee of Rāma, who is one of the incarnations of Viṣṇu

Virupakṣa temple, Paṭṭadkal, 9th century

16

Lakṣmī, goddess of fortune, the consort of Viṣṇu

Bengal, 11th century

17

Rāvaṇa, demon-king of Ceylon, a devotee of Śiva

Virupakṣa temple, Paṭṭadkal, 9th century

18

Bhairava, the Terrible, the destructive aspect of Śiva

Chaturbhuja temple, Khajuraho, 10th century

19

The *liṅga* of Śiva, who is the undivided causal principle
Udayapur (Gwalior state), 12th century

20

The Hermaphrodite, Ardhanārīśvara, symbol of the union of Śiva and Śakti, his consort

Central India, 11th century

21

Śiva, lord of yoga, doing penance

Bhuvaneśvara, 9th century

22

Skanda or Kumāra, one of Śiva's sons, the handsome and ever young captain of the gods' army

Bhuvaneśvara, 9th century

Śiva and an aspect of his power, Pārvatī, Daughter of the Mountain, or space

Central India, 12th century

24

Kālī, Time, a fearful form of the consort of Śiva and one of ten objects of transcendent knowledge or aspects of the power of Śiva

Rāmgaṛh (Rajputana), 12th century

25

A *ḍākinī*, an attendant of Kālī, surrounded by demons, drinking blood on a battlefield
Khandarya Mahadeva temple, Khajuraho, 10th century

Durgā killing the buffalo-demon

Telika temple, Bhuvaneśvara, 11th century

Gaṇapati, Pārvatī's son, and Siddhi, Success, one of Gaṇapati's two wives
Khajuraho, 10th century

28

A form of Brahmā

Pārśvanātha Jain temple, Khajuraho, 11th century

A *nāga*

Janjira (Central India), 12th century

29

30

A flying *gandharva*, a celestial harmony

Duladeva temple, Khajuraho, 11th century

31

An *apsaras*, a heavenly courtesan
Chaturbhuja temple, Khajuraho, 11th century

32

A seer, or *ṛṣi*

Bengal, early 19th century. Wood

not to be feared," "the deliverer, the first divine physician; blue-necked and red-colored, with a thousand eyes, the bearer of a thousand quivers." In another hymn he is three-eyed (Tryambaka),[5] sweet-scented, increaser of prosperity. In the *Atharva Veda* he is the protector of cattle, but his character is fierce. The fearful Rudra is pictured with a hundred heads, a thousand eyes. Nothing is hidden from him, nothing escapes his power. It is he who punishes the evildoer.

"Rudra gives to the sinner the tortures of hell." (Mahīdhara's commentary on the *Vājasaneya Saṁhitā* of the *Śukla Yajur Veda* 16.33. [329])

From the point of view of life, destruction appears fearful and is dreaded. "Rudra is the god that kills." (*Atharva Veda* 1.19.3. [330]) Men speak of him with terror. "He is death . . . the demon . . . the cause of tears." (*Atharva Veda, Sūkta,* 16.6.26. [331]) They invoke him with anguish.

Do not slaughter our father or our mother.
(*Ṛg Veda* 1.114.7. [332])

Do not strike us in our sons or in the length of our life. Be not cruel!
Do not injure us in our cattle or our horses.
Do not slay our brave men in your anger, O lord of tears!
(*Śvetāśvatara Upaniṣad* 4.22. [333])

For him the priest and the warrior are but food, and death is the condiment.
Who knows when he will come?
(*Kaṭha Upaniṣad* 2.25. [334])

Anyone who performs a function of destruction participates in the Rudra principle. Life, which can exist only by destroying life, is a manifestation of Rudra.

"O Maitreya! Anyone who destroys anything of the animate or inanimate world thus belongs to the Destroyer; he becomes the death-giving embodiment of the fearful Torturer-of-Men (Janārdana)." (*Viṣṇu Purāṇa* 1.22.39. [335])

First acknowledged as the Transcendent-God (Mahā-deva) in the *Śukla Yajur Veda*, Rudra appears as the Supreme God in the Upaniṣads.

He is without beginning, middle, or end:
the One, omnipresent,
wonderful, the joy of the mind, the consort of Peace-of-the-Night (*Umā*),
the supreme deity, the supreme lord,
three-eyed, blue-throated, tranquil.

5 See note 3. Also *Ṛg Veda* 7.59.12.

He is the Creator, the lord of sleep,
and Indra, the lord of heaven;
indestructible, supreme, self-resplendent.
He is the Pervader, the life breath,
the fire of destruction, and the devoured offering (the Moon).
He is all that has been or shall be,
eternal.
Knowing him, one crosses beyond death.
There is no other way to liberation.

(*Kaivalya Upaniṣad* 6–9. [336])

As the active principle of destruction, the lord of tears is the ruler of the universe. "Rudra, the terrible, the one without a second, through his powers rules the worlds. He dwells within all creatures. He is the protector. Having created all beings, he merges them together at the end of time." (*Śvetāśvatara Upaniṣad* 3.2. [337])

"This Transcendent-God (Mahā-deva) is all-pervading yet nowhere seen; he is the creator, the ruler, suzerain of the Immense Being, of the Pervader, and of the king-of-heaven (Sureśa, i.e., Indra). All celestial beings, from the Immense Being to the evil spirits, worship him." (*Mahābhārata* 13.14.3–4; 13.45.3–4, Kumbakonam ed. [338])

The Name Rudra

The origin of the name Rudra remains obscure; we know only symbolic etymologies. The Brāhmaṇas say that when Rudra was born he wept. His father, the lord-of-progeny (Prajāpati), asked the reason, and on being told that he wept because he had no name, he called the child Rudra (from the root *rud*, "to weep"). The same story appears in the *Padma Purāṇa* (ch. 8), the *Kūrma Purāṇa* (1.10), the *Viṣṇu Purāṇa* (1.8).

The *Bṛhad-devatā* also takes the name to mean "the howler." "Because he-howled (*arodīt*) in the sky, giving rain and lightning to men, he is praised by four seers as 'the howler' (Rudra)." (Ibid. 2.34. [339]) The *Mahābhārata* (12.10369) compares his laughter to the fearful hollow sound of the battle drum.

Rudra means also the "remover of pain." "*Rut* is the name given to the three forms of pain [physical, mental, and spiritual] found in the world. The cause of pain is also called *rut*, and he is Rudra, the 'remover of pain' because he drives away all forms of pain." (*Śabda-cintāmaṇi*. [340])

Rudra may further mean the "red one." This may also be the original meaning of "Śiva" in some non-Aryan tongue. In Tamil the word for red is *śev-*, *śivappu*.

In the Purāṇas and the Upaniṣads the name Rudra means the lord of tears.

"He is Rudra because he causes [men] to cry." (*Kūrma Purāṇa* 1.10.24. [341])

"At the time of destruction he destroys the living beings and makes them cry, hence he is the lord of tears." (*Viṣṇu-sahasra-nāma Bhāṣya* 26. [342]) "When the breath of life leaves the body, it causes men to lament. [The life breath] is thus called Rudra because it makes them cry." (*Bṛhad-āraṇyaka Upaniṣad* 3.9.4. [343])

The Personification of Anger

This world is governed by fear. Rudra is "the Great Fear, the upraised thunderbolt" (*Kaṭha Upaniṣad* 5.3; *Kena Upaniṣad* 3.2 [344]), "whose anger in war even the gods fear" (*Rāmāyaṇa* 1.1.4 [345]). "Out of fear of him the wind blows, out of fear the sun shines, out of fear fire and the king of heaven and death rush to their work." (*Taittirīya Upaniṣad* 2.8.1. [346])

The anger of divinity is the source of fear. As the supreme ruler, the lord of tears is thus called the Wrathful (Caṇḍa), the Fury (Caṇḍikā), the Furious (Bhīma), the Fearful (Ugra), the Terrible (Ghora), the Frightful (Vibhīṣaṇa). (*Mahābhārata* 12.10.370; 10.375.) In Rudra anger itself is worshiped.

"I salute thee, wrath of the lord of tears." (*Vājasaneya Saṁhitā* 16.1. [347])

In the Purāṇic myth the birth of Rudra is connected with the anger (*manyu*) of the lord-of-progeny (Prajāpati).

The Fire That Kills

First among the forms of destruction comes fire. Agni, the lord of fire, is thus a manifestation of Rudra. In the *Ṛg Veda* Agni is often called Rudra and identified with him. "Agni is Rudra." (*Śatapatha Brāhmaṇa* 5.3.1.10; 6.1.3.10. [348]) [6] "This all-pervading subtle fire is the very god Rudra." (Ibid. 9.1.1.1. [349])

"Agni is the name of Rudra. Agni has two shapes, the one fearful, the other benevolent (Śiva)." (*Aitareya Brāhmaṇa*, as quoted in *Kalyāṇa*, Śiva aṅka, p. 50. [350]) "Agni is called Rudra." (*Nirukta* 10.1.7. [351])

"Because he made all the worlds, this Rudra was named Agni." (*Atharva Saṁhitā* 7.87.9. [352]) All that burns pertains to Rudra. The heat of the sun is

6 Also *Taittirīya Saṁhitā* 5.4.3.1.

the "breath of Rudra" (*rudra-prāṇa*). As the personification of the sacrificial fire, Rudra is called the Herdsman (Paśupati) (see below, pp. 205, 209). In alchemy mercury, believed to be "solar heat" stored between the layers of the earth, is called *rudra-vīrya*, the "semen of Rudra."

Bhairava (the Terrible)

In his most destructive aspect Rudra becomes Bhairava, the fearful destroyer, who takes pleasure in destruction. According to the *Taittirīya Saṁhitā* (6.2.3), Rudra attacked the three cities of the *asuras* and destroyed them. This may be the origin of the myth of the burning of the three cities.

The Lord-of-Elements or Lord-of-Ghosts (Bhūteśvara)

The *Aitareya Brāhmaṇa* (3.33) calls Rudra lord-of-the-elements (Bhūtaman). This is also the meaning of Bhūteśvara. In later mythology, however, the term *bhūta* is taken to represent ghosts and evil spirits and Bhūteśvara appears as the lord of ghosts.

As the lord of ghosts Rudra "haunts graveyards and places of cremation, wearing serpents round his head and skulls for a necklace, attended by troops of imps, and trampling on rebellious demons. He sometimes indulges in revelry, and, heated with drink, dances furiously . . . the dance called Tāṇḍava, while troops of drunken imps caper around him." (Dowson, *Dictionary of Hindu Mythology*, p. 298.)

Death, the Remover (Hara)

As the power of devastation which sweeps away and destroys all things, Śiva is named Hara, the "remover"; this aspect of Śiva is identified with sickness and death as well as with that all-dispatching power which, in the end, destroys the universe.

"He is the Remover (Hara) because he takes everything away, because he destroys all things."

In the *Mahābhārata* (13.1146), Rudra is "he who sweeps away all beings" (Sarva-bhūta-hara). He is also the "remover of the eyes of Bhaga" (Bhaga-netra-hara), since he blinded Bhaga, the Āditya who distributes to the gods their shares of the sacrifice. (Ibid. 10.249.) He is the "remover of the offerings of Ritual Skill" (Dakṣa-kratu-hara), for he steals away the fruit of the sacrifice. (Ibid. 10.253.)

Hara is disease (*Mahābhārata* 7.2877) and his messenger is fever (ibid. 12.10259). He is death (ibid. 13.7497), which destroys indiscriminately the good and the bad (ibid. 12.2791). At the end of the ages he devours all he has created (ibid. 9.2236). He draws in the universe and swallows up all things (ibid. 13.941–43).

Rudra, as the lord-of-sleep (Śiva), is also the remover of pain because sleep removes all suffering.

In another etymology "Hara is taken to mean the 'giver of wonders.'" (*Śivatoṣiṇī*, commentary on the *Liṅga Purāṇa* 1.65.143. [353])

Śiva, the Auspicious, the Lord of Sleep

"THE MORE abstract form of Rudra is called Śiva in the ancient scripture." (*Liṅga Purāṇa* 1.3.10. [354]) According to the *Siddhānta-kaumudī* (1032 [355]), the name Śiva comes from the root *śīṅ*, which means "sleep." "All sleep in him, hence he is the lord of sleep." (Ibid., *Uṇādi Sūtra* 1.153. [356])

In the hymns of the Vedas the word *śiva*, meaning "auspicious," is only an adjective applied to the peaceful aspect of Rudra.

"May you appear to us, O Rudra, dweller among the mountains, with that form of yours which suggests no evil, which is auspicious (*śiva*),

> *not terrifying, most kindly to us.*
> *O dweller among the mountains! Protector of mountains!*
> *make gentle* (śiva) *the arrow which you hold in your hand*
> *ready to be thrown.*
> *Injure not man or things."*
>
> (*Śvetāśvatara Upaniṣad* 3.5–6. [357])

The idea, common to all primitive peoples, of propitiating what one fears by speaking of it indirectly and with gentle names made of the adjective "auspicious" (*śiva*) another name of Rudra. This appellation was to become his usual name in the Upaniṣads. Later it superseded the older names in popular religion. The two names, Rudra and Śiva, are now used as equivalents, yet theoretically Rudra represents the fearful, manifest aspect, Śiva the peaceful, transcendent aspect of the *tamas* tendency, that which alone remains when the two other tendencies come to rest.

When beings are tired of action, of life, of knowledge, of pain and pleasure, and seek the rest of dreamless sleep, they enter into "Śiva, the changeless state, the abode-of-joy (Śambhu), in whom the universe comes to rest and sleeps." (Quoted in Karapātrī's "Śrī Śiva tattva," *Siddhānta*, II, 1941–42. [358])

This rest in sleep is the ultimate mercy of the Creator. Even Indra, the king of heaven, who possesses all the means of enjoyment, is said to long in the end for the peace of nonexistence (*Bhāgavata Purāṇa*). Śiva, the undifferentiated, nondual state, is the supreme goal of the yogis, who "know Śiva to be the nondual undifferentiated Fourth-stage (*turīya*) that is peace." (*Māṇḍūkya Upaniṣad* 7. [359])

We fear death that is eternal sleep because of our failure to understand its significance. Man, in his world of illusion, fears death, even though it means for him liberation from bondage, all that is to be desired.

"The yogi [even] fears him, seeing an object of fear in what is but freedom from fear." (Gauḍapāda's *Māṇḍūkya Upaniṣad Kārikā* 3.39. [360])

"As the worms of the bitter *nim* fruit seem tortured when placed in sugar, so also the ignorant worm, who seeks the pleasures of the world of duality, fears the joy of the nondual, of the unmanifest, since he can find there no trace of the songs and dance and play of this world. Yet those who attain knowledge realize that it is there only that the essence of true joy can be found. Rudra, fear of the ignorant, appears to the wise as the auspicious Śiva, the ambrosia of all joy." (Karapātrī, "Śrī Śiva tattva," *Sanmārga*, 1946, p. 114.)

As the Cosmic Being, Śiva is made of all the principles of the elements. "Fire is his forehead, the sun and moon are his eyes, the directions of space are his ears, the Veda is his voice, the wind that pervades the world is the breath which raises his chest, his feet are the earth. He is the inner self of all living beings." (*Muṇḍaka Upaniṣad* 2.1.4. [361])

The Lord of Knowledge, Maheśvara

The transcendent-divinity (Maheśvara), the lord of knowledge, represents a state where all differentiation ceases to exist, "where the individuality merges into that greater being which is in ourselves yet existed before we were born, before creation arose. This true Self of all beings is the unqualified transcendent divinity, Maheśvara." (Karapātrī, "Maheśvara," *Sanmārga*, 1946.)

"This divinity is by itself more vast than all that has place in the universe, hence the wise call him the transcendent divinity." (*Brahma-vaivarta Purāṇa*, Prakṛti khaṇḍa, ch. 53. [362])

From the cosmological point of view Maheśvara is another name for the Indestructible-Person (*akṣara puruṣa*). It is this Indestructible Person who, as the world's creator, is generally aimed at through the singular personal term "God." Each of the component-parts (*kalā*) of the Akṣara Puruṣa is also God, that is, appears to us as being the whole indivisible totality. Just as an infinite number, an infinite distance, an infinite quantity, all of which are fictions, may appear to us as part of a general Infinite in which quantity, number, distance are no longer distinct entities but seem to merge into their common quality, that is, infinity; so, similarly, each divinity, that is, each transcendent aspect of creation, appears to man to merge into an indivisible undifferentiated Immense Being. The God who is above all the gods, the indivisible whole of all the deities, is the transcendent divinity, the Great God, Maheśvara. This unity of all that exists is represented by the unity of the three elements which constitute the nature of the cosmos, of the cosmic sacrifice: Might (Indra), the Devourer (Agni), and the Devoured (Soma), the three main aspects of Śiva.

In the Purāṇas, as in the Upaniṣads, Maheśvara is the deity of transcendent knowledge.

"It is from Maheśvara that knowledge is to be sought." (*Karma-locana,* quoted in *Śabda-kalpa-druma,* II, 507. [363])

"I bow to the abode of all science, the Great Lord, Maheśvara. From his breath sprang the eternal word (the Veda) and from the word the universe." (Sāyaṇa's *Ṛg Veda Bhāṣya,* quoted in *Kalyāṇa,* Śiva aṅka, p. 169. [364])

"He is the Ruler (Īśāna), master of all the forms of knowledge. He is the Lord (Īśvara) of all the elements." (*Mahānārāyaṇa Upaniṣad* 47. [365])

In Maheśvara are said to be co-ordinated the three energies from which knowledge arises, the powers of understanding (*jñāna*), will (*icchā*), and action (*kriyā*). Śiva as Maheśvara is therefore worshiped for intellectual achievement.

"He is the king of the world, the lord of tears, the great seer from whom the gods are born and into whom they merge in the end. May he, who first saw the birth of the universal Intellect, endow us with understanding." (*Śvetāśvatara Upaniṣad* 4.12. [366])

"Seeking enlightenment, I take refuge in him who first established the Creator, him from whom sprang forth the Vedas, the resplendent god by whom intellect is illumined." (*Śvetāśvatara Upaniṣad* 6.18. [367])

The Māheśvara Sūtra

Every science can lead us to the common spring of all the sciences. Yet there are four approaches which are considered as leading more directly to the understanding of higher reality. The teaching of these four sciences is symbolically attributed to Śiva. They are Yoga, the method of suprasensorial perception; Vedānta, the theory of metaphysics or the understanding of suprasensorial reality; the study of Language, that is, the relation of words or verbal symbols to ideas; and Music, the perception of the relation of numbers to ideas and forms. It is believed that the theory of these four forms of knowledge can be derived from a mysterious formula called the *Māheśvara Sūtra*, said to have sprung from the small drum of Śiva during the cosmic dance through which the universe was shaped.[7]

The *Māheśvara Sūtra* contains all the possible articulate sounds arranged in a symbolic order said to be the key to the structure and the significance of all language. It represents one of the esoteric word-formulae in which the ancient Śaiva wisdom was condensed and which are believed to constitute the earliest revelation. According to some strict followers of Śaivism, the transfer of the symbolic value attributed to word-symbols to the magic incantations and poetic descriptions of the Vedic hymns could only be a new re-velation (i.e., unveiling) of the ancient wisdom following the Aryan conquest. The term *veda*, taken to mean the pure "beginningless knowledge," should be understood as referring not necessarily to the Vedic hymns but to these ancient formulae or *mantras*, which do not pertain to any particular known language and which have remained the key to the secret knowledge transmitted by Hindu esoteric groups.

In the theory of language a fundamental distinction is made between the word and its meaning. Śiva, being the substance of knowledge, is identified with the meaning of words. The word itself, the instrument through which we grasp the meaning, is a form of energy and is thus assimilated to the power of Śiva, the active principle of his manifestation represented as his consort. "Śiva is the meaning, his consort the words." (*Liṅga Purāṇa* 3.11.47. [368])

"The beloved of Śiva, his divine Energy, is the support of all the words, while Śiva himself, whose brow the crescent moon (the cup of Soma) adorns (i.e., as the yogi whose vital powers have been sublimated), is the support of all meanings." (*Vaiyākaraṇa-mañjūṣā*. [369])

Time (Kāla), the All-Destroyer

Before anything exists, time is. Time is the first condition for the existence of the universe. Although the "point of view of cosmology" (Sāṅkhya) takes time to be a corollary of space, the point of view of logic (Nyāya), as well as that of metaphysics (Vedānta), considers time as prior to space. Time thus understood is distinct from the relative time we perceive. It is Transcendent-Time (*mahā-kāla*), absolute, eternal, measureless, ever present. It is also called the "rodlike undivided time" (*akhaṇḍa daṇḍāyamāna*). The divisions of relative time as we perceive them are merely an apparent division of continuous Time

7 The story of the circumstances in which the grammarian Pāṇini obtained the *sūtras* from the Great God is told in the *Kathā-sarit-sāgara*, the *Hara-carita-cintāmaṇi*, the *Bṛhat Kathā-mañjarī*, and the *Nandikeśvara Kāśikā*.

due to the motion of the planets. Relative time is experienced differently by different kinds of beings. The planets whose motions determine the rhythms of relative time, the process of the phenomenal world, may well be regarded as the agencies of the eternal laws which rule over our destinies, and viewed under this aspect they are spoken of as deities. So long as we are subject to the rule of the planetary rhythms we remain shut up within the realm of relative existence. It is only when the relative succession of time lapses, or somehow loses its significance, that we can attain rest within absolute time.

Śiva, as the Destroyer, is identified with Time (Kāla). (*Mahābhārata* 13.7497, 1161, 1188, 942.)

"You are the origin of the worlds and you are Time, their destroyer." (*Mahābhārata*, Anuśāsana parvan, 45.313. [370])

Perceptible manifestation can take place only within space-time. *Sattva*, the centripetal tendency, is the principle of location, of space, while *tamas*, the centrifugal tendency, is the essence of absolute time, the measure of the expansion by which things are destroyed. Relative or cyclic time, on the other hand, which is the effect of the circular motion of the planets, is related to space and pertains to the revolving tendency, *rajas*, through which all substances, all things, are born. The *Viṣṇu*, *Bhāgavata*, and *Padma Purāṇas* therefore state that the Immense-Being (Brahmā), the embodiment of the revolving tendency, is the form of relative time.

Yet "the time by which the worlds come to an end is different from the time which measures life. Time is thus of two kinds, gross and subtle, manifest and unmanifest." (*Sūrya-siddhānta* 1.10. [371])

The Divinity of Time

"In the *Viṣṇu Purāṇa* (1.2) it is said that, when the three fundamental tendencies balance one another, the flow that is the universe ceases to be. Then Nature and Person, Prakṛti and Puruṣa, stand apart. At that time the manifest aspect of the supreme causal state, upon which rest Nature and Person, now separate, is eternity or eternal time. Absolute time is thus the aspect of a transcendent reality which, at the time of creation, links Nature and Person and which separates them when the world dissolves.

"The word 'Time' is therefore used in a theological acceptation to represent the union of the lord of sleep, the manifest substratum, Śiva, and his power, his consort Śivā, the oneness of the illusionist (*māyin*) and his power of illusion (*māyā*)." (Yogatrayānanda, "Kāla tattva," *Śiva-rātrī*, p. 177.)

When identified with the lord of sleep or with transcendent-divinity

(Maheśvara), eternal, indivisible Time is known as Transcendent or Absolute-Time (*mahā-kāla*).

Relative time measures all growth and decay, all existence. This elusive power, which destroys all, is the only measure of life. Time is therefore the power of Rudra, the power of death, the All-Destroyer.

"I am Time (Kāla), inclined toward destroying the worlds," says the Cosmic Being of the *Bhagavadgītā* (11.52 [372]). The *Mahābhārata* (1.1.273 [373]) refers to "Time which digests the elements, Time which devours all beings."

"All this world, existence and nonexistence, joy and pain rest upon Time." (*Mahābhārata* 1.1.272. [374])

Relative time is also sometimes identified with the Binder (Yama), the ruler of the kingdom of death. (*Mahābhārata* 13.1, etc.)

The Lord of Yoga

The state attained by the yogi who has silenced his mind is the root of knowledge. It is there that he can grasp the unmanifest source of manifestation. All the teachings of yoga and the process of liberation are witnessed by the yogi in the cavern of his heart as the form of Maheśvara. Maheśvara is thus the great Yogi, the teacher of all that is beyond the reach of sensorial experiment. To him is attributed the revelation to mankind of the technique of yoga.

Śiva is himself represented as the perfect ascetic (Mahā Yogi), in whom is centered the perfection of austerity, penance, and meditation, through which unlimited powers are attained. He is shown naked, "clad in space" (*dig-ambara*), "loaded with matted hair" (*dhūr-jaṭi*), his body smeared with ashes.

Since the methods of yoga, different in this from those of ritual, are open to everyone able to follow its disciplines, Śiva, the Yogi, is accused, in the Aryan scripture, of being the teacher of the low-born, the god who revealed the secret of the higher truth to those who are unqualified for ritual practice.

Śaṅkara (the Giver of Joy) and Śambhu (the Abode of Joy)

"Because he creates (*kṛ*) joy (*sukha-śam*), because he is the source of boundless joy, Śiva, the supreme formless being, is named the Giver-of-Joy (Śaṅkara)." (*Śivatoṣiṇī*, commentary on the *Liṅga Purāṇa* 1.6.22. [375])

Śambhu is the Abode of Joy. Transcendent joy is the symbol of transcendent experience, that is, absolute knowledge.

The Hermaphrodite

The neutral, uncreative substratum first divides itself into substance and energy, into a male and a female principle. When these again unite, a spark appears which is lust, the source of the flow of life.

It is this lust which is the apparent origin of manifestation. The division into a male and a female constituent represents an attempt to explain the appearance of the spark of lust out of the neutral substratum.

The union of Śiva and Śakti is their basic reality. This is symbolized in the Hermaphrodite (Ardhanārīśvara), half male, half female, whose nature is pure lust.

"When existence and consciousness unite, their union is pleasure and in this pleasure lies their purpose. Their separate existence is but an appearance." (Karapātrī, "Liṅgopāsanā-rahasya," *Siddhānta,* II, 1941–42, 153.)

The symbolism of the Hermaphrodite is equivalent to that of the *liṅga* and the *yoni.*

From the point of view of cosmology, "the power of deliberation (*vimarśa*) and the power of expression (*prakāśa*) first manifest themselves respectively in 'the determinant of space,' the point-limit (*bindu*) from which manifestation begins, and 'the determinant of time,' the primordial-vibration (*nāda*). Space is represented as female, time as male. Their union in the Hermaphrodite is known as Lust (Kāma)." (Karapātrī, "Śrī Śiva tattva," *Siddhānta,* II, 1941–42, 114.)

"The male principle is also represented as Fire, the devourer, while the female principle is Soma, the devoured offering. The Hermaphrodite is then the embodiment of the cosmic sacrifice, the image of the universe." (Vijayānanda Tripāṭhī, "Devatā tattva," *Sanmārga,* III, 1942.)

Śiva can unite only with himself, for "perfect beauty can see only itself reflected in itself. No other mirror would reflect perfection. Hence divinity is 'by its own beauty bewildered.' [376] The spark of lust appears which is born when Śiva and his power, Śakti, become one, and from the emotion of love springs forth the universe." (Karapātrī, "Liṅgopāsanā-rahasya," p. 154.)

"He divided his body into halves, one was male, the other female. The male in that female procreates the universe." (*Manu Smṛti* 1.32. [377])

The Forms of Rudra-Śiva

The Elemental Forms of Rudra

THE POWER OF DESTRUCTION, the power of Rudra, manifests itself through all the elements, the forces of nature. Rudra is the fire that kills, the water that kills, the wind that destroys, the man that murders. As the power behind the elements Rudra is represented under eight forms, mentioned in the *Śatapatha Brāhmaṇa* (6.3.1) as the forms of the multicolored-fire (*citra-agni*) or the fiery-breath (*āgneya-prāṇa*), which are the fiery forms of Śiva.

Like all the aspects of Śiva, the elemental forms of Rudra have a dual aspect, the one fearful, the other benevolent. Some of them happen to be more usually envisaged in their benevolent than in their fearful aspect. (*Śatapatha Brāhmaṇa* 63.1.9–17.)

"Existence (Bhava), the Archer (Śarva), the lord-of-tears (Rudra), the Herdsman (Paśupati),[1] the Fearful (Ugra) and Great (Mahān, i.e., Mahādeva), the Tremendous (Bhīma), the Ruler (Īśāna), these are the eight names. In each of these divine wisdom spreads. They are the dwelling place of him who is all that is to be desired and before whom I bow." (*Śiva-mahimna Stotra* 28. [378])

1. The Archer (Śarva)

Śarva represents the element earth, the nourisher, the support of life, the hunter who brings food. He is also an equivalent of the god of love whose arrows are the five senses.

"The support of all beings, animate or inanimate, the deity whose substance is earth is called Śarva by all the knowers of the Scripture. Earth is his nature;

1 Rudra is already called Śarva, Bhava, Paśupati, in *Śatapatha Brāhmaṇa* 1.7.3, 8.

he is the ruler of all. His wife, the Disheveled (Vikeśī), is the earth goddess and his son is [the planet] Mars (Aṅgāraka)." (*Liṅga Purāṇa* 2.13.3–4. [379])

2. *Existence (Bhava)*

Bhava, always associated with Śarva, is the element water. He is sometimes shown as an attendant of Śiva and is then equated with Parjanya, the god of rain.

"Bhava, the knowers of the Veda say, is the all-powerful god. He is the nature of the life of the worlds. His consort is called Peace-of-the-Night (Umā) by the sages; his son is the planet Venus. He is the reservoir of the seed of the seven worlds; he is the one protector of the seven worlds." (*Liṅga Purāṇa* 2.13.5–6. [380])

3. *The Herdsman (Paśupati)*

The *Aitareya Brāhmaṇa* (3.33) calls Rudra the "Herdsman" (Paśupati), the feeder of sacrifices. Paśupati here represents the element fire, the embodiment of the ritual sacrifice, the giver of life.

"The Lord-Herdsman (Paśupati) is known to the sages as the embodiment of fire. The beloved wife of the Herdsman is the Invocation-at-Offering (Svāhā). His son is said to be Ṣaṇmukha, the six-faced [lord-of-war] (Skanda)." (*Liṅga Purāṇa* 2.13.7. [381])

4. *The Ruler (Īśāna)*

Īśāna is the embodiment of air, the purifier, the regent of the northeastern direction.

"All-pervading, nourisher of all that has a body, the spirit of air is called the Ruler (Īśāna) by the sages. The consort of this divine Īśāna, creator of the worlds, whose nature is wind, is said to be the Auspicious-Goddess (Śivā). His son is Swiftness-of-Mind (Manojava)." (*Liṅga Purāṇa* 2.13.8–9. [382]) (See also below, p. 211.)

5. *The Tremendous (Bhīma)*

Bhīma is the embodiment of ether, the source of all that is. "Fulfiller of the desires of all living or lifeless beings, the embodiment of ether is called the Tremendous (Bhīma) by the sages. The ten-directions-of-space (*diśā*) are the wife of this divine Bhīma of great fame. His son is Creation (Sarga)." (*Liṅga Purāṇa*, 2.13.10–11. [383])

6. *The Lord-of-Tears* (*Rudra*)

Rudra is the embodiment of the sun, the celestial form of fire, which brings forth and dries up life.

"The solar deity, source of all splendor, giver of liberation and enjoyment, is called Rudra, the lord of tears, by the gods. The wife of this solar Rudra, inspirer of devotion, is the Shining-Goddess (Suvarcalā). His son is Saturn (Śani), the slow mover." (*Liṅga Purāṇa* 2.13.12–13. [384])

7. *The Great-God* (*Mahā-deva*)

Śiva is the reproductive power, perpetually creating again that which he destroys. He is the Supreme Lord, the Great-God (Mahā-deva) symbolized by the phallus (*liṅga*), the instrument of reproduction and the source of pleasure, from which flows the seed of life whose storehouse is the Moon, the cup of ambrosia. The *liṅga* is worshiped alone or combined with the *yoni*, or female organ, representing Śiva's consort, Energy (Śakti).

"Known as the embodiment of all that is gentle (i.e., the Moon), the Great-God (Mahā-deva) is mentioned by the wise as made of the sacrificial-elixir (*soma*). The gods say that the wife of this great god made of ambrosia is the Red-One (Rohiṇī). His son is the planet Mercury (Budha)." (*Liṅga Purāṇa* 2.13.14–15. [385])

8. *The Fearful* (*Ugra*), *or the Thunderbolt* (*Aśani*)

The thunderbolt, Aśani, is a spark of the fire-of-the-universal-destruction (*vaiśvānara-agni*). The thunderbolt is also the name given to the sacrificer, the Yajamāna, who kills the victim.

"Support of offerings to gods and Ancestors, ever the devourer of offerings, self of the sacrificer, the great and fearful god Ugra is known to the wise. Others call him the Ruler (Īśāna). His wife is Initiation (Dīkṣā). His son is the Libation (Santāna)." (*Liṅga Purāṇa* 2.13.16–18. [386])

The Five Components (*kalā*) of Śiva and the Manifestation of Speech

THE PROCESS of the manifestation of thought into speech is equated with the process of cosmic manifestation through which the lord-of-sleep (Śiva) gives birth to the universe. This process takes place in five stages, which are called joy (*ānanda*), knowledge (*vijñāna*), thought (*mana*), life-breath (*prāṇa*), and physical-life (*bhūta*), the last itself divided into speech (*vāc*) and food (*anna*).

"From food springs the life breath of all beings. From breath thought, from thought knowledge, and from knowledge joy, the matrix of all. The Cosmic Person is thus fivefold, and all that exists has a fivefold nature. . . . Having realized this in mind and in heart, the wise cross beyond death." (*Nārāyaṇa Upaniṣad* 79. [387])

These five elements of the manifestation of thought are impersonated in five deities which are called the five "components" (*kalā*) of Śiva.[2]

1. The Conqueror-of-Death (Mṛtyum-jaya)

The Conqueror-of-Death (Mṛtyum-jaya) represents the being-of-pure-joy (*ānanda-maya-mūrti*).

The state of the perfectly silenced mind is represented as perfect peace, unconditioned enjoyment. Enjoyment is the source and the end of all activities. The urge for pleasure, which is the relative, manifest form of enjoyment, is the impeller of action. Life is meant for enjoyment, is sustained by enjoyment. If there was only the prospect of pain, no being would remain alive. It is only in the hope of heavenly joy that beings seek anything but pleasure.

The yogi who, through introspection, has reached within himself the silent region beyond thought, beyond knowledge, has attained the experience of pure enjoyment, and "reaching that essence of enjoyment, he becomes all joy." (*Taittirīya Upaniṣad* 2.7. [388])

2. The Southern-Image (Dakṣiṇā-mūrti)

The Southern-Image (Dakṣiṇā-mūrti) represents the being-of-knowledge or -intellect (*vijñāna-maya-mūrti*).

In the unmanifest substratum of intellect, the motionless ocean of joy, appears the first movement which blurs its waters. This is the beginning of an idea, the inner vision which the mind tries to express in words.

The faculty which perceives the idea is known as intellect (*buddhi*). It is the instrument of knowledge. Knowledge is the power of the intellect. Its total cosmic form is represented by the solar-sphere (*sūrya-maṇḍala*) from which are issued all planets and their contents: the living beings and the forms and ideas contained in the solar system. Since nothing exists on the earth which

2 We follow here the description given by Giridhara Śarmā Caturvedi in "Śiva mahimā," *Kalyāṇa*, Śiva aṅka, p. 41.

is not issued from the sun, the sun must contain the potentiality of all that is to be known. The sun is the sum total of all knowledge.

The sun stands in the center of the solar world. In symbolic orientation the center is called the north. From the north to the south, from the center to the periphery, knowledge comes down like the rays of light. The aim, the end, of knowledge is represented as a flow toward the south, as the Southern-Image (Dakṣiṇā-mūrti). This flow toward the south, toward disintegration, is also the way of death. The Southern Image is therefore considered the presiding deity of death.

The Southern Image is shown standing on the rhythm-of-the-letters (*varṇa-mātṛkā*). To take form, knowledge will depend upon the device of language. The word is the manifested form of knowledge.

The Conqueror of Death and the Southern Image are predominantly enlightenment (*prakāśa-pradhāna*). They are consequently shown as white in color.

3. The Lord-of-Lust (Kāmeśvara)

The lord of lust, Kāmeśvara, represents the mental-being (*mano-maya-mūrti*).

The idea visualized by the intellect is now seized by the mind, which tries to reduce it to words, to put it in code, so that it may become transmissible. In its universal form the mental being is known as the "lord of lust," for the mind is predominantly desire. Mind is made of lust, of ambition.

"Lust appeared first, wandering over all. It appeared before and is the seed of thought." (*Nṛsiṁha-pūrva-tāpinī Upaniṣad* 1.1. [389])

The color of the lord of lust is red, the color of desire. The Tantras explain that the lord of lust should be worshiped seated with his consort on a bed made of the five evil spirits (*preta*) which are the five forms of sensorial perception that furnish him with their vain images.

4. The Herdsman (Paśupati)

The Herdsman (Paśupati) represents the being-of-life (*prāṇa-maya-mūrti*).

The words which have been shaped by the mind are now brought forth by the vital breath. They become perceptible, alive. This power which brings forth into manifestation, into life, the subtle vibration of thought is the life breath identified with the being-of-life and represented as the five-faced herdsman, Paśupati, lord of the earth, who, through the instruments of rule that are the five vital energies (*prāṇa*), guides the immense herd of creatures, the changing forms of manifestation.

We have already met Paśupati as the embodiment of fire among the elemental forms of Rudra (p. 205). The Herdsman represents both the life energy or inner fire and the ritual fire, these being the two forms of combustion through which men live and gods are sustained. All life is a transformation. It is through the sacrificial fire that the victim enters into a divine world. The Herdsman is a typical figure of ancient Śaivism. He appears as the Ruler of the Earth, the friend of life, the guide of each species in its development. There is a form of Paśupati for each world. Already the Vedas picture Rudra as living in the forests and mountains, ruling over animals tamed and wild. The Śaiva mythology shows him as the divinity of life, the guardian of the earth, who wanders naked through the rich forest, lustful and strong. He teaches the highest and most secret knowledge to the most humble. He brought to the earth the arts of music and dancing and the dramatic art through which wisdom can be imparted to the crowd.

The Herdsman is often equated with Prajāpati, the lord of progeny, the guiding spirit of the natural world.

Everything in the universe is made of three parts: an inner spark, which is the life principle or soul, a substance or body, and a linking element made of the life energies and rhythms. These are called, respectively, the Herdsman (Paśupati), the animal (*paśu*), and the reins or noose (*pāśa*).

None can exist independently of the rhythms of life, and these rhythms are the link of the body with the inner spark or spirit. Thus the Herdsman, the "reins," and the "animal" are inseparable from one another.

"All beings from the Creator to lifeless matter are known as the animals (*paśu*), 'the herd' of the wise God of gods who causes the world to move. Being their lord, the all-powerful Rudra is known as the Herdsman." (*Liṅga Purāṇa* 2.9.12–13. [390])

Thus the body or external form of the universe, like that of the individual being, is part of the herd or the evolving-aspect (*vikāra*) of creation. This includes its physical and mental characteristics. The Herdsman procreates all the species from his own substance and binds them with the laws of Nature (*prakṛti*) through which he keeps them in his control. Thus "the twenty-four life-energies (*tattva*) are the reins" (*Liṅga Purāṇa* 2.9.13 [391]). All the laws that guide the movements of the stars of the seasons or the behavior of living species are part of the reins (*pāśa*). These laws also regulate the rhythms of life (*prāṇa*), the evolution of Nature, the growth of all things.

"In the earthly sphere the earth itself is the Herdsman, the earth's attraction and rhythms are the reins, all plants and living creatures are the herd." (Giridhara Śarmā Caturvedi, "Paśupati evam Prajāpati," *Kalyāṇa,* Śiva aṅka, p. 41.)

The *Mahābhārata* (5.3825) depicts Paśupati sitting on the ridge of the Himavat mountains, shining like the fire at the end of the ages. In 12.10.212 we find him on the mountain Meru, on a peak called Sāvitra, and in 7.3465 on Mount Mandara. On the north side of Mount Meru is a lovely *karṇikāra* forest, full of the flowers of all the seasons of the year, where, surrounded by heavenly spirits, Paśupati, the beloved of Peace-of-the-Night (Umā), rejoices. (Ibid. 6.218 and 13.6339.)

According to the *Śatapatha Brāhmaṇa* (1.7.4.1–3),[3] Rudra agreed to be born in order to punish the lord-of-progeny (Prajāpati), who had cast lustful glances on his own daughter. Rudra accepted the lordship of the animals and, himself taking an animal form, he attacked the lord of progeny. Even today men can meet him in the form of an animal or of a hunter or as the star Rohiṇī in the sky.

5. *The Lord-of-the-Elements (Bhūteśa)*

The lord of the elements, Bhūteśa, represents the physical-being or body-of-food (*anna-maya-mūrti*), who is the being-of-speech (*vāṅ-maya-mūrti*).

The connection of the body with the life energies is dual. These energies express themselves through the body and are sustained by the body. This double relation is represented by speech (*vāc*) and food (*anna*). Speech is the outward projection of the mind, and food is the substance of life breath and thought.

All physical matter used in the making of physical bodies is spoken of as food. The body is entirely made of food, and is food for other bodies. The spoken word is also the materialized, the transmissible, form of thought moving from body to body as the food of the mind.

The Ruler of Space, the Five-faced

AS THE ruler of the five directions of space, of the five elements, of the five human races, of the five senses and all that is ruled by the number 5, Śiva is shown as five-faced (*pañcānana*).

"His five faces are pearly, yellow, cloudlike (dark-blue), white, and red in color. He has three eyes and, on his brow, the crescent moon; he holds a spear, a sword, a hatchet, a thunderbolt, and a flame, a king serpent, a bell, an elephant

3 Also *Aitareya Brāhmaṇa* 3.33.

hook, and a noose. One of his hands shows the gesture of removing fear. He is timeless, limitless. His resplendent limbs shine like a thousand moons." (*Tantra-sāra*. [392])

The significance of the five faces of Śiva is explained in the *Liṅga Purāṇa* (2.14–15). There is some divergence as to their colors and attributes between the *Liṅga Purāṇa*, the *Śiva Purāṇa*, the *Viṣṇu-dharmottara Purāṇa*, the *Rūpa-maṇḍana*, the *Śiva-tattva-nidhi*, etc.[4]

One of the five faces looks upward; the others face the four directions. Sometimes it is the *liṅga* of Śiva which is represented with five faces as the progenitor of the five orders of creation.

According to the *Mahābhārata* (13.6384–90), the three faces that look east, north, and west seem mild like the moon, but that which turns to the south is fearful. The eastern face rules the world, the face that looks toward the north enjoys the company of Peace-of-Night (Umā). The western face is gentle and brings happiness to all living creatures, but that which looks toward the south is terrible and destroys all.

The five aspects represented by the five faces of Śiva are sometimes made into separate deities.

1. *The Ruler (Īśāna)*

The face of Śiva that looks upward represents the enjoyer-of-nature (Kṣetra-jña). Transparent like crystal, it is called the Ruler (Īśāna). "The embodiment of all the forms of learning, Īśāna is the master of all knowledge." (*Śivatoṣiṇī*, commentary on the *Liṅga Purāṇa* 1.65.96. [393]) Īśāna is connected with the element air, the sense of touch, and the hand, the organ of touch. As a solar aspect of Śiva, Īśāna is sometimes shown as copper-colored.

As a separate deity, Īśāna is five-faced.

"I bow to Śiva as Īśāna, the Ruler, who has five faces. Followed by the She-Goat (the power of Nature, Prakṛti), he holds in his hands the Vedas, an elephant hook, a noose, a hatchet, a skull, a drum, a rosary, a trident, and he shows the gestures of removing fear and granting boons." (*Śivatoṣiṇī*, 1.1.16. [394])

2. *The Supreme-Man (Tat-puruṣa)*

The eastern face of Śiva is yellow. This face corresponds to that which is enjoyed, that is, Nature (*prakṛti*). It is called the Supreme-Man (Tat-puruṣa). It

4 The colors listed here are those given in the *Śiva Purāṇa* (*Rudra Saṁhitā* 1.4–36). The *Rūpa-maṇḍana* and the *Viṣṇu-dharmottara* give other colors. Their texts, however, often seem corrupt.

is connected with the earth, the sense of smell, and the anus as organ of action.

As a separate deity, "the Supreme Man is the color of the blazing thunderbolt, or he is like gold. He has four faces and three eyes. He wears a yellow garment and yellow ornaments. He dwells forever in gladness with his consort, the solar-hymn (Gāyatrī)." (*Śivatoṣiṇī* 1.1.13. [395])

"As the source of the knowledge that leads to liberation, the Supreme Man is identified with Peace-of-Night (Umā), one of the main powers of Śiva." (Karapātrī, "Śrī Śiva tattva," *Siddhānta*, II, 1941–42, 11.)

3. *The Nonfearful (Aghora)*

The southern face of Śiva is blue or blue-black. It represents the principle-of-intellect (*buddhi tattva*) or the eternal-law (*dharma*). It is called Aghora, the "nonfearful," and is connected with the element ether, the sense of hearing, and the organ of speech.

As a separate deity, Aghora appears "holding ax, shield, elephant hook, noose, spear, skull, drum, and rosary. He is four-faced. I contemplate in my heart the nonfearful divinity of shining darkness." (*Śivatoṣiṇī*. 1.1.14. [396])

4. *The Left-hand–Deity (Vāma-deva)*

The western face of Śiva is red. It represents the notion of I-ness (*ahaṁkāra*) and is called Vāma-deva, the "left-hand deity." It corresponds to the element fire, the sense of sight, and the feet as organs of action.

As a separate deity, "we worship in our hearts the left-hand deity dressed in red and adorned with red ornaments. His color is that of the lotus's heart. Two of his hands show the gestures of granting boons and removing fear. The others hold a rosary and a hatchet." (*Śivatoṣiṇī* 1.1.12. [397])

5. *The Suddenly-born (Sadyojāta)*

The northern face of Śiva is white. This face represents the mind. It is called the Suddenly-born (Sadyojāta) and corresponds to the sacrificial elixir (*soma*), to the water element, the sense of taste, and the sex organ.

The Suddenly-born may be represented as a separate deity. "May we be protected by the Suddenly-born, the leader of Delight (Nanda), Enjoyment (Sunanda), and other [attendants of Śiva]. His color is that of the jasmine or the full moon or mother-of-pearl or crystal. He holds the Vedas and a rosary and shows the gestures of granting boons and removing fear." (*Śivatoṣiṇī* 1.1.11. [398])

The Image of Śiva

As we have seen, Śiva, like all deities, is envisaged under various aspects and each of these aspects not only bears a different name but is represented by different symbols in different images. For each aspect of Śiva there is a *yantra* or numerical-geometrical representation, a *mantra* or symbolic formula, and an anthropomorphic image. The most common symbol of Śiva is the phallus (*liṅga*). Śiva's power of manifestation is shown by the *liṅga* inserted in the *yoni* or female emblem. This is the representation of Śiva found in every one of his temples.

The most common anthropomorphic image of Śiva shows him as "beautiful, three-eyed, with the crescent moon on his brow. From the crown of his matted hair flows the Ganges, emblem of purity, white as milk. His arms are strong and smooth like the trunk of an elephant. He is smeared with ashes and adorned with shining armlets. A garland of pearls and a snake surround his neck. He wears a tiger skin. Two of his hands hold a trident and an ax. The two other hands show the gestures of 'granting boons' and 'removing fear.' " (Karapātrī, "Śrī Śiva tattva," *Sanmārga*, 1946.)

"Śiva, the lord of sleep, appears seated with his consort, Umā, the Peace-of-the-Night, on a bull as white as the Himalayan peaks. Men and serpents, musician-angels (*gandharva*), celestial-humans (*kinnara*), the gods, their king Indra, and their teacher Bṛhaspati are ever seen worshiping him. The spirits of darkness, the antigods (*asura*), the daimons (*daitya*), the genii (*yakṣa*), evil-spirits (*bhūta*), ghosts (*preta*), evil-elves (*piśāca*), magicians (*vetāla*), mermaids (*ḍākinī*), witches (*śākinī*), scorpions, serpents, and even tigers are serving him." (Giridhara Śarmā Caturvedi, "Śiva mahimā," *Kalyāṇa*, Śiva aṅka, p. 57.) Thus Śiva rules over both the spirits of light and those of darkness.

The White Color

ŚIVA IS PICTURED as white as camphor. "His limbs shine like jewels." (*Śiva Purāṇa* 1.21.82. [399])

The all-pervading consciousness whose form is knowledge is compared to light. Enlightenment is the nature of the centripetal-tendency (*sattva*). Śiva, being the embodiment of the centrifugal-tendency (*tamas*), is made of darkness and should therefore be black. But, as we have already seen (pp. 22 f.), the two opposite tendencies being inseparable, darkness is surrounded by light and light is enveloped in darkness. Hence Viṣṇu, who is all *sattva*, is shown outwardly black and Śiva, who is all *tamas*, appears white.

According to Giridhara Śarmā Caturvedi ("Śiva mahimā," p. 57), "white is the basis of all colors. No dyer can dye something white. All other colors are superimposed on white. White exists before and remains after all other colors. That in which all is found but where no differentiation takes place can be called white. This is the nature of divinity. All the shapes of the world are potentially in Śiva yet remain undifferentiated. Difference is the work of ignorance, the power which by suppressing one color causes another to appear. Since all things coexist in Śiva without differentiation, his outward color can only be white."

According to the *Mahābhārata* (12.10364), Śiva is called "the white one" because he wears a shining white garment, and his garland, his sacred thread, his bull, and his banner are all white.

In the *Ṛg Veda* (2.33) Rudra is tawny in color.

The Three Eyes

THE THREE eyes of Śiva represent the sun, the moon, and fire, the three sources of light that illumine the earth, the sphere of space, and the sky. The Purāṇas and Upaniṣads speak of "him whose eyes are sun, moon, and fire." (*Bhasmajābāla Upaniṣad* 1. [400]) Through his three eyes Śiva can see the three forms of time, past, present, and future. (*Mahābhārata* 10.1251.) The three eyes are said to shine like three suns. (Ibid. 13.846.)

"The frontal eye, the eye of fire, is the eye of higher perception. It looks mainly inward. When directed outward, it burns all that appears before it. It is from a glance of this third eye that Kāma, the lord of lust, was burned to ashes and that the gods and all created beings are destroyed at each of the periodical destructions of the universe." (Karapātrī, "Śrī Śiva tattva," *Siddhānta*, II, 1941–42, 116.)

Having three eyes, Śiva is commonly called Tri-netra, Try-ambaka (*Ṛg Veda* 7.59.12; *Meghadūta* 1.58), Try-akṣa, Tri-nayana (*Meghadūta* 1.52).

In the *Mahābhārata* (13.6362) a legend is told of the way Śiva came to have a third eye. One day the beautiful Daughter-of-the-Mountain (Pārvatī) went behind Śiva and, in play, placed her hands over his eyes. Suddenly the world was covered with darkness and all life seemed suspended. All beings trembled in fear. The lord of the universe had closed his eyes and the light of the world was extinguished. Then a third eye flamed forth, like a sun, on his forehead and darkness disappeared.

The Moon

ŚIVA BEARS on his head as a diadem the crescent of the fifth-day moon.

"The Moon is Soma, the sacrificial offering. Placed near the fiery third eye, the crescent moon shows the power of procreation co-existent with that of destruction." [1] The moon is also the cup of offering placed near the yogic center of fire located between the brows. It is the chalice of semen, the power of sublimated eros, near the fire of penance.

The crescent or digit of the moon is also the measure of time in counting the days and months. The cycle of the years is represented by the serpent.

The Ganges

THE GANGES flowing from the crown of Śiva's head represents the causal-waters (*ap*). The Ganges is said to purify all things. It is the essential instrument of ritual purification. Hence, "holding the Ganges on his head, he [Śiva] brought into his power the means of the liberation of the world." (Karapātrī, "Śrī Śiva tattva," *Siddhānta*, II, 1941–42, 116.)

The Matted Hair

THE JAṬĀ, Siva's knot of matted hair, represents the lord of wind, Vāyu, who is the subtle form of *soma*, the flow of offering. It is therefore connected with the Ganges, the manifest *soma*, flowing from Śiva's head.

The *Ṛg Veda* (2.33) mentions Rudra's matted hair.

1 Karapātrī, "Śrī Śiva tattva," *Siddhānta*, II, 1941–42, 116.

The Tiger Skin

THE TIGER is the vehicle of Śakti, the symbol of the power of Nature (*prakṛti*). Śiva is beyond the power of Nature. He is its master and carries the skin of the tiger as a trophy.

A legend says that once Śiva wandered in a forest in the form of a naked mendicant. The wives of the sages were bewitched by his beauty. The sages, in an attempt to overpower him, dug a pit, and through magic formulae caused a tiger to rush out of it. Śiva slew the tiger and taking its skin wore it as a garment.

The *Vājasaneya Saṃhitā* (3.61; 16.51) of the *Śukla Yajur Veda* mentions that Rudra is clad in skin.

The Four Arms

THE FOUR arms of Śiva are the sign of universal power. They represent the four directions of space and show mastery over the elements. This symbol corresponds to that of the cross (see p. 353) and of the wheel (see p. 354, s.v. "The Star Hexagon").

In some of his aspects Śiva has ten arms (*Mahābhārata* 13.1154). These also represent the directions of space and are connected with his five-headed form.

The Trident

THE TRIDENT of Śiva is the symbol of the three qualities of Nature, the three *guṇas*, and hence of the three functions of Creator, Preserver, and Destroyer. In the microcosm the trident represents the three subtle arteries of the body, *iḍā*, *piṅgalā*, and *suṣumnā*, which, according to the theory of yoga, ascend from the root center at the base of the spinal cord to reach the "lotus of a thousand petals" at the summit of the head.

The trident is also the giver of punishment on the spiritual, subtle, and physical planes.

"As the giver of the three punishments (*śūla*) to the evildoer, you shine like the Law, holder of the trident." (*Śaiva Siddhānta-sāra.* [401])

The trident is called *triśūla* or, more commonly, *śūla*. It is also called the Victorious (Vijaya) (*Mahābhārata* 12.14551). With his trident Śiva destroyed King Māndhātar and all his army (ibid. 13.860).

As the trident-bearer Śiva is named Śūlin (*Meghadūta* 5.34), Śūladhara, or Śūlapāṇin.

The Spear Pāśupata

THE FAVORITE weapon of Śiva is the fearful spear called the Herdsman's-Staff (Pāśupata), with which he kills the genii (*daitya*) in battle and with which, at the end of the ages, he destroys the universe. Śiva gave this spear to Arjuna after their fight. (*Mahābhārata* 3.11985; 13.851.) This spear is also called the Head-of-the-Immensity (Brahmaśiras). (Ibid. 1.5306; 3.1644.)

The Ax, the Bow (Pināka), and the Club Khaṭvāṅga

ŚIVA POSSESSES a sharp battle-ax (*paraśu*). He gave it to Paraśu-Rāma, who, with its help, destroyed the princely order of the *kṣatriyas*. (*Mahābhārata* 13.864.)

So that he may assist the gods, Śiva always holds in his hand a bow resembling the rainbow, which is made of a powerful serpent with seven heads and poisonous teeth. (*Mahābhārata* 13.849, 6396).

"Because he carries a bow called Pināka, Rudra, the true image of Śiva Giver-of-Peace (Śaṅkara-Śiva), is called Pinākin (the bowman)." (*Śivatoṣiṇī*, commentary on the *Liṅga Purāṇa* 1.6.25. [402])

The bow is also sometimes called Ajagava (the southern sunpath).

Khaṭvāṅga (the striking limb) is a club with a skull at its end.

The Serpent

ŚIVA CARRIES a snake around his neck. Snakes always surround his image, and a snake is coiled around his phallus (*liṅga*).

Śiva is beyond the power of death, yet is himself always surrounded with death. He alone can drink the deadly poison to free the world from its effect. In cosmology the serpent is taken to represent the spiral, which is the symbol of the cycles of time. But the main meaning attached to the serpent is to represent the basic dormant energy, akin to the sexual power, which is coiled at the base of the spinal cord and which is the support of the yogi in his attempt to conquer the higher worlds during his inward journey. This energy, source of all spiritual conquests, is called Kuṇḍalinī (the coiled), the serpent power.

The Noose and the Garland of Skulls

ŚIVA CARRIES a noose (*pāśa*) with which he binds refractory offenders.

At the time of destruction Śiva remains alone. The universe is then compared to the remnant of a funeral pyre, a heap of ashes and calcinated bones (*ruṇḍa-muṇḍa*). Śiva is shown covered with these ashes and wearing a garland of skulls (*ruṇḍa-muṇḍa-dhārī*).

"At the end of the ages, tossing a skull on the vast funeral pyre of the universe, you remain alone, O God! adorned with skulls, as the sole refuge of whatever consciousness is left, upholding the elements." (*Śaiva Siddhānta-sāra.* [403])

The garland of skulls is also said to represent the perpetual revolution of ages and the successive appearances and disappearances of the human races.

The Ashes

ŚIVA IS said to have burned the universe and all the gods including Viṣṇu and Brahmā with a glance of his third eye, and to have rubbed their ashes (*vibhūti*) on his body.

The yogis, as a sign of their discipline, rub themselves with the ashes of the ritual fire. This gives to their naked bodies a strange, fearful whiteness and protects them from the mild cold of the tropical winter. For the man of complete renunciation the ashes may be those of the funeral pyre.

In Yoga the ashes are a symbol of the sublimated power of procreation. The semen of the man who observes perfect chastity is consumed inside his body. This burned energy is believed to give a peculiar beauty and radiance to his body. This brilliance of the yogi is spoken of as the glow of the ashes of his semen. As the lord of continence, Śiva, who burned Kāma, the god of lust, to ashes, himself appears smeared with ashes.

The crack-of-fire (*bhṛgu*) is the name given to the inner fire of the subtle centers of the body, which burns to ashes the water or semen (*retas*).

"The seed that came through these exhausted, burned, and heated [centers] was roasted. It was roasted, hence it became Bhṛgu, 'the crack of fire.' Bhṛgu's nature is combustion." (*Gopatha Brāhmaṇa* 1.1.3. [404])

Śiva is called "the lord of the cracks-of-fire" (Bhṛgu-pati).

The Bhṛgus, envisaged as a group of deities whose name is derived from *bhrāj*, "to shine," are a mythical race of beings who discovered fire (*Ṛg Veda* 10.46.2 [405]) and brought it to man (ibid. 1.58.2 [406]; 1.95.2 [407]).

The Hourglass-shaped Drum, the Ḍamaru

THE TWO complementary principles, the *liṅga* and the *yoni*, are graphically represented by the fiery triangle with upward apex and the watery triangle with downward apex. When the triangles penetrate one another to form the hexagon, this is taken to show the state of manifestation. When they part, the universe dissolves.

The instant when their apexes alone are in contact is the point-limit (*bindu*), from which manifestation begins. This is shown in the hourglass shape which is that of the Ḍamaru, the drum of Śiva, from which all the rhythms of manifestation are said to have come forth (see p. 354, s.v. "The Star Hexagon").

The Bull

THE VEHICLE of Śiva is a bull (*vṛṣa* or *vṛṣabha*), white as snow, with a huge body and soft brown eyes. Its neck is thick; its horns are as hard as diamonds. With their sharp red points it tears up the earth. (*Meghadūta* 1.52. [408]) It has broad shoulders, sleek sides, and a black tail and is decorated with a golden girth. Its hump resembles the top of a snow-covered mountain.

According to the *Mahābhārata*, this bull was given to Śiva by Ritual-Skill (Dakṣa), who is sometimes spoken of as the Creator Dakṣa-Brahmā (ibid. 13.6401) or as the lord of progeny, Prajāpati (ibid. 13.3722). The bull is also the emblem which appears on Śiva's banner. Śiva is thus Vṛṣāṅka, he "whose emblem is the bull," and Vṛṣabha-dhvaja, he "whose banner is the bull."

The bull which wanders about, anxious to find a mate, is taken as the embodiment of the sex impulse. Most living creatures are governed by their instincts; they are ridden over by the bull. They are merely the appendage of their reproductive powers.

But Śiva is the master of lust. He rides on the bull. With one glance of his third eye, the eye of higher perception, he reduces to ashes the Seducer-of-the-Mind (Madana), the god of love, who disturbs his meditation.

Only those who have attained knowledge are the masters of their impulses, can ride on the bull, and utilize for other ends the power of transmitting physical life.

"Among those who have mastered the bull you are the bull keeper. O Lord! riding on the bull, you protect the worlds." (Quoted in Karapātrī's "Liṅgopāsanā-rahasya, *Siddhānta*, II, 1941–42. [409])

The experiments of the yogis have led them to the discovery that sex energy is the very energy that man can utilize for the conquest of his own self. The sexually powerful man, if he controls himself, can attain any form of power, even conquer the celestial worlds. On the other hand, men of weak temperament are unqualified for great adventures, physical or mental. The sex impulse must therefore never be denied or weakened. Thus yoga opposes exaggerated austerities. The man of strong powers is the vehicle of Śiva.

The bull of Śiva is called the Joyful (Nandi) or the lord-of-gladness (Nandikeśvara). He is also called the Wanderer (Bhṛṅgi). He is the embodiment of justice and virtue, the qualities of the strong.

Nandi is most commonly shown in the form of a bull lying down before the image of Śiva. Worshipers touch his testicles before entering the temple. They are the source of life.

Nandikeśvara is represented in human form but with a bull's head. He is considered one of the mythical teachers of music and dancing.

The Lion

TO CLIMB on his mount, Śiva sets foot on the lion Pot-bellied (Kumbhodara).

"Know that I am the servant of Śiva, the friend of [his lieutenant] Nikumbha. My name is Pot-bellied. When Śiva wishes to climb on his bull, white as the pleasure mountain Kailāsa, he first honors my back with the touch of his feet." (*Raghuvaṁśa* 2.35. [410])

This pot-bellied lion represents greed for food. Food is the unavoidable step toward lust. Unless man controls his food, he cannot succeed in controlling his impulses. "Lust is a great eater," says the *Bhagavadgītā* (3.37 [411]).

Kāśī, the Resplendent City

KĀŚĪ, the resplendent city of Śiva,[2] is now called Vārāṇasī (Benares). Śiva's most sacred temples are here. Kāśī is believed to be the world's oldest city, built by the first king in a forest carpeted with the sacred *kāśa* grass (*Saccharum spontaneum*). Hence "Kāśī is where the *kāśa* grass grows" [413]. In this forest Kumāra (Kārttikeya), the son of Śiva, was born.

Kāśī represents the city-of-knowledge (*jñāna-purī*). In the microcosm

2 "Kāśī is that by which all is illumined." (*Kāśīmukti-viveka* of Sureśvara. [412])

"Kāśī" is the name given to the summit of the head, where knowledge is said to dwell. The "lotus of a thousand petals" at the summit of the head is thus Kāśī-purī (the resplendent city).

This inner "Kāśī" is situated at the point where the three subtle arteries of the body unite. Hence it is said to stand on the trident of Śiva. Similarly the earthly Kāśī, the holy Benares, is at the point where the three Ganges cross one another. These are the celestial Ganges or Milky Way, the earthly river, and the subterranean stream called the "Underworld Ganges" (Pātāla Gaṅgā). The Underworld Ganges is said to come down from the Himālayas, but unlike the earthly river, it descends toward the south.

There are five main temples of Śiva in which *liṅgas* symbolizing the five elements are worshiped. In Kāśī is the water *liṅga*, in Kāñcī (Conjeeveram) the earth *liṅga*, in Chidambaram the ether *liṅga*, in Kālahasti the air *liṅga*, in Tiruvannamalai the fire *liṅga*.

The Liṅga

THE WORD *liṅga* means "sign." "The distinctive sign through which it is possible to recognize the nature of someone is called a *liṅga*." (*Śiva Purāṇa* 1.16.106. [414]) The Principle (*brahman*), being without form, is *liṅga*-less. "Śiva is signless (sexless), without color, taste, or smell, beyond word and touch, without quality, changeless, motionless." (*Liṅga Purāṇa* 1.3.2–3. [415])

This unmanifest being can be perceived only through his creation, which is his sign, his *liṅga*. The existence of the unqualified substratum is known only from this sign. The *liṅga*, the phallus, giver of life, is one of the shapes under which the nature of the shapeless can be represented.

Yet "it is not the *liṅga* itself which is worshiped but the owner-of-the-*liṅga*, the Progenitor, the [Supreme]-Man (*puruṣa*). The *liṅga* leads to the Supreme Man, to Śiva, whose symbol it is." (*Śiva Purāṇa* 1.16.106–107. [416])

The *Liṅga* Is the Universe

"FROM THE signless comes forth the sign, the universe. This sign is the object of word and touch, of smell, color, and taste. It is the womb of the elements, subtle and gross." (*Liṅga Purāṇa* 1.3.3–4. [417])

"Basic-Nature (*pradhāna*) is thus called the *liṅga*. The owner-of-the-*liṅga* is supreme divinity." (*Liṅga Purāṇa* 1.17.5. [418])

"The root of the *liṅga* is the signless. The *liṅga* itself is Unmanifest-Nature (*avyakta*). Thus Śiva himself is sexless. The *liṅga* is the thing-of-Śiva." (*Liṅga Purāṇa* 1.3. [419])

"Śiva as the undivided causal principle is worshiped in the *liṅga*. His more manifest aspects are represented in anthropomorphic images. All other deities are part of a multiplicity and are thus worshiped in images." (Karapātrī, "Śrī Śiva tattva," *Siddhānta*, II, 1941–42.)

"The Sun is envisaged as the progenitor of the worlds, hence its symbol is that of procreation." (*Śiva Purāṇa* 1.16.105. [420])

The *Yoni*

"MANIFEST NATURE (*vyakta*), the universal energy, is shown as the *yoni,* or female organ, embracing the *liṅga.* Only under the shape of a *liṅga,* giver of seed, can Śiva be enveloped by the *yoni* and become manifest.

"The symbol of the Supreme-Man (*puruṣa*), the formless, the changeless, the all-seeing eye, is the symbol of masculinity, the phallus or *liṅga.* The symbol of the power that is Nature, generatrix of all that exists, is the female organ, the *yoni.*" (Karapātrī, "Liṅgopāsanā-rahasya," *Siddhānta,* II, 1941–42, 154.)

The *liṅga* stands in the *yoni,* which is the power of manifestation, "the womb of the real and the unreal." (*Śukla Yajur Veda, Vājasaneya Saṁhitā* 13.3; *Taittirīya Saṁhitā* 4.2.8.2. [421]) "The universal womb in which all that is individual ripens." (*Śvetāśvatara Upaniṣad* 5.5. [422])

The *liṅga* fecundates this womb.

"The vast Immensity [the principle of intellect] is the womb in which I [Kṛṣṇa] deposit my seed. From it are born [Manifest Intellect, the first element] and then [in hierarchy] all the elements [and all the creatures]." (*Bhagavadgītā* 14.3. [423])

"Because she is the source of development, Nature (*prakṛti*) is compared to a womb." (*Śiva Purāṇa* 1.16.101. [424]) "The womb is Nature, basis of all. The enjoyer is Śiva. He is the giver of enjoyment. There is no other giver." (Ibid. 1.16.102–103. [425])

The *liṅga* is the universal fecundator and as such is fundamentally one. But for each form of existence there is a different womb to be fecundated. Thus the different species are spoken of as *yonis.* The Purāṇas speak of 8,400,000 different kinds of beings, of *yonis.*

Although phallic worship has no place in Vedic ritual, the phallus-god (Śiśna-deva) is mentioned in the *Ṛg Veda* (7.12.5; 10.99.3) and in the *Nirukta* (4.29).

The Union of the Principles

IN THE unmanifest state there is a perfect balance. Then all the gods appear as one; there is no perceptible duality, no distinction of a positive and a negative force. As soon as the first tendency toward manifestation appears in the undifferentiated substratum duality is already present. This duality has the character of complementary poles of attraction, a positive and a negative tendency, which will be manifested in the whole of creation by male and female characteristics. There can be no creation without the relation of opposites. There could be no creation from Śiva alone or from Nature (*prakṛti*) alone. The union of a perceiver and a perceived, of an enjoyer and an enjoyed, of a passive and an active principle, of a male and a female organ, is essential for creation to take place. The union of Supreme Man and Nature is represented in the copulation (*maithuna*) of the lord-of-sleep (Śiva) and Faithfulness (Satī), that is, Energy (Śakti).

Transcendent manhood is the immanent cause of creation; transcendent womanhood, the efficient cause. In the microcosm these principles are mainly apparent in the sex organs, which represent the most essential physical function of all beings. Everything in Nature centers around procreation, is intended to ensure the continuity of life. It is in the union of the *liṅga* and the *yoni* that divinity, the power to create, is most directly apparent in man. There cannot be procreation without such union, and there cannot be divine manifestation without their cosmic equivalent. It is only through the understanding of the *liṅga* and the *yoni* that we can understand the mystery of creation.

The entire Vedic ritual is seen as an equivalent of the ritual of love.

> "*The first call is the invocation-of-the-deity* (hiṅkāra).
> *The request is the preliminary-laudation* (prastāva).
> *To lie down with the woman is the hymn-of-glory* (udgītha).
> *To lie facing the woman is the chorus* (pratihāra).
> *The climax is the concluding-hymn* (nidhana).
> *The going apart is the concluding-hymn* (nidhana).
> *Thus is the hymn of the left-hand-[fiery]-god (Vāmadeva) woven upon the act of love.*

"He who knows that this hymn of the left-hand [fiery] form [of Śiva] is woven upon the act of love procreates himself anew at each intercourse. He reaches the full length of his life, lives long, becomes great in offspring and cattle, great in fame.

"One should never abstain [from any woman]. That is the rule." (*Chāndogya Upaniṣad* 2.13.1, 2. [426])

The Divine Lust

IN THE Causal Being first arises the desire to create. "He desired, let me create. May I be many." (*Taittirīya Upaniṣad* 2.6.1. [427])

"Born of the first dualism, of the distinction of Person and Nature, desire, the attraction of opposites, is the supernatural eros. Linked to Nature by desire, the Cosmic Person gives birth to innumerable worlds. This desire, this inclination toward pleasure, is a part of himself." (Karapātrī, "Liṅgopāsanā-rahasya," p. 153.)

"Desire is part of the Indweller (Vāsudeva)." (*Bhāgavata Purāṇa* 10.55.1. [428])

"Pleasure dwells in the sex-organ (*upastha*), in the cosmic *liṅga* and *yoni* whose union is the essence of enjoyment. In the world also all love, all lust, all desire, is a search for enjoyment. Things are desired for the pleasure they contain. Divinity is the object of love because it is pure enjoyment. Other things are objects of temporary love since they bring us only a temporary satisfaction.

"The desire of the lustful man for a woman exists because he sees her as the form of his pleasure, the source of his enjoyment. In the joy of possession the pain of desire is for one instant relieved and man experiences pleasure, which is the end of his desire, and the perception of his inherent nature, which is enjoyment.

"All enjoyment, all pleasure, is the experience of divinity. The whole universe springs forth from enjoyment; pleasure is found at the root of everything. But perfect love is that whose object is not limited, love without attributes, the pure love of love itself, of the transcendent being-of-joy." (Karapātrī, "Liṅgopāsanā-rahasya," p. 153.)

The Śiva principle is the totality of the procreative power found in the whole universe. All individual procreation is a fragment of it. "From the relation of *liṅga* and *yoni* the whole world arises. Everything therefore bears the signature of the *liṅga* and the *yoni*. It is divinity which under the form of all individual *liṅgas* enters every womb and procreates all beings." (Karapātrī, "Liṅgopāsanā-rahasya," p. 163.)

"It is he alone who dwells in every womb." (*Śvetāśvatara Upaniṣad* 5.2. [429])

"The seed of both [Śiva and Satī] fell on the back of the earth and filled the world. From this seed all the Śiva-*liṅgas* seen in the underworld, on earth, and in heaven became manifest. From these are made all the Śiva-*liṅgas* of the past and those of the future. The *liṅga* of Śiva appears from the radiance of both." (*Nārada Pāñcarātra* 3.1. [430])

The Father, Owner of the *Liṅga*

ENVISAGED AS the source of manifestation, Śiva and Śakti are represented by the organs of procreation. The owner of the *liṅga* is the unknowable unmanifest stage.

In a less abstract symbolism, the unknowable entity of whom the *liṅga* is the sign can be replaced by the father, the manifest form of the phallus-bearer.

The Total Being envisaged as the entity of which procreation is the characteristic and the *liṅga* the symbol is often spoken of as the Father.

"O son of Kunti! The beings born in all the wombs rise from the womb of the Immensity. I am the Father, the giver of seed." (*Bhagavadgītā* 14.4. [431])

"I am the father of the world." (Ibid. 9.17. [432])

"Like a mother and a father, principial Nature and the Supreme Person give birth to all forms. In the world men desirous of progeny fecundate women, and likewise the Supreme Being, desirous of progeny, of multiplicity, fecundates Nature." (Karapātrī, "Liṅgopāsanā-rahasya," p. 153.)

As we have seen with respect to the bull of Śiva, it is the function, the organ, that is important and permanent. The individual carrying the organ is but its temporary servant. The tendency to replace the symbol that is the organ of procreation by the figurative image of a father is a substitute which brings in unnecessary anthropomorphic elements and a lowering of the degree of abstraction of the deity represented.

Bīja, the Seed

SEMEN IS the essence of life. It is the best offering, the purest form of the sacrificial-elixir (*soma*). All beings are born of an offering of semen cast into the fire of lust. Agni, the lord of fire, is shown devouring the semen which flows from the *liṅga* of Śiva. This semen is worshiped under many names. It is stored in the Moon; it is the Ganges flowing from the head of the *liṅga*. All the forms of offering, all the beverages that bring forth life and immortality, are represented as the forms of the semen of Śiva.

The meaning of Agni and Soma, the meaning of the ritual sacrifice, is best understood as the offering of the seed of life into the sacred fire of love.

Semen is spoken of as *bīja* (the seed), *soma* (the offering), *candra* (the moon), *vīrya* (the male essence).

The Worship of the *Liṅga*

IT IS through the mastery of sex that we become powerful in the physical as well as the mental sphere. It is through the union of sexes that new beings, new lives, come into existence. This union is thus the link between two worlds, the point where life manifests itself, where the divine spirit becomes incarnate.

The shape of the organ which performs this ritual is, verily, a symbol—the visible form of the divine creator. When the Hindus worship the *liṅga,* they do not deify a physical feature, they merely recognize the divine, eternal form manifest in the microcosm. It is the human phallus which is a divine emblem of the eternal causal form, the all-pervading *liṅga.* The phallus is divinity "projecting [from the body] by the breadth of ten fingers" (*Puruṣa Sūkta* 1 [433]). "Those who do not recognize the divine nature of the phallus, who do not measure the importance of the sex ritual, who consider the act of love as low or contemptible or as a mere physical function, are bound to fail in their attempts at physical as well as spiritual achievement. To ignore the sacredness of the *liṅga* is dangerous, whereas through its worship the joy of life (*bhukti*) and the joy of liberation (*mukti*) are obtained." (Karapātrī, "Liṅgopāsanā-rahasya.")

"He who spends his life without honoring the phallus is verily unfortunate, sinful, and ill-fated. If we put in balance the worship of the *liṅga* as against charities, fasts, pilgrimages, sacrifice, and virtue, it is the worship of the giver of pleasure and liberation, the remover of adversity, that prevails." (*Śiva Purāṇa* 1.21.23–24, 26. [434])

"He who worships the *liṅga* knowing it to be the First Cause, the source of consciousness, the substance of the universe, is nearer to me [Śiva] than any other being." (*Śiva Purāṇa* 1.18.159. [435])

"Just as we worship in the Sun, the giver of light, the sum of all individual eyes, so also in the *liṅga* we worship Śiva, who pervades all individual generative powers. It is not a particular eye we worship and of which we make images but the Sun, the eye totality, the giver of sight, the source of visibility. Similarly it is the Śiva totality which is worshiped and of which images are made." (Karapātrī, "Liṅgopāsanā-rahasya," p. 154.)

According to the Purāṇas, the Śiva-*liṅga* is an eternal symbol and its worship has existed from the earliest ages of mankind. In the *Mahābhārata* the worship of the *liṅga* is commended.

"Who is it whose semen was offered in sacrifice in the beginning of the world into the mouth of Fire, of Agni, the teacher of the gods and the antigods? Is the golden mountain [Sumeru] made of any other semen? Who else in the world goes naked, and who can sublimate his sex power? Who made of his beloved the half of his own self and who could not be conquered by the Bodiless [god of lust]? Rudra, the God of gods, creates and therefore destroys, O king of heaven! See how the world bears everywhere the signature of the *liṅga* and the *yoni.* You know also that the changing three worlds sprang forth from the semen poured out by the *liṅga* during the act of love. All the gods, the Creator (Brahmā), the king-of-heaven (Indra), the lord-of-fire (Agni), the Pervader (Viṣṇu), the genii and the powerful demons whose desires are never satisfied, all acknowledge that nothing exists beyond the Giver-of-Joy (Śaṅkara). . . . This Ruler of the Worlds is the cause of causes. We never heard that the phallus of any other being was worshiped by the gods. Who is more desired than he whose *liṅga* is ever worshiped by Brahmā, Viṣṇu, and all the gods and thyself." (*Mahābhārata*, Anuśāsana parvan, 14.211–232. [436])

Different Forms of *Liṅga*

The Liṅga *of the Universe*

The shapeless is represented through many symbols such as ether, the pillar of light, and the universe's egg. All these refer to Śiva manifest and united to his power.

The earth is the womb, and space is the *liṅga*, erect above its pedestal. And just as only a part of divinity is in contact with Nature, so also only part of space is in contact with the earth.

"Space is the *liṅga*, the earth the altar. In it dwell all the gods. It is called the 'sign' because all dissolve in it." (*Skanda Purāṇa.* [437])

The Cosmic Egg

Totality is often represented in the form of an egg. The universe appears to man like an egg divided into halves, sky and earth. The egg is also considered the source of life, in which both male and female forms are united. This shape, too, is called a "sign," a *liṅga.*

In the Tantras, the phallus is the more common symbol, but in the Purāṇas the egg shape is often referred to as the *liṅga.*

The Principle (*brahman*) can be said to have the form of a curve which surrounds the universe and forms the cosmic egg, the "golden egg resplendent like a sun" of Manu (1.9 [438]).

The Formless Mass

Another symbol of the first causal stage is a shapeless object representing chaos. This also is called a *liṅga,* a sign. Several of the celebrated images of

Śiva, such as that of Kedāra-nātha in Benares and Amara-nātha in Kashmir, are shapeless mounds.

The Altar's Fire

In the sacrificial ritual, the fire, image of the Destroyer, is called a *liṅga*, an "auspicious light" (*śiva jyotis*). The altar represents woman and the hearth (*yajña kuṇḍa*) is the *yoni*.

The Arrow

The arrow (*bāṇa liṅga*) is taken as the symbol of the number 5 because of the five arrows of the god of love through which he perturbs the five senses. The arrow is thus symbolically connected with the principles of human perception and with the five spheres of the senses or elements. The arrow *liṅga* is represented with five faces.

The Linga *of Light*

The Śiva principle is the axis of manifestation developing from the point-limit (*bindu*), the center of the universe. This axis is represented as an endless pillar of light. When the inner vision of pure knowledge is attained, the *liṅga* of light is seen everywhere piercing the world.

In Yoga the root center at the base of the spinal cord is called the hearth, or *yoni*. Its shape is that of the female organ. The fiery energy coiled in its center can be made to rise upward along the path of realization. The uncoiled energy is then called the *liṅga* of light.

"In the middle of the lowest subtle center of the body, said to be the triangle of desire-knowledge-action, stands this self-born *liṅga*, shining like a thousand suns." (*Śiva Purāṇa*. [439])

All the other centers of the body are *yonis* and have in their middle a *liṅga* representing the all-pervading power of knowledge.

The "Supreme Sign," Mahā-liṅga

"Person and Nature, Puruṣa and Prakṛti, are one yet distinct, and though distinct are one. They exist only in relation to each other. From the point of view of the Principle they are manifest, yet from the point of view of the world they pre-exist creation. It is their undivided state, the stage when the sign (*liṅga*) is one with the signless (*aliṅga*), which is called the Supreme-Sign, Mahā-liṅga. This state is the changeless (*nirvikāra*) stage of divinity, conceived as independent of anything else (*nirālamba*)." (Gopinātha Kavirāja, "Liṅga-rahasya," *Kalyāṇa*, Śiva aṅka, p. 476.)

The Self-born, Svayambhū

"The principle of knowledge which pervades Nature is the everlasting sign of divinity; this motionless, signless potentiality of knowing is the seed of creation, the supreme sign. Out of Unmanifest Nature first arises, of itself, the possibility of being known. This is the Self-born sign, the *svayambhuva-liṅga*. From the possibility of knowing we can apprehend the existence of Nature yet unmanifest." (Karapātrī, "Liṅgopāsanā-rahasya," p. 163.)

The Phallic Image

THE ŚIVA-*liṅga* is represented erect and is divided into three parts. The lowest part is square and is hidden in the pedestal. This is called the Brahmā part. The second part, which is octagonal and is grasped by the *yoni*, is called the Viṣṇu part. The third part, which is cylindrical and rises above the *yoni*, is the Rudra part.

"At the root is Brahmā; in the middle, Viṣṇu, lord of the three worlds; above is the fierce Rudra, the Great God, the eternal giver of peace, whose name is the sacred syllable AUM. The altar of the *liṅga* is the Great Goddess; the Liṅga is the true divinity (Maheśvara)." (*Liṅga Purāṇa* 1.73.19–20. [440])

The part of the *liṅga* of Śiva grasped by the *yoni* shows the source of creation, the First Principle, in contact with Nature. "The substance of the pedestal is the universal mother; the *liṅga* itself is pure consciousness." (*Śiva Purāṇa* 1.11.22. [441])

The greater part of the *liṅga* remains untouched by Nature, forever aloof (*udāsīna*). "One quarter of him [the Puruṣa] is the universe with all its being and elements. The three quarters above are the Immortal." (*Puruṣa Sūkta* 3. [442])

The length of the *liṅga* outside the *yoni* is said to be ten fingerbreadths. The hidden part of the *liṅga* is divinity veiled by ignorance (*avidyā*); the part exposed beyond the *yoni* is divinity unveiled.

In image-making the three parts of the *liṅga* are to be either equal or divided according to certain proportions. From the Brahmā part downward, the proportions of the three parts in a *liṅga* worshiped by priests (*brāhmaṇa*) should be in the relation of the numbers 4, 5, 6 or 7, 7, 8. Those worshiped by warriors (*kṣatriya*) should be 5, 6, 7 or 5, 5, 6. Those worshiped by merchants (*vaiśya*) should be 6, 7, 8 or 4, 4, 5. Those worshiped by workers (*śūdra*) should be 7, 8, 9 or 3, 3, 4.

The *yoni* when represented alone is spoken of as the chalice or water-vessel (*argha, jalaharī*). Its shape is sometimes that of a conch.

The Triangle

THE *yoni* is symbolized by the triangle of Nature made of the three fundamental-qualities (*guṇa*), the ascending illumination, the descending obscurity, the dynamic creativeness. The pure Śiva essence stands above Nature, unsoiled by the three qualities, while in his qualified aspect Śiva as Rudra becomes, in the trinity, the ruler of disintegration.

From the point of view of creation Śiva is the giver-of-seed (*bījavan*), Viṣṇu the receptacle, the *yoni*, Brahmā the seed which unites both. "He is the giver of seed, you are the seed, and I am the eternal *yoni*." (*Liṅga Purāṇa* 1.20.73. [443])

In the stage beyond manifestation the *yoni* is represented by the circle, the central point being the root of the *liṅga*. But in differentiated creation the three qualities become distinct and the circle is changed to a triangle. These are essential figurations in the symbolism of *yantras*. Nothing can be surrounded by less than three lines. The Tantras call this the root-triangle (*mūla-trikoṇa*).

The *liṅga* stands for liberation in all the triangles of nature, be it the triangle of the individuality, physical-mental-intellectual (*viśva-taijasa-prajñā*), or that of the total cosmic body, physical-mental-intellectual (*virāṭ-hiraṇyagarbha-īśvara*). The *liṅga* is the Fourth unmanifest stage in the triangle of wakefulness-dream-sleep. It is the monosyllable AUM in the three Vedas. It is the first undifferentiated notion (*parā-vāc*) in the triangle of ideation-wording-utterance (*paśyantī-madhyamā-vaikharī*).

Brahmā, the Immense Being

Brahmā, the Space-Time or Revolving Principle

THE POSSIBILITY of a form, of a perceptible reality, depends on the existence of a "place" where it can appear and expand, that is, on the existence of an oriented medium (in our world space-time) which is the result of an equilibrium between two opposites, between the centripetal and the centrifugal principles. It is a balance between concentration and dispersion, between a tendency toward existence and a tendency toward annihilation, between light and darkness, between Viṣṇu and Śiva.

The source of the manifest world is therefore neither Viṣṇu nor Śiva, neither concentration nor dispersion, but the result of their opposition, their equilibrium, the third tendency called *rajas*. The Immense-Being (Brahmā), masculine or personified form of the Immensity (*brahmān*), represents the possibility of existence resulting from the union of opposites. Hence Brahmā is the source, the seed, of all that is.

This third tendency manifests itself as a revolving, space-creating, and time-creating power. Without the movements that create the appearance of a division in absolute space and time, the substratum of unoriented, boundless Immensity would offer no room for existence. Brahmā is the balance of forces from which measurable extension originates. He is the nature of all form, of all perceptible existence, of all the spheres and their movements, of all the rhythms that create the divisions of relative time. As the principle of space-time the third tendency is called the Immense-Being (Brahmā), which represents the boundless waste in which space and time originate. But since this Being represents a polarized immensity, his name has a gender. He is the first personal stage of existence.

The *Mahābhārata* (Śānti parvan, 357.21) says that the notion-of-individual-existence (*ahaṁkāra*) appeared first and from it Brahmā was born.

The personified creator appears to arise from the polarizations of the abstract impersonal Brahman. The pure Brahman is beyond-quality (*nirguṇa*). Only when "spotted through by the power of illusion" (*māyā-śabala*) does it become the qualified-Brahman (*saguṇa brahman*), immanent cause of the universe.

The Immense-Being (Brahmā) is thus a name given to the fiction of a personified creator of an efficient-cause (*nimitta*) of creation. This Immense Being is also the Golden-Embryo (Hiraṇya-garbha), from which the universe develops, and the lord-of-progeny (Prajāpati), who, "born before all the gods" (*Muṇḍaka Upaniṣad* 1.1 [444]), nourishes and protects creation.

The illusion (*māyā*) which is movement or action appears as the original, the Nonevolved (*avyākṛta*), form of Nature (*prakṛti*). In other terms, the reflection-of-consciousness (*cidābhāsa*) deposited within the passive nonevolved Nature (i.e., Viṣṇu or the womb) before the creation of the universe by the transcendent Lord, the active power (i.e., Śiva) or giver of seed, is the first individual being, the Self-born–Immense-Being (Svayambhū-Brahmā), who dwells in the unmanifest city, the abstract plan of the universe, as the source of the Cosmos (*virāṭ*) and of the perceptible worlds. From him all the forms of existence arise.

When we attempt to analyze any form of existence, we find at its base a surprisingly precarious state of balance between different forms of being, a strange equilibrium in Nature which prevents the excessive predominance of one thing over another. It is difficult for us to realize that it is this balance which is the real principle of things. Creation does not proceed with forms that develop independently and then come to balance one another. It starts from a state of balance from which opposing tendencies, opposing species, opposing forces, develop evenly. It is this state of balance, this causal equilibrium, which is the sign of the Creator, the third tendency, Brahmā, the energy from which the universe springs forth.

The "Immense Being" is a cosmological notion which first appears in some of the Brāhmaṇas and Āraṇyakas. The name Brahmā is not found in the Vedas and the Brāhmaṇas, where the active creator is merely known as the Golden-Embryo (Hiraṇya-garbha) or the lord-of-progeny (Prajā-pati). A passage of the *Maitrī Saṁhitā*, possibly an interpolation, mentions his four faces and the lotus. This may be the earliest mention of some of his iconographical characteristics. In Buddhism, Brahmā rules over the second and third heavenly spheres (*loka*). The older part of the *Mahābhārata* defines him as the original deity from whom the world is born.

Although from a certain point of view Brahmā can also be considered the all-inclusive divinity, "the source of the universe presiding over all creation, preserving like Viṣṇu, destroying like Śiva" (*Mārkaṇḍeya Purāṇa* 46.14 [445]), in later popular Hinduism his powers as creator are arrogated by Viṣṇu and Śiva and he is overshadowed. His place is taken by Śakti, the female principle, whose definition includes almost all of Brahmā's characteristics and who almost entirely replaces him as the principle of creation under a garb more appealing to popular imagination. The definition of Śakti as the Energy resulting from the union of opposing principles is practically identical to that of Brahmā.

It is under the feminine form of Śakti that the Creator remains the chief object of worship and rituals among large sections of Hindus. These even claim that the worship of Śakti is the only religion suited to the conditions of the modern age.

The Names of Brahmā

AS THE source of the manifold forms of creation, the Brahmā principle can be envisaged under different aspects which are given different names. Many of these names, like many of the early tales of Brahmā, were transferred to Viṣṇu when Viṣṇu developed into the most prominent deity of later Hinduism.

From the cosmological point of view Brahmā is the Golden-Embryo (Hiraṇya-garbha), the ball of fire from which the universe develops. The *Mahābhārata* considers him as born from the embryo which took shape in Viṣṇu's mind when he began to think of creation. (Ibid., Ādi parvan, 1.45; and *Skanda Purāṇa* 5.1.3.) The Vedas, envisaged as the Eternal-Law (Dharma), the scheme of the universe, spring from Brahmā and return into him. As the first individual entity manifested, he is the Self-born (*svayam-bhū*). All other beings are his progeny; hence he is the lord-of-progeny (Prajā-pati), the Patriarch (Pitā-maha).

Brahmā is the Abode-of-Man (Nārāyaṇa),[1] a name also interpreted to mean "he who dwells in the [causal] waters (*nara*)." This last meaning corresponds to the common description of Brahmā.

"All was only water in which the earth was formed. Thence arose Brahmā, the Self-born." (*Rāmāyaṇa* 2.110.3. [447])

1 "This divine Brahmā, called Nārāyaṇa, created all beings." (*Viṣṇu Purāṇa* 1.4.2. [446])

Later Nārāyaṇa became almost exclusively an epithet of Viṣṇu.

Brahmā is also the Great-Lord (Bṛhas-pati), the lord of speech, the First-Seer (Ādi-kavi), the god of asceticism. He is the Ordinator (Vidhi or Vedhas), the Shaper (Druhiṇa or Śāstṛ). He is the Sustainer (Dhātṛ or Vidhātṛ), the World's-Master (Lokeśa), the Supreme-Ruler (Parameṣṭhin), Everlasting (Sanat). He is also called the Undivided-Impulse (Dru-ghaṇa).

After the universal destruction Viṣṇu falls asleep, floating on the causal waters. When creation again arises, Brahmā appears on a lotus having the form of the earth, which springs from the navel of Viṣṇu.[2] Hence Brahmā is called Navel-born (Nābhi-ja), the Lotus (Kañja), Having-a-Lotus (Sarojin), Lotus-born (Abja-ja, Abja-yoni, Kañja-ja).

The universe's architect, Viśva-karman, is an aspect of Brahmā. To Brahmā himself is attributed a treatise on architecture (*Matsya Purāṇa* 252.2) and a work on politics said to contain a hundred thousand couplets.

The Worship of Brahmā

AS THE creating principle Brahmā is not usually worshiped. Men's aspirations go toward liberation or toward divine contemplation, and this leads them toward Śiva and Viṣṇu. Brahmā is worshiped by the angels, the seers, the lords of progeny, who are the entities upon whom rest the management and organization of the manifest universe. There are, however, representations of Brahmā in most temples and his name is invoked in rituals. His image is still worshiped in Puṣkara, near Ajmeer in Rajputana.

The *Skanda Purāṇa* (1.1.6; 3.2.9–15; 3.1.14) gives a number of reasons why Brahmā is not today an object of worship. One of them is that he was condemned by Śiva never to be worshiped by mortals because he lied, pretending he had reached the summit of the *liṅga* of light. (Ibid. 1.1.6.)

The Tales of Brahmā

MANY OF the speculations found in the Brāhmaṇas regarding the origin of man and the story of creation center around the figure of Brahmā.

A golden egg was produced in the causal boundless waters, from which came forth the lord of progeny, Prajāpati. From him was born a daughter,

2 *Matsya Purāṇa* 169.2; *Mahābhārata*, Vāma parvan, 273.45; *Bhāgavata Purāṇa* 3.8.15.

She-of-the-Hundred-Forms (Sata-rūpā), who is also called Speech (Vāc or Sarasvatī), the solar-hymn (Sāvitrī), the triple-hymn (Gāyatrī), Twilight (Sandhyā, i.e., the junction of light and darkness), the "consort of the Immense Being" (Brahmāṇī), etc. (*Matsya Purāṇa* 3.) The incest of Brahmā and his daughter Speech is related in the *Matsya* and *Śiva Purāṇas*. From them was born the Lawgiver Son-of-the-Self-born, Svāyambhuva Manu, the progenitor of man, and from him in turn all creatures. From Brahmā's mind were also manifested the law of the universe, the Veda, and those who perceive it, the seers or *ṛṣis*, who are also counted among the lords of progeny, the Prajāpatis. (*Brahmāṇḍa Purāṇa* 2.9.)

Brahmā is thus the source of all knowledge and his consort, Sarasvatī, is knowledge itself. He taught the transcendent-knowledge (*brahma-vidyā*) to Atharvan (*Muṇḍaka Upaniṣad* 1.1.2) or to Parameṣṭhin (*Bṛhad-āraṇyaka Upaniṣad* 2.6.3; 4.6.3). He also taught the *Brahma Upaniṣad* to Prajāpati (*Chāndogya Upaniṣad* 3.11.4).

In the *Śatapatha Brāhmaṇa*, Manu, the supreme lawgiver, created the waters and placed in them a seed which became a golden egg in which he himself was born as Brahmā, the progenitor of the worlds.

In the *Aitareya Brāhmaṇa*, the Creator is shown in the form of a buck and his daughter as a red deer, Rohitā.

The story of the boar who raised the earth from beneath the water seems to have been originally a tale of the Brahmā cycle that was later transferred to Viṣṇu. Brahmā, becoming a boar, raised the earth and created the world, the sages, and the lords of progeny. (*Śatapatha Brāhmaṇa*, *Liṅga Purāṇa*, *Matsya Purāṇa* 3.30–40; *Rāmāyaṇa*.) From Brahmā was born the Light (Marīci), whose son was Vision (Kaśyapa). Kaśyapa gave birth to the Resplendent (Vivasvat), that is, the Sun, from whom in turn was born the Lawgiver and ancestor of men, Manu, sometimes identified with the Adam of Semitic tradition.

The forms of a tortoise and of a fish (later considered avatars of Viṣṇu) seem to have been originally attributed to Brahmā. "Formerly, at the commencement of the ages, the lord of progeny took the shapes of a fish, a tortoise, a boar." (*Viṣṇu Purāṇa* 1.4.8 [448]) Although, in the *Viṣṇu Purāṇa*, the name Prajāpati came to be attributed to Viṣṇu, it was not so originally.

In the *Rāmāyaṇa* Brahmā appears bestowing boons on Rāma and extending his favors also to Rāvaṇa and other demons who are the descendants of his son Smooth-Hair (Pulastya). Brahmā also created the lovely Ahalyā who became the wife of the sage Gautama.

In the Purāṇas Brahmā often appears as a patron of the enemies of the gods. Through his favor Bali, king of the genii (*daitya*), obtained almost universal dominion.

Ritual-Skill (Dakṣa) sprang from the thumb of Brahmā, who was present when Rudra disturbed the great sacrifice that Dakṣa performed. This quarrel is described mainly in the *Liṅga Purāṇa* but is often referred to in the other Purāṇas.

Brahmā was the priest who celebrated the marriage of Śiva. He drives the chariot of Śiva. He created the four eternal youths or princes (*kumāra*), the chief of whom is Everlasting-Youth (Sanat-kumāra). These also are called his sons.

Brahmā is the inventor of that imitation of creation that is the theatrical art. Music, dancing, and stagecraft are said to have been revealed by him.

The Brahmā Icon

BRAHMĀ HAS four heads. Originally he had five but one was burned by the fire of Śiva's third eye. He is therefore called four-headed (*catur-ānana*), four-faced (*catur-mukha*), eight-eared (*aṣṭa-karṇa*). His color is red or pink.

He has four arms. In his hands he may hold the four Vedas, or he may hold the Vedas in one hand and in the other various accessories such as a scepter, one or two ritual ladles (see the *Mānasāra*), a string of beads, his bow Parivīta (enveloping), a water jug. He is usually shown as a bearded man in the maturity of age.

Brahmā's vehicle is the swan or goose, symbol of knowledge. Hence he is said to be riding-on-the-swan (Haṁsa-vāhana). He is also shown standing on the lotus that springs from Viṣṇu's navel.

Brahmā's residence is the Immense-Grove (Brahma-vṛnda), that is, the universe.

The Golden Embryo, Hiraṇyagarbha

"AS THE Golden Embryo, Brahmā is first among the gods. He has no beginning; he dwells in the center of the earth's lotus." (*Mārkaṇḍeya Purāṇa* 46.21. [449])

The Golden Embryo is identified with the Indestructible-Person (*akṣara puruṣa*), that is, the everlasting plan from which all destructible forms are made. In the theory of the creation by the word, the Indestructible (*akṣara*) is the name given to the prototypes of the letters of the alphabet which are the permanent substratum of all language. When we say, "I pronounce the letter *a*," or, "I write the letter *a*," we refer to a permanent entity we call *a* which we may represent in any form we please but which exists even when neither uttered nor represented; it is therefore a permanent entity. Speech (Vāc), which is the manifestation of Knowledge (Sarasvatī), is the consort of this indestructible-principle-of-speech (*akṣara-brahmā*) that is identified with the Golden Embryo.

The Golden Embryo, principle of all vibration or movement, expresses itself "in the form of a vibrating energy" (*spandana-śakti-rūpa*). It divides itself into the causal mass of potentialities (the causal waters, *rayi*) and the breath-of-life (*prāṇa*) pictured as the wind that creates the waves in the causal ocean from which all forms develop. In the microcosm this breath of life becomes the breath that causes the places of articulation to vibrate and thus gives birth to manifest speech.

When the tendency toward manifesting itself, that is, vibrating, begins to develop, the Golden Embryo divides itself into water and breath. When creation begins, water and breath again unite, that is, Brahmā and his daughter copulate. The word *rayi* means both "water" and "wealth" (see p. 117). Wealth is always compared to a flowing water (cf. Sarasvatī).

In the cosmic sacrifice, the Moon, which is the essence-of-life (*soma*), is identified with water (*rayi*), while the Sun, the Āditya (sovereign principle), is the breath-of-life (*prāṇa*), for breath is born of heat as are all the forms of wind.[3]

The Lord-of-Progeny (Prajā-pati)

IN THE Vedas the Creator is known as the lord-of-progeny (Prajā-pati). We have already seen that this name was also taken to refer to one of the main aspects of Śiva (p. 209), and used as a name of Viṣṇu (p. 236).

In every case the name Prajāpati refers to the creative aspect, that is, the Brahmā aspect, of divinity. In hymn 10.129 of the *Ṛg Veda*, Prajāpati, moved by desire and fear of loneliness, exerts his "heat" and duplicates himself.

"The source of what *is not* and of what *is* is, verily, the lord of progeny, who is the Immense-Being (Brahmā), the Indestructible (*akṣara*) [i.e., the instrument of speech], as well as the thing said (*vācya*)." (*Bṛhad-devatā* 1.62. [450])

In the Upaniṣads Prajāpati is the manifesting form of Brahmā.

3 See Śaṅkara Tīrtha, "Bhagavān Hiraṇya-garbha," *Siddhānta*, III, 1942–43, 19.

"In the beginning this [world] was just water. That water emitted the Real (*satya*) and the Real is the Immense-Being (Brahmā). From the Immense Being came forth the lord-of-progeny (Prajā-pati), and from the lord of progeny the gods. Those gods worship the Real (i.e., Brahmā)." (*Bṛhad-āraṇyaka Upaniṣad* 5.5.1. [451])

"Prajāpati is connected with the cosmic sacrifice, the Yajña, because all creatures are born of an offering of life, live by sacrificing life, and are, in the end, themselves sacrificed." (Vijayānanda Tripāṭhī, "Devatā tattva," *Sanmārga*, III, 1942, no. 3.)

As the manifestation of the revolving-tendency (*rajas*), the source of all cosmic movement, "Prajāpati is also the symbol of the year . . . , the cycle of life, the cycle of seasons on which life depends. He is the light which guides the evolution of life. The luminaries that shine in the day, the night, and the twilight are his components. These are the sun which illumines the day, the moon which illumines the night, and fire shining in the twilight." (Woodroffe, "Ṣaḍadhva," *Kalyāṇa*, Śakti aṅka, 1938, p. 585. See also *Kāmakalā-vilāsa*, p. 55.)

The year can be envisaged as the sum of all the days, nights, and twilights. When the year is represented as the wheel of time, "out of a total of 360 days or rays, 108 rays are said to be made of fire, of twilight, 116 rays to be made of sun, of daylight, 136 rays to be made of moon, of night. These are the symbolic numbers associated with the three luminaries. In the microcosm they correspond to the divisions (*kalā*) of the subtle energies which make the body act." (Woodroffe, "Ṣaḍadhva," *Kalyāṇa*, Śakti aṅka, p. 586.)

These energies are centered in the heart. Hence "the heart is the lord of progeny, is the Immense-Being (Brahmā), and is everything." (*Bṛhad-āraṇyaka Upaniṣad* 5.3.1. [452])

The lord of progeny divides himself into different entities that are the manifest beings who rule over the creation of the world, the establishment of cosmic order and of the world's order, the relation of men and gods. These too are known as lords of progeny, and are depicted as the sons, the manifestations, of the Immense Being. They represent the entities most often referred to under the name of "God." The seers (*ṛṣi*), the mysterious beings who revealed the divine law to man, are the manifestations of the power-of-knowledge (Sarasvatī), the consort of the Immense Being, and are often identified with the lords of progeny.

The myths of the lords of progeny are found in the Purāṇas.[4] In a later "humanist" interpretation, "lord of progeny is a name given to the man qualified

4 See Part Five for descriptions of the seers (pp. 316–24) and the lords of progeny (p. 317).

for ritual action and knowledge." [5] The lord of progeny is thus the embodiment of the laws that create harmony between the worlds and the teacher of moral duties, which mean abiding by these laws. These duties vary for different sorts of beings.

"The three kinds of children of the lord of progeny, gods, men, and antigods, dwelt with their father as students.

"Having completed their time of study, the gods said: 'Please speak to us.' He then spoke to them the syllable *da*. 'Did you understand?' 'We understood. You said to us, "Restrain yourselves" (*dāmyata*).' 'Bless you (AUM),' said he, 'you did understand.'

"Then the men said to him: 'Please speak to us.' He spoke to them the syllable *da*. 'Did you understand?' 'We understood. You said to us, "Give" (*datta*).' 'Bless you (AUM),' said he, 'you did understand.'

"Then the antigods said to him: 'Please speak to us.' He spoke to them the syllable *da*. 'Did you understand?' 'We understood. You said to us, "Be merciful" (*dayadhvam*).' 'Bless you (AUM),' said he, 'you did understand.'

"The divine voice resounds like thunder, repeating, '*Da! Da! Da!* "Restrain yourselves, give, be merciful." ' " (*Bṛhad-āraṇyaka Upaniṣad* 5.2.1–3. [454])

The Creation of the World

THE MYSTERY of creation can be approached from different points of view, the main ones being the theological, the empirical, and the cosmological. We are familiar with the theological myths of creation,[6] as we are with the empirical explanations of science. Indian cosmology envisages the appearance of the universe as a succession of intentions pictured as a desire, that is, a lack of balance, appearing in the causal continuum. This lack of balance gives rise to more and more elaborate forms of manifestation.

At the origin of manifestation, the first tension that appears in the undifferentiated cosmic mind is a vague desire-to-create (*sisṛkṣā*). This, in turn, gives rise to a particularized desire-to-act (*vicikīrṣā*), said to represent the state of nonexistence-prior-to-existence (*prāg-abhāva*).[7]

5 Śaṅkarācārya, *Viṣṇu-sahasra-nāma Bhāṣya*. [453])

6 For the myth of Brahmā's creation, see *Padma Purāṇa*, Sṛṣṭi khaṇḍa, 3, and *Brahmāṇḍa Purāṇa* 2.9.

7 One of the four forms of nonexistence, the three others being nonexistence-after-destruction (*pradhvaṁsa-abhāva*), nonexistence-at-all-times (*atyanta-abhāva*), nonexistence-in-something-else (*anyonya-abhāva*).

A question arises as to why the first impulse to create should ever appear in the Cosmic Being. So long as the three fundamental-qualities (*guṇa*) remain in a state of balance there is no reason why such an impulse should ever arise. What is therefore the cause of the first lack of balance? This has been attributed to latent traces of activity remaining from other creations. If there had been nothing left from other universes the present one could not have appeared. There is no question here of anteriority, since relative or successive time exists only within the universe and absolute time is omnipresent. The remains of the destroyed universes should not be understood as traces of gross or subtle matter—these may wholly return to their causal state of latent energy—but they are conceived as forms of power, or energy, into which all substance, all form, as well as relative space and time, can be ultimately withdrawn.

We can imagine that in the state preceding creation the fruits of action remaining unrewarded from previous creations and which have been in their unperfected maturity (*aparipakva*) the cause of destruction may become in their matured state (*paripakva*) the cause of creation. This imprint of action is called *bīja-śakti*, the seed power. When, in the preliminary stage of any creation, the seed energy begins to grow into a desire to create, this desire, which is the first conscious impulse, directs the unconscious will toward action. The desiring consciousness is represented as the giver-of-seed (*bījin*). When it finds something to which to apply its will, that is, a receptacle, it becomes the " 'possessor of *māyā*,' the illusionist (*māyin*) who creates the universe. . . ." (Karapātrī, "Śrī Bhagavatī tattva," *Siddhānta*, V, 1944–45, 23.)

"Lust, the primal seed and germ of the spirits, existed first. . . . The seers, looking into their hearts, discovered the kinship of the existent and the nonexistent." (*Ṛg Veda* 10.129.4. [455])

Every action, every movement, every impulse, starts a chain of reactions which is theoretically endless. Since substance appears to be illusory, it is action, the motion that characterizes its form, and the energy that characterizes its nature that are eternal. Action is found at the origin of all form.

The creative impulse in the cosmic substratum is but the result of the unfulfilled repercussions or actions which took place in destroyed universes. When asked how actions can keep alive when all the forms that bear their mark have ceased to be, the Vedāntist answers: "Just as by the strength of a resolve to wake up at a certain time, taken before going to sleep, we can wake up at that exact time, the decision to wake up having remained outside the realm of the state of sleep; so, by the strength of the divine resolve taken when the universe is dissolved, the state of equilibrium comes to an end at a given moment, the previous actions bear fruit, and the state of nonexistence-previous-to-existence comes to an end. Actions having ripened, the polarization (*vṛtti*), the appearance-that-is-substance (*māyā*), arises. In the substratum, the Immensity (*brahman*), thus polarized by ripened actions, appears as a beginning of space-time, a point-limit (*bindu*) that is the first perceptible form of Unmanifest-Nature (*avyakta*)." (Karapātrī, "Śrī Bhagavatī tattva.")

When it manifests itself, *māyā*, the stuff from which the illusion-that-is-substance is made, becomes known as Nature (*prakṛti*). It can be considered to be an unconscious mass of energy which comes to life when the cosmic consciousness is awakened and reflects itself in it. The cosmic consciousness is by itself changeless, like the solar light, yet, when mirrored in the ocean of Nature, it gives rise to waves, and clouds, and wind, and life. As the mirror of changeless consciousness, Nature, by itself unconscious, becomes the source of all manifest consciousness.

"Just as the poker in the fire acquires the burning nature and light-giving properties of fire, so unconscious Nature, in contact with the reflection of the Cosmic Man, becomes conscious and manifests the universe. In a womb into which seed, the essence of man's nature, is poured, a child is conceived; similarly, when the reflection of the Cosmic Man, his likeness, appears in unconscious Nature, consciousness invades her.

"When the consciousness reflected in Unmanifest-Nature (*avyakta*) is turned inward, toward nonexistence, this is the Fourth-stage (*turīya*), the stage beyond the three forms of manifestation (gross, subtle, and causal). When it is turned outward it is known as the causal-body (*kāraṇa deha*). From this Unmanifest, outwardly directed, arises the whole of the spatial universe, with all subtle and gross forms." (Karapātrī, "Śrī Bhagavatī tattva.")

The Cosmic Being, as the illusionist, is both the immanent cause, the substance, of the universe and its efficient cause, its builder. The part of the Cosmic Being connected with the universe is but a fragment of his totality.

"One quarter of him is the assemblage of elements which form the universe, the three other quarters are his immortal splendor." (*Puruṣa Sūkta* 3. [456])

The Cosmic Being thus pervades the universe as both its substance and its ruler. As such he is of three kinds:

As the provider of forms to the universe he is its substance (*sṛṣṭa*). This aspect is called Viśva, the spatial universe.

As the consciousness that dwells in the universe and rules over it, he is the indweller (*praviṣṭa*). This aspect is called Viśva-cara, the "driver of the universe."

As the changeless entity, forever undisturbed by the coming and going of universes, he is the aloof-one (*vivikta*). This aspect is called Viśvātīta, "beyond the universe."

"I stand aloof while a part of myself supports the whole universe." (*Bhagavadgītā* 10.42. [457])

The Myth of Creation

THE UPANIṢADS give us a vivid picture of the personified Universal Being and the myth of creation.

"In the beginning, verily, all this did not exist. From non-Being Being (*sat*) was produced. That Being changed itself into a Self, an Ātman." (*Taittirīya Upaniṣad* 2.7.1. [458])

Thus, from the very first, the notion of "being" is linked with that of "a being," a self, a center of consciousness.

"Verily, in the beginning this self was alone—there was no other winking thing. He thought: 'Let me now create the worlds.' " (*Aitareya Upaniṣad* 1.1.1, Gītā Press ed.; 4.1, Adyar ed. [459])

With the self thus appear thought and will prior to all substance.

"He was afraid. Therefore one who is alone is afraid. He thought, 'Since there is nothing else than myself, of what am I afraid?' Therefore, verily, his fear departed, for of what should he have been afraid? It is from a second that fear arises." (*Bṛhad-āraṇyaka Upaniṣad* 1.4.2. [460])

Fear and desire are the basic emotions from which creation arises.

From the first desire, the primordial eros, is formed the original notion-of-individual-existence (*aham-tattva*), the notion "I" linked to that of "self."

"First there was the Self, the Ātman, in the form of the Cosmic-Man (*puruṣa*). He looked and saw nothing but himself. He first said, 'I am'; hence his name is 'I.' So that even today a man first says, 'I am . . .' and then tells his name." (*Bṛhad-āraṇyaka Upaniṣad* 1.4.1. [461])

"He desired: Would that I were many! Let me procreate myself! He warmed himself. Having warmed himself, he created this world, whatever there is here. Having created it, he entered it. Having entered it, he became both the perceptible and what is beyond, both the defined (*nirukta*) and the undefined, both the based and nonbased, both knowledge (*vijñāna*) and unknowing, both the true (*satya*) and the false (*anṛta*). As the real, he became whatever there is here. That is what they call 'the Real.' " (*Taittirīya Upaniṣad* 2.6.1 [462])

"This existence desired, 'May I be many and procreate'; and he created the

Fire-that-is-Thought (*tejas*). This Fire wished, 'May I be many and procreate,' and from it the causal-waters (*ap*) appeared. Therefore, when men are warm, they perspire, from heat springs forth water. This water wished, 'May I be many and procreate,' and it gave birth to food grains. Therefore, when it rains, food grains multiply." (*Chāndogya Upaniṣad* 6.2.3–4. [463])

"The lord-of-progeny (Prajā-pati), verily, was longing for issue. He warmed himself. Having warmed himself, he produced a pair, water (*rayi*, fem., i.e., semen) and breath (*prāṇa*, masc.), thinking, 'These will procreate for me many kinds of beings.'

"The sun, verily, is this breath of life; the Moon, indeed, is these waters.

"From the waters everything is made, both what is manifest and what is unmanifest. Therefore all manifestation (*mūrti*) is water." (*Praśna Upaniṣad* 1.4–5. [464])

"Verily, he had no pleasures. Therefore one alone has no pleasures. He desired a second. He became as large as a woman and a man in close embrace. He divided himself into two. Therefrom arose a husband and a wife. Hence it is that everyone is but half a being. The vacant space is filled by a wife. He copulated with her. This is how men were created." (*Bṛhad-āraṇyaka Upaniṣad* 1.4.3. [465])

"From the Self, verily, space (*ākāśa*) arose; from space, wind (*vāyu*); from wind, fire; from fire, water; from water, earth; from earth, herbs; from herbs, food; from food, man." (*Taittirīya Upaniṣad* 2.1.1. [466])

"He created these worlds: the causal-waters (*ambhas*), light (*marīci*), death (*mara*), the earthly-waters (*ap*)." The causal waters are beyond heaven, the sky is their support; the world of light is the sphere of space; the world of death is the earth; the earthly waters are below.

"He thought: 'Now here are worlds. Let me create world guardians.' From the waters he drew forth and shaped a being.

"He hatched it.

"When it had been hatched, its mouth was separated, egglike; from the mouth came forth speech (*vāc*) and from speech fire.

"The nostrils were separated; from the nostrils came forth the life breath; from breath the wind.

"The eyes were separated; from the eyes came forth sight; from sight the sun.

"The ears were separated; from the ears came forth hearing; from the hearing the quarters of heaven.

"The skin was separated; from the skin came forth the hairs; from the hairs the plants and trees.

"The heart was separated; from the heart came the mind; from the mind the moon.

"The navel was separated; from the navel came forth the outward breath (*apāna*); from the outward breath sprang death (*mṛtyu*).

"The virile member was separated; from this virile member came forth semen and from semen the earthly-waters (*ap*)." (*Aitareya Upaniṣad* 1.1.2–4, Gītā Press ed.; 4.1, Adyar ed. [467])

"First produced from the mind of Brahmā, anxious to create, were the four classes of beings, [which range] from the gods to insentient things. . . .

"From his buttocks came forth the antigods (*asura*). He cast away that body, which became night.

"In another body he experienced delight; thus from his mouth he created the gods. He then cast away that body, which became the day.

"In another body he created the Ancestors (*pitṛ*). He then abandoned that body, which became the morning twilight. . . . Then in another body made of passion and darkness he created hungry monsters, demons (*rākṣasa*) and genii (*yakṣa*). The hair of the Creator gave birth to the serpents. . . . When he hatched the earth, the Fragrances [i.e., the celestial musicians] (*gandharva*) were born. He breathed in their words, hence they are known as 'Fragrances.' . . . Then he created birds and cattle: goats from his mouth, sheep from his breast, cows from his loins, and from his feet, horses, asses, camels, hares, deer, and mules.

"Plants and trees were created from the hair of his body." (*Mārkaṇḍeya Purāṇa* 48.3–26. [468])

Once the Creator became separated into a male and a female. "The female thought: 'How can he copulate with me when he has just created me out of himself? Come, let me hide.' She became a cow. He became a bull and copulated with her. Thus cattle were born. She became a mare; he a stallion. She became a female ass, he a male ass; he copulated with her. Thence hoofed animals were born. She became a she-goat, he a goat; she a ewe, he a ram. Thus, indeed, he created all, whatever pairs there are, even down to the ants." (*Bṛhad-āraṇyaka Upaniṣad* 1.4.4. [469])

"In the beginning the world was peopled only with 'priests and sages' (*brahma*). Being of but one kind, it could not develop. He [Brahma] created further a superior form, the princely order and also those who are princes among the gods, the lord-of-heaven (Indra), the lord-of-the-waters (Varuṇa), the lord-of-offering (Soma), the lord-of-tears (Rudra), the lord-of-rain (Parjanya), the king-of-justice (Yama), the lord-of-death (Mṛtyu), and I, the lord-of-space (Īśāna). There is nothing higher than a king, and at the royal sacrifice (Rājasūya) the priest sits below the king. Upon the princely order alone is this honor conferred. The priestly order is the source of the princely order. Therefore, although the king attains supremacy, he depends upon the priest as his own source. So whoever injures the priest destroys himself. He fares the worse as he injures one who is better.

"He was to develop yet further. He created the craftsmen (*viś*) and the [minor] gods who are mentioned in groups, such as the spheres-of-existence (Vasus), the divinities-of-life (Rudras), the sovereign-principles (Ādityas), the universal-principles (Viśva-devas), the genii-of-the-winds (Maruts).

"He was to develop yet further. He created the lowest class, which is attached to the soil, and [in heaven] the Nourisher (Pūṣan). Verily, this earth is the Nourisher, for she nourishes every thing that lives." (*Bṛhad-āraṇyaka Upaniṣad* 1.4.11–13. [470])

The Creation of Man

"ONCE CREATED, the gods fell into the moving ocean. He brought them hunger and thirst.

"They prayed: 'Find for us an abode where we may dwell and eat.'

"He brought them a bull. They said: 'This is not sufficient.'

"He offered them a horse. They said: 'This is not enough for us.' He offered them a man. They said: 'Well done, for a man, verily, is a thing well done.'

"He said: 'Enter into your abodes.'

"Fire became speech and entered the mouth. Wind became breath and entered the nostrils. The sun became sight, and entered the eyes. The directions of space became hearing, and entered the ears. Plants and herbs became hairs, and entered the skin. The moon became mind, and entered the heart. Death became the outward-breath (*apāna*), and entered the navel. Waters became semen, and entered the virile member.

"Hunger and thirst said to him: 'Find us an abode.' He said: 'I shall give you a place among the gods. I make you partakers among them.'

"Hence, whenever oblation is made, hunger and thirst share it." (*Aitareya Upaniṣad* 1.2.1–5, Gītā Press ed.; 4.2, Adyar ed. [471])

"He thought: 'Now here are worlds and world guardians. Let me create food for them.'

"He hatched the waters. From the heated [waters] a tangible-substance (*mūrti*) came forth. That substance is food.

"Food, once created, attempted to escape.

"He sought to seize it with speech, but speech could not grasp it. If it could be grasped with speech, one would be satisfied merely by saying 'food.'

"He sought to grasp it with breath, but breath could not grasp it. If it could be grasped with breath, one would be satisfied merely with breathing food.

"He sought to grasp it with sight, but sight could not grasp it. If it could be grasped with sight, one would be satisfied merely with seeing food.

"He sought to grasp it with hearing, but hearing could not grasp it. If it could be grasped with hearing, one would be satisfied merely with hearing food.

"He sought to grasp it with the skin, but the skin could not grasp it. If it could be grasped with the skin, one would be satisfied merely with touching food.

"He sought to grasp it with the mind, but the mind could not grasp it. If it could be grasped with the mind, one would be satisfied merely with thinking of food.

"He sought to grasp it with his virile member, but the virile member could not grasp it. If it could be grasped with the virile member, one would be satisfied merely with emitting food.

"He then sought to grasp it with the outward breath (*apāna*—the digestive energy). He swallowed it. This grasper of food is like the wind (*vāyu*), and those who live on food (*annāyu*) are like the wind.

"He thought: 'How could all this exist without me?'

"He thought: 'Where should I dwell?'

"He thought: 'If it is speech that utters, breath that breathes, sight that sees, hearing that hears, skin that feels, mind that thinks, the outward breath (*apāna*) that expels, the virile member that gives forth, then who am I?' So he opened the seam [of the scrotum] and entered by that door. This door is named 'the cleft' (*vidṛti*). It is the abode of pleasure.

"He has three abodes, three [places where he] rests. This is his abode (the eye). This is his abode (the mind). This is his abode (the heart)." (*Aitareya Upaniṣad* 1.3.1–12, Gītā Press ed.; 4.3, Adyar ed. [472])

The Creation of the Ritual Sacrifice

"PRAJĀPATI hatched the worlds. Warming them, he extracted their essences: fire from the earth, wind from space, the sun from the sky.

"He hatched these three deities. Warming them, he extracted their essences: from fire, the Meters (*Ṛk*); from the wind, the Contents (*Yajus*); from the sun, the Extension (*Sāman*).

"He hatched this threefold knowledge. Warming it, he extracted its essence: the *mantra*-of-the-earth (*bhūr*) from the Meters (*Ṛk*); the *mantra*-of-space (*bhuvas*) from the Contents (*Yajus*); the *mantra*-of-the-sky (*svar*) from the Extensions (*Sāman*).

"So, if [in the ritual sacrifice] there should come a defect connected with meters, one should make an oblation in the householder's (*gārhapatya*) fire, uttering the *mantra*, 'To earth (*bhūr*)! Hail!' Through the essence of the meters, by the power of the *Ṛg Veda*, one mends the injury done to the sacrifice.

"If there should come a defect connected with the contents, one should make an oblation in the Southern (*dakṣiṇa*) fire with the words, 'To space (*bhuvas*)! Hail!' Through the essence of the contents, by the power of the *Yajur Veda*, one mends the injury done to the sacrifice.

"If there should come a defect in connection with the development (the singing), one should make an oblation in the eastern-fire (*āhavanīya*) with the words, 'To the sky (*svar*)! Hail!' Through the essence of extension, by the power of the Sāman chant, one mends the injury done to the sacrifice." (*Chāndogya Upaniṣād* 4.17.1–6. [473])

The Opening of the Cosmic Egg

IN THE beginning this world was merely non-Being. Then it existed. It developed. It turned into an egg. It lay for a year. It was split. One of the two egg-shell parts became silver, the other gold.

"That which was of silver is this earth. That which was gold is the sky. The outer membrane became the mountains. The inner membrane is the clouds and mist. The veins are the rivers. The fluid within is the ocean." (*Chāndogya Upaniṣad* 3.19.1–2. [474])

"He [9] desired: 'May a second self of me be produced!' He who is hunger and death copulated mentally with speech (*vāc*). The semen produced became the year. Before that there was no year. He bore it for a time as long as a year. After that time he gave it birth. Once it was born, it opened its mouth. [The child] cried, '*Bhāṇ!*' That, indeed, became speech.

"He thought: 'Verily, if I kill it, it will make only a little food for me.' With Speech, with that [second] self, he brought forth the whole world, whatsoever exists here: the Meters (the *Ṛg Veda*), the Contents (the *Yajur Veda*), the Ex-

9 Virāṭ-rūpa Agni (i.e., Fire considered as the causal body of the universe), which Śaṅkarācārya, in his commentary on these verses, identifies with Prajāpati.

tension (the *Sāma Veda*), the rhythms (*chandas*), the sacrifices, men, and cattle." (*Bṛhad-āraṇyaka Upaniṣad* 1.2.4–5. [475])

The Duration of the Universe

"BRAHMĀ'S LIFE is one hundred years." (*Mārkaṇḍeya Purāṇa* 46.22. [476])

Once created, the world remains unaltered for one day of Brahmā, a period of 2,160,000,000 human years. The world and all that is therein is then consumed by fire, but the sages, the gods, and the principles of the elements survive. Brahmā sleeps during the night. When he awakes, he again restores creation, and this process is repeated until he completes his hundredth year, a period which it requires fifteen figures to express in human years.

The duration of each of the four Yugas, or ages of the world, in human years is as follows:

Kṛta Yuga	1,728,000
Tretā Yuga	1,296,000
Dvāpara Yuga	834,000
Kali Yuga	432,000

One thousand cycles of the four Yugas make one day of Brahmā; 360 such days make a year. Brahmā's life lasts for one hundred years. When this period is ended Brahmā himself ceases to exist. He and all the gods and sages and the whole universe are resolved into their constituent elements.

FOUR

The Divine Power (Śakti) as the Goddess

Śakti, the All-pervading Energy

Power as Divinity

NOTHING CAN exist unless there is some ground for its existence, some substratum from which it may rise. There must also be some possibility and some reason for existence. We have seen that the universal substratum was called the Immensity (*brahman*) and that the mechanical potentiality of manifestation lay in the form of opposing tendencies represented as cohesion (Viṣṇu) and disintegration (Śiva), their balance, the space-time creating principle, being known as the Immense-Being (Brahmā).

The tension between the opposites from which motion arises in the substratum is depicted as the first appearance of energy (*śakti*). It is from manifest energy, and not merely from the opposition from which it springs forth, that existence arises. Energy does not pertain to one or the other of the opposites nor to their mere opposition. It is something more, something new. Once manifestation has taken place, it appears as the substance of everything, pervading everything. It can be represented as the power of Śiva or that of Viṣṇu or that of Brahmā. As the power of their combined form, Īśvara, it becomes the Supreme-Goddess (Bhagavatī), the Resplendent-One (Devī). It can even be conceived as the power which appears in the neutral Immensity, as the maelstrom from which existence and the three basic-tendencies (*guṇa*) themselves appear to arise; it is then called Illusion (Māyā). From the point of view of cosmology this power, when manifest, is called Nature (*prakṛti*).

Being the creative aspect of divinity, the power through which creation arises, through which the gods are born and procreate, Energy is pictured as female. The notion of divinity rests upon that of power. The gods are the most powerful of beings.

"The quality of being divine appears in that in which there is most energy. It is only when the qualityless, shapeless, motionless substratum becomes 'spotted through' by the great Energy, center of limitless energies, that the universe can be created, maintained, and destroyed. Without energy, Śiva, the lord of sleep, is unable to create or destroy, is as powerless as a corpse. The divinity of divinity rests upon Energy.

" 'She is the power of the Self; she it is who creates appearances.' " (Karapātrī, "Śrī Bhagavatī tattva," *Siddhānta*, V, 1944–45, 160. [477])

In the *Liṅga-arcana Tantra* we read: "Devoid of senses, the eternal lord of sleep is merely the form of the Void. He has no visible form. What can be expected from the worship of nothingness?

"Without the great Daughter-of-the-Mountain (Pārvatī), ever glorified as his supreme dread energy, the corpse of Rudra is never worshiped. This primordial goddess is known as 'the coiled,' Kuṇḍalinī. Her substance is Brahmā-Viṣṇu-Śiva. She envelops Śiva with her three and a half veils. . . . Only because he is united with Energy is the eternal lord of sleep a doer of actions. This is why the Goddess is worshiped as a *liṅga* surrounded by a *yoni*."

"The quiescent aspect of Śiva is, by definition, inert. . . . Activity is the nature of Nature (*prakṛti*). . . . For this reason the female form is represented in sexual union as being above (*viparīta*) the male. When the *devī* is shown standing above Śiva . . . [this also represents] the liberating aspect of the Mother." (Woodroffe, *The Serpent Power*, p. 27 n., with changes.)

Among the Śāktas, who are the worshipers of the Goddess, the source of existence, considered female, becomes the main representation of divinity. God is woman.

Yet power is ever inseparable from him who possesses it. So the all-powerful Energy cannot be really distinct from the substratum from which it arises. The concept of Śakti is necessary to justify the appearance of the perceptible universe out of an inaccessible, motionless substratum.

The word *śakti*, meaning "energy," is found in the Vedas, where its equivalent, *śacī* (divine grace), represents Energy, personified as the consort of Indra, the divine might. The notion of Śakti as the supreme power seems to appear fully only in the *Śvetāśvatara Upaniṣad*, one of the Śaivite Upaniṣads.

In the common Hindu theology, Śakti is but another name for the manifesting power, the creative principle. It takes the place of Brahmā, the Cosmic-Embryo (Hiraṇya-garbha). In later mythology the concept of Śakti comes to include both the notions of a concentrating, illuminating power that is Viṣṇu and an active space-time principle that is Brahmā to form the complement of the male, positive, ultimate knowledge that is Śiva.

Descending from the earliest prehistoric Śaivism, the eternal couple Śiva-

Śakti represented in the male and the female emblems, the *liṅga* and the *yoni*, pervades the whole of later Hinduism. The *liṅga* embraced by the *yoni* forms the central object of worship and tends to reduce to a minor position all the other ways of representing divinity.

Energy is the source of everything, the origin of the phenomenal world but also of the conscious plan of its creation, and the principle of knowledge or perception through which its existence, real or apparent, can be known. Thus the Goddess is also represented as Consciousness or as Knowledge. Without her the gods are dead, inactive, unknown, nonexistent. Knowledge (*jñāna*) without action (*kriyā*) is dead knowledge, and so is feeling (*rasa*) without strength (*bala*).

The Goddess is the source of all, the universal creator.

"The gods, approaching the resplendent Goddess, asked her, 'Who are you?' The Goddess replied, 'I am the form of the Immensity; from me the world arises as Nature and Person (*prakṛti-puruṣa*).' " (*Devī Upaniṣad* 1–2. [478])

"She is the form of all that is conscious. The origin, the knowledge, the perception of reality, the instigator of intellect." (*Devī Bhāgavata Purāṇa* 1.1. [479])

She is realized in the microcosm as the ultimate goal of Yoga.

"In the principial-aperture (the *brahma-randhra*, behind the forehead) each man finds me, the lady-of-the-spheres (Bhuvaneśvarī), who am the shape of the Principle, beyond the Fourth [unmanifest] stage." (*Bhuvaneśvarī Upaniṣad.* [480])

The *Devī Sūkta* of the *Ṛg Veda* describes her as supreme, all-pervading divinity.

The Goddess says:

"I wander with the principles-of-life (Rudras), with the spheres-of-existence (Vasus), the sovereign-principles (Ādityas), and the all-pervading-gods (Viśvadevas). I am the support of Might (Indra), of Fire (Agni), of the law-of-man-and-gods (Mitra-Varuṇa), of the horse-headed gods-of-agriculture (the Aśvins). I am the support of the *soma* wine which flows from the crushing stone; I am the support of the Shaper (Tvaṣṭṛ), of the Nourisher (Pūṣan), of the Inherited-Share (Bhaga). I am the giver of the fruit of action to the performer of the ritual sacrifice, which nourishes the gods with offerings.

"I am the Kingdom, the giver of wealth, the knower [of the essence of things]. I come first in all rituals. The gods have established me in various abodes. My sphere is wide. I dwell in all things.

"From me comes the food you eat, all that you see, all that has breath (*prāṇa*), and all the words you hear. Those who do not acknowledge me are destroyed. Study and hear what I say with respect. I am the pleasure of gods and men.

"I make everyone whatever he wishes to be, feared or great, a man of vision or intellect. I draw the bow of the lord-of-tears (Rudra) to kill the tribes of the enemies of knowledge. I fight for the people. I enter the sky and the earth. I give birth to the father and I am his head. I spring forth from the waters (*ap*) of the ocean. From there I spread into the universe. I touch the sky with my body. I blow like the wind, creating the worlds. My greatness expands beyond the sky and the earth." (*Ṛg Veda* 10.125.1–8. [481])

As the source, the plan of the universe, Energy first appears as a consciousness. Knowledge, that is, the perception of the existing universe, is its manifest form. There is a conscious plan for everything and therefore a possibility of knowing, a knowledge related to everything. The knowledge of the universe is the transcendent-knowledge (*mahā-vidyā*), whose form is identical to that of the all-powerful Goddess, and fragments of which are expressed in the revealed scripture, the Veda.

The knowledge of the cosmos is called *virāṭ-vidyā;* that of the manifest universe is *viśva-vidyā*. The main aspects of existence as perceived from the point of view of man are represented in the ten forms of the Goddess, the ten objects-of-transcendent-knowledge (*mahā-vidyā*) which are her most commonly worshiped aspects.

Origin and Worship of the Goddess

THE CONCEPTION of supreme divinity as a woman, a mother, a womb, does not seem to have had at first any place in the Aryan Scriptures, which are the religious books of a patriarchal society. But the prehistoric cult of the mother goddess can be found there too, as in all other religions, latent, ready to spring forth. Some of the peoples who came to be integrated into the Hindu fold had always worshiped the divine Mother.

The Goddess is mentioned in the epics under a number of names. Many of her myths and their meanings are given in the Purāṇas, particularly the *Brahma-vaivarta*, the *Kūrma*, the *Garuḍa*. A number of hymns-of-praise (Māhātmyas), such as the *Devī Māhātmya*, are dedicated to her. In the Tantras, the Goddess is the all-embracing, absolute divinity. For a great number of Hindus she represents "God," supreme, yet within the reach of the worshiper.

The *Kālī Upaniṣad* and the *Tārā Upaniṣad* advocate the worship of the Goddess as the symbol of the Unqualified Principle, the Immensity, the Brahman.

"To be freed from the world, one should worship the Witness of All, the transcendent Energy, whose shape is the Self and in whom are found neither the manifest world nor its pleasures." (*Sūta Saṁhitā.* [482])

"She is said by the learned to be of two kinds, unqualified and qualified. Those bound by attachment should worship her qualified form, and those without attachment her unqualified form." (*Devī Bhāgavata Purāṇa* 1.8.40. [483])

"For those who seek pleasure or those who seek liberation, the worship of the all-powerful Goddess is essential. She is the knowledge-of-the-Immensity (*brahma-vidyā*); she is the mother of the universe, pervading the whole world." (Karapātrī, "Śrī Bhagavatī tattva.")

"The fearful-goddess (Caṇḍikā), devoted to her devotees, reduces to ashes those who do not worship her and destroys their merits." (*Devī Māhātmya.* [484])

The Consorts of the Three Gods

BEING THE power of manifestation of the three tendencies (*guṇa*), the Goddess appears at the root of the three aspects of existence as Reality, Consciousness, and Experience (*sat-cit-ānanda*).

As Reality she is the power-of-co-ordination (*sandhinī*), that is, the power of the centripetal tendency visible in the sun. She is pictured as the Left-handed-One (Vāmā), who is the power-of-action (*kriyā*), that is, of causation. She is the power of multiplicity, Lakṣmī (the goddess of hundreds of thousands), that is, the goddess of fortune, consort of Viṣṇu.

As Consciousness she is the power-of-understanding (*saṁvit*), the power of the revolving tendency, visible in the Moon and pictured as "the Elder" (Jyeṣṭhā). She is the power of volition, the power of the flow of knowledge, Sarasvatī, goddess of learning and consort of Brahmā.

As Experience or Joy she is the power-of-delight (*āhlādinī-śakti*), of enjoyment, the power of the centrifugal, disintegrating tendency, visible in fire, the destroyer. She is pictured as the Fierce (Raudrī). She is the power of cognition, of realization, of transcendent knowledge, the destroyer of the world of illusion, the consort of Śiva. She is also called Beyond-Reach (Durgā).

Creation arises from this triple form of power.

"According to the plan formed in the divine mind, Energy (Śakti) arose from the radiance of Reality-Consciousness-Experience. From Energy sprang forth the principial vibration, the point-limit from which the manifest world begins." (Quoted in Karapātrī's "Śrī Bhagavatī tattva," *Siddhānta*, V, 1944–45. [485])

"The manifest forms of Existence-Consciousness-Experience, which are action, knowledge, and desire, are the beginning of creation. They are the law (*dharma*) that governs divinity, a law which is not distinct from divinity itself. It is the nature of the Immensity. The Scripture describes this nature of divinity as 'spontaneous knowledge, strength, and action.' [1] The law that rules the nature of divinity is identical with the Divine Energy. Because of its uncontrollable intensity, it is spoken of as the Wrathful (Caṇḍī). This Energy takes the form of the Transcendent-power-of-Time (Mahā-Kālī), of the Transcendent-power-of-Multiplicity (Mahā-Lakṣmī), of the Transcendent-power-of-Knowledge (Mahā-Sarasvatī), according to the task to be performed. To see in this Supreme Wrath a male or a female merely depends on the inclination of the worshiper. In male terms she is known as the transcendent lord of tears, Mahā-Rudra, in female terms as Wrath (Caṇḍī) or Beyond-Reach (Durgā)." (Karapātrī, "Śrī Bhagavatī tattva.")

The Progenitors of the Gods

"REALITY, that is, the power-of-multiplicity (Lakṣmī), enthroned on the pure lotus of knowledge, became bi-form as a man and a woman. The names given to the male form are the Immense-Being (Brahmā), the Support (Dhātā), etc., while the female names are Beauty (Śrī), Lotus-Lady (Kamalā, Padmā), Fortune (Lakṣmī), etc.

"The Power of Time, which is also the power of experience or power of delight, became bi-born. The male had a blue throat, red arms, fair thighs, and the moon as a diadem; the woman was beautiful, fair. The male names were Lord-of-Tears (Rudra), Giver-of-Happiness (Śaṅkara), Pillar (Sthāṇu), Matted-haired (Kapardī), Three-eyed (Tri-locana). The female names were Triple-Knowledge (Trayī-vidyā), Wish-Cow (Kāma-dhenu), Language (Bhāṣā), the Lettered (Akṣarā), the Syllabled (Svarā).

"As to the couple that sprang forth from the power of consciousness, the names of the male were Pervader (Viṣṇu), Dark-One (Kṛṣṇa), Lord-of-the-Senses (Hṛṣī-keśa), Indweller (Vāsu-deva), Giver-of-Rewards (Janārdana). The female's names were Peace-of-the-Night (Umā), Fair-One (Gaurī), Faithfulness (Satī), Wrathful (Caṇḍī), Beautiful (Sundarī), Fortunate (Subhagā), Lady-of-Sleep (Śivā)." (Karapātrī, "Śrī Bhagavatī tattva.")

The Flowing-One (Saras-vatī), the Divinity of Knowledge

THE POWER of Brahmā, represented as both his daughter and his consort, is the goddess of speech, the Flowing-One (Saras-vatī). She represents the union of power and intelligence from which organized creation arises.

[1] *Svābhāvikī jñāna-bala-kriyā.*

Speech is the power through which knowledge expresses itself in action. Sarasvatī is the source of "creation by the Word," which runs parallel to the visible "creation in terms of forms." She is the goddess of eloquence, of wisdom, of learning, the patroness of arts and of music. She revealed language and writing to man. She is the mother of poetry.

The name of Sarasvatī is of rather obscure origin. It is sometimes thought to refer to the pool of knowledge. The name is that of a sacred river, called the Sarsuti; although now dried up, it is mentioned in the *Ṛg Veda* as "She who goes pure from the mountains as far as the sea." According to the *Mahābhārata*, the river was dried up by the curse of the sage Utathya. *Saras*, which means fluid, refers to anything that flows and as such applies to speech and thought as well as water. Other names of Sarasvatī are Eloquence (Bhāratī), Transcendent-Knowledge (Mahā-vidyā), Speech (Vāc), Transcendent-Word (Mahā-vāṇī). She is the Noble-One (Āryā), the Power-of-the-Immense-Being (Brahmī), the Wish-Cow (Kāma-dhenu), the Womb-of-the-Seed or Womb-of-the-Elements-of-Speech (Bīja-garbhā), Divinity-of-Wealth (Dhaneśvarī), etc.

Sarasvatī is depicted as a graceful woman, white in color, sitting on a lotus with a slender crescent on her brow. She is shown with either two or eight arms. In the latter case her attributes are a lute (*vīṇā*), a book, a rosary, and an elephant hook, but she is also shown with an arrow, a mace, a spear, a discus, a conch, a bell, a plow, and a bow (Karapātrī, "Śrī Bhagavatī tattva," p. 183). She is beautifully pictured in the *Harṣa-carita*.

On the day consecrated to Sarasvatī none may read books or play musical instruments. These are cleaned, placed on an altar, and worshiped as the abodes of the goddess.

The Divinity of Speech, Vāc

SPEECH (Vāc) appears personified in the *Ṛg Veda* as the vehicle of knowledge. "She (Vāc is feminine) 'enters into the seers.' She gives power and intelligence to those she loves. She is the 'mother of the Vedas,' the consort of the lord-of-heaven (Indra), containing all the worlds within herself. 'Hence Vāc is everything.' " (*Aitareya Āraṇyaka* 3.1.6. [486])

To create the world, the lord-of-progeny (Prajāpati) unites with Speech. In the *Atharva Veda* (8.10.24 and 11.8.30) she appears as the Wish Cow and is identified with the Cosmos (Virāj).

The *Padma Purāṇa* describes Speech as the daughter of Ritual-Skill (Dakṣa) and as ever present in all rituals. She is the wife of Vision (Kaśyapa) and the mother of the emotions, pictured as the Fragrances or celestial-musicians (*gandharva*). She also gives birth to the uncreated potentialities, represented as celestial dancers, the water-nymphs (*apsaras*).

One of the main aspects of Vāc is "the Triple Hymn" (Gāyatrī). This name applies particularly to a Vedic meter of twenty-four (three times eight) syllables and to a sacred verse in this meter considered to be the essence of the Vedas and pictured as their mother. Gāyatrī is the patroness of the Noble Ones, the Āryas; they alone are permitted to utter her name. In addition, she is the wife of Brahmā. She is also called the Hymn-to-the-Sun (Sāvitrī). This hymn to the Sun is called Gāyatrī at dawn, Sāvitrī at midday, and Sarasvatī at sunset.

The Goddess of Fortune, Lakṣmī

THE POWER of the all-pervading Preserver, Viṣṇu, is represented as the power of multiplicity or goddess of fortune, She-of-the-Hundred-Thousands (Lakṣmī). She is also the goddess of beauty and is then known as Śrī.

Both "Lakṣmī" and "Śrī" are found in the Vedas in the sense of "fortune." But Fortune is depicted as a major goddess only in the epics. The *Taittirīya Saṁhitā* makes Fortune and Beauty the two wives of the solar-principle (Āditya). The *Śatapatha Brāhmaṇa* describes Beauty as born from the lord-of-progeny (Prajāpati). Beauty is also the mother of Lust (Kāma). When the ocean was churned by the gods and the antigods, she sprang from the waves, a lotus in her hand. She is also represented seated on a lotus floating on the ocean of milk. The *Viṣṇu Purāṇa* says that Fortune was first born as a daughter of the Crack-of-the-Ritual-Fire (Bhṛgu) united to the Hymns-of-Praise (Khyāti). Fortune is thus the fruit of the ritual-sacrifice (*yajña*).

As the consort of Viṣṇu Fortune appears with him in every one of his descents (*avatāra*) or incarnations. "She appeared as the Lotus-Lady (Padmā or Kamalā) when the Remover-of-Sorrow (Hari) was born as a dwarf. She was the Earth (Dharaṇī) when he was Rāma of the Ax." (*Viṣṇu Purāṇa* 1.9.143. [487]) So as to be the consort of Rāma, Fortune appeared from a furrow made by the plow in the Earth. She was called Furrow (Sītā). She was then said to represent the lustful aspect of Viṣṇu, the power of delight inherent in Fortune.

According to the *Agastya Saṁhitā*, Śiva, the lord of sleep, performed great austerities to obtain the vision of Rāma, the Charming, the delight of the Earth. Rāma told him, "If you wish to know my inner nature, you should worship my transcendent power-of-delight (*āhlādinī-śakti*). Without her I stand nowhere.

"O Giver-of-Peace (Śambhu), you should ever worship my transcendent power of delight. As the Charming (Rāma), I am dependent upon her. Without her I could not for an instant remain in existence; she is my innermost life." (*Agastya Saṁhitā*. [488])

Then Śiva worshiped the goddess, and she appeared before him. Praising her, he said:

"I bow to the lotus feet of the daughter of Videha, whose youthfulness and grace attract the minds of the yogis. She destroys the three kinds of pain [spiritual, mental, physical]. The sages, the swans of knowledge, ever wait upon her. She is the store of pollen from which the bee of intellect drinks." (*Agastya Saṁhitā*. [489])

When Viṣṇu appeared as Kṛṣṇa, Fortune became Rukminī. She will appear as the goddess of destruction when he comes as Kalki at the end of the ages. She is the goddess Beyond-Reach (Durgā).

Other names of Fortune are the Jewel (Hīrā), the Powerful-One (Indirā), the Ocean-born (Jaladhi-jā), the Fickle-One (Cañcalā or Lolā), the Mother-of-the-World (Loka-mātā).

Lakṣmī is sometimes represented with four arms, but more usually with two. She holds a lotus. She has no temples but is worshiped in every home on all important occasions. The day dedicated to her worship is observed all over India.

Fortune's opposite is Misfortune (A-lakṣmī), fearful and ugly, also known as the Elder-Sister (Jyeṣṭhā).

Destiny or Transcendent Fortune, Mahā-Lakṣmī

ENVISAGED AS Destiny or Transcendent-Fortune (Mahā-Lakṣmī), this divinity embodies the characters of all the gods.

"She who springs forth from the body of all the gods has a thousand, indeed countless, arms, although her image is shown with but eighteen. Her face is white, made from the light streaming from the lord-of-sleep (Śiva). Her arms made of the substance of Viṣṇu are deep blue; her round breasts made of *soma*, the sacrificial ambrosia, are white. Her waist is Indra, the king of heaven, and is therefore red. Her feet, sprung from the Creator Brahmā, are also red, while her calves and thighs, sprung from Varuṇa, the lord of the waters, are blue. She wears a gaily colored lower garment, brilliant garlands, and a veil. Starting from the lower left, she holds in her hands a rosary, a lotus, an arrow, a sword, a hatchet, a club, a discus, an ax, a trident, a conch, a bell, a noose, a spear, a stick, a hide, a bow, a chalice, and a waterpot.

"He who worships the Transcendent Divinity of Fortune becomes the lord of all the worlds." (Karapātrī, "Śrī Bhagavatī tattva.")

Success (Rādhā), the Personification of Devotion

IN SOME Tantras the main companion of Attraction (Kṛṣṇa) is Success (Rādhā), his childhood companion and beloved, who never became his lawful consort. She is the presiding deity of life and of the life-energies (*prāṇa*), sometimes considered an aspect of Śiva. Rādhā means "achievement," "success."

The Powers of Procreation, Development, and Destruction, Pārvatī, Śakti, and Kālī

LIKE ŚIVA himself, the power of Śiva is envisaged under three main aspects: a creative, all-pervading active aspect called Energy (Śakti), a permanent, peaceful, all-pervading, spatial aspect named Pārvatī, the Daughter of the Mountain (i.e., Ether personified), a destructive, all-pervading time aspect known as the Power-of-Time (Kālī).

"The lord-of-sleep (Śiva), the phallus clasped by the womb that is his energy, gives forth the seed of the spatial universe. When conceived as a personified entity, the lord of sleep appears inactive while his energy seems alive. As the instrument of Śiva's procreating power, this energy is the Power-of-Lust (Rati). She then appears to be the very opposite of the power of destruction that is Kālī, the Power of Time. When Energy, which is also the power-to-think (*vimarśa*), unites with the lord of sleep, this leads to a state of agitation, of unrest (*unmanā*), from which creation springs forth. When she is aloof from him, this leads to the state of sleep, of equalization (*samānā*), in which the world dissolves." [2] When Śakti clasps Śiva, the universe is shaken. She is the all-pervading power of lust, of enjoyment, and also the power of liberation, for liberation from Nature's bonds is not a neutral state but an active fight.

As Satī, the Faithful, Śiva's beloved threw herself into the ritual fire so that the cosmic sacrifice might be completed. She is therefore represented as the daughter of Ritual-Skill (Dakṣa), as Dakṣiṇā,[3] the wealth offered during the sacrifices.

Pārvatī is a gentle goddess, daughter of the axial mountain, from which

2 Karapātrī, "Śrī Bhagavatī tattva."

3 In the "Five Nights of Nārada" (*Nārada Pāñcarātra*), it is said that, in the beginning of creation, everything was female except the Giver-of-Peace (Śaṅkara-Śiva). Brahmā, Viṣṇu, Dakṣa, and many others performed austerities to evoke the goddess of time, Kālikā, who appeared and permitted them to ask a boon. The gods said, "You must become the daughter of Ritual-Skill (Dakṣa) and seduce Śiva."

the earth energy springs forth. The mountain (*parvata*) or the Snow-capped-One (Himavat) is a symbol of ether. The peaks of the mountains are regarded as the places from which the earth energy flows into the ether. Hence dwelling on top of a hill is not advisable and only places of worship may be built there. The mother of Pārvatī is Menakā, who represents intellect (*buddhi*). Born of Ether and Intellect, Pārvatī is the conscious substance of the universe. Pārvatī is also the chief of all the elves and spirits that wander about the earth. She is the leader of Śiva's attendants, the "categories" (*gaṇa*).

It is under her fierce aspect as the Power-of-Time (Kālī), the power of disintegration closely connected to the power of liberation, that the consort of Śiva is mainly worshiped. She is then shown under a fearful form. She is a fierce-looking goddess, fond of intoxicants, of lust, of bloody sacrifices. Cruel and orgiastic rituals are performed in her honor by the followers of the Tantra cult.

The Power-of-Enjoyment (*āhlādinī-śakti*)

WHEN OPPOSITES unite, the lack of balance, the tension, from which all things are born, is removed and pleasure is experienced. Hence it is thought that the state of permanent stability is a state of perpetual enjoyment, a state of bliss. For the living being it is only in the union of opposites that the state of joy appears. Only during the brief moment when two beings become one, when desire is satisfied, is a fragment of joy experienced. This state is the closest image of the state of liberation.

"When the presiding deity of life (Prāṇa) and that of intellect (Buddhi), united in man, are not in coition, not in the state of enjoying one another, when they are not in the state of balance, the living being cannot be liberated; the supreme aim of existence, which is complete liberation from the triple form of pain, spiritual, mental, physical, cannot be realized.

"The methods of liberation which allow Life and Intellect to become one depend either on the control of the mind through a mental-process (*vicāra*) or on the control of vital impulses by regulating the life-breath (*prāṇa*); the last method is that of introspection as taught by Yoga." (Yogatrayānanda, *Śrī Rāmāvatāra kathā*, p. 55.)

"At the time of the birth of the world, the knowing faculty, in the form of Root-Nature (*mūla prakṛti*), unites with Energy (Śakti), the ruling deity of life and intellect, which ever instigates and controls all living beings. The whole world, moving or inert, from the Cosmic Man onward depends on these two powers. Liberation is easy for him who gains their favor." (*Devī Bhāgavata Purāṇa* 9.50.6–8. [490])

"Through the perceptible goddess-of-the-spheres (Bhuvaneśvarī), who is the form of Root Nature, the world became manifest. A dual energy appeared in the form of Achievement (Rādhā), the presiding deity of the life-energies (*prāṇa*) in their cosmic unity or their manifestations in individual beings, and in the form of Durgā, the presiding deity of intellect (*buddhi*) in its cosmic unity or its manifestation in individual beings." (*Devī Bhāgavata Ṭīkā*, ibid. [491])

"This dual Energy, presiding deity of life and intellect, is called [the all-powerful goddess], the universal ruler. [The gift of] liberation depends on it. Liberation depends on the union of intellect and life, their uniting and going apart. The other gift is the grace of life and intellect, which is difficult to reach." (*Devī Bhāgavata Ṭīkā*, ibid. [492])

Being the power of enjoyment, of divinity, the Goddess is described as the consort of Śiva.

"The qualityless Supreme Self takes shelter in you. You are the woman whence he derives pleasure, the lady of the spheres." (A Tantra quoted in Yogatrayānanda's *Śrī Rāmāvatāra kathā*. [493])

The whole concept of the union of opposites as creating a state of bliss, as the pacified state representing eternal happiness, the experience of the Absolute, is pictured in the union of the sexes, in the symbol of the *liṅga* and the *yoni* forever united.

"Nature (*prakṛti*), made of the five principles-of-the-elements (*tattva*), is the vulva into which enters this phallus of light which represents the power of illumination of the Immensity. When it is said that the Lady-of-the-Mountain (Pārvatī) took the shape of a vulva to catch hold of this phallus, this means that, becoming Nature, namely, becoming the five principles of the elements, she became the support of the world's egg, of the created universe. This is why her symbol is the number 5.

"The world knows that the Lady of the Mountain, the beloved of Śiva, is represented by the number 5 (i.e., has the form of an arrow).

"The vulva, the arrow, and the number 5 are considered equivalent symbols. The word arrow is a symbolic expression for the number 5. It is used for the god of lust, Kāma, because of his five arrows (the five senses), for Śiva because of his five faces, and for the Lady of the Mountain because of the five principles of the elements. Although static electricity (*vidyut-puñja*) pervades all the elements, it dwells more particularly in water and in mountain ranges.

Since Pārvatī is the five elements (i.e., is like a mountain range), the phallus of light enters her. When the mass of static energy falls into her womb, that is, into earth or water, it becomes stabilized. Otherwise it reduces everything to ashes. Thus arises the myth of the Lady of the Mountain becoming a vulva to catch hold of the phallus of fire that was burning the world." [4] This is also the meaning of the dry tree embraced by the leafless creeper (*aparṇā*); the leafless creeper is an equivalent of the vulva that is Pārvatī, while the Changeless Being is the dry tree or phallus.

The Amorous, Lalitā

DIVINITY CAN be conceived as a playful being for whom the world is a toy, a game. Playfulness personified as the Supreme Cause is called Lalitā. Lalitā is then represented as an amorous, playful girl whose form is the universe.

The Divinity of Lust, Kāmeśvarī

"THE FAVORABLE aspect of the Supreme Being envisaged without attributes is called the Transcendent-Ruler-of-the-Left-Hand (Mahā-vāmeśvara), while the favorable aspect of the Supreme Being when endowed with the attributes which pervade his limbs with the joy of existence is known as the Divinity-of-Lust (Kāmeśvarī).

"In the hand of the Divinity of Lust are a noose, an elephant hook, a bow made of sugar cane, and an arrow. Attachment is said to be the noose, intellect the elephant hook, the mind the sugar-cane bow; words and the objects of the senses are the arrows of flowers. In another version 'the noose is the power of desire, the elephant hook represents knowledge, the brilliance of the bow and arrow is the power to act' [494]." (Karapātrī, "Srī Bhagavatī tattva.")

The Names of the Goddess

AS THE gentle companion of Śiva's pleasures the Goddess is mainly known as the Daughter-of-the-Mountain (Pārvatī) or the Mountain-born (Adri-jā or Giri-jā), the Daughter-of-the-Snow-capped-One (Haima-vatī). She is also the Earth-born (Ku-jā), the Fair-One (Gaurī), the World's-Most-Fair (Jagad-Gaurī), the Peace-of-the-Night (Umā). Auspicious (Śivā), she is the Mother (Ambikā), the Mother-of-the-World (Jagad-mātā), the Giver-of-Existence

4 Karapātrī, "Liṅgopāśanā-rahasya," *Siddhānta*, V, 1944–45.

(Bhavānī). She is the Youngest (Avarā), the Virgin (Kanyā), the Virgin-Girl (Kanyā-kumārī). She is the Sustainer-of-the-World (Jagad-dhātrī), the Auspicious-Power-of-Time (Bhadra-Kālī), the Giver-of-Food-and-Plenty (Annapūrṇā), the Shining-One (Devī), the Consort-of-the-Great-Lord (Mahā-devī). As the embodiment of lust she is Wanton-eyed (Kāmākṣī), Her-very-Name-is-Lust (Kāmākhyā). She is the Rubbing- or Squeezing-One (Mṛḍā, Mṛḍānī), Noble (Āryā), Rich (Ṛddhi), Pearl-eared (Karṇa-moṭī), Recognizable-from-her-Lotus (Padma-lāñcanā); she is Always-Auspicious (Sarva-maṅgalā). Like-a-Bee (Bhrāmarī), she is Śiva's-Messenger (Śiva-dūtī).

She is the Goddess Beyond-Reach (Durgā), the Endless (Anantā), the Everlasting (Nityā).

Fearful, she is Tawny-Dark (Piṅgā), Spotted (Karburī), Naked (Koṭarī), Violent (Caṇḍī), Dark (Śyāmā), Terrible (Bhairavī). She is the Fearful-Goddess (Bhīmā-devī), the Power-of-the-Antigods (Mahāsurī), the Fierce (Rājasī), Red-toothed (Rakta-dantī); she is the Mother-of-the-God-of-War (Skanda-mātā), the Victorious (Vijayā)

The *Caṇḍī Māhātmya,* one of the hymns of praise dedicated to her, depicts her as Ten-armed (Daśa-bhujā), Riding-on-a-Lion (Siṁha-vāhanī or Siṁha-rathī). She is the "Destroyer of the Buffalo-Demon" (Mahiṣa-mardinī),[5] the Disheveled (Mukta-keśinī).

Being addicted to austerities, she is the Leafless (Aparṇā), the Widow (Kātyāyanī), Grass-robed (Śākambharī).

From Śiva she obtains names which are the feminine form of his, such as the Tawny-One (Bābhravī), the All-Powerful (Bhagavatī), the Ruler (Īśānī), Divinity (Īśvarī), Dwelling-in-the-Kalinjar-Mountain (Kālañjarī), Adorned-with-Skulls (Kapālinī). She is the Sentiment-of-Love (Kauśikī), the Savage-Girl (Kirātī), the Great-Goddess (Maheśvarī), the Goddess-of-Tears (Rudrāṇī), Universal (Śarvāṇī), Auspicious (Śivā), Three-eyed (Tryambakī).

5 For the story, see p. 288.

The Ten Objects-of-Transcendent-Knowledge (mahā-vidyā)

EVERY DAY we see the twilight dissolve into darkness. Midnight is the hour of deepest obscurity, the time most remote from the day. If we compare the cycle of the day to that of the ages, the midnight of the universal night will be the time of absolute silence over which the universal power of destruction, the transcendent power of Time, Mahā-Kālī, rules unchallenged.

The whole cycle of existence, like that of the day and night, can be divided into ten main parts connected with the symbolism attached to the number 5 — the five aspects of Śiva and the five aspects of the Goddess united as day and night.

The ten aspects of the cycle of time are conceived as an epitome of the entire creation, a summary of all the stages of existence, of all that is to be known. They are the ten aspects of the power of Śiva. To know them is equivalent to knowing the secret of the universe. They are the energies of which the universe is the pulsation, the outer expression.

These ten energies are called the ten objects of transcendent knowledge, the Mahā-vidyās. They are the source of all that is to be known, the various aspects of the divine night. Through the language of their symbols appears a picture of our destiny. They are ultimately the powers of destruction, hence Manu speaks of night as a fearful demoness (3.280), but it is through the destruction of all that appears to us desirable and by facing what appears to us most fearful, namely, the power of time, of death, that we can become free from bondage and attain the aim of our existence, the limitless supreme bliss of nonexistence.

THE FIRST OBJECT OF TRANSCENDENT KNOWLEDGE: Kālī, the Power of Time, and the Night-of-Eternity (Mahā-rātrī)

The Cycles of Time

We have seen that Śiva, as eternal time, was considered the substratum from which all the secondary cycles of time and the energies which rule them are formed, beginning with the cycles of creation and including all the cycles which determine the existence of universes, of solar systems, of atoms, and the cycles which rule the existence of species, of life, and of each day, each moment, each life.

The cycle of the day and night is, for us, the closest image of the cycle of time. It is a constant reminder of the rhythmic pattern of creation and dissolution of all that exists.

The Eternal Night

Absolute time is the measure of an eternal night. The concentrations of energy which give rise to light, to divisible time, are only temporary phenomena implying a location and some form of relative time. The state of deep sleep bears some resemblance to the absolute quiescence which spreads everywhere when the universe dissolves and all beings and forms enter into eternal sleep in the lap of the boundless night.

Deep sleep is for us an image of the total peace that follows the dissolution of the universe, of the stage where nothing remains but the transcendent power of Time, Mahā-Kālī, the absolute night.

We saw that the word Śiva can be derived from the root *śiṅ*, which means "to sleep." Hence Śiva is described as he in whom "all goes to sleep," "he who puts all things to sleep," etc. His power is represented by the eternal night in which all goes to sleep.

As absolute eternal time, Śiva is beyond the universe. He is the "Beyond the beyond" (*parāt paraḥ*) of the Upaniṣads. The absolute, indivisible night (Mahā-rātrī) is the abode of the Transcendent-power-of-Time (Mahā-Kālī).

"From the 'Hymn to the Night' (*Rātrī Sūkta* of the *Ṛg Veda* 10.127) we can understand that there are two divinities of night, the one experienced by mortal beings, the other by the divine Being; the one experienced by all the spheres and in relation to which all activities come daily to rest, the other in which the activity of divinity also comes to rest. This absolute night is the night of destruction, and is the nature of the Power-of-Time (Kālī). Nothing then remains except the transcendent Immensity checkered with its power of illusion. This stage is the stage of Unmanifest-Nature (*avyakta*)." (Karapātrī, "Śrī Bhagavatī tattva," *Siddhānta*, V [1944–45].)

"Night has for its substance the power of illusion of the Immensity (*brahmamāyātmikā*); the nature of night is dissolution into supreme divinity (*parameśalayātmikā*). The principle presiding over this absolute night is celebrated as the goddess-of-the-spheres (Bhuvaneśī)." (*Devī Purāṇa*. [495])

The approaching night, in her display, spreads over the twilight, which is but the reflected remnant of an apparent consciousness, itself but the veiling-power (*āvaraṇa-śakti*) of ignorance (*avidyā*), of unconsciousness. It seems to us impossible that night may ever entirely drive away twilight, as well as all remnants of thought or perception, but the absolute night is the ultimate form of consciousness, and when perception of all appearances vanishes, she appears supremely resplendent. By comparison with her, twilight and dawn are but obscurity. Just as dawn vanishes when the sun rises, so also the veiling power of ignorance dissolves when illumined by the power of consciousness. When the veiling power which appears to us as light is consumed to its root, and "previous deeds" (*prārabdha*) cease to bear consequences, then the nontranscendent darkness which is the root-of-unknowing (*mūla-ajñāna*) is forever destroyed.

"May the divinity of night (Rātrī), the transcendent power of consciousness (*cit-śakti*), be pleased, so that we may nestle in happiness like birds in their nests at night. Dwellers in the villages, their cows and horses, the birds of the air, men who travel on many a business, and jackals and wild beasts, all welcome the night and joyfully nestle in her; for to all beings misguided by the journey of the day she brings calm and happiness. Then all comes to rest. Even those beings who have never heard the name of the lady-of-the-spheres (Bhuvaneśvarī) come to her lap, where they sleep as happily as unconscious children. O merciful! O power of consciousness! O enfolding darkness! O divinity of night! Overlook our deeds; take us away from the killers who harm us, the wolf that is sin, and the she-wolf that is never-ending desire. Remove us from lust and the other passions which rob us of wisdom and wealth, and be for us the ship of gladness that brings us to the other shore and leads us to beatitude." (Karapātrī, "Śrī Bhagavatī tattva.")

The word *rātrī* (night) is symbolically derived from the root *rā*, "to give," and is taken to mean "the giver" of bliss, of peace, of happiness.

Kālī, the Power of Time

The chief quality of the eternal night is eternity, that is, the transcendent power of Time, Mahā-Kālī, also called the Origin (Ādyā) or the First-Power (Prathamā). Conceived as a divinity, the Power of Time is represented as a goddess, consort of the aspect of Śiva known as Transcendent-Time (Mahā-Kāla).

Time (Kāla) is that "which dissociates all things." It is considered the cosmological aspect of Śiva, the Destroyer. "I am Time, ever inclined to destroy the worlds," says the *Bhagavadgītā*. Kālī, the feminine form of the word *kāla*, is taken to represent the "energy "or "power" of time.

The Image of Kālī

The *Kālī Tantra* depicts the image of Kālī:

"Most fearful, her laughter shows her dreadful teeth. She stands upon a corpse. She has four arms. Her hands hold a sword and a head and show the gestures of removing fear and granting boons. She is the auspicious divinity of sleep, the consort of Śiva.

"Naked, clad only in space, the goddess is resplendent. Her tongue hangs out. She wears a garland of heads. Such is the form worthy of meditation of the Power of Time, Kālī, who dwells near the funeral pyres." (*Kālī Tantra.* [496])

THE CORPSE

Kālī is represented as the supreme night, which swallows all that exists. She therefore stands upon "nonexistence," upon the corpse of the ruined universe. So long as the power that gives life to the universe remains predominant it is favorable (*śiva*), but when it is without strength it becomes as a corpse (*śava*). Hence it is said that without *i*, symbol of his power, the lord-of-life (Śiva) is a corpse (*śava*). The lifeless body is indeed the symbol of whatever is left of the manifested universe when it reverts to the sole control of eternal time. At the time of universal destruction, the Power of Time, the power of destruction, is all that remains. It can well be represented as standing upon the debris of a universe in ruins, which lies powerless as a corpse.

THE FEARFUL APPEARANCE

At the end of the fight, when the warrior "finishes" the vanquished enemy and remains alone on the field of battle, his appearance inspires no emotion but fear. Who could dare to look him in the face? So terrible is Kālī. Her dread appearance is the symbol of her boundless power of destruction.

THE LAUGHTER

The conqueror laughs in his triumph. That laughter is the expression of absolute dominion over all that exists. It mocks at those who, in the folly of their vanity, hope to escape.

THE FOUR ARMS

The four arms of Kālī represent the four directions of space identified with the complete cycle of time. Completeness is usually represented by the four corners. With her four arms, she stands as the symbol of the fulfillment of all and of the absoluteness of her dominion over all that exists. In the strict language of symbolism four arms always represent the idea of absolute dominion. This is also the meaning of the cross.

THE SWORD

The sword represents the power of destruction.

THE SEVERED HEAD

The warrior keeps as a trophy the head of his victim. This trophy shows to the living the fate they must expect. The severed head in the hand of the Goddess reminds all living beings that there is no escape from the Omnipotence-of-Time (Kālī).

THE HAND REMOVING FEAR

So long as there is existence, there is fear of destruction. Fear is inherent in all forms of existence; fear is the law of all that exists. "Out of fear of him fire burns; out of fear the sun shines." (*Kaṭha Upaniṣad* 2.3.3. [497])

All that has a limit fears what is beyond its limit. Only absolute time (*mahā-kalā*) which pervades all things and has no limit knows no fear. The Upaniṣads say that he alone who exists "beyond the beyond" "exists without fear." Kālī, the power of time that destroys all, is the embodiment of all fear, while she herself is beyond fear; she alone who is beyond fear can protect from fear those who invoke her. This is the meaning of the hand removing fear.

THE GIVING HAND

All the pleasures of the world are transient; all human joy is but a momentary and feeble perception of our true nature, which is unbounded joy. But such perception cannot last and is soon veiled by pain. True happiness can only exist in that which is permanent. Only the Power of Time is permanent; it alone can grant happiness. Thus Kālī is the giver of bliss. This is represented by her giving hand.

THE GARLAND OF SKULLS

Life and death are inseparable. There is no life without death, no death without life. Hence there must be a common support for life and death. She who supports the living as well as the dead is the supreme happiness. She is the only help of the living and the only help of the dead. All life rests on her, and on her also depends whatever remains after life. Death is not immediate, total annihilation. The dead leave traces behind which also rest upon her; hence she is represented as wearing on her breast a garland of skulls, the skulls that once carried life and are left behind as the reminders of death.

THE NAKEDNESS

The universe which is created and pervaded by the eternal power of time is also its veil. "Having created it, he entered it." (*Taittirīya Upaniṣad* 2.6. [498]) When the universe is destroyed, the Power of Time remains without a veil, naked. Hence the Goddess is "clad in space" (*digambarā*), having the vast emptiness of space as her only vesture.

THE FUNERAL PYRE

She is to be found near the funeral pyre of the world in destruction. There alone is she to be attained. Hence she is spoken of as dwelling near funeral grounds.

THE BLACK COLOR

Being the embodiment of the tendency toward dispersion or obscuration (*tamas*), Kālī is black. But why should the primordial energy, "of whom the sun and the moon are the eyes" and "by whose light the world is illumined," [1] be spoken of as black, as dark like the fearful clouds of the hour of destruction? It is replied that she is dark because she is the ultimate energy, in which all distinctions disappear. In the Power of Time all colors dissolve into darkness. All shapes return to shapelessness in the all-pervading darkness of the eternal night.

The Dual Aspect of Kālī

In the hierarchy of manifestation, Kālī stands as the highest, the most abstract, aspect of divinity. In a world where joy is linked with attachment, she represents a stage beyond all attachments and thus appears to us fearful. To reach supreme bliss man has to abandon, one after another, all the things dear to him, all that is his joy as a living being. It is not surprising that the stage attained by renouncing all that seems desirable should appear from outside as the most fearful darkness. Yet it is only by facing this inevitable reality, which seems at first the sum of all terrors, that man may gradually realize that this stage which terrifies him represents the essence of all that is to be desired, the bound-

1 *Kālī Tantra.*

less supreme bliss. If the supreme stage, the stage beyond manifestation, was but nothingness, death would mean annihilation, and Kālī, as the one who destroys all that is manifest, would be nothing more than the embodiment of universal fear. But beyond forms, beyond death, beyond existence, there is a supreme stage which is absolute joy. Kālī is fearful only relatively, from the point of view of existence and worldly enjoyment. When, in the course of man's spiritual adventure, the relative is transgressed, his individuality dissolves into the primordial infinite joy.

Kālī, the power of destruction, has thus a dual aspect. She is, from the point of view of finite existence, the fearful destroyer of all that exists. As such she is known as the Power of Time and her male counterpart, known as Kāla in cosmology, is called Rudra, the lord of tears, or Bhairava, "the wrathful," in the religious scriptures. But when all is destroyed and the Power of Time is appeased, the true nature of the eternal night reveals itself as limitless joy, as eternal peace. In this respect Kālī is known as the Transcendent-Night (Mahā-rātrī) or as the Power-of-Ether (Pārvatī). Her counterpart is known as the auspicious lord-of-sleep (Śiva) or the Abode-of-Joy (Śambhu).

The Purāṇas and the Tantras describe eight main representations of Kālī corresponding to the eight main aspects of Śiva. These aspects of Kālī are called Dakṣiṇā, Bhadrā, Guhyā, etc.

In some of the Hindu Scriptures Kālī is given a prominent place. In the chapter of the *Mahābhārata* just preceding the *Bhagavadgītā* Arjuna invokes the three aspects of Kālī.

"I bow to you, leader of the Realized, noble-goddess (Āryā) who dwells in heaven. O tenebrous maiden garlanded with skulls, tawny, bronze-dark, I bow to you who are the auspicious Power of Time, the Transcendent-power-of-Time (Mahā-Kālī)." (*Mahābhārata* 6.23.4–5. [499])

THE SECOND OBJECT OF TRANSCENDENT KNOWLEDGE: Tārā, the Star, the Power of Hunger, and the Night-of-Anger (Krodha-rātrī)

THE STAR (Tārā) is the power of the Golden-Embryo (Hiraṇya-garbha), the first cosmic location from which the world develops. As soon as the germ of life appears, hunger is born. Nothing exists but by devouring something else. The embryo wants only food. Only through combustion, through devouring some fuel, some food, can the universe survive and develop. This perpetual hunger is the source of the cosmic sacrifice, as well as of all the forms of existence and life. The nature of the Golden Embryo can well be said to be hunger. His power lies in his ability to devour. The name given to this pure, this absolute, hunger is "the Star" (Tārā).

Tārā appears in the cosmic immensity as a source of light, a combustion, a devouring. "In the night of time, which is the state of universal dissolution, light [the first combustion, the first satisfied hunger] appears as a star. This light is the nature, the source, of all thought [for thought is also an energy, a combustion] and is the instrument of knowledge illuminating its object." (Karapātrī, "Śrī Bhagavatī tattva.")

The word *tārā* means a star, but the Tantras take its etymology to mean "that which leads to the other shore."

"She who brings us to the other shore (*tarati*) is Tārā." [2]

"She who deserves to be served by Brahmā, Viṣṇu, and the Great-God (Maheśvara), she who creates, nourishes, and destroys the world, who supports the universe and destroys the fear inherent in existence, she who alone can prevent rebirth is the Supreme Energy, the boat with the help of which the ocean of the world may be crossed." (A Tantra quoted in Hīrānanda Śāstrī Gauḍ's "Tārā-rahasya," *Kalyāṇa*, Śakti aṅka, p. 224. [500])

Because it was all hunger, the Golden Embryo was at first terrible, devouring all substance, all form, all thought, all knowledge. When it found food, it became pacified. Thus Tārā has a dual aspect, the one fierce, fearful, all-devouring, the other pacified and luminous. This is also the nature of the sun and of all beings.

Hunger need not be merely a desire for physical foods. The search for knowledge, the desire for strength, are also forms of hunger. All that leads man toward his goal comes therefore under the form of a desire, a hunger, and is part of the kingdom of Tārā.

Tārā and Kālī

In the waste of the boundless all-devouring Time, the all-devouring hunger appears. Tārā is but a manifestation of Kālī with whom she shares the dominion of the void that is the substratum of the universe.

"In the Great Void, the sphere of the Egg-of-Immensity that is the universe (Brahmāṇḍa), there exist fifty forms of void. Five of these are the kingdom of the power-of-hunger (Tārā); the rest belong to the power-of-time (Kālī)." (Quoted in Karapātrī's "Śrī Bhagavatī tattva." [501])

2 *Taratyanayā sā tārā.* (Quoted in the *Devī-sahasra-nāma.*)

"The Transcendent-power-of-Time (Mahā-kālī) was the ruling-deity (*adhiṣṭhātrī*) of universal-destruction (*mahā-pralaya*). The fearful Tārā is the deity of the 'destruction of a solar system' (*sūrya-pralaya*). To destroy is the law (*dharma*), the nature of both deities. Therefore there is little difference in the 'mental picture for meditation' (*dhyāna*) of both deities." (Motilāl Śarmā Gauḍ, "Daśa Mahā-vidyā," *Kalyāṇa*, Śakti aṅka, p. 89.)

In the cycle of day and night, Tārā represents early dawn, the hunger, the desire, that first appears after the calm of sleep, after the rule of Kālī. Hence Tārā rules from midnight to dawn. This is the Night-of-Anger (Krodha-rātrī) when every living thing prepares to destroy and devour other lives, other beings.

The Representation of the Void

In its peaceful aspect, the power of hunger is merely spoken of as a void.

"She is the transcendent form of the Void, the divider (*kalā*), the Supreme-Beauty (Mahā-sundarī). Beautiful, she commands the king of kings. Boundless, she is the ruler of the vast universe.

"She is the Great Void, the Star from which all was gradually evolved and which leads all toward liberation from the endless [cycle of life]." (*Mahāsundarī Tantra.* [502])

"All deities are aspects of the Void. The universe arose from the Void and dissolves into the Void. Seeing the Void as the goal of the universe, the sages, leaving a world of delusion (*moha*), dissolve into the Void, into the changeless shape of the Immensity." (Hīrānanda Śāstrī Gauḍ, "Tārā-rahasya," p. 225.)

So long as food is provided, so long as offerings are poured into the fearful solar fire, the cosmic sun is at peace, but if food is lacking the sun becomes the Fearful-Star (Ugra-Tārā) and devours the worlds.

Other Aspects of Tārā

Jains and Buddhists worship the goddess Tārā. For the Buddhists as for the Hindus hunger is eternal. In the Buddhist Scripture Tārā is represented as the power of Avalokiteśvara. In the Tantras she is the consort of the Never-decaying (Akṣobhya) aspect of Śiva.

"O great goddess, without decaying, Śiva, the lord of sleep, drank the *hālāhala* poison, hence he is known as the Never-decaying (Akṣobhya). The transcendent power of illusion, ever in lustful dalliance with him, is the Star, Tārā." (*Tārā Tantra.*[3] [503])

3 Texts of the Tantras from which some of the quotations are drawn, namely, nos. 503, 504, 510, 512, 514–18, are available in *Śākta Pramoda* (Bombay, 1931).

In the Jain tradition this divinity appears under the name of Su-tārā or Su-tārakā, the "Good Star." According to the Śvetāmbara sect she is a semi-goddess, a *yakṣinī*, and is the ruling-deity (*śāsana-devī*) of the Jain prophet Suvidhinātha. Among the primitive tribes of India she is worshiped as Tārā.

The Mother-Star (Tārā-ambā) mentioned in the *Brahmāṇḍa Purāṇa* seems to be a different deity.

The Image of Tārā

Tārā is always depicted in her fearful form with four arms entwined with poisonous snakes and serpents in her matted hair. She holds a head and a chalice, for in her fearsome mood she drinks blood, the sap of the world.

"Standing firmly with her left foot forward resting on a corpse, she laughs loudly—transcendent. Her hands hold a sword, a blue lotus, a dagger, and a begging bowl. She raises her war cry, *huṁ!* Her matted tawny hair is bound with poisonous blue snakes. Thus the terrifying Tārā destroys the unconsciousness of the three worlds and carries them on her head [to the other shore]." (*Tārā Tantra*. [504])

"She shines upon a white lotus arisen from the water, pervading the world. She holds in her hands scissors, a sword, a skull, and a blue lotus. Her ornaments are snakes, which form a girdle, earrings, a garland, armlets, bracelets, anklets. She has three red eyes, fearful tawny tresses, a wagging tongue, fearful teeth. Round the hips she wears the skin of a panther. She wears a diadem made of bleached bones. One should meditate on Tārā, the mother of the three worlds, who is seated on the heart of a corpse, her face resplendent with the power of the Never-decaying (Akṣobhya)." (*Tārā Tantra*, quoted in Hīrānanda Śāstrī Gauḍ's "Tārā-rahasya," *Kalyāṇa*, Śakti aṅka, 1938. [505])

As the star Tārā is the ship's pilot and is shown holding a rudder. A ship is shown on her image at Kanheri.

The Worship of Tārā

The Tantras specify that the goddess is to be worshiped according to the Buddhist ritual. Otherwise her worship remains fruitless.

"The proper way to worship me is the Buddhist way. O Tormentor of Men! That way one man alone knows; none other knows its inner significance." (*Lalitā-upākhyāna*. [506])

In the *Ācāra Tantra*, the sage Vasiṣṭha is said to have vainly attempted to worship this divinity and to have lost courage. Then a voice from the sky told him to worship in the Chinese way (*cīnācāra*). He went to China and learned to worship Tārā and succeeded in pleasing the goddess.

THE THIRD OBJECT OF TRANSCENDENT KNOWLEDGE: Ṣoḍaśī, the Girl-of-Sixteen, the Power of Perfection, and the Divine-Night (Divya-rātrī)

THE SUN is the source of our universe. Everything that exists on the earth, substance, form, thought, knowledge, etc., must trace its origin to the solar substance. The peaceful manifest aspect of the Golden-Embryo (Hiraṇya-garbha) which appears to us as the sun, the source of our life, is connected with the number 5 and with the five elements and is represented in the five-faced Śiva. In him the full cycle of perfected being, of accomplished creation, is realized, hence he is also associated with the number taken to represent perfection, totality, that is, the number 16. The power of the five-faced Śiva is known as the Girl-of-Sixteen. In every form of existence perfection is linked with this number. In human life sixteen years represent the age of accomplished perfection, after which decline sets in; sixteen days form the completed lunar cycle from the new moon to the full moon. The full moon is the moon of sixteen days. The Girl-of-Sixteen rules over all that is perfect, complete, beautiful.

After dawn, after the hour of the Star (Tārā), comes the hour of perfection. The young sun has risen in its fullness; its fierceness has not yet appeared. It seems gentle, bright, auspicious (*śiva*). In the morning sun men worship the Progenitor, the principle that gives life to the three worlds and to all the mortals and immortals.

The Girl-of-Sixteen, the power of Śiva as the ruler of the three worlds, is, according to the *Ṣoḍaśī Tantra*, identified with the Belle-of-the-Three-Cities (Tripura-sundarī), said to be the light radiating from the three eyes of Śiva to illumine the worlds. Hence she is "the Girl-of-Sixteen in whom the three forms of light unite." (Ibid. [507])

Indra, the wielder of the thunderbolt, is a solar aspect of Śiva, hence he is sometimes identified with the Girl-of-Sixteen.

"Indra is Ṣoḍaśī" (*Śatapatha Brāhmaṇa* 4.2.5.14. [508])

In the *Ṣoḍaśī Tantra* [509] we find the description of the Girl-of-Sixteen:

"I salute the auspicious goddess who shines like the orb of an infant sun, has four arms and three eyes, and holds a noose, an elephant hook, an arrow, and a bow."

As a form of the eternal night, Ṣoḍaśī is the Divine-Night (Divya-rātrī), the night of perfection.

THE FOURTH OBJECT OF TRANSCENDENT KNOWLEDGE:
Bhuvaneśvarī, the Lady of the Spheres, the Power of Knowledge, and the Night-of-Realization (Siddha-rātrī)

ONCE THE three worlds have been created, the universe matures, the Girl-of-Sixteen (Ṣoḍaśī) makes place for the resplendent lady-of-the-spheres (Bhuvaneśvarī), consort of the Three-eyed Śiva (Tryambaka). Creation now becomes a powerful flow, a constant evolving, over which rules the Sovereign Goddess. As the ruler of the universe she is also known as the Queen-of-Queens (Rāja-rājeśvarī).

She is depicted in the *Bhuvaneśvarī Tantra.*

"With the moon as her diadem, with large breasts and three eyes, smiling, she shines like the risen sun. Her hands grant boons, allay fears, and hold an elephant hook and a noose. I bow to the fear-inspiring lady of the spheres." (*Bhuvaneśvarī Tantra.* [510])

"With the ambrosia made from the lunar essence, that is, the seed, the sacrificial offering, *soma*, she quenches the thirst of the world. This is why the all-powerful goddess has the moon, the cup of *soma*, as her diadem. She takes care of the three worlds and feeds them, so one of her emblems is the gesture-of-granting-boons (*vara mudrā*). The sign of her kindness is her smile. The emblems of her ruling powers are the elephant-driving hook and the noose.

"The lady of the spheres is represented with various attributes. In the lower of her right hands she holds a chalice, in the upper right hand a mace, in the upper left hand a shield, in the lower left hand the *bilva* fruit, called the fruit-of-Fortune (*śrī-phala*). On her head are a serpent, a *liṅga*, and a *yoni.* Preciously colored like molten gold, the all-powerful goddess wears a divine garland and gold ornaments.

"Her marvelous radiance illumines the universe. The fruit in her hand shows her as the giver of the fruit of actions. Her club is the 'power to act' or 'power of dispersion' (*vikṣepa śakti*). The 'power of knowing' (*jñāna śakti*) is her shield; the 'tendency toward liberation, toward the Fourth stage' (*turīya vṛtti*), is the chalice which contains the sap of existence, that is, delight in the Self. The *liṅga* is the male principle (*puruṣa tattva*), the Cosmic Man; the *yoni* represents Nature (*prakṛti tattva*). The serpent is 'Time' (*kāla tattva*).

"Placed on her head, the serpent, the *liṅga*, and the *yoni* show her to be the manifest form of the Transcendent-Immensity, the Para-Brahman, which supports the trinity of Nature, Person, and Time (*kāla*).

"The lady of the spheres, as the embodiment of transcendent knowledge that sustains the world, is said to represent the totality of the everlasting knowledge, fragments of which are revealed in the Vedas. The lady of the spheres is not really different from the divinity of knowledge, Sarasvatī, the power that protects the worlds, although her attributes appear to be distinct." (Karapātrī, "Śrī Bhagavatī tattva.")

As a form of the eternal night Bhuvaneśvarī is the Night-of-Realization (Siddha-rātrī), the veil made of knowledge which surrounds the universe.

THE FIFTH OBJECT OF TRANSCENDENT KNOWLEDGE:

Chinnamastā, the Beheaded, the Power of the Sacrifice, and the Night-of-Courage (Vīra-rātrī)

ONCE THE world has reached a state of stability, it continues to exist, depending for its sustenance on destruction, on burning, on devouring. The cosmic sacrifice expresses this constant process, and the ritual sacrifices performed by man have for their purpose a conscious co-operation with the cosmic life; this is the purpose of rites in all religions, and ritual is always a form of sacrifice.

The aspect of Śiva which presides over the cosmic sacrifice is the Headless (Kabandha).

The Vedic ritual of sacrifice consists in beheading the victim.

"The sacrifice is indeed beheaded." (*Śatapatha Brāhmaṇa.* [511]) Hence the power of the sacrifice is shown in the Beheaded (Chinnamastā).

The first offering from which life springs forth is an offering of semen; the full offering is the blood of a mature victim. From the latter offering is derived the food upon which we live. The taking of life, the feeding upon life, when understood as a participation in a cosmic, eternal process, can become a means of realization, instead of being merely an unconscious participation in a cosmic process. Hence the conscious man should partake only of sacrificed flesh, and the first fruits of all produce should be offered to the deity.

The whole system of the created universe is divided into five forms of ritual sacrifice. The Beheaded rules over them all. Among men the five sacrifices are those to the elements (*bhūta yajña*), to men (*manuṣya yajña*), to Ancestors (*pitṛ yajña*), to gods (*deva yajña*), and to the Immensity (*brahma yajña*). The last is identified with the study of the Scripture.

Details regarding the symbolism of beheading can be found in the Purāṇas in the tale of Hayagrīva, where the head of the sleeping Viṣṇu is cut off.

At the end of the ritual sacrifice there is a ceremony called the "joining of the head" (*śiro-sandhāna*), in which the head is symbolically reattached to the body of the victim. This represents the consummation of the cycle, the ultimate resurrection of all forms, without which the meaning of the sacrifice would remain incomplete.

The solar radiation (*pravargya*) is also a constant offering. The life of the sun, poured into the world so that it may live, is the essence from which food (*anna*) takes its substance. This solar radiation is compared to a perpetual beheading of the sun and as such the Beheaded represents the life-giving and life-destroying power of the sun.

In Buddhism the Beheaded is shown as the Power-of-the-Thunderbolt (Vajra-yoginī). Her philosophical form is Prajñā-pāramitā.

The Tantras describe the Beheaded as follows:

"Her left foot forward in battle, she holds her severed head and a knife. Naked, she drinks voluptuously the stream of the blood-nectar flowing from her beheaded body. The jewel on her forehead is tied with a serpent. She has three eyes. Her breasts are adorned with lotuses. Inclined toward lust, she sits erect above the god of love, who shows signs of lustfulness. She looks like the red China rose." (*Chinnamastā Tantra.* [512]) Her eyes are blue.

As a form of the eternal night Chinnamastā is the Night-of-Courage (Vīra-rātrī) when the victim is brought to the altar of sacrifice.

THE SIXTH OBJECT OF TRANSCENDENT KNOWLEDGE:
Bhairavī, the Fearful Goddess, the Power of Death, and the Night-of-Death (Kāla-rātrī)

CHINNAMASTĀ represents the end of things, the spectacular moment when the victim is sacrificed, beheaded; life, existence, comes to an abrupt end.

But this sudden end is only the culmination of a process that began long before. Destruction begins from the very first moment of existence. Death is ever present, ever at work, in everything. This aspect of death is called the perpetual-destruction (*nitya-pralaya*).

The fire of destruction is believed to dwell in the southern direction. Yama, the king of death, is the ruler of the south, while Soma, the "essence of life," of love (*sneha tattva*), dwells in the north. The aspect of Rudra representing the divinity of death is the southern aspect. It is called the Southern-Image (Dakṣiṇā-mūrti) or the Time-of-the-Fearful (Kāla-Bhairava).

The power of this all-pervading ruler of death is the Fearful-Goddess, Bhairavī, also called the Fearful-Goddess-of-the-Three-Cities (Tripurā-Bhairavī). All that the lady-of-the-spheres (Bhuvaneśvarī) protects, the Fearful Goddess ceaselessly destroys. She is the Tangible-Demoness (Aparā-Ḍākinī), ever near, ever to be felt. Her soft and gentle hand slowly, voluptuously, silently, does the work of death.

"Softly smiling, you shine with a crimson glow that may be compared to a thousand newly risen suns. You wear a silken veil and a garland of skulls. Blood smears your breast. Three voluptuous eyes adorn your lotus face; the moon is your diadem. Your lotus hands show the gestures of victory, of wisdom, the granting of boons, and the allaying of fear." (*Tripurā-bhairavī Tantra.*[513])

THE SEVENTH OBJECT OF TRANSCENDENT KNOWLEDGE:
Dhūmāvatī, the Smoky One, the Power of Poverty, and the Night-of-Frustration (Dāruṇa-rātrī)

ONCE ALL is destroyed, the universe goes into smoke; hence the power of ultimate destruction is called the Smoky-One (Dhūmāvatī). She has destroyed the body of things, that is, the male emblem that is the universe, hence she is called a widow (*vidhavā*). Nothing is left for her to own, hence she is utterly destitute. She is the goddess-of-poverty (Daridrā), of frustration, of despair, identified with Mis-fortune (A-lakṣmī) and with the divinity-of-disease-and-misery (Nirṛti), "the fearful poverty that is Nirṛti" [514].

Her visage can be seen in the destitute, the beggars, the lepers, the diseased. She dwells in the wounds-of-the-earth (*kṣatavikṣatā-pṛthivī*), in deserts, ruined houses, tatters, hunger, thirst, widowhood, quarrels, the mourning of children, etc.

"She appears as a woman of unhealthy complexion, restless, wicked, tall, with a dirty robe and disheveled hair. With gaps in her teeth, she looks like a widow, and holds in her hand a winnowing basket. Her eyes seem cruel, her hands tremble, her nose is long. She behaves deceitfully and is sly in her looks. Insatiably hungry and thirsty, she inspires fear and is the instigator of quarrels." (*Dhūmāvatī Tantra.* [515])

Dhūmāvatī rules over the rainy season. For four months the solar light is hidden by the evil water-spirit (*asura-āpya-prāṇa*). This corresponds in the cosmic cycle to the night of the gods when the spirits of darkness rule. The night of Dhūmāvatī is the Night-of-Death (Kāla-rātrī). No ritual can be performed during that time, no pilgrimage, no marriage, no initiation. At the end of that period the rule of light returns and the festival of lights (*dīpāvalī*) takes place. The peaceful reign of Kamalā begins.

THE EIGHTH OBJECT OF TRANSCENDENT KNOWLEDGE:
The Deceitful, Crane-headed Bagalā, the Power of Cruelty, and the Second Night-of-Courage (Vīra-rātrī)

IN ALL those who create is found a subtle desire to destroy all but themselves. This desire to kill, to destroy, is reflected in the heart of every microcosm, of every living being. This secret desire which, without our knowledge, guides many of our actions is represented as a woman with the head of a crane, the gentle-looking crane being considered the most deceitful of all animals. This goddess is called the Crane-headed, Bagalā-mukhī.

The Crane-headed presides over all the subtle forms of killing. She is the goddess of black magic, of poisons. She rules over the subtle perception which make us feel at a distance the death or misery of those we know. She incites men to torture one another. She revels in suffering.

"I bow to the two-armed goddess who with the right hand grasps the tongue of her enemy and with her left hand tortures him. She holds a mace and is clad in yellow." (*Bagalāmukhī Tantra.* [516])

Her consort is the One-faced (Ekavaktra) Rudra.

The night of Bagalā is identical to that of Chinnamastā. It is the Night-of-Courage (Vīra-rātrī), the time of suffering.

THE NINTH OBJECT OF TRANSCENDENT KNOWLEDGE:
Mātaṅgī, the Elephant Power, the Power of Domination, and the Night-of-Delusion (Moha-rātrī)

THE ELEPHANT, king of beasts, is the mount of kings and the symbol of royal power, the power of domination. Indra, the king of heaven, is shown riding on an elephant. Śiva, as the world ruler, the dispenser of justice, the embodiment of kingly virtues, the destroyer of evil, is known as the Elephant (Mataṅga).

After the terror of the night appears the reassuring sunlight. The demons are defeated; Mātaṅgī, the Elephant power, establishes the rule of peace, of calm, of prosperity.

"We meditate on Mātaṅgī, the Elephant power, delight of the world. Dark, with a white crescent in her garland, and with three lotus eyes, she sits resplendent on a jeweled throne, fulfilling the wishes of her devotees. Her two feet are honored by the hosts of the gods. She shines like a blue lotus, resembling the forest fire which consumes the abode of the demons. Holding in her four beautiful lotus hands a noose, a sword, a shield, and an elephant hook, she gives to those who invoke her all they may wish for." (*Mātaṅgī Tantra.* [517])

The day is, however, a dream, a mirage that appears in the eternal night. As a form of night, Mātaṅgī is therefore the Night-of-Delusion (Moha-rātrī).

THE TENTH OBJECT OF TRANSCENDENT KNOWLEDGE: The Lotus-Girl, Kamalā, the Power of Wealth, and the Night-of-Splendor (Mahā-rātrī)

THE LOTUS-GIRL (Kamalā) is the consort of the Everlasting-Śiva (Sadā-Śiva) who protects the world and can be identified with an aspect of Viṣṇu. She is the embodiment of all that is desirable, the exact counterpart of the Smoky-One (Dhūmāvatī). The signs of the zodiac in which the two divinities are said to dwell are in opposition. Kamalā rules over the auspicious Rohiṇī sign (Taurus), giver of wealth, while Dhūmāvatī dwells in the Jyeṣṭhā sign (Scorpio) which brings poverty.

"With a golden complexion, bathed in the stream of ambrosia flowing from golden vessels held by the trunks of four white elephants, she looks like the abode of snow, the Himālaya. Her hands grant boons, allay fear, and hold two lotuses. She has a brilliant diadem. Her hips, like ripe fruits, are loosely draped in a silken garment. We bow to her who stands upon a lotus." (*Kamalā Tantra.* [518])

Kamalā is identified with Lakṣmī, the goddess of Fortune. Many of the popular representations of Lakṣmī are really images of Kamalā.

The aspect of the eternal night corresponding to Kamalā bears the same name, Mạhā-rātrī, as the night of Kālī but is interpreted to mean the Night of Splendor.

Some Other Aspects of the Goddess

THERE ARE as many aspects of the Goddess as there are gods or aspects of creation. Among the goddesses a few are more prominently worshiped. But this seems to have varied considerably in different periods.

Umā

THE WORD *umā* is said to mean "light," although it is often interpreted as meaning "the peace of the night," a very suitable name for the consort of the lord-of-sleep (Śiva). The first known mention of the Goddess as Umā is in the *Kena Upaniṣad*, where she is a mediatrix between Brahmā and the other gods. As a divinity she is sometimes identified with Speech (Vāc).

"Umā is the eternal knowledge, whose shape is limitless space. In every part of the boundless energy of Rudra dwells his power of illusion as the seed (*bīja*) of the universe, just as the power of the mighty banyan tree dwells in every tiny seed. Umā is the power of germination; she is orderly creation and as such different from Māyā, who is incidental, indiscriminate happening." (Śaṅkarānanda Giri, "Umā," *Kalyāṇa*, Śakti aṅka, p. 48.)

"From the point of view of the 'philosophy of nondual power' (Śakti-advaita), light, the nature of which is pure knowing, is considered to be the 'essence called the lord of sleep' (Śiva tattva). The conscious thought (*vimarśa*) that appears within this light is its power (*śakti*). Together with light, the existence of a power of perception of thought-form is a necessity. Without light there could be no perception and without perception no light. A conscious mind must be present at every stage. Even when the veils of ignorance are removed, the possibility of thought remains by itself as an oriented motion." (Karapātrī, "Śrī Bhagavatī tattva," *Siddhānta*, V, 1944–45, 173.)

The Unborn or the She-Goat (Ajā)

THE WORD *ajā* means both "she-goat" and "the unborn." The she-goat is taken as the symbol of Unmanifest Nature (*avyakta*).

"One single she-goat (*ajā*), red, white, and black, gives birth to many small ones which look just like her. One he-goat, enjoying her, follows her. The others, having enjoyed her, abandon her." (*Taittirīya Āraṇyaka* 10.10.1. [519])

"Like the She-Goat, Nature (*prakṛti*), made of the three qualities, gives birth to the world. First to be born is the universal Intellect, the transcendent-principle (*mahat*). In it, too, are found the three fundamental qualities. Its black quality is the tendency toward disintegration, the nature of which is to veil. Its white quality is the tendency toward concentration, the nature of which is to give light. Its red quality is the revolving tendency, the nature of which is enjoyment. Some of the goats, after enjoying the spotted she-goat whose children are likewise spotted, still follow her, while others, having enjoyed her, abandon her. So also some living beings, after enjoying Nature, follow her who, spotted with the three qualities, procreates the world, while others, having enjoyed her, proceed toward another goal." (Karapātrī, "Śrī Bhagavatī tattva," p. 174.)

The Destroyer-of-the-Genii (Cāmuṇḍā)

CĀMUṆḌĀ IS an emanation of intellect symbolized by the goddess Beyond-Reach (Durgā). The *Mārkaṇḍeya Purāṇa* (87.5–7) gives a description of her: "From the forehead of the Mother (Ambikā, i.e., Durgā), contracted with frowns, sprang forth a black goddess of fearful aspect. She carried a sword, a noose, and a heavy mace. Round her neck was a garland of dead corpses. Dry, withered, and hideous, she was dressed in the hide of an elephant. Her mouth open, her tongue hanging out, her eyes bloodshot, she filled the quarters of heaven with her shouts."

The Coiled-Energy (Kuṇḍalinī)

IN THE microcosm the Goddess appears as a dormant energy, coiled like a serpent but able, when she wakes up, to destroy the illusion of life and lead to liberation.

In the macrocosm this coiled energy, when it begins to move and manifests itself, gives birth to the universe. When it coils round the supreme Śiva, the universe goes to sleep.

The Mother (Ambikā)

UNDER HER main manifest aspect, which is Nature (*prakṛti*), the Goddess is the mother of the world. She is invoked in the form of the solar-hymn (Sāvitṛ) in the twilight rituals (*sandhyā*) which every twice-born should perform at the conjunction of day and night and at midday and midnight.

As the world's mother the Goddess appears ever merciful. She forgives all, and is kind even to ungrateful sons, for "a bad son may be born, never a bad mother." (Śaṅkarācārya, *Aparādha-kṣamāpaṇa Stotra.* [520])

"She fights her enemies with skill, yet shows mercy toward them. She remains at heart a mother. Purifying her sons with her arrows, she sends them to heavenly worlds. Verily, all are the sons of the Mother. Who could be her enemy?" (Karapātrī, "Śrī Bhagavatī tattva," p. 174.)

The Seven-Mothers (Sapta-Mātṛkās)

THE GODDESS is depicted under seven motherly forms called the Seven Mothers or Mātṛkās. These in the "creation by the word" are identified with the seven matrices or vowels (five pure, two mixed: *e*, *o*), the basis of all language, language being the instrument of transmitted knowledge.

The seven mothers are called: the Power-of-the-Immense-Being (Brahmāṇī), consort of Brahmā; the Power-of-Universal-Dominion (Maheśvarī), consort of Śiva; the Power-of-Youth (Kaumārī), consort of Skanda; the Power-of-Pervasion (Vaiṣṇavī), consort of Viṣṇu; the Power-of-the-Boar (Vārāhī), consort of Varāha, the Boar incarnation; the Power-of-Might (Indrāṇī), consort of Indra; the Destroyer-of-Demons (Cāmuṇḍā).

Indrāṇī

INDRĀṆĪ, the consort of the king-of-heaven (Indra), is sometimes called Śacī (eloquence). She is also called Paulomī because she was the daughter of the demon Puloman. Indra killed Puloman and made her his wife.

Indrāṇī corresponds to the Sujātā of Buddhism.

The Destroyer of the Buffalo-Demon (Mahiṣa-asura-mardinī)[1]

A LONG WAR had been waged between the gods, led by Indra, and the antigods. The king of the antigods, the genie Mahiṣa (the Powerful), won the war and established himself in heaven. The gods wandered homeless on the earth. Then, guided by Śiva and Viṣṇu, they concentrated their powers which came forth from the mouth of each one in the form of a jet of fire. These flames united into a blazing sphere which took the shape of a goddess. The power of Śiva formed the head, that of Yama the hair, that of Viṣṇu the arms, that of the Moon the breasts, that of India the waist, that of Brahmā the feet. From the power of the Sun came the toenails, from the Vasus the fingernails, from Kubera the nose, from Prajāpati the teeth, and from Agni the eyes, from the Twilight (Sandhyā) the brows, from Vāyu the ears. Each god handed over his weapons to the goddess.

Riding a lion, the goddess whose name is Durgā (Beyond Reach) defeated the armies of the antigods and fought the genie Mahiṣa. Mahiṣa took many shapes to fight her and, finally, that of a buffalo, symbol of death. She pierced the throat of the buffalo, and when the genie tried to escape from the animal's body, she cut off his head with a sword and could thereafter restore heaven to the gods.

Minor Forms of the Goddess: *Yoginīs*, *Ḍākinīs*, *Grahīs*, *Bhairavīs*, and *Śākinīs*

Yoginīs are the attendants of Durgā. Originally they were eight, but later they became thirteen, then sixty-four. They are represented as ogresses or sorceresses.

The *ḍākinīs* are female imps, eaters of raw flesh. They are attendants of Kālī. Pūtanā, the demoness who attempted to poison the child Kṛṣṇa, was a *ḍākinī*.

The *grahīs* (seizers) are witches who enter into newborn babies and cause them to die.

Bhairavīs (fearful ones) are fearful-looking female servants of Śiva and of Durgā.

The *śākinīs* (able ones) are female demons, attendants of Durgā.

1 This story is told in the *Mārkaṇḍeya Purāṇa*, ch. 82 and 83. These chapters are reproduced in the *Durgā Saptaśati*. The same story is told more briefly in several other Purāṇas and in the *Mahābhārata*.

FIVE

Secondary Gods

{ 24 }

The Sons of Śiva

Gaṇapati or Gaṇeśa, the Lord of Categories

EVERYTHING WHICH our senses can perceive or our mind can grasp can be expressed in terms of kind, of category. Hence it is logical for us to consider category" as a fundamental element of existence. "All that can be counted or comprehended is a category (*gaṇa*)," [1] "the word 'category' meaning any collection of things." [2] The principle of all the classifications through which the relations between different orders of things, between the macrocosm and the microcosm, can be understood is called the lord-of-categories (Gaṇapati).

"Gaṇapati, the ruler of all categories," [3] can be identified with divinity in its perceptible manifestation. "I bow to you, lord of categories. You alone are the visible form of the principle. You alone are the creator, you alone are the sustainer, you alone are the destroyer, you alone are unmistakably the Principle-of-All (*brahma*), the true Self." (*Gaṇapati Upaniṣad* 2. [524])

"O Lord of Categories, thou art the lord, the seer of seers, unrivaled in wealth, king of elders, lord of the principle of principles. Hear us and take thy place, bringing with thee all enjoyments." (*Ṛg Veda* 2.31.1. [525])

The principle of categories transcends intellect. "The lord of categories rules over the universal-Intellect (*mahat-tattva*), and the principles-of-the-elements (*tattva*) derived from it." (Quoted in Karapātrī's *Śrī Bhagavat tattva*, p. 645. [526])

The Cult and the Names of Gaṇapati

Though named indirectly in the *Taittirīya Āraṇyaka* and in an interpolated passage of the *Maitrāyaṇī Saṁhitā*, Gaṇapati appears in his present form only

1 Karapātrī, *Śrī Bhagavat tattva* [521], p. 638.
2 Ibid. [522]
3 Ibid. [523]

with the *Mahābhārata*. The *Agni Purāṇa* and *Yājñavalkya Smṛti* briefly describe a ritual for him. In the *Yājñavalkya Smṛti* he is shown as a demoniacal being. He plays a significant part in Tantrism. The *Prapañcasāra Tantra* gives an elaborate description of him. For the followers of the Gāṇapatya sect he is the supreme divinity. He is one of the five divinities of the *smārta* cult. Several Purāṇas place him above the trinity (*trimūrti*).

Gaṇapati is sometimes identified with the Great-Lord (Bṛhaspati), the teacher of the gods, already mentioned in the *Ṛg Veda*.

The lord of categories is the patron of letters, of schools. He is the scribe who writes down the Scriptures. "You, leader of categories, are the writer of this [*Mahā-*] *Bhārata*." (*Mahābhārata* 1.1.77. [527]) The Brāhmaṇas accept him as the god of learning.

Success (Siddhi) and Prosperity (Ṛddhi) are Gaṇapati's wives.

Gaṇapati has many names. The main ones are Gaṇeśa (lord of categories), Vighneśvara (lord of obstacles), Vināyaka (great leader), Gajānana (elephant-faced), Gajādhipa (lord of elephants).

Gaṇeśa is also king-of-the-elders (Jyeṣṭha-rāja); he is first among the great and presides over the assembly of the gods.

The Birth of Gaṇapati

According to the *Śiva Purāṇa*, once Śiva's consort, the Lady-of-the-Mountain (Pārvatī), was disturbed by her lord, who entered the house while she was bathing.

Worried not to have a servant of her own to guard her door, she rubbed her body, and from some scurf she gathered a being was born whom she called her son and used as a guard. His name was Gaṇapati. When the boy attempted to prevent Śiva from entering the house, the god sent his squires against him and in the battle Gaṇapati's head was cut off. On seeing Pārvatī's sorrow over this deed, Śiva severed the head of the first living being that came his way and joined it to the child's body. This happened to be the head of an elephant.

In another myth (in the *Brahma-vaivarta Purāṇa*) it is the evil glance of Saturn (Śani) which blew off the child's head.

The Meaning of Gaṇapati and Its Relation to the Number Principle

Gaṇapati stands for one of the basic concepts of Hindu mythological symbolism, the identity of the macrocosm and the microcosm or, in religious terms, the notion that man is the image of God. This notion of the divinity of man and the immanence of God should be present before the mind whenever one begins anything, hence one should first bow to Gaṇeśa. Not only is he worshiped at the beginning of every enterprise, his image is seen at the entrance of every house, of every sanctuary.

The identity of the macrocosm and the microcosm can be observed in the permanence of the relations found as the substratum of all the aspects of the perceptible universe. These relations can best be expressed in terms of number. Hence number is easily seen as the common element of all forms, the all-pervading unity of all substance.

Elephant and Man [4]

Gaṇapati is represented as an elephant-headed man to express the unity of the small being, the microcosm, that is man, and the Great Being, the macrocosm, pictured as an elephant. The word "man" (*nara*) is defined as meaning "divinity qualified." The microcosms are the progeny of the Cosmic Being, hence "the beings born of the [universal] Man are known to the sages as men." (*Mahābhārata* 5.70.10. [528])

The word *gaja* (elephant) is taken to mean "the origin and the goal." "The stage reached by the reintegrated being, the yogi, in his experience of ultimate identification (*samādhi*) is called *ga*, the 'goal'; and the principle called *ja*, the 'origin,' is that from which the syllable-of-obeisance, AUM, is said to be issued through a process of multifold reflection." [529] The elephant is thus a symbol of the stage "whence existence begins" (*Brahma Sūtra* 1.1.4. [530]) and "whence the syllable AUM issues, from AUM as for the *Veda* the [universal law, i.e., the] *Veda*, and from the *Veda* the universe" [531].

The man part of Gaṇapati, representing the manifest Principle, is inferior to the unmanifest, shown as the elephant. The elephant part is therefore the head.

Thou Art That

In terms of the world a man cannot be an elephant, yet this can be true in terms of divinity, for divinity is that in which opposites coexist. This becomes evident when we trace each symbol to its essential meaning. The sacred utterance which represents Gaṇapati is "Thou art That" (*tat tvam asi*).

"Thou [the living being] art the visible form of That [the supreme essence]." (*Gaṇapati Upaniṣad* 2. [532])

4 The following description of Gaṇapati is based mainly on Swāmi Karapātrī's *Śrī Bhagavat tattva.*

The neuter pronoun "That" (*tat*) represents "the limitless, transcendent principle whose [nature] is truth and knowledge" (*Taittirīya Āraṇyaka* 8.1.1 [533]), aloof from all attributes. The pronoun "Thou" (*tvam*) represents "the qualified principle whose form is the universe." Both "That" and "Thou" are welded into an indivisible identity by the third term, "art" (*asi*), that is, by existence.

Human existence is the co-ordination of the absolute and the relative, of That and Thou. True knowledge is the realization of this unity.

The image of Gaṇapati constantly reminds us of the reality of this apparently impossible identity. Man is truly the image of the cosmos. All realization lies within himself. Through the study of our inner impulses and of our inner structure we can understand the nature of the universe.

The Remover of Obstacles

The lord of categories is the destroyer of obstacles.

"I bow to the son of Śiva, to the embodiment of the giver of gifts who destroys obstacles." (*Gaṇapati Upaniṣad* 15. [534])

After explaining the meaning of this text, Sāyaṇācārya adds: "He it is who, by giving immortality, removes the fear inherent in time and duration." (Commentary on ibid. [535]. Cited in Karapātrī's *Śrī Bhagavat tattva*, p. 646.)

In the *Skanda* and *Maudgala Purāṇas* is found the story of Prince Pleasing-to-All (Abhinandana), who offered a great sacrifice to the gods but omitted to invite Indra, the king of heaven. Hearing of this, Indra was angry; he summoned Time (Śiva as Kāla), the destroyer, and ordered him to put an end to the sacrifice. Time then took the shape of the genie Obstruction (Vighna-asūra), who killed Prince Abhinandana, and then wandered through the world, sometimes visible, sometimes invisible, obstructing all rites. Bewildered, Vasiṣṭha and the other sages went to the Creator Brahmā, seeking his protection. He ordered them to pray to the lord of categories, who alone is beyond Time, which no other deity has the power to conquer.

Vanquished by Gaṇeśa, the genie Obstruction placed himself under his protection and served him obediently. Thus it is that Gaṇeśa is also called lord-of-obstruction (Vighna-rāja). Should any work be undertaken without praying to and worshiping Gaṇeśa, obstacles will inevitably occur. Hence, in the auspicious "Invocation preliminary to all Sacrifices" (*Puṇyāha-vācana* [536]), we hear, "May the two gods Obstruction and its master be pleased."

The Image of Gaṇapati

Like every other Hindu deity, Gaṇapati can be represented through various symbols. There is therefore a *mantra* or sound representation, a *yantra* or graphic representation, and an icon or image of Gaṇapati.

The *mantra* or sound image of Gaṇapati is the monosyllable AUM uttered at the beginning of every rite. Its meaning is also expressed in the sacred formula *tat tvam asi*, "Thou art That," which represents the fundamental identity of the macrocosm and the microcosm.

The *svastika* is the graphic symbol of Gaṇeśa. It is made of a cross representing the development of the multiple from the basic unity, the central point, but each of its branches is bent so that it does not aim toward the center. This is intended to show that we cannot reach the basic unity directly through the outward forms of the universe. Hence the way toward the principle (*tattva*) is said to be "crooked."

There is also an elaborate diagram called the Gaṇeśa *yantra*, used for ritual worship. Another symbol of Gaṇapati is the stone Svarṇabhadra.

In the *Gaṇapati Upaniṣad* (11–14 [537]) the image of the deity is described.

> *He has one tusk and four arms.*
> *Two of his hands hold a noose and a hook, while two other hands*
> *show the gestures of removing fear and granting boons.*
>
> *A mouse is seen on his flag.*
> *Red, obese, he has ears like winnowing baskets;*
> *he is dressed in red; his limbs are painted with red sandal paste.*
>
> *He is worshiped with red flowers.*
> *Unfailing, merciful, the origin of the worlds,*
> *he appears at the beginning of creation,*
> *alone, beyond Nature, beyond the Cosmic Person.*
> *He who meditates on his form becomes great among the reintegrated.*

THE TUSK

Gaṇapati has only one tusk. According to the *Maudgala Purāṇa* [538], "the word 'one' is the symbol of illusion (*māyā*); from it everything has sprung. The tooth (or tusk) is the support of existence; it is therefore the impeller of illusion."

Gaṇapati has only one tooth because in him are united the qualified or manifest being which is illusion (*māyā*) and the nonmanifest unqualified being which is the support of illusion, the illusion-giver (*māyin*).

THE TRUNK

Gaṇapati's trunk is bent. "His face, shape of the Self, is crooked." (Quoted in Karapātrī, *Śrī Bhagavat tattva*, p. 642. [539])

"While the outward form of the world appears intelligible for mind and words, divinity cannot be directly understood and is therefore said to be crooked. [Gaṇapati's] trunk is also said to be bent because he is the master of obstacles." (Ibid. [540])

The trunk of Gaṇapati is sometimes represented as bent to the right and sometimes to the left. These directions correspond to the two ways in which obstacles can be got round and the supreme goal reached. These are the right-hand and the left-hand ways. This meaning applies also to the *svastika*, whose arms can be bent to either side.

THE FOUR ARMS

As the universal ruler, Gaṇapati has four arms. It is he who established the four kinds of beings. It is he also who instituted the four castes and the four Vedas.

"In heaven this child will establish the predominance of gods, on earth that of men, in the nether world that of the antigods and serpents. O priest! he causes the four principles of the elements to move and is therefore four-armed.[5] There are many kinds of quaternary; he has established them all." (Ibid. [541])

To catch delusion (*moha*), the enemy of all seekers, he holds the noose. The driving hook is the insigne of the ruler of the universe, and the hand granting boons shows him as the fulfiller of desires. The hand allaying fear shows that Gaṇapati is beyond the realm of time, of death, to which all fear pertains.

THE MOUSE

The vehicle of Gaṇapati is the mouse (*mūṣaka*). The mouse is the master of the inside of everything. The all-pervading Ātman is the mouse that lives in the hole called Intellect, within the heart of every being. It is the real enjoyer of the pleasures of all creatures. Like the mouse, this self of all is a thief, because, unnoticed, it steals away all that people possess. It hides itself behind the

5 The fifth element, ether, is ever motionless.

inscrutable shapes of illusion, and no one knows that this inner ruler takes for himself the pleasures people believe they enjoy. "It is he who is benefited by all penance." (*Bhagavadgītā* 5.29. [542])

The word *muṣa* (mouse) comes from the root *muṣ*, "to steal" (*Dhātu-pāṭha* 17.25 [543]). Although it steals from people the things they enjoy, the mouse has no concern whether those enjoyments are virtues or vices. Similarly, the inner ruler of everything, hidden under the inscrutable illusion, enjoys the pleasures of all, but remains unaffected by vice or virtue.

"The mouse is his vehicle, glorious for all to behold. Eternal wisdom (the Vedas) named him the 'Mouse Rider.' The root *muṣ* means 'to steal.' Theft is the support of the Immense-Being (Brahmā), essence of all names and shapes, yet ever remaining hidden. Being the cause, in all enjoyments he is the real enjoyer of the pleasure. Those deluded by I-conceit alone are unaware of this. He is the All-Enjoyer [Īśāna], the sovereign Lord (Īśvara), established in us like a thief. The impeller of mankind, he is said to be a mouse." (Quoted in Karapātrī's *Śrī Bhagavat tattva*, p. 643. [544])

Gaṇapati is obese because all manifestation is contained in his belly, yet he himself is not contained in anyone.

"Many vast universes were born from his belly, of this there is no doubt." (Quoted in Karapātrī's *Śrī Bhagavat tattva*, p. 644. [545])

The ears of the god resemble winnowing trays because he winnows the words that men address to him. He throws away the dust of vice and virtue. Real values alone then remain to be apprehended.

"Only by winnowing does corn, dust-mixed, become dust-free and fit for every man to desire as his food." (Quoted in Karapātrī's *Śrī Bhagavat tattva*, p. 644. [546])

"Thus, O lovely one! he who neglects the worship of the winnowing ears will never find the Absolute buried under the changing forms of appearances." (Quoted in Karapātrī's *Śrī Bhagavat tattva*, p. 644. [547])

"Men seek the protection of the winnowing ears, and reject the impurities of all that changes, in order that the Great Being may establish itself in their midst and they may become one with him." (Ibid. [548])

Kumāra, the Adolescent

"TORMENTED BY the antigod Tāraka, the gods, with Indra at their head, went to the world of the Self-born, the Creator." (*Kumāra-saṁbhava* 2.1.)

The Creator said: "Only the seed of Śiva can produce a hero who will defeat the powers of evil." But Śiva, the great Yogi, was lost in meditation. Kāma, the god of lust, attempted to attract his attention and was reduced to ashes by a single glance of Śiva's third eye. The goddess Pārvatī began to practice austerities. But it was only after a long penance that she won the notice of the Lord of Yoga. Once Śiva was aroused, none could bear his fiery seed. It fell into the mouth of Fire (Agni) and was afterward received by the Ganges, to be finally thrown into a thicket of *kāśa* grass called the Forest-of-Arrows (Śaravana). This seed of life gave birth to the "Jumper" or the "Spurt of Semen" (Skanda), who was called the Chaste-Adolescent (Kumāra) since he remains forever young and single. Skanda was thus conceived without the participation of a female being.

He was reared by the six Pleiades (Kṛttikās); hence he is known as Kārttikeya (Son of the Pleiades). He developed six faces to drink their milk. He was made the lord of war, the secret-chief (*guha*) of the gods' army, and he defeated the antigods Mahiṣa and Tāraka (*Mahābhārata* 3.14610 and 8.4181), whose power, gained through austerities, had threatened that of the gods. The leadership of the gods' army is said to have been the main purpose of his birth. He is sometimes considered not only as the son but as an avatar of Śiva.

It is commonly said that the army of the gods is Skanda's only wife, hence he remains forever single; yet according to another tradition he is represented as married to the Army (Senā), pictured as a daughter of Brahmā, or to the Virgin (Kaumārī).

Kumāra's strength is immense. Once, as a boy, he thrust his spear into the ground, challenging anyone to pull it out or even shake it. Viṣṇu took hold of the lance with his left hand and moved it. Immediately the earth shook, with its mountains, forests, and seas. But when the *daitya* Prahlāda tried to pull up the spear, he could not accomplish the feat and fainted. (*Mahābhārata* 12.12320.)

Skanda is shown as an adolescent with one or six heads, two or twelve arms. Dressed in red, he holds a bow and some arrows, a sword, a thunderbolt, and an ax. His spear, which never misses its mark, returns to his hand after killing his enemies. He rides on a peacock called the Year (Paravāṇi); his emblem is the rooster. His banner, a gift from Fire (Agni), is as red as the fire of destruction and flames high above his chariot.

The cult of Skanda is an ancient one. Patañjali mentions his images, and Kushan coins bear his name. He was worshiped in northern India under the Guptas. He was the favorite deity of the Calukyas. Today, however, he is worshiped almost exclusively in southern India. Women must not worship him. It has been suggested that he may have been originally a genie of children or of the dead. Several ancient South Indian divinities were identified with him, particularly the Boy (Murugan),[6] the Spear-bearer (Velan), the Red-One (Śeyyān or Śeyyavan). Attempts to make him a deification of Alexander or a form of Soma or to take him for the Dionysos of Megasthenes have proved unfounded.

The name of Skanda first appears in a passage, possibly an interpolation, of the *Maitrāyaṇi Saṁhitā* and in the *Gṛhya Sūtras,* where he appears in a demoniacal role he will maintain later. The *Chāndogya Upaniṣad* identifies him with Sanat-kumāra. His story is found among others in the *Śiva Purāṇa* and the *Mahābhārata* and is retold in the celebrated poem of Kālidāsa, the *Kumāra-saṁbhava* (mainly in parts that pass as apocryphal). His cult is also described in the Tantras. The *Skanda Purāṇa,* the largest of the Purāṇas, claims to be an epitome of his teachings. There is also a treatise on archery attributed to him.

Skanda has many names. He is the Adolescent (Kumāra), the Son-of-the-Pleiades (Kārttikeya), the Secret-One (Guha), the Offspring-of-Rudra (Rudra-sūnu), Dear-to-the-Brāhmaṇās (Subrahmaṇya), the Great-Captain (Mahā-sena), the Lord-of-Armies (Senā-pati), the Captain-of-the-Realized (Siddha-sena), the Spear-holder (Śakti-dhara), the Son-of-the-Ganges (Gaṅgā-putra), Born-in-the-Thicket (Śara-bhū), Vanquisher-of-the-demon-Tāraka (Tāraka-jit), Six-faced (Ṣaṇmukha or Ṣaḍānana), Son-of-the-Purifier or Son-of-Fire (Pāvaka), etc. The *Mahābhārata* (3.14630) mentions thirty-one of his names.

In yoga, Skanda is the power of chastity. According to Vāsudeva Śaraṇa Agravala (*Kalyāṇa,* Śiva aṅka, p. 501): "The power of the virile seed, preserved through penance and complete chastity, is called Skanda (the spurt of semen) or Kumāra (the adolescent). So long as, in the practice of yoga, complete control is not attained, Kumāra is not born, and the mind is ever put in check by desires, that is, the gods are defeated by the demons. It is only by making his sublimated seed rise through the central inner channel of the subtle-body (*suṣumnā*) up to the 'mouth of fire' (*vahni-mukha*) in the sixth center, where it is consumed, that the yogi becomes complete master of his instincts. It is then that Skanda is born. The yogi who can master his body and his mind even in sleep can use his sexual powers for intellectual and spiritual ends. He then becomes really an adept, an image of Śiva."

The Pleiades are divinities of fire envisaged in its gentle and beneficent

6 Murugan was a Dravidian god of war, the heroic son of the fearful Korrovei. Graceful and amicable, he had six faces, twelve arms, and the rooster as an emblem. He was worshiped with flower offerings and orgiastic dances.

aspect. These six nurses of Kumāra are connected with the six subtle centers through which Kumāra develops.

Kumāra rides on the peacock, the killer of serpents, for he defeats the most subtle instincts that bind the spirit of man in his body. Kumāra changes poison into ambrosia. The serpent, furthermore, represents the cycle of the years. The peacock is thus the killer of Time.

In cosmology, Kumāra is identified with the solar energy which dwells in the higher sphere of the earth beyond the sphere of air and gives rise to the cycle of the year (*saṁvatsara-agni*). He is thus the form of Rudra called the Blue-and-Red (Nīla-lohitā). (*Śatapatha Brāhmaṇa*, Brahma khaṇḍa, 6.1.3.)

Minor Gods and Genii

AMONG the heavenly beings, the presiding deities of different spheres, species, and elements are called the everlasting-gods (*nitya devatā*). They are surrounded by minor powers over whom they rule. Among these are the regents-of-the-directions (Loka-pālas), the lords-of-progeny (Prajāpatis), and the deities-protecting-towns-and-villages (*grāma-devatā*).

"The Fragrances [or celestial harmonies] (*gandharva*) and the Essences [or unmanifest potentialities] (*apsaras*) are the celestial beings born of the centripetal *sattva* tendency, the tendency toward light. They are the [minor] forms of the Pervader, Viṣṇu.

"The speedy-ones (*yakṣa*) or spirits of the earth, the heavenly-humans (*kinnara*), and the genii (*daitya*) are the kinds of supernatural beings born of the revolving *rajas* tendency. They are therefore aspects of the Creator, Brahmā.

"The night-wanderers (*rākṣasa*), serpents (*nāga*), and ghosts (*preta*) are the supernatural beings born of the obscuring tendency, *tamas*, or tendency toward dispersion. They are aspects of the lord of sleep, Śiva, and are shown as his attendants.

"The main minor deities are the powers-of-realization (*yoginī*), the minor ruling-powers or fairies (*upanāyikā*), and the village-goddesses (*grāma-kālī*).

"The saints, that is, the human beings who, following the path of merit, have reached heaven and are enjoying its pleasures, are also counted among the gods." [1]

The Attendants of Śiva

THE MAIN attendants of Śiva are the *gaṇas*, the "categories," which include all the minor deities which are counted in groups. They are under the command

[1] Vijayānanda Tripāṭhī, "Devatā tattva," *Sanmārga*, III, 1942.

of the lord-of-categories (Gaṇa-pati). They dwell on the Pleasure-Mountain (Kailāsa).

The main *gaṇas* are of nine kinds: the Ādityas, the Rudras, and the Vasus, which are respectively the divinities of the sky, the atmosphere, and the earth (see pp. 112 ff., 102 ff., 85 ff.). Besides these important *gaṇas*, there are the ten Universal-Principles (Viśvas or Viśvadevas), the Satisfied (Tuṣitas), the sixty-four Shining-Ones (Ābhāsvaras), the forty-nine divinities-of-the-winds (Anilas), the Princely-Ones (Mahārājikas), the Means-of-Realization (Sādhyas).

Evil spirits, such as ghosts (*preta*), monsters (*piśāca*), wandering-souls (*bhūta*), ogresses (*ḍākinī*), vegetation-spirits (*śākinī*), and the fearful-spirits (*bhairava*), are also counted among the attendants of Śiva.

The Universal-Principles (*Viśvas or Viśvadevas*)

According to the *Viṣṇu Purāṇa* and other Purāṇas, the Viśvas are the sons of Viśvā, daughter of Ritual-Skill (Dakṣa).

The number of Viśvas is variously counted between ten and thirteen. They are:

1. Vasu, the Dwelling Place
2. Satya, Truth
3. Kratu, Will, Intelligence, Sacrifice
4. Dakṣa, Ritual Skill
5. Kāla, Time
6. Kāma, Lust
7. Dhṛti, Forbearance
8. Kuru, the Northern Ancestor
9. Purū-ravas, Cry of Abundance (a being dwelling in the atmosphere)
10. Mādrava, Cry of Joy

To these are sometimes added:

11. Rocaka, Pleasantness, or Locana, Sight
12. Dhvani, Fame
13. Dhuri, Leadership

The two last can also be considered as one being.

We have already met Vasu among the gods of the Vedas and Kāla as one of the aspects of Śiva (see pp. 85 ff. and 200 f., respectively.) Besides these, the two most important of the universal principles are Ritual-Skill (Dakṣa) and Lust (Kāma).

The Satisfied (*Tuṣitas*)

The Tuṣitas are the sons of the Progenitor-of-Knowledge (Veda-śiras), the ancestor of the priestly class, and his wife Satisfaction (Tuṣitā).

The Shining (Ābhāsvaras)

The Ābhāsvaras are a class of sixty-four deities which rule over all the forms of spiritual and physical enlightenment.

The main ones are twelve: "Ātmā (the soul), Jñātā (the knower), Dama (restraint), Dānta (patience), Śānti (peace), Jñāna (knowledge), Sama (tranquillity), Tapas (penance), Kāma (lust), Krodha (anger), Mada (intoxication), Moha (delusion)." (Tārānātha Tarkavācaspati's Dictionary [549]. Quoted in Monier-Williams, *A Sanskrit-English Dictionary*, s.v. Ābhāsvara.)

The Means-of-Realization (Sādhyas)

The Sādhyas, or Means of Realization, are different from the Realized (Siddhas) (see below).

"The Sādhyas live upon the fifth nectar [i.e., the Upaniṣads]. Brahmā is their mouth. . . .

"They enter the form [which seems to quiver in the center of the sun] and spring forth from that form." (*Chāndogya Upaniṣad* 3.10.1, 2. [550])

According to the *Agni Purāṇa* (Gaṇabheda adhyāya [551]), "the Sādhyas are twelve. They are named: Manas (mind), Mantā (thought), Prāṇa (life), Nara (man), Apāna (digestive breath), Vīryavān (brave), Vibhu (powerful), Haya (horse), Naya (prudent), Haṁsa (swan), Nārāyaṇa (refuge of man), Prabhu (lord)."

The Realized (Siddhas)

"SUCH human beings as have attained liberation and thus are included within the limits of Patañjali's definition of the gods are also divinities, but there remains a difference between beings who have become deities after having been through the bondage of life and gods eternally unbound. The human being who dissolves into Basic-Nature [Pradhāna] may appear again and find the fruit of his action waiting for him, while a divinity is forever free." (Yogatrayānanda, *Śrī Rāmāvatāra kathā*, p. 101.)

The Siddhas are often mentioned in the *Mahābhārata*. They are perfect and blessed spirits who dwell mostly in the sacred Uttara-Kuru land far in the north. (Ibid. 6.254.)

Siddhapura, the city of the Siddhas, is, however, described in the *Āryabhaṭīya*, a fourth-century work on astronomy, as situated in a country where the sun rises when it sets in Laṅkā (Ceylon) and it is midday in Romaka (Alexandria).

The Skillful-Craftsmen (Ṛbhus)

THE ṚBHUS were men who attained immortality by performing with skill a large number of propitiatory rites. As immortals they are beyond the reach of desire, beyond happiness and suffering, beyond the reach of time, a state that all the gods wish to reach.

The Ṛbhus are the sons of Good-Archer (Sudhanvan), whose eye is like the sun (Sūracakṣus). They are identified with the deities of the year (*Ṛg Veda* 1.7.30) and are thought possibly to be connected with an ancient division of the year.[2] They take rest in the house of the sun during the twelve intercalary days of the winter solstice. They are subtle guardians of the ritual sacrifice.[3] Elsewhere they are shown as three clever craftsmen, Inventiveness (Ṛbhu), Strength (Vāja), and Skill (Vibhvan), who dwell in the solar sphere. They fashioned the chariot of the twin Aśvins, the palaces of Indra, the miraculous cow of Bṛhaspati, the ax (?) of Tvaṣṭṛ. They gave back youth to their parents. They usually accompany Indra.

The Bearers-of-Wisdom (Vidyā-dharas)

THE BEARERS OF WISDOM resemble men but have magic powers and change form at their fancy. They are aerial spirits, generally benevolent. They live in the northern mountains, where they have cities and kings. They can intermarry with humans, who then themselves become Vidyādharas. When warriors fight with courage Vidyādharas shower a rain of flowers on them (*Mahābhārata* 2.408).

The Vidyādharas are mentioned in Buddhist and Jain mythology. The *Nāgānanda* of Harṣa is a play based on a legend of the Vidyādharas.

The Essences (*apsaras*)

THE *apsarases* are the unmanifest potentialities, the possible worlds, which exist in the divine Mind but may never come to exist physically. As their name indicates, they are essences of the waters, being forms that take shape within

2 Louis Renou, *L'Inde classique*, I, 328.
3 Vijayānanda Tripāṭhī, "Devatā tattva."

the causal ocean. "O king! when the water (*ap*) was churned, beautiful women appeared from its essence (*rasa*). These are called the essences-of-the-waters (*apsaras*)." (*Rāmāyaṇa* 1.45.31. [552]) In the *Nirukta* (2.5.13) Yāska explains their name as "moving in the waters" (*ap-sāriṇī*). They are also said to be the daughters of Vision (Kaśyapa). In later mythology they are represented as water nymphs, eternally young women who are the courtesans and the dancers of heaven. They are called the women-of-the-gods (*surāṅganā*), the daughters-of-pleasure (*sumad-ātmajā*).

The *apsarases* were born during the churning of the ocean. "Since no one married them, they became public women." (*Rāmāyaṇa* 1.45.35. [553]) They are sometimes shown as the consorts of the Fragrances (*gandharva*), who live with them in their ocean dwellings. Sometimes they appear as spirits of midair. They are depicted as uncommonly beautiful, with lotus eyes, slender waists, and large hips. By their languid postures and sweet words they rob those who see them of their wisdom and their intellect. They seduce the ascetics whose austerities might endanger the supremacy of the gods.

Their number is large; the Kāśī khaṇḍa of the *Skanda Purāṇa* speaks of thirty-five million. They are divided into hosts (*gaṇa*). The *Vāyu Purāṇa* names fourteen of these hosts, the *Harivaṁśa* seven. Twelve *apsarases* are especially prominent. One of them, Menakā, seduced the sage Viśvāmitra and became the mother of Śakuntalā. Rambhā, another, was seized by Rāvaṇa. Tilottamā caused the death of the demons Sunda and Upasunda. Urvaśī is already mentioned in the *Ṛg Veda* (4.2.18; 5.41.19; 7.33.11; 10.95.10; 10.95.17).

The *apsarases* are not prudish, and willingly dispense their favors. Their amours on earth have been numerous. One can master them by stealing their clothes while they bathe. They choose lovers among the dead fallen on the battlefield. They have the power of changing their form, are fond of playing dice, and give luck to those whom they favor. They also produce madness, and the *Atharva Veda* gives charms and incantations against them.

The Fragrances (*gandharva*)

THE FRAGRANCES (*gandharva*), or celestial harmonies, are shining celestial beings dwelling in the sky; they are aspects of the sun. The Vedas speak of "the Gandharva" in the singular. Sāyaṇa mentions him as a solar deity. The *Ṛg Veda* (10.123.7) says that the Gandharva stood upon the firmament and, like the Sun, generated precious rain. This Vedic Gandharva knew and revealed the secrets of heaven and the divine Truth, hence his connection with the goddess of speech, Vāc.

The *gandharvas* wear fragrant garments and feed on the fragrance of herbs and the smell of stagnant water. They are associated with Soma, the elixir of life, whose dwelling place they guard but whom they sometimes try to monopolize. They are said to possess limitless sexual power and to be attracted by women. They play the part of lovers, give or refuse fecundity. They steal the fetus, disturb the mind with wine, gambling, and love. A *gandharva* is spoken of as having cured Varuṇa of his loss of virility with the help of an aphrodisiac plant.[4] In later Saṁhitās or Brāhmaṇas they are connected with the human embryo and are invoked in the nuptial rites. They are shown as having great influence over unmarried girls and as taking possession of human beings.

According to Sāyaṇa, the term *gandharva* is taken to represent the macrocosm, "the primeval universal life-force enveloped in the cosmic shell," while in the microcosm it represents the vital breath.[5]

In later mythology the *gandharvas* appear as benevolent singers and musicians. They play the *vīṇā* and know the most beautiful modes. They are teachers of musical knowledge. Their king is the Owner-of-the-Wonder-Chariot (Citra-ratha). Their place in the heavenly hierarchy is near that of the *devas.*

The *Viṣṇu Purāṇa* says that the *gandharvas* were born of Brahmā but later mentions them as sons of Vision (Kaśyapa). The *Harivaṁśa* makes them spring from Brahmā's nose. Their cities are splendid. A mirage is called a "city of the *gandharvas*" (*gandharva-nagara*).

The *gandharvas* are often shown with a human torso and a bird's or horse's head. They are connected with the *kinnaras*, *kimpuruṣas*, and *cāraṇas*, who are also musicians of the gods. They may be connected with the centaurs and with initiatory groups constituted in a sect.[6]

They are sometimes called *gātus* and *pulakas*. In the *Mahābhārata*, a particular people dwelling in the hills and the wilds is called the Gandharvas.

The Wanderers (*cāraṇa*)

THE *cāraṇas* are the panegyrists of heaven. They admire heroes and sing their praise. They are also dancers.

4 See B. Rāmacandra Śarmā, "Some Aspects of the Vedic Gandharva and Apsarases," *Poona Orientalist*, XIII (1948), 65.
5 See B. Rāmacandra Śarmā, op. cit.
6 Louis Renou, *L'Inde classique*, I, 329.

The Heavenly-Humans (*kinnara*)

THE *kinnaras*[7] are mythical beings with a human body and the head of a horse (or with a horse's body and the head of a man). They are musicians who sing the praise of the gods and are sometimes regarded as a variety of *gandharva*. They are attached to the service of Kubera.

The Village-Angels (*grāma-devatā*) and Village-Goddesses (*grāma-kālī*)

THE *grāma-devatās* are tutelary village deities who look after the welfare of humans.

"The *grāma-kālīs* also are protective deities, belonging to the same class as the *nāgas*. They are the divinities of villages and forests." (Vijayānanda Tripāṭhī, "Devatā tattva.")

The Ancestors (*pitṛ*)

THE FIRST progenitors of the human race, as well as all the ancestors burned or buried with the proper rites, are worshiped under the name of Ancestors (*pitṛ*).

They are considered as equal to the gods, though sometimes opposed to them. They are immortals and share in the glorious life of the gods. The rites known as Śrāddha (homage) are performed in their honor, and offerings called Piṇḍas (bodies) are presented to them. Manu (3.284) says: "One must consider the Ancestors as gods."

The *pitṛs* dwell in the sphere of space (*bhuvas*) or in the sphere of the Moon. They are the regents of the constellations Maghā and Mūla.

Genii (*daitya* and *dānava*)

"THE *daityas* and *dānavas* are supernatural beings who dwell in the lower worlds yet enjoy heavenly pleasures. They are among the first children of Vision (Kaśyapa) and are thus counted among the *asuras*, the elder brothers of the gods. They are said to have been relegated to an inferior status because they

7 The Indian *kinnara* and Greek *kentauros* (centaur) are words of the same origin.

were proud, cruel, and seekers of pleasure." (Vijayānanda Tripāṭhī, "Devatā tattva.")

The name of the *dānavas* came from their mother, Danu, one of the daughters of Ritual-Skill (Dakṣa) and wife of Vision (Kaśyapa). The name of the *daityas* came from Diti, another daughter of Dakṣa and wife of Kaśyapa. The genii Golden-eyed (Hiraṇyākṣa), Golden-Vesture (Hiraṇyakaśipu), etc., are *daityas*. The Maruts also are sons of Diti. The most powerful of the *dānavas* is Vṛtra but the most famous is their king, the architect Maya.

The Serpents or Dragons, the Ever-moving (*nāga*)

THE *nāgas* are linked with the antigods. They are represented as half human, half serpent. They are possessed of great courage and are quick and violent. They are handsome and wear jewels, crowns, and large earrings.

They belong to different tribes; some are blue, some red, and some white. All are dangerous, having large limbs and tusks full of poison. Some have three, others seven, and others again ten heads. (*Mahābhārata* 1.2162; 5.3622.) The *nāgas* are also known as serpents (*sarpa*), creeping-creatures (*pannaga*), those creeping-on-their-chests (*uraga*), those creeping-on-their-shoulders (*bhujaṅga*), goat-eaters (*ajagara*).

The *nāgas* have three kings, Vāsuki, Takṣaka, and Śeṣa. Śeṣa (remainder) is the giant serpent which lies under the earth and supports its weight. Śeṣa is said to represent the "remainder" of destroyed universes when, during the divine night, the power of creation recoils upon itself.

The *nāgas* are said to descend from the Fragrant (Surabhi), the fabulous cow, daughter of the non-Aryan sage Vision (Kaśyapa). In another version they were born from the union of Vision and Chalice-of-Immortality (Kadru), a daughter of Ritual-Skill (Dakṣa). In this case they are taken as the symbols of the cycles of time.

The *nāgas* dwell in an underworld, the serpent-world (*nāga-loka*), which is an immense domain crowded with palaces, houses, towers, and pleasure gardens. This serpent world is also called Pātāla or Niraya. Its main city is the City-of-Pleasures (Bhogavatī) ruled by Vāsukī. According to the *Varāha Purāṇa*, three of the lower worlds, Pātāla, Atāla, and Sutāla, belong to the *nāgas*. The *nāgas* also live on the earth but dwell there in the caves of inaccessible mountains. Their favorite countries are the banks of the river Ikṣumatī, the Naimiṣa forest on the shores of the Gomatī, the northern banks of the Gaṅgā, and the Niṣada country. They also dwell under the sea.

Though enemies of the gods, the *nāgas* are not unfavorable to men, and they intermarry with them. Arjuna thus married the *nāga* girl Ulūpī.

The legend of the *nāgas* appears to come from a mixture of elements, on one side the cult of serpents considered as the genii of trees and rivers and, on the other, memories of non-Aryan clans who worshiped serpents.

Today the *nāgas* are still worshiped as deities in most villages of southern India. The serpent seems to have been the totem of the ancient Dravidians, and until comparatively recent times there were dynasties of kings who were pictured with a cobra's hood in eastern and southern India. The aboriginal tribe known today as the Nāgas in Assam seems, however, to be of a different origin. According to the *Rāja Taraṅginī*, the Nāgas were the first inhabitants of Kashmir.

The Night-Wanderers (*rākṣasa*)

THE *rākṣasas* are of three sorts: some are genii, similar to the *yakṣas* and *daityas;* others are titans, powerful enemies of the gods; others are fearful demons and ogres. The *rākṣasas* devour human beings, animate dead bodies, disturb sacrifices, harass pious men, and afflict mankind in many ways. They are children of darkness who wander at night. Their rule is unchallenged until midnight. They haunt forests, mountains, and deserts, which resound with their fearful roars.

The *rākṣasas* can take any form they like: human, animal, monstrous; but they always look fearful, large, and strong, with flaming eyes, sharp, prominent teeth, and a tongue of unusual length.

When the monkey Hanuman, the envoy of Rāma, secretly entered the city of Laṅkā, he saw *rākṣasas* of every shape and form. "Some of them frightened the eye; others seemed beautiful. Some had long arms and fearful shapes; some were fat, some were lean; some were like dwarfs, some prodigiously tall. Some had only one eye, some only one ear. Some had monstrous bellies, hanging breasts, projecting teeth, and crooked legs; others, beautiful to behold, were richly adorned. Some had two legs, some three legs, some four legs. Some had the heads of serpents, some the heads of donkeys, some the heads of horses, and some even the heads of elephants." (*Rāmāyaṇa*, Sundara kāṇḍa, sargas 4 and 17.)

Various origins are attributed to the *rākṣasas.* They are said to be descendants of the non-Aryan seer Pulastya or to have been born from Brahmā's foot and a daughter of Ritual-Skill (Dakṣa). According to the *Viṣṇu Purāṇa,* they were born to Rākṣas, a son of Vision (Kaśyapa), and Khaśā, a daughter of Ritual Skill.

The ten-headed Rāvaṇa, who ruled over Laṅkā and was the enemy of Rāma, is the most celebrated king of the *rākṣasas.*

The demoniac aspect of the *rākṣasas* is much lessened in the Dravidian version of the *Rāmāyaṇa.* There is some ground to think that they may have been assimilated to the dark-skinned inhabitants of South India.

The marriage by capture is called by Manu the *rākṣasa* form of marriage.

A number of names and epithets describe the character of the *rākṣasas.* They are killers (*hanūṣa*), devourers-of-offerings (*iṣṭipaca*), strong-after-dusk (*sandhyābala*), roaming-at-night (*kṣapāṭa, naktañ-cara, rātri-cara, niśā-cara, śamanī-ṣada*), devourers-of-men (*nṛjagdha* or *nṛcakṣas*), eaters-of-raw-flesh (*palāla, palāda, palaṅkaṣa, kravyāda*), drinkers-of-blood (*asra-pa, asṛk-pa, kauṇa-pa, kīlāla-pa, rakta-pa*), biters (*dandaśūka*), gluttons (*praghasa*), dirty-faced (*malina-mukha*), etc.

The Eaters-of-Raw-Flesh (*piśāca*)

THE *piśācas* are usually mentioned together with the *rākṣasas* and are sometimes identified with them. They are also associated with the *asuras* and the *yakṣas.* Like the *rākṣasas,* they are hideous, repellent, and bloodthirsty. Their name appears in the *Atharva Veda.* Kashmir tradition places them in Central Asia. Like the *nāgas,* they are half fabulous, half human. An aberrant Prākṛt, the Paiśācī, is attributed to them. The lowest form of marriage, that by rape, is associated with their name.

The Sorcerers (*yātu* or *yātudhāna*)

THE *yātus* or *yātudhānas* are similar to the *rākṣasas* but were originally distinct from them. They are also associated with the *dasyus* or primitive tribes. They are magicians and sorcerers. Their name is of Vedic origin. In the Purāṇas they are identified with the *rākṣasas.*

The *yātudhānas* are said to have been born of Vision (Kaśyapa) and Good-Taste (Su-rasā).

Twelve *yātudhānas* are named in the *Vāyu Purāṇa.*

The Vampires (*vetāla*)

THE *vetālas* are vampires who animate dead bodies. The Tantras describe *vetāla* forms of black magic.

The Ghosts (*preta*)

THE *pretas* are ghosts. They are spirits who have gone from the world of the living but have not reached liberation nor entered new living bodies. They are under the direct rule of Yama, the king of the dead, and are among the attendants of Śiva.

"They are cruel and instigate trouble. They love unclean places and people. Man comes easily under their influence when impelled by his lower emotions such as fear.

"The *pretas* themselves are in a state of suffering and bear constant pain." (Vijayānanda Tripāṭhī, "Devatā tattva.")

The Wandering-Souls (*bhūta*)

THE *bhūtas* also are ghosts; the term often covers all demoniac beings.

Bhūtas are the souls of people who died a violent death; they are not always distinct from the *pretas*. They are shown following armies or poisoning trees, water ponds, and fields. They haunt trees and abandoned houses. In northern India today they are still worshiped and given offerings by many low-caste people, who practice forms of magic connected with them.

The Fearful-Spirits (*bhairava*)

VĪRABHADRA and the eight other *bhairavas* are represented as the fearful attendants of Rudra, but they are also sometimes considered as his aspects.

{ 26 }

Other Deities

Kāma (Eros), the Divinity of Lust

KĀMA is one of the universal principles or Viśvadevas. In the *Atharva Veda*, Lust, or Kāma, is mentioned as the supreme divinity, the impeller of creation.

"Lust was born first. Neither gods nor Ancestors nor men can equal him.

"You (i.e., Lust) are above them all and forever great." (*Atharva Veda* 9.2.19. [554])

Fire (Agni) is but a form of Lust. "When [Fire and Lust] are distinguished from each other, Lust is the higher form of the other deity." (*Atharva Veda* 9.2.24. [555])

Lust is said to be self-born (*ātma-bhū*), born of no other (*ananya-ja*), unborn (*aja*), springing from the heart of the Immense-Being (Brahmā) or from the Primeval-Waters (Irā-ja). The *Taittirīya Brāhmaṇa* makes him the son of the Inherent-Law-of-Things (Dharma) and calls his wife Devotion (Śraddhā). According to the *Harivaṁśa*, he is the Son-of-Fortune (Lakṣmī-putra).

In the Purāṇas, Lust's wife is Desire (Rati or Revā). His younger brother is Anger (Krodha). Lust has a daughter called Thirst (Tṛṣā) and a son called the Unopposed (Aniruddha, also an array or particular arrangement of the various cosmic elements that constitute the entity called Viṣṇu).

Lust, or Kāma, is the presiding deity of the mind, the god of beauty and youth. He is pictured as a proud adolescent, riding a parrot. He has two or eight arms. He holds a bow made of sugar cane; the bowstring is a line of bees; the five arrows are made of five fragrant flowers which inspire lust, the blue lotus, the jasmine, the mango flower, the *champak*, and the *śirīṣa*. On his red banner is a dolphin (*makara*). He is attended by heavenly dancers, the Essences (*apsaras*), and by celestial musicians, the Fragrances (*gandharva*). (*Mahābhārata.*) He is worshiped with garlands of red *aśoka* leaves.

In an ancient myth, retold in the *Rāmāyaṇa,* the gods, perturbed by the power of the antigod Tāraka, sent Kāma to awaken Śiva from his meditation.

The angry god, disturbed by Lust, reduced him to ashes with the fire that flashed from his central eye. Hence Lust became the Bodiless (Anaṅga). Moved by the plaints of Desire (Rati), Śiva allowed Lust to be reborn as Pradyumna, the son of Kṛṣṇa (and another of the arrays of Viṣṇu).

Kāma is worshiped by the yogis, for he alone, when pleased, can free the mind from desire. This is also one of the reasons why erotic images must be carved around the temple and on the door of the sanctuary. It is not pleasure but desire that binds man and is an obstacle to his spiritual progress.

"He who hankers after pleasure with a view to enjoying it becomes addicted to desire. The sage partakes of sensual pleasures as they occur, with a detached mind, and does not become addicted to desire." (*Gopāla-uttara-tāpinī Upaniṣad* 15. [556])

The Vedāntists make a difference between "the process by which the ruler of the universe deposits his seed in the womb of Nature which is the real Eros (*sākṣāt-manmatha*) and the mere drop of lust which spreads through the universe as the worldly Eros, the perturber of the mind.

"The seduction of divinity embodied in Attractiveness (Kṛṣṇa) toward its own manifestation represented in Success (Rādhā) is the true Eros. The divine beauty is so marvelous that God himself is bewildered by it. Lust (Kāma), seeing the jewellike toenails of Kṛṣṇa, was intoxicated. He lost all notion of manhood and womanhood and said, 'Even if I have for countless lives to practice austerities I must in the end be born a shepherdess of Cow Land to caress the toenails of Kṛṣṇa.' But already Kṛṣṇa, enamoured of himself, had resolved to experience lust for his own self; he manifested his own Nature in the cow-herd girls and enjoyed them." (Karapātrī, "Liṅgopāsanā-rahasya," *Siddhānta,* II, 1941–42.)

The Seed-of-Lust (Kāma-bīja)

IN COSMOLOGY lust appears as born of the union of a watery principle represented as the moon and a fiery principle, or life breath, assimilated to the sun.

"Prajāpati, the lord of progeny, wished to procreate. He hatched himself and invented copulation. 'From the union of semen (the Moon) and breath (the Sun) I shall obtain many sons.' " (*Praśna Upaniṣad* 1.4. [557]) In the *mantras*, the syllables that represent "Water (Ab-bīja), the sound *K;* Earth (Pṛthivī-bīja), the sound *L;* Lust, the sound *Ī;* and the Moon [whose symbol is the nasal half letter] are joined together to form the seed-of-lust (Kāma-bīja), that is, the syllable *klīṁ* that stands for Lust in all ritual formulae." (Brahma-yogin's commentary on the *Gopāla-pūrva-tāpinī Upaniṣad* 1.11–13. [558])

Kāma has many names. He is Remembrance (Smara), the Churner-of-the-Heart (Manmatha), the Killer (Māra), connected with the Māra of Buddhism. He is the Owner-of-Arrows (Īṣma), Born-of-Water (Kañjana), the Slave (Kiṅkara).

He is also Intoxication (Mada), Volupty (Rama or Ramaṇa), Born-of-Passion (Bhāva-ja), Born-of-the-Mind (Mano-ja). He is the Son-of-Attraction (Kārṣṇi), the Son-of-Illusion (Māyī or Māyā-sūta), the Beloved-of-Fortune (Śrī-nandana). He is the Beautiful (Abhi-rūpa), the Inflamer (Darpaka or Dīpaka), Tense (Gadayitnu, Gṛdhu, Gṛtsa), Desirous (Kāmana, Kharu), the Inflamer-of-the-Creator (Kandarpa), Happy (Kantu), Wanton (Kulākeli), the Deluder (Mohī), the Flame-of-Honey (Madhu-dīpa), the Bewilderer (Muhira), the Crackling-Fire (Murmura), the Stalk-of-Attachment (Rāga-vṛnta), Having-Beauty-for-his-Weapon (Rūpāstra), Voluptuous (Śatanārīca), Destroyer-of-Peace (Śamāntaka). He is the Teacher-of-the-World (Saṁsāra-guru), the Womb-of-Volupty (Śṛṅgāra-yoni), the Spicy (Titha), the Handsome (Vāma). Flowers-are-his-Weapons (Kusumāyudha), His-Bow-is-of-Flowers (Puṣpa-dhanus), His-Arrows-are-Flowers (Puṣpa-śara).

The Architect-of-the-Universe (Viśva-karman)

VIŚVAKARMAN, the architect of the gods, is a demiurge, duplicate of Prajāpati. His name first appears as an epithet of Sāvitṛ. But he has a distinct individuality in the more recent part of the *Ṛg Veda.*

"In the Purāṇas, Prabhāsa, the wife of Vasu, most faithful and expert in Yoga, is the mother of the universe's architect. All the flying chariots of the gods, all their weapons, are his work. It was he who built the golden city of Laṅkā, the city of Dwarakā and the Śrīvigraha city of Jagannātha. He is identified with the craftsman Tvaṣṭṛ. The wife of the Sun, All-Knowing (Saṁjñā), is his daughter. He had two sons, World-Shape (Viśva-rūpa) and Dark-Cloud (Vṛtra). He built up the whole universe through a universal-sacrifice (Sarva-medha) and completed the work by sacrificing himself.

"He is the presiding deity of all the craftsmen. Nala, the king of the monkeys, who made the great bridge through which Rāma invaded the island of Ceylon, was his partial incarnation. The Hindu architect worships him for the improvement of his work on the day when the sun enters the Bhādrapada constellation. On that day no tool belonging to the building craft may be used. The worship of Viśvakarman is now more especially observed in Bengal." (Vijayānanda Tripāṭhī, "Devatā tattva," *Sanmārga*, III, 1942.)

The Architect-of-the-Antigods (Maya)

MAYA is the ruler of the underworld called Sutāla. He is a devotee of Śiva. On earth he dwells on the Devagiri mountain (near Delhi). He worked for men as well as for the *daityas*, of whom he is the architect and artificer. His skill is in no way inferior to that of Viśvakarman. The *Mahābhārata* speaks of a hall he built for the Rājasūya sacrifice of the Pāṇḍavas. He is often mentioned in the *Harivaṁśa*.

"The greatest wonder created by Maya was the Triple-City (Tri-pura), three fortresses of gold, silver, and iron that could move at will in the air, on earth, and in water. He gave these cities to his sons. These cities would come together only once in a thousand years, and it was only then that they were vulnerable. In the golden city was a well of ambrosia. Śiva destroyed the cities but saved Maya.

"The father of Maya was the Sagacious (Vipracitti). His daughter was the Thin-waisted (Mandodarī), who married Rāvaṇa, the *rākṣasa* king of Laṅkā. Maya had four sons: the Magician (Māyāvī) and the War-Drum (Dundhubhi) were killed in a war with Vālin, king of the monkeys; the third, the Sky (Vyoman), approached Kṛṣṇa, who gave him a place in heaven; the fourth was called Thunder-Lust (Vajra-Kāma).

"When Agni, with the help of Kṛṣṇa and Arjuna, devoured the forest of Khāṇḍava, protected by Indra, the god of rain, Maya was practicing austerities in the forest. Every creature who tried to escape was destroyed. Maya alone was saved by Kṛṣṇa. As a reward he built the assembly hall of Yudhiṣṭhira.

"Maya is the teacher of magicians. He created the science of magic, or "snare of Indra" (*indrajāla*), and all the attainments of magic (*āsurī-siddhi*). He is still worshiped today by all magicians." (Vijayānanda Tripāṭhī, "Devatā tattva.")

The Seizer (Rāhu)

RĀHU, the spirit who causes eclipses by attempting to devour the sun and the moon, is the *dānava* most often mentioned. He is also called Radiance-of-Soma (Svarbhānu).

The myth of Rāhu is connected with the churning of the ocean and the strife of the gods and antigods for the possession of the ambrosia and the sovereignty of the world.

According to the *Mahābhārata* (1.1103–18), Rāhu is the son of the Sagacious (Vipracitti). He is therefore the brother of Maya. His mother is the Lioness (Siṁhikā).

"While the gods were sharing the nectar, a *dānava* named Rāhu, disguised as a god, was drinking his share; the Sun and the Moon discovered him when the nectar had only reached his throat, and they informed the other gods. Viṣṇu instantly cut off with his discus the *dānava's* head, which was thrown into the sky and began to utter piteous cries, while the headless trunk fell upon the ground and, rolling thereon, made the earth tremble, with her mountains, forests, and islands. From that time a quarrel has existed between Rāhu's head and the sun and the moon, and to this day it always attempts to swallow the sun and the moon." (*Bhāgavata Purāṇa* 10.8.9.)

The tail of Rāhu became Ketu, the monster which gives birth to comets and meteors.

In astronomy Rāhu is considered to be the Dragon's Head, the ascending node of the moon, that is, the point where the moon's orbit crosses the ecliptic. This point is classified among the planets (*graha*). Rāhu is also the regent of the southwest quarter.

The Cow

THE cow is a symbol of the earth, the nourisher. Its cult, which holds a great place in modern Hindu ritual, is mentioned in the *Atharva Veda*.

According to the *Kālikā Purāṇa* (adhyāya 91), the Wish-Cow (Kāmadhenu) was born of Fragrance (Surabhi), daughter of Ritual-Skill (Dakṣa), and the seer Vision (Kaśyapa). The bull of Śiva, the Wanderer (Bhṛṅgi), is the son of this wish cow sired by Vetāla, one of Śiva's attendants. Through penance Bhṛṅgi obtained the favor of Śiva and became his vehicle and his emblem.

For the bull of Śiva see Nandikeśvara (p. 220).

The Seers (*ṛṣi*)

THE SEERS are mysterious beings connected with the origin of man and the origin of knowledge. Although represented as human sages, they are considered eternal powers who appear every time a new revelation is needed. "The power called by the name of 'seer' refers to the 'Law of the universe' (*dharma*) as it manifests itself enveloped in revelation (*veda*). These powers represent the basic energies that combine to create life." [1] The seers are the beings who "see" the divine law and express it in terms of creation as well as in terms of knowledge. The word *ṛṣi* seems, however, to be of obscure origin.[2]

In later mythology the seers are mere human sages and are countless. They are divided according to their origin and achievements into *brahma-ṛṣis* or priestly seers, *rāja-ṛṣis* or kingly seers, and *deva-ṛṣis* or divine seers, that is, seers who have attained the status of gods.

The main seers are said to be seven, although ten and sometimes twelve are commonly mentioned. The ten seers are often identified with the ten lords of progeny. The seven main seers dwell in the sky as the seven stars of the Great Bear. They are connected with the divinities of the elements.

According to the *Śatapatha Brāhmaṇa*, the seers are the authors of the Vedic hymns. Their names are Gautama, Bharadvāja, Viśvāmitra, Jamadagni, Vasiṣṭha, Kaśyapa, and Atri.

But according to the *Padma Purāṇa* (Sarga khaṇḍa, adhyāya 11) and to the *Mahābhārata* the seers are cosmic principles. They are called: Marīci (light), Atri (devourer), Aṅgiras (fiery), Pulaha (bridger of space), Kratu (inspiration), Pulastya (smooth hair), Vasiṣṭha (owner of wealth).

Manu calls them lords of progeny and adds three names: Dakṣa (ritual skill) or Pracetas (awareness), Bhṛgu (crack of fire), and Nārada (giver of advice).

The *Brahmāṇḍa Purāṇa* gives the same list. To these is sometimes added Agastya (the mover of mountains). This brings the total number of the seers to twelve.

The wives of the seven seers are, respectively, Sambhūti (fitness) for Marīci, Anasūyā (without spite) for Atri, Lajjā (modesty) for Aṅgiras, Kṣamā (forgiveness) for Pulaha, Sannati (humility) for Kratu, Prīti (love) for Pulastya, Arundhati (faithfulness) for Vasiṣṭha.

Some of the seers play an important role in the shaping of the universe, the creation of gods and men. Pulastya and Pulaha are the seers of the antigods. Kaśyapa is the progenitor of all beings: gods, antigods, animals, and men. His thirteen wives were the daughters of Ritual-Skill (Dakṣa).

The stability of the world results from the rituals performed thrice daily, at dawn, midday, and sunset, by the seven seers, and the recitation of the sacred triple-song (Gāyatrī) by all the twice-born at the same hours.

1 Motilal Śarmā Gauḍ, *Īśopaniṣad Vijñāna Bhāṣya.*
2 Louis Renou, *L'Inde classique,* I, 531.

The names of the seven seers differ for each cycle-of-creation (*manvantara*).[3]

In the first *manvantara*, ruled by the Lawgiver Son-of-the-Self-born (Svāyambhuva Manu), the seers are Marīci, Atri, Aṅgiras, Pulastya, Pulaha, Kratu, Vasiṣṭha. (*Harivaṁśa* 7.8.)

In the second *manvantara*, ruled by the Son-of-the-Self-luminous (Svārociṣa Manu), they are Ūrjastambha, Prāṇa, Dattoli, Ṛṣabha, Niścara, Arva, and Vīra. (*Mārkaṇḍeya Purāṇa* 67.4.)

In the third *manvantara*, ruled by the Son-of-the-Highest (Auttama Manu), they are the seven sons of Vasiṣṭha (*Mārkaṇḍeya Purāṇa* 73.13): Rajas, Gātra, Ūrdhvabāhu, Mavana, Anava, Sutapas, and Śukra (*Kūrma Purāṇa* 12).

In the fourth *manvantara*, ruled by the Son-of-Darkness (Tāmasa Manu), they are Jyotirdhāma, Pṛthu, Kāvya, Caitra, Agni, Balaka, and Pīvara. (*Mārkaṇḍeya Purāṇa* 73.13.)

In the fifth *manvantara*, ruled by the Son-of-Opulence (Raivata Manu), they are Hiraṇyaromā, Vedaśrī, Ūrdhvabāhu, Vedabāhu, Sudhāmā, Parjanya, Vasiṣṭha. (*Mārkaṇḍeya Purāṇa* 75.73–74.)

In the sixth *manvantara*, ruled by the Son-of-Vision (Cākṣuṣa Manu) they are Sumedhā, Virajā, Haviṣmān, Unnata, Madhu, Atināmā, Sahiṣṇu. (*Mārkaṇḍeya Purāṇa* 76.54.)

In the present, or seventh, *manvantara*, ruled by the Son-of-Brightness (Vaivasvata Manu), the seven seers are the authors of the Vedic hymns: Atri, Vasiṣṭha, Kaśyapa, Gautama, Viśvāmitra, Bharadvāja, Jamadagni. (*Mārkaṇḍeya Purāṇa* 79.9–10.)

In the eighth *manvantara*, ruled by the Kinsman-of-the-Sun (Arka-sāvarṇika Manu), the seers will be Gālava, Dīptimān, Paraśurāma, Aśvatyāmā, Kṛpa, Ṛṣyaśṛiṅga, Vyāsa. (*Mārkaṇḍeya Purāṇa* 80.4.)

In the ninth *manvantara*, ruled by the Kinsman-of-Ritual-Skill (Dakṣa-sāvarṇika Manu), the seers will be Medhātithi, Vasu, Satya, Jyotiṣman, Dyutimān, Sabala, Havyavāhana. (*Mārkaṇḍeya Purāṇa* 94.8.)

In the tenth *manvantara*, ruled by the Kinsman-of-the-Immensity (Brahma-sāvarṇika Manu), the seers will be Āpa, Bhūti, Haviṣmān, Sukṛtī, Satya, Nābhāga, Vasiṣṭha. (*Mārkaṇḍeya Purāṇa* 94.10–14.)

In the eleventh *manvantara*, ruled by the Kinsman-of-Eternal-Law (Dharma-sāvarṇika Manu), the seers will be Haviṣmān, Variṣṭha, Āruṇi, Niścara, Anagha, Viṣṭi, Agnideva. (*Mārkaṇḍeya Purāṇa* 94.19–20.)

In the twelfth *manvantara*, ruled by the Kinsman-of-the-Destroyer (Rudra-

3 For an explanation of the term *manvantara* see p. 327.

sāvarṇika Manu), the seers will be: Dyuti, Tapasvī, Sutapā, Tapomūrti, Taponidhi, Taporati, and Tapodhṛti. (*Mārkaṇḍeya Purāṇa* 94.25.)

In the thirteenth *manvantara*, ruled by the Kinsman-of-Light (Deva-sāvarṇika Manu) or the Son-of-Brightness (Raucya Manu), the seers will be: Dhṛtimān, Avyaya, Tattvadarśī, Nirutsuka, Nirmoha, Sutapā, Niṣprakampa. (*Mārkaṇḍeya Purāṇa* 94.30.)

In the fourteenth *manvantara*, ruled by the Kinsman-of-Might (Indra-sāvarṇika Manu) or the Son-of-Might (Bhautya Manu), the seers will be: Agnidhra, Agnibāhu, Śuci, Mukta, Mādhava, Śuka, Ajita. (*Mārkaṇḍeya Purāṇa* 100.31.)

The Fiery (Aṅgiras)

The Fiery (Aṅgiras) is the manifestation of Fire (Agni) as the power of enlightenment. He is the teacher of transcendent-knowledge (*brahma-vidyā*). He is also one of the ten lords of progeny. One of the ten sons born of Brahmā's mind, he sprang forth from the mouth of Brahmā. According to the *Matsya Purāṇa*, he was one of the three sages produced from the sacrifice of Varuṇa. Agni is sometimes said to be his son, although, according to the same Purāṇa, it is he who was adopted by Agni. The main wives of Aṅgiras are Tradition (Smṛti) and Devotion (Śraddhā); but he also married several of the daughters of Ritual-Skill (Dakṣa) and two daughters of Friendliness (Maitreya).

His four sons, born of Devotion (Śraddhā), are Fire (Agni), Cosmic-Revolution (Saṁvarta), Pervading-Truth (Utathya), and Great-Teacher (Bṛhaspati), the teacher of the gods.

Aṅgiras's four daughters, born of Śraddhā, are the goddess Sinīvālī (the first day of the new moon, giver of fecundity), Kuhū (the new-moon day), Rākā (the full-moon day), and Anumati (acceptance, the last day before the full moon, which is the day when gods and Ancestors receive oblations with favor). A fifth daughter, Akūpārā (the unbounded), is from another bed.

Aṅgiras gave sons to the wife of Rathītara, a *kṣatriya* who was childless. These sons, possessors of Brahmanical knowledge, were later called the descendants of Aṅgiras, and all are personifications of light. The Vedic hymns (*Ṛk*), the Giver-of-Offerings (Havismat), and Mankind are the offspring of the Fiery. He is connected with all luminous objects and has been identified with the planet Jupiter and a star in Ursa Major.

Aṅgiras is the priest of the gods and the lord of sacrifices. A number of Vedic hymns are attributed to him. He is one of the Lawgivers and the author of a work on astronomy.

The Owner-of-Wealth (Vasiṣṭha)

The Owner-of-Wealth (Vasiṣṭha) is connected with the spheres-of-existence (Vasus) and represents the power of wealth, basis of ritual sacrifices. Vasiṣṭha is the owner of the wish cow called Delight (Nandinī), itself daughter of the Fragrant (Surabhi), which, by granting all he could wish for, made him the master of all the objects-of-pleasure (*vasu*).

Vasiṣṭha is the author of a number of hymns of the *Ṛg Veda.* A law book is also attributed to him. According to the *Ṛg Veda* Vasiṣṭha was the family priest of King Sudāsa. The *Mahābhārata* mentions him as the priest of the kings of the solar race, in particular Rāmacandra.

Vasiṣṭha was the son of the celestial nymph Urvaśī, his fathers being Mitra and Varuṇa. He is counted among the ten lords-of-progeny (Prajāpatis), ancestors of the human races.

In the Purāṇas he appears as the arranger of the Vedas. He had seven sons, including Aurva and the Sukālins.

The Universal-Friend (Viśvāmitra)

The Universal-Friend (Viśvāmitra) represents the power of the social laws that link men to one another. He is also the embodiment of will and longevity and the author of a great number of hymns of the *Ṛg Veda.* A law book, a work on archery, and a work on medicine are attributed to him.

Viśvāmitra raised himself from the princely to the priestly class. He was an opponent of Vasiṣṭha and, like him, lived at the court of Sudāsa, king of the Tṛtsus. He went over to the Bharatas but could not prevent their defeat. He was the friend and counselor of the young Rāmacandra.

Ritual-Skill (Dakṣa)

Ritual-Skill (Dakṣa) represents the power of rites that link men with gods. He is also the source of life, the progenitor. As a Vedic Āditya he is considered the universal father of gods, men, and antigods. Dakṣa is mentioned in the *Ṛg Veda* (10.72.4–5), the *Śatapatha Brāhmaṇa* (2.4.4.1), and the *Saṅkhyāyana Brāhmaṇa* (4.4).

"He is the lord of progeny, who brings forth the moving universe. His worship is ordained together with that of Yama, the lord of death, and of his assistant, Citragupta." (Vijayānanda Tripāṭhī, "Devatā tattva.")

The present ruler of life on earth is known to the Purāṇas as Ritual-Skill (Dakṣa). The first Dakṣa existed at the time of the first lawgiver, Svāyambhuva

Manu. According to the *Bhāgavata Purāṇa* (4.1), he was born from the right thumb of the Creator Brahmā. His wife was called Prasūti and was the daughter of Svāyambhuva Manu himself. Dakṣa had by her sixteen daughters, thirteen of whom were married to Eternal-Law (Dharma), one called Offering (Svāhā) to Fire (Agni), the fifteenth, Invocation-at-Offering (Svadhā), to the Ancestors, and the sixteenth, Faithfulness (Satī), to Śiva. The second Dakṣa was born during the rule of Cākṣuṣa Manu, the son of Māriṣā and the ten Awarenesses (Pracetases). In obedience to the order of the Creator he undertook to procreate living beings. He took as his wife the Dark-One (Aśinī), daughter of Profundity (Vīraṇa), another lord of progeny. First he produced ten thousand sons called Joyful-Horses (Haryaśvas). All were of identical nature. When ordered by their father to spread creation, they started practicing austerities to this end. But the seer Nārada persuaded them to renounce worldly inclinations and they refused to procreate. A second time Dakṣa created ten thousand sons, the Multicolored-Horses (Śabal-āśvas) or Simple-natured-Horses (Saral-āśvas). They, too, followed the teachings of the seer, and took monastic vows. Dakṣa's anger was great. He cursed the seer: "Thou shalt never stay in one place for more than twice twenty minutes."

Brahmā calmed the anger of the lord of progeny. So far procreation had been only a mental process. Dakṣa now indulged in physical procreation and to his wife sixty daughters were born. He married ten of them to Eternal-Law (Dharma), thirteen to the sage Vision (Kaśyapa), four to Tārkṣya, twenty-seven to the Moon (Soma), two to Bhūta, two to Aṅgiras, and two to Kṛśāśva (*Bhāgavata Purāṇa* 6.5–6).[4] All the living beings on the earth—gods, demons, men, and animals—are born from the thirteen girls married to Kaśyapa. These girls are known as the World Mothers (the twenty-seven girls married to the Moon form the lunar mansions).

Apart from the two Dakṣas mentioned generally, four others are known to the Purāṇas. They are: (1) the Clan-maker (Gotra-kāra), who belonged to the Aṅgiras clan; (2) the son of Aṅgiras and Surūpa (*Matsya Purāṇa* 196.2); (3) the son of Bhṛgu and Paulomī (*Mārkaṇḍeya Purāṇa* 195.13); and (4) the son of Bāṣkala (*Brahmāṇḍa Purāṇa* 3.5.38–39).

"Having had a quarrel with Śiva, Dakṣa decided that he must be given no share in a ritual sacrifice he offered to all the other gods. Seeing that there

4 According to the *Harivaṁśa* (1.3) and *Viṣṇu Purāṇa* (1.15), ten daughters were given to Dharma, thirteen to Kaśyapa, twenty-seven to the Moon (Soma), four to Ariṣṭanemin, two to the son of Bhṛgu, and two to Kṛśāśva. The number of Dakṣa's daughters is not given in these texts.

was no part for her husband in her father's offerings, Satī, Dakṣa's youngest daughter, destroyed herself through the fire of her anger. Śiva, desperate at the loss of his beloved, sent the monster Vīrabhadra to take revenge. Vīrabhadra sacrificed the head of Dakṣa in the Southern fire, the fire of Death. Then, pacified by the prayer of all the gods, Śiva allowed Dakṣa to live again with the head of the first living being that was met. A goat (henceforth the principal sacrificial animal) was the first living being found. And since then Dakṣa Prajāpati has had a goat's head. Dakṣa's name means 'skilled.' He is a ritual expert. Ritual is a difficult technique. It is through the ritual sacrifice that all beings are created. Even the gods worship Ritual Skill. By pleasing him one gains ability and craftsmanship." (Vijayānanda Tripāṭhī, "Devatā tattva.")

The Crack-of-Fire (Bhṛgu)

The Crack-of-Fire (Bhṛgu) represents the power of knowledge. He is the alleged author of two Vedic hymns. He is one of the ten lords of progeny created by Manu.

The Mover-of-Mountains (Agastya)

The Mover-of-Mountains, or Mover-of-the-Unmoving[5] (Agastya), represents the power of teaching. He is the teacher of grammar, medicine, and other sciences and is the author of several Vedic hymns and of a book on medicine. Indra taught him the *Jaiminīya Upaniṣad Brāhmaṇa* (see 4.15.1; 4.16.1). Agastya was, like Vasiṣṭha, the child of Mitra-Varuṇa and Urvaśī. He is said to have been born in a water jar (*Bṛhad-devatā* 5.134).[6] The *Ṛg Veda* (7.33.13) mentions his birth. He was of small stature and is pictured as a dwarf, yet he swallowed the ocean (*Mahābhārata* 3.105; *Padma Purāṇa* 1.19) and compelled the Vindhyā mountains to prostrate themselves before him. (*Mahābhārata* 3.104; *Devī Bhāgavata Purāṇa* 10.3.7.)

The wife of Agastya is Lohāmudrā, the daughter of the king of the Videhas. The *Ṛg Veda* (1.179.4) mentions a conversation between her and her husband.

In the *Aitareya Brāhmaṇa* (5.16) Agastya is said to have made peace between Indra and the Maruts, who had had a quarrel.

5 For the derivation of the word *agastya* from *gam*, "to move," and *aga*, "unmoving" or "mountain," see *Rāmāyaṇa* 2.11.

6 The birth of Agastya is also mentioned in the *Matsya Purāṇa* 61.201; *Padma Purāṇa*, Sṛṣṭi khaṇḍa, 22; *Mahābhārata* 3.98, 7.157, 185, 12.344; *Brahmāṇḍa Purāṇa* 3.35.

Agastya is further mentioned in *Ṛg Veda* 1.165.13–15; 1.166–69; 1.170.2 and 5; 1.171–78; 1.179.3–4; 1.180–91; *Taittirīya Saṁhitā* 7.5.5.2; *Taittirīya Brāhmaṇa* 2.7.11.1; *Kāṭhaka Saṁhitā* 10.11; *Maitrāyaṇi Saṁhitā* 2.1.8; *Pañcaviṁśati Brāhmaṇa* 21.14.5.

King Nahuṣa, who acted for Indra during an absence of the king of heaven, asked the seven sages to carry him in a palanquin when he was on his way to make love to Indra's wife. Agastya was so short that he could not walk fast enough, and the king abused him. In anger, Agastya cursed the king and he became a serpent. Later Kṛṣṇa released him from the curse.

Agastya gave divine weapons to Rāma so that he could kill the demons during his stay in the forest. (*Rāmāyaṇa* 3.11.) The *Rāmāyaṇa* (3.12) mentions that all the gods used to come with Indra to visit the sage in his hermitage.

At one time two demon brothers, Vātāpi and Ilvala, were ill-treating the sages. Agastya killed Vātāpi and swallowed Ilvala. (*Rāmāyaṇa* 3.12.)

Agastya conquered southern India and taught Vedic rites to its inhabitants. His hermitage is said to have been in the extreme south.

His cult was carried from the Tamil country to Indonesia.

The Devourer (Atri)

The Devourer (Atri) is the power of detachment. He is the author of a number of Vedic hymns. One of the ten lords of progeny, he was born from the mind of the Immense-Being (Brahmā) and sprang forth from his eyes. When the sons of Brahmā were destroyed by a curse of Śiva, Atri was born again from the flames of a sacrifice performed by Brahmā. His wife in both manifestations was Without-Spite (Anasūyā). She bore him three sons, Datta, Durvāsas, and Soma, in his first life and a son, Nobility (Aryaman), and a daughter, Purity (Analā), in the second.

Atri shines as one of the stars of the Great Bear and is the author of a code of law. In the Purāṇas he is said to have produced the Moon from his eyes while he was practicing an austere penance.

Inspiration (Kratu)

Inspiration (Kratu) represents the power of intelligence. He was one of the ten sons born of the mind of Brahmā. He is one of the lords of progeny and a progenitor of mankind.

He married Action (Kriyā) or the Horse-headed (Hayaśiras) and is the father of the sixty thousand Vālakhilyas, the thumb-sized sages who surround the chariot of the Sun. (*Bhāgavata Purāṇa* 4.1.39.)

The Giver-of-Advice (Nārada)

The Giver-of-Advice (Nārada) represents the power of persuasion. Author of some of the hymns of the *Ṛg Veda*, he is associated with Parvata and acts as messenger between men and gods. He is fond of spreading discord; hence his epithet is strife-lover (Kalipriya). He appears among the ten lords of progeny as a son of Brahmā, having sprung from his thigh.

He is later represented as the friend of Kṛṣṇa and the inventor of the lute, the *vīṇā*. He is the alleged author of a code of law.

Light (Marīci)

Light (Marīci) is connected with the Maruts. He is considered to be one of the sons born of the Creator (Brahmā) or one of the ten Patriarchs created by the first lawgiver (Manu). He was the father of Vision (Kaśyapa).

Vision (Kaśyapa)

Vision (Kaśyapa) [7] represents the power of procreation. He is the universal progenitor of men, gods, and demons, all born from his thirteen wives, who were the daughters of Ritual-Skill (Dakṣa).

Vision is the son of Light (Marīci), himself a son of the Immense-Being (Brahmā).

Bṛhaspati (the Great Master), the Teacher of the Gods

"THE WIFE of the seer Fiery (Aṅgiras), because of an error she had committed, gave birth to a dead child. Brahmā advised her to practice the son-giving (*puṁsavana*) austerities. Having learned the technique of these austerities from Eternal-Youth (Sanat-kumāra), the seer's wife was able to please the All-Powerful. She bore a son called the Great-Master (Bṛhaspati), who is the presiding deity of mental powers and the teacher of the gods." (Vijayānanda Tripāṭhī, "Devatā tattva.")

The Great Master is the teacher of the "science of light" (*jyotir-vijñāna*, i.e., astrology and astronomy). He is the ruler of the Sun and the Moon. Seated on his chariot, called Sound-of-the-Wise-Rules (Nīti-ghoṣa), he controls the movement of the planets. He is represented as golden in color. The seer Skylark (Bharadvāja) is his son.

Bṛhaspati is mentioned in the *Ṛg Veda* as born in the sky with seven faces and seven rays (4.50.4). He has sharp horns (10.155.2). He holds a bow, arrows, and a golden ax (2.24.8; 7.97.7). Red horses are yoked to his chariot (7.97.6). He released the cows stolen by Indra while the god was fighting a demon (2.23.18). Bṛhaspati defeats his enemies and breaks their forts (6.73.2). Prayers are offered to him before starting battle (1.40.8). He favors his devotees

7 For the symbolical etymology of the word *kaśyapa*, see p. 95, n. 6.

(2.25.1). No ritual sacrifice can be complete without invoking this teacher of the gods.

The Great Master is mentioned under several names. The main ones are: the priestly-lord (Brahmaṇas-pati), the lord-of-assemblies (Sadasas-pati), the king-of-elders (Jyeṣṭha-rāja), the lord-of-[heavenly]-hosts (Gaṇa-pati).

He is the seer who perceived and wrote one of the hymns of the *Ṛg Veda* (10.72). The wife of Bṛhaspati is called Speech (Dhenā) (*Gopatha Brāhmaṇa* 2.9) or the Great-One (Bṛhatī) or Speech (Vāṇī). The Great Master himself is called Bṛhaspati because he is her husband. (*Bṛhad-āraṇyaka Upaniṣad* 1.3.20, 21.)

Bṛhaspati worshiped Śiva for a thousand years in the Field-of-Light (Prabhāsa Kṣetra). As a reward, Śiva then made him the planet Jupiter. (*Skanda Purāṇa.*) As a planet his wife is the Star (Tārā). She was seduced by the Moon and bore a son who is the planet Mercury (Budha). Tārā later came back to her husband.

A book of law and a book of politics are attributed to Bṛhaspati.

"The *Bṛhaspati Saṁhitā* contained a large collection of the teachings of the teacher of the gods regarding the giving of alms. Only a fragment of this text is now available. Some traditional authorities consider that the atheistic philosophy now attributed to Carvāka was originally his creation and was undertaken to discourage the antigods from performing the ritual sacrifices (*yajña*), charities (*dāna*), and penance (*tapas*), etc., through which they had acquired godlike powers." (Vijayānanda Tripāṭhī, "Devatā tattva.")[8]

Śukra, the Teacher of the Genii

"ŚUKRA, the son of the seer Bhṛgu, because of his enmity toward Bṛhaspati, agreed to be the teacher of the genii (*daitya*). Bṛhaspati's son, Beauty (Kaca), learned from him the science of reviving the dead. When, during the ritual sacrifice offered by the *daitya* king Bali, Vāmana, the dwarf avatar of Viṣṇu, began to ask for land, Śukra attempted to prevent him from realizing his aim. Because Śukra thus created obstacles toward the giving of charity, Viṣṇu made one of his eyes sightless. Since then his name has become synonymous with being one-eyed.

"Śukra is the presiding deity of semen. In the visible world his form is the planet Venus. His influence is described in the treatises on astrology. Śukra is

8 See also Durgādatta Tripāṭhī, "Deva guru Bṛhaspati," *Siddhānta*, IV, 1943–44, 54–66.

considered the inventor of political science, and is said to have composed the *Śukra-nīti*, the most famous code of behavior and politics. His sons Impetuous (Caṇḍa) and Eclipse (Marka) taught this science to the genie Golden-Vesture (Hiraṇya-kaśipu)." (Vijayānanda Tripāṭhī, "Devatā tattva.")

Pṛthu, the First King

PṚTHU, the first king, is the inventor of agriculture. Through his invention, the earth, becoming a cow, was milked.

He was born from his dead father's arm, which the sages rubbed, or, in another story, from a fire consecrated by the gods. He is the distributor of wealth and the originator of royal investiture and of the principle of royal government. The earth was named *pṛthivī* after him.

Manu, the Lawgiver

THE FOURTEEN progenitors and lawgivers of the human race in fourteen successive creations are known as Manus.

The first was the Son-of-the-Self-born (Svāyambhuva), procreated by the Immense-Being (Brahmā) after he had divided himself into male and female halves. From this Manu were born the ten Great-Seers (Mahā-ṛṣis) or lords-of-progeny (Prajā-patis).

The Manu of the present age is the Son-of-Light (Vaivasvata). His story is linked with that of the deluge.

Manu is mentioned in the Vedas as the progenitor of mankind (*Ṛg Veda* 1.80.16, etc. *Taittirīya Saṁhitā* 2.1.5.6; *Atharva Veda* 14.2.41).

The story of the deluge and Manu are mentioned in the *Śatapatha Brāhmaṇa* (1.8.1.1).

Manu is a performer of sacrifices (*Ṛg Veda* 10.63.7; *Taittirīya Saṁhitā* 1.5.1.3, etc.).

According to the *Mahābhārata* (12.343.40), it was the first Manu, Svāyambhuva, who wrote the treatise on morals and politics known as *Manu Smṛti*. According to Kullūka's commentary on *Manu Smṛti*, the lord-of-progeny (Prajāpati) himself wrote this work, which originally had a hundred thousand verses. These were later condensed by Manu. A Tantric text also is attributed to Manu.

In the history of creation, one day and night of the Immense Being is called a *kalpa*. This day is divided into fourteen parts. One Manu rules over each of these parts, which are called *manvantaras* (reign of a Manu). Each *manvantara* lasts two and a half equinoxial precessions, that is, 4,320,000 human years. There are thus fourteen Manus in a *kalpa*, and for the rule of each Manu a different set of the seven sages, different gods, a different Indra, and different avatars appear.

The names of the fourteen Manus are: Son-of-the-Self-born (Svāyambhuva), Son-of-the-Self-Luminous (Svārociṣa), Son-of-the-Highest (Auttama), Son-of-Darkness (Tāmasa), Son-of-Opulence (Raivata), Son-of-Vision (Cākṣuṣa), Son-of-Brightness (Vaivasvata), Kinsman-of-the-Sun (Arka-sāvarṇika), Kinsman-of-Ritual-Skill (Dakṣa-sāvarṇika), Kinsman-of-the-Immensity (Brahma-sāvarṇika), Kinsman-of-the-Eternal-Law (Dharma-sāvarṇika), Kinsman-of-the-Destroyer (Rudra-sāvarṇika), Kinsman-of-Light (Deva-sāvarṇika or Raucya), Kinsman-of-Might (Indra-sāvarṇika), or Son-of-Might (Bhautya).

SIX

The Representation and the Worship of Deities

{ 27 }

The Representation of Deities

The Worship of the Manifest Forms

THE human mind is bound by form. It cannot reach the formless; it cannot conceive it, still less concentrate on it. Hence forms and symbols are the inevitable intermediaries in a process in which the mental mechanism is discarded and supramental states of being are realized. We can approach the Unmanifest only through manifestation. It is the initial, the least formal, aspect of each field of manifestation which we may call a deity. The word "religion," like the word "Yoga," means "link." A religion that would speak only of the Unmanifest would be a contradiction in terms. There can be no direct relation between the individuality of man and unmanifest being. All religion aims at creating contacts with subtle yet manifest forms of divinity.

"Those who feel attracted to the contemplation of the Unmanifest (*avyaktā*) are faced with a problem, because a being imprisoned in a body cannot grasp the ways of the Unmanifest." (*Bhagavadgītā* 12.5. [559])

All religion is an attempt to establish contacts with manifest divinity.

"He who tells anyone that he should worship the qualityless, shapeless being acts like the doctor who advises his patient to drink celestial ambrosia. We need not question the existence of ambrosia and its curative value. We merely know that no doctor will give such advice. It is said that from the drops fallen from the urn of divine ambrosia all the medicinal plants were born. These plants constitute the source of our pharmacopoeia; for the remedy, as defined in the ancient medical science, is that which acts against the disease and which is within the reach of the patient. Similarly the spiritual guide, the *guru*, understanding the nature and the qualifications of the seeker, tells him the particular form of divinity he should worship." (Vijayānanda Tripāṭhī, "Devatā tattva," *Sanmārga*, III, 1942.)

The Representation of Deities

NAME and form are for man the two essential aspects of manifestation, form being the direct expression of an idea in the Creator's mind and name the parallel process of the manifestation of the same idea through the human mind. "Verily, in the beginning the world was not differentiated. It became differentiated just by name and form; so that everything has a name and a form. Even today things are differentiated just by name and form, so that [we describe them] saying, 'It has such a name, such a form.' " (*Bṛhad-āraṇyaka Upaniṣad* 1.4.7. [560]) It is only when the perception of the divine thought and the name are superimposed, that is, when divine creation and human creation unite, that things really exist. The world comes to life.

The basic energies of the universe, which are the deities, can be approached through a mental creative process, that is, through words or through the perception of created forms. Deities are therefore represented in terms of both words and forms.

In these two fields there are different degrees of abstraction. We can represent a deity through the description of its characteristics, its picture in words, or through symbolic elements of sound, that is, thought-form (*mantra*) or magic words, which correspond to its nature, though they may seem to us otherwise meaningless. Similarly we can picture a deity in an image portraying a number of symbolic attributes, or we can represent it through a diagram, a geometrical abstraction. These abstract or magic diagrams are known as *yantras*.

The representation of deities through thought-forms and magic diagrams, *mantras* and *yantras*, being more abstract, is more accurate than an image. These forms constitute the nearest representations of the nature of a deity, and are therefore more efficacious in rites. Descriptive pictures of deities are for the assistance of worshipers who need a pictorial medium as a support, to enable them to concentrate their thoughts on abstractions.

Like all the aspects of manifestation, language develops from simple, elemental principles into complex multiple forms. The fundamental basic monosyllables which are the elements of language have been connected with universal principles as yet hardly differentiated, and are called the "basic thought-forms" (*bīja-mantra*). They are considered the root of all language.

The elementary graphic figures representing the same principles are the root-diagrams, the *mūla-yantras*, which form ideograms, which all writing utilizes.

The descriptions and stories of deities and their representation in anthropomorphic, zoomorphic, or vegetal figures are symbolic commentaries on these ideograms. They utilize as symbols the more intricate, that is, more manifest, forms of Nature (*prakṛti*), and are meant for minds which cannot easily grasp a greater degree of abstraction.

An intermediary degree of symbolic representation is conveyed through conventional gesture and through the relation of sounds. The two outstanding applications are the sacred arts of dancing and music. Traditionally these have been considered essential means of making abstract concepts accessible to the common mind.

"[The gods asked:] 'Since it is not proper that the Vedas be heard by those of low birth, you should create a fifth Veda for all classes of people.'

"[Brahmā replied:] 'I shall compose a fifth Veda, called the Theatrical Art, based on history, which will convey the meaning of all the Scriptures and give an impulse to the arts. It will give good advice and moral lessons, rich in meaning, that lead to good conduct, prosperity, and fame. It will show the line of proper conduct to the future world.' " (*Nāṭya Śāstra* 1.4.13–15. [561])

Mantras and *yantras* are therefore the abstract symbols, *mudrā* (gesture) and *svara* (musical notes) are the subtle representations, and image and myth are the gross representations of the principles known as deities.

The Thought-Forms, or Mantras

MANU, the Lawgiver, is represented as having been the first being to perceive the thought-forms of objects and to have taught these thought-forms to man and explained their relation with their objects, thus creating the first language. The thought-forms are envisaged as the subtle forms or subtle bodies of things and are permanent, indestructible formulas from which the impermanent physical forms can always be derived. The language that Manu taught was the primeval language, the eternal, true language made of root-words (i.e., meaningful basic monosyllables). Sanskrit is believed to be the language most directly derived from this original speech, while all other languages are its more or less corrupt forms.[1]

To the original or true language belong the sacred utterances used in worship and called *mantras*. The word *mantra* means "thought-form." Through the understanding of the inner significance of the *mantra* we can realize the nature of that which it represents.

As the abstract patterns from which manifestation is derived, the *mantras* are in a way identical to deities. They represent the nature of deities and are inseparable from them. The power of the deity is inherent in its name, its formula, its *mantra*, which becomes the subtle vehicle through which contacts can be established between deity and worshiper. Through adequate *mantras* any sort of being can be evoked. *Mantras* are therefore the key to all rituals in all religions and are also used in most forms of magic.

"Verily, the body of the deity arises from its basic thought-form [or seed-*mantra*]." (*Yāmala Tantra*. [562])

Each deity is represented by a distinct *mantra*, and it is only through these

1 See Baradā Kantha Majumdar, in *Principles of Tantra* (ed. Woodroffe), Introduction, II (1916), xxxv–xxxvi, or p. 603 (1952 ed.).

mysterious sounds that images can be consecrated and become "alive." [2] It is the power of the *mantra* which brings down the deity and makes it enter the image.

As the links between different worlds, the bridges between different orders of things, the *mantras* are the instruments through which man can reach beyond the limits of his perceptions. "A *mantra* is so called because through it the thought (*manana*) that is knowledge of the world and protection (*trāṇa*) from transmigration can be attained." (*Piṅgala Tantra.* [563])

"It is called a *mantra* because the thought of it protects." (*Mantra Mahārṇava,* quoted by Devarāja Vidyā Vācaspati, "Tantra men Yantra aur Mantra," *Kalyāṇa,* Śakti aṅka, p. 390.)

The first perception of a *mantra* is always attributed to a direct contact between a human being and a divinity. The *mantra* has to be first directly received from a divine incarnation or to be witnessed by a seer as a supranatural vision. Hence "he who [first] utters the *mantra* is its seer." (*Sarvānukramaṇī.* [564]) The *mantra* is further defined by metrical characteristics connected with the linear characteristics of the corresponding *yantra;* these features refer to the order of things to which the *mantra* belongs. The *mantra* represents a definite deity whom it praises and pleases; "that of which it speaks is the deity" (ibid. [565]). It may further have a particular action or purpose for which it is used.

The Basic-Thought-Forms (*bīja-mantra*)

THE NUMBER of sound-elements used in all languages to form "articulate syllables" or *varṇas* is limited by the capabilities of the human vocal organ and the aptitude for differentiation of the ear. These elements are common to all languages, although most languages use only a part of them.

These sound-elements of language are permanent entities, independent of the evolution of language, and can be spoken of as everlasting or eternal. The Tantras attribute to them an independent existence and describe them as living, conscious sound-powers, equated with the deities.

These basic sound-powers have correspondences in all the spheres of manifestation. Each form grasped by the mind or the senses has an equivalent in terms of sound, a natural name.

The main monosyllabic *mantras* are called basic-thought-forms or seed-*mantras* (*bīja-mantra*).

2 The transmutation of bread and wine in the Roman Catholic ritual is done through a *mantra* and cannot be done without it.

Each element of the utterance of a *mantra* corresponds to a given notion which originates in the place of its articulation, the nature of the muscular action by which it is produced, its relative pitch, duration, etc. These elements lead to the attribution of common characters to each category of letter or articulate unit of speech. Hence the vowels and the simple consonants are female, sibilants and simple aspirates are neuter. Gutturals are priestly and suited for the invocation of deities. Cerebrals, palatals, and dentals are warriors, suited for the magic words of action and duty. Labials and liquids are traders, suited for persuading and propitiating. The sibilants and aspirates are workmen, used in the lower forms of magic.[3]

Several elements of articulation may combine to form the monosyllables which are called seed-*mantras* and which represent the complex nature of the basic energies or deities. These powerful monosyllables are the roots of the power of speech and produce echoes in all the aspects of manifestation. The primordial language is believed to have been made of such ideophones and was therefore essentially monosyllabic. The syllables which express the elemental forces of Nature (*prakṛti*) are the true names of the deities and their images. The gods are bound to respond to these sounds.

Other Kinds of *Mantras*

THERE IS an almost endless number of *mantras*.[4] The whole of the sacred text of the Vedas is believed to be made of magic words. *Mantras*, however, have to come down through a direct verbal transmission from the seer who first

3 The sound-elements of language are based upon differences in pitch, volume, and duration superimposed on the vowels or lasting sounds that can be produced in five main places of articulation. There are therefore five simple vowels, which can be short or long, to which are added four mixed vowels; nine vowels in all.

At each place of articulation there can also be four kinds of occlusion (with outward effort or inward effort, both of which can be simple or aspirate). There is, furthermore, a nasal for each place of articulation; a semivowel for four of them, an aspirate for one, and a sibilant for three of them. In all, there are thirty-three consonants (excluding the three semiconsonants, visarga, upadhmānīya, and anusvara).

The nine vowels combine with the thirty-three consonants. Semivowels and sibilants can be further combined with other consonants within a single syllable. All these sounds can be nasalized and, in addition, can have five different pitches, easily recognizable.

This gives us a total of $9 + 297 + 1{,}188 + 891 = 2{,}385 \times 2 = 4{,}770 \times 5 = 23{,}850$ possible monosyllabic sounds.

4 The main *mantras* are said to number seventy million and the secondary *mantras* to be countless.

experienced them; otherwise they are not considered alive. *Mantras* cannot be learned from a book nor can they be revived when their transmission has been broken. While the seed-*mantras* are monosyllabic, others may have the form of a sentence. Their structure is ruled by the symbolism of numbers, hence the main Śiva *mantra* has five syllables, the main Viṣṇu *mantra* eight, the solar *mantra* twelve, etc. Most of the important *mantras* used in Hindu rituals possess, besides their inner suprasensorial significance, an exoteric meaning in the Sanskrit language. The exoteric meaning is an aid to memory but is not necessarily directly connected with the inner significance of the *mantra,* though it may be an outward praise of the deity represented. There are also *mantras* which have no outward meaning in any language or system of sounds existing at present but whose celestial resonance and efficacy is great; such are the *śabara* (wild) *mantras* used in some forms of magic ritual all over India.

Mantras are classified in different categories according to the effect.

"Wise men should know *mantras* to be of four kinds, called Sure (Siddha), Helpful (Sādhya), Accomplished (Susiddha), and Enemy (Ari)." (*Viśva-sāra Tantra.*) "The Sure-*mantras* bring results unfailingly within a specified time, the Helpful-*mantras* bring results when used with rosaries and offerings, the Accomplished-*mantras* bring results immediately, the Enemy-*mantras* destroy those who utter them." (*Mantra Mahodadhi* 24.23. [566])

A particular *mantra* can belong to any of these categories according to the way it has been transmitted and the qualifications of the worshipers.

"Hindu life is pervaded by *mantras.* The entire existence of a peasant or a prince is regulated by them. The purposes of *mantras* are numerous; they are used for: (1) attaining liberation, (2) worship of the manifest forms of divinity, (3) worship of the lesser gods and genii, (4) communicating with deities, (5) the acquisition of superhuman powers, (6) the feeding of Ancestors and gods, (7) communicating with ghosts and spirits, (8) warding off evil influences, (9) exorcising devils, (10) the cure of diseases, (11) preparing curative water, (12) destroying plants, animals, or men, (13) eliminating poisons from the body, (14) influencing others' thoughts and actions, (15) bringing men, beasts, lesser deities, and ghosts under control, (16) the purification of the human body." (Baradā Kantha Majumdar in *Principles of Tantra* [ed. Woodruffe], Introduction, II [1916], xxxviii, or p. 606 [1952 ed.], quoted with slight changes.)

Mantras are also a means of increasing one's powers:

"Uncommon powers of the mind can be the result of birth, drugs, *mantras,* austerities, and divine contemplation." (Patañjali, *Yoga Sūtra* 4.1. [567])

The Chief Basic Thought-Forms, or Seed *Mantras*

1. *The Seed-of-the-Immensity* (brahma-bīja) *or Thought-Form-of-the-Knowledge-of-the-Immensity* (brahma-vidyā mantra)

SOUND: AUM.

MEANING: "I bow," or "I agree," or "I accept," in the primeval language. "Verily, this syllable is assent: for whenever a man assents to anything he says simply, 'AUM.' This indeed is a realization; that is, assent is." (*Chāndogya Upaniṣad* 1.1.8. [568])

DEFINITION: This *mantra* is also called "that which leads to the other shore" (*tārā* or *tāriṇī*). It is considered the source of all *mantras*.

"*A, U, M* are the three letters, and these letters are the three tendencies, the revolving, the cohesive, and the disintegrating. Next comes the half letter, representing the Unqualified, which is perceived only by the yogi." (*Dattātreya Tantra Saṁhitā*. [569])

"*A* represents Brahmā, the revolving-tendency (*rajas*), the red color, the form of the universe (the Destructible Person, *kṣara puruṣa*) or Cosmic Body (the Glorious, *virāṭ*), the state of wakefulness, the power of action.

"*U* represents Viṣṇu, the tendency toward concentration (*sattva*), the white color, the Law of the universe (the Indestructible Person, *akṣara puruṣa*), the Cosmic Intellect (the Embryo of Splendor, Hiraṇyagarbha), the state of dream, the power of thought, the unmanifest world.

"*A* and *U* together mean 'truth,' 'immortality.'

"*M* represents Śiva, the tendency toward disintegration, the black color, the causal substratum (the Changeless Person, *avyaya puruṣa*), the Cosmic Consciousness, the All-knowing (*sarva-jña*), the state of deep sleep, the power of consciousness.[5]

"This half letter (*M*) is the basis of all things, but this basis is not-straight (*kūṭastha*), that is, is not within the reach of mind and words." (Karapātrī, "Śrī Bhagavatī tattva," *Siddhānta*, V, 1944–45.)

AUM is said to represent also the One Being pervading space, time, and forms (Chalāri on *Tantra-sāra Saṅgraha*).

NUMBER OF REPETITIONS: Either 300,000 or thrice ten times a day by householders, and on all occasions by ascetics (*Tantra-sāra*).

PURPOSE: Leads to realization, to liberation from bondage, to the attainment of Supreme Reality.

5 According to Durgā Dāsa, *A* stands for Viṣṇu, *U* for Śiva, *M* for Brahmā.

RITUAL USE: At the beginning of all rituals.

REFERENCES: *Chāndogya Upaniṣad, Tantra Tattva-prakāśa, Tantra-sāra,* etc.

Going further in the analysis of this one syllable, the Upaniṣads distinguish eight components in it.

"This one syllable is formed of eight subtle sound-elements. It has an eightfold character, is divisible into eight parts.

"*A* is the first, *U* the second, *M* the third. The nasalization (*bindu*) is the fourth; the sound (*nāda*) is the fifth; the duration (*kāla*) is the sixth; the resonance within time (*kālātīta*) is the seventh. In addition to these, its timeless resonance is the eighth." (*Tāra-sāra Upaniṣad,* 2.1. [570])

Taken as the symbol of Divinity, AUM appears as the form from which the universe develops. The three letters therefore have equivalents in all the forms of manifestation (see chart on p. 340).

From the basic syllable AUM spring forth all the elemental sounds, the "seed utterances" (*bīja-mantra*) which are the root of all the aspects of manifestation, the keys to all language, the powerful sound-elements from which the magical power of the *mantras* is derived.

"AUM. This syllable is the whole world. It is the past, the present, the future. Everything is just the word AUM. And whatever else there is that transcends threefold time, that, too, is just the word AUM." (*Māṇḍūkya Upaniṣad* 1.1. [571])

An important class of literature deals with the implications of the single syllable AUM taken as the most abstract symbol of divinity and the instrument of realization.

"The syllable AUM has Speech (Vāc) for its deity, or else it is addressed to the Ruler-of-Heaven (Indra), or else it belongs to the Supreme-Ruler (*parameṣṭhin*), or it is addressed to the totality of the gods or to the Immensity or to the gods in general. The principle represented by the syllable *ka* is its deity." (*Bṛhad-devatā* 2.125. [572])

Taken as the symbol of the union of the three gods, AUM appears as the first thought-form from which the universe develops.

"The first unit (the letter *A*) of the syllable is the terrestrial world (the seven continents surrounded by the seven seas). The letter *A* stands also for the 'Knowledge of Meters,' the *Ṛg Veda*. Brahmā, the Creator, is its presiding deity, and the eight spheres of existence, the Vasus, are the deities exercising their beneficial influence over it. The twenty-four-syllabled Gāyatrī is its meter. The householder's (*gārhapatya*) fire is its fire.

EQUIVALENTS OF THE LETTERS OF AUM

	A	U	M
Meters:	Gāyatrī (24 syllables)	Triṣṭubh (44 syllables)	Jagatī (48 syllables)
States:	waking-consciousness (*jāgrata*)	dream (*svapna*)	deep-sleep (*suṣupti*)
Periods (*sāvana*):	morning	midday	evening
Cycles:	24 years	44 years	48 years
Gods:	of the elements (Vasus)	of the sky (Ādityas)	of the sphere-of-space (Rudras)
Season:	spring	summer	winter
Offering:	the offered-butter (*ājya*)	the fuel (*idhma*)	the act-of-offering (*havis*)
Ritual utterance:	"Earth" (*bhūr*)	"Sky" (*svar*)	"Space" (*bhuvas*)
Spheres:	earthly	heavenly	intermediary
Veda:	Knowledge-of-meters (*Ṛk*)	Knowledge-of-contents (*Yajus*)	Knowledge-of-extension (*Sāman*)
Elemental deity:	Fire (Agni)	Sun (Āditya)	Wind (Vāyu)
Manifestation of speech:	voice (*vāc*)	mind (*manas*)	breath (*prāṇa*)
Priestly function:	The Hotṛ (making offering)	The Adhvaryu (performing ritual)	The Udgātṛ (singing)
Quality:	extension (*rajas*)	cohesion (*sattva*)	disintegration (*tamas*)
Ritual fire:	of the home (*gārhapatya-agni*)	of Ancestors (*dakṣiṇa-agni*)	of invocation (*āhavāna-agni*)
Goddess:	Ambā	Ambikā	Ambālikā
Deity:	Brahmā (the Creator)	Viṣṇu (the Preserver)	Śiva (the Destroyer)
Power:	of action (*kriyā*)	of knowledge (*jñāna*)	of will (*icchā*)

NOTE. From Vāsudeva Śaraṇa Agravala, "Śiva kā svarūpa," *Kalyāṇa*, Śiva aṅka, p. 492.

"The second letter is the intermediary world. This is the letter *U*, it stands for the 'Knowledge of Inner Reality,' the *Yajur Veda*, glorifying the sacrifice. The All-Pervader, Viṣṇu, the sustainer of the worlds, is its presiding deity. The eleven Rudras (representing the five organs of perception, the five organs of action, and the mind) are the deities exercising their beneficent influence over it. The meter is the forty-four-syllabled Triṣṭubh. Charity is the Southern (*dakṣiṇa*) fire.

"The third letter, *M*, is the celestial world. It is the 'Knowledge of Extension,' the *Sāma Veda*, composed of hymns that are chanted. Rudra, the Destroyer, is its presiding deity, and the twelve sovereign principles, the Ādityas, who stand for the twelve solar months, are the deities exercising their beneficial influence over it. The forty-eight-syllabled meter Jagatī is its meter. The invocation (*āhvana*) with which oblations are offered in its fire is '*bhuvas*' (to Space).

"The half letter *ardha-mātrā* at the end of that sacred syllable completes its fourfold character. It represents the lunar world, the 'Knowledge of Subtle Correspondences,' the *Atharva Veda*, composed of hymns (those specially used in the six observances and revealed to the seer Atharvāṅgiras). The rain of fire which reduces the three worlds to ashes is the presiding deity, and the forty-nine deities of the wind, the Maruts, are the deities exercising their beneficent influence over it. The ten-syllabled meter Virāṭ is the meter. The Ekarṣi Fire of the Atharva ritual is the fire. This letter shines inward in all the quarters of the thought-form and is [the king of thought-forms], the soul of the fourfold letter in its gross, subtle, seed, and witness stages." (*Nṛsiṁha-uttara-tāpinī Upaniṣad* 3.1–5. [573])

2. *The Seed-of-Consciousness or Seed-of-Speech* (vāg-bīja)

SOUND: AIṀ.

DEFINITION: This *mantra* is also called Sārasvata (pertaining to knowledge), or Sārasvatī (pertaining to the goddess of knowledge). It represents the form of consciousness embodied in the goddess Sarasvatī, the consort of Brahmā.

"*AI* represents Sarasvatī. The nasalization means the removing of pain. This is the seed-utterance of Sarasvatī. With it the 'Word' is worshiped." (*Varadā Tantra*. [574])

PURPOSE: Acquiring knowledge and wisdom, mastery over words, and power of speech.

REFERENCES: *Tripurā-tāpinī Upaniṣad, Karpūra-stava, Varadā Tantra*, etc.

3. *The Seed-of-Illusion* (māyā-bīja) *or Seed-of-Energy* (śakti-bīja)

SOUND: HRĪṀ.

DEFINITION: This *mantra* represents *māyā*, the power of illusion. It stands for the lady-of-the-spheres (Bhuvaneśvarī), the dispeller of sorrow. It is the root from which develop ether and the other elements of the manifest world, the principle ever liberated, unbound by the triple form of time.

"*H* means Śiva. *R* is his Nature, Prakṛti. *Ī* means Transcendent-Illusion (*mahā-māyā*). The sound is the 'progenitor of the universe.' The nasalization means the removing of sorrow. The lady of the spheres should be worshiped with this [*mantra*]." (*Varadā Tantra.* [575])

PURPOSE: Conquest of the Unmanifest, of the power of Nature. Transgressing the laws of time and space.

REFERENCES: *Tripurā-tāpinī Upaniṣad* 1.13; *Karpūra-stava* 2; *Varadā Tantra*, etc.

4. *The Seed-of-Existence or Seed-of-Fortune* (lakṣmī-bīja)

SOUND: ŚRĪṀ.

DEFINITION: This *mantra* represents the goddess of fortune and multiplicity, Lakṣmī, the consort of Viṣṇu.

"*Ś* represents the transcendent divinity of Fortune. *R* means wealth. *Ī* is satisfaction. The sound means 'limitlessness.' The nasalization means the dispelling of sorrow. This is the seed utterance of the goddess Lakṣmī through which she should be worshiped." (*Varadā Tantra.* [576])

PURPOSE: Gaining worldly wealth, power, beauty, and glory.

REFERENCES: *Tripurā-tāpinī Upaniṣad, Varadā Tantra*, etc.

5. *The Seed-of-Desire* (kāma-bīja)

SOUND: KLĪṀ.

DEFINITION: This *mantra* represents the form of joy, of pleasure, the procreative aspect of the power of Śiva in the form of his consort, the Transcendent-Goddess (Maheśvarī).

"*K* represents Eros (Kāmadeva) or Kṛṣṇa, the incarnation of divine lust. *L* means the lord of heaven, Indra. *Ī* means satisfaction. The nasalization is the giver of both pleasure and pain. This Seed of Desire is spoken to you out of love, O Great Goddess." (*Varadā Tantra.* [577])

PURPOSE: Gaining transcendent knowledge and also pleasure, victory, and royal power.

REFERENCES: *Tripurā-tāpinī Upaniṣad, Karpūra-stava* 3, *Varadā Tantra*, etc.

6. *The Primordial-Seed* (ādya-bīja) *or Seed-of-the-Power-of-Time* (kālī-bīja)

SOUND: KRĪṀ.

DEFINITION: This *mantra* represents the power of time, the power of death, the destructive aspect of Śiva, and thus the goddess Kālī, the power of time.

"*K* is Kālī. *R* is the Brahman. *Ī* is the transcendent power of illusion. The sound is the 'Mother of the universe.' The nasalization is the dispelling of sorrow. The goddess Kālī should be worshiped with this *mantra* for the pacifying of all pain." (*Varadā Tantra*. [578])

PURPOSE: Gaining detachment, power over death, transcendent knowledge.

REFERENCES: *Tripurā-tāpinī Upaniṣad, Mahānirvāṇa* and *Varadā Tantras*, etc.

Other Seed *Mantras*

DUṀ is Durgā, the goddess Beyond Reach.
HAUṀ is Śiva, the lord of peace, and also the seed of speech.
HUṀ protects from anger and demons.
GAṀ is Gaṇapati, the unity of the macrocosm and the microcosm.
GLAUṀ is Gaṇapati as giver of mental powers.
KṢRAUṀ is the Man-Lion, the aspect of Viṣṇu that destroys evil.
STRĪṀ delivers from difficulties.
PHAṬ is the weapon which can destroy anything.
STRAUṀ is the giver of lust.
PREṀ is used for enchantments and magic.
KHA kills.
AṀ is the noose with which to catch anything.

The Seed *Mantras* of the Elements

YAṀ, Air. Its color is black, its symbol the hexagon, its vehicle the black antelope.

LAṀ, Earth. Its color is yellow, its symbol the square, its vehicle the elephant. It is also the *mantra* of Indra, the king of heaven.

RAṀ, Fire. Its color is red, its symbol the triangle, its vehicle the ram.

VAṀ, Water. Its color is white, its symbol is the crescent or the arc of a circle (or the triangle apex downward), its vehicle is the crocodile.

HAṀ, Ether. Its color also is white, its symbol is the point or the circle, its vehicle is the white elephant.

The *Chāndogya Upaniṣad* 1.13.1–3 [579]) gives distinct liturgical seed-*mantras:*

HĀ-U, the Earth. "Verily, the sound *hā-u* is this world (for it occurs in the *Rathantara Sāman*, which is identified with the earth)."

HĀ-I, Wind. "The sound *hā-i* is wind (for it occurs in the *Vāmadeva Sāman*, which has for its subject the origin of wind and water)."

ATHA, the Moon (or sperm). "The sound *atha* (take this) is the moon (or sperm) (for everything is established on food and the Moon [sperm] consists of food)."

IHA, the self. "The sound *iha* (here) means oneself (for 'here' is where one's self is)."

I, Fire. "The sound *i* is Fire (Agni) (for all *Sāmans* sacred to Agni end with the sound *i*)."

U, the Sun. "The sound *U* (up) is the Sun (for people praise the Sun when it goes up (*ūrdhvam*)."

E, Invocation. "The sound *e* is invocation (for people call, saying, '*Ehi*' (come)."

O-HŌ-I, the Viśvadevas. "The sound *o-hō-i* is the Viśvadeva gods (for it occurs in the *Sāman* to the Viśvadevas)."

HIṀ, the lord of creatures. "The sound *hiṁ* is Prajāpati (for Prajāpati is undefined and the sound *hiṁ* is also indistinct)."

YĀ, Food. "*Yā* is food (for everything here moves [*yati*] through the help of food)."

VĀC, the Cosmic Body. "*Vāc* is the Cosmic-Body (*virāj*) (for it occurs in the *Sāman* to Virāj)."

HUṀ, the Undefined. "The sound *huṁ*, the variable thirteenth interjection, is the Undefined."

The Expanded *Mantras*

SOME *mantras* are formed by combining the *bīja-mantras* to represent more complex notions.

The Mantra *of the Supreme-Energy* (parā Śakti)

SOUND: AUṀ KRĪṀ KRĪṀ KRĪṀ HŪṀ HŪṀ HRĪṀ HRĪṀ SVĀHĀ.

DEFINITION: This is the *mantra* of the Supreme Goddess, containing all the forms of Energy. It is used for her worship.

PURPOSE: To acquire all attainments.

REFERENCES: *Karpūrādi Stotra* 5 [580]; *Karpūra-stava* 5.

Flying through the Void (khecari bīja)

SOUND: HA SA KHA PREṀ.

DEFINITION: HA is the Sun, the lord of life, and also space. SA is power. KHA is space and the power to kill. PREM is the magical power for all enchantments.

PURPOSE: Moving through space.

REFERENCE: *Tripurā-tāpinī Upaniṣad* 3.12. [581]

Gāyatrī (the Protector of the Vital Energies) [6]

TEXT: AUM! *Bhūr Bhuvaḥ Svaḥ! Tat savitur vareṇyam bhargo devasya dhīmahi; dhiyo yo naḥ pracodayāt.* AUM. (*Ṛg Veda* 3.62.10 [582])

MEANING: "AUM. O terrestrial sphere! O sphere of space! O celestial sphere! Let us contemplate the splendor of the solar spirit, the Divine Creator. May he guide our minds [toward the attainment of the four aims of life [7]]. AUM."

DEFINITION: This is the most important *mantra*. Every twice-born should recite it during the three meditations of morning, midday, and sunset. It should not be uttered by women nor by men of low birth. It has twice twelve syllables, hence it is a solar *mantra*.

NUMBER OF REPETITIONS: Twelve.

RITUAL USE: During the three rituals of the day for Brahmaṇas.

REFERENCES: *Chāndogya Upaniṣad* 3.12; *Bṛhad-āraṇyaka Upaniṣad* 5.15, etc.

Brahma Gāyatrī

TEXT: *Parameśvarāya vidmahe para-tattvāya dhīmahi; tan no Brahmā pracodayāt.*

6 For the signification of the word, see *Bṛhad-āraṇyaka Upaniṣad* 5.14.4.
7 See the Brahma *mantra*, p. 346, and the *haṁsa-mantra*, p. 348.

MEANING: "May we know the Immense Being! Let us contemplate the transcendent Reality. And may that Being guide us."

DEFINITION: This form of Gāyatrī may be uttered by all.

PURPOSE: The attainment of realization by all.

REFERENCE: *Mahānirvāṇa Tantra* 3.109–11. [583]

Brahma Mantra

TEXT: AUM. *Sat-cid-ekaṁ Brahma.*

MEANING: "AUM. The Immensity is Unity, Existence, Consciousness."

PURPOSE: This *mantra* helps to fulfill the four aims of life, Righteousness, Prosperity, Pleasure, and Liberation.

REFERENCE: *Mahānirvāṇa Tantra* 3.12. [584]

Rudra Mantra

TEXT: AUM. *Trayambakaṁ yajāmahe sugandhiṁ puṣṭivardhanam Urvārukam iva bandhanān mṛtyor mukṣīya māmṛtāt.*

MEANING: "AUM. We worship the three-eyed Lord, fragrant, giver of strength, who liberates from death. May he make us free from the bonds of death."

DEFINITION: This *mantra* is the main *mantra* of the lord of tears, Rudra, the destructive aspect of Śiva.

PURPOSE: To remove all the signs of death, to prevent the withering of the body.

REFERENCES: *Uḍḍīśa Tantra* 94; *Mahānirvāṇa Tantra* 5.211. [585]

*The King-of-*Mantras (mantra-rāja)

TEXT: *Śrīṁ, Hrīṁ, Klīṁ, Kṛṣṇāya Svāhā.* (*Mantra Mahārṇava.* [586])

MEANING: "*Śrīṁ, Hrīṁ, Klīṁ,* Oblation to the Dark One."

DEFINITION: This *mantra* invokes the three aspects of the Supreme Goddess and Kṛṣṇa, the embodiment of divine love.

PURPOSE: To inspire divine love and lead to liberation.

The Pacifying of Misfortune

TEXT: AUM *haṁ hāṁ, hiṁ hīṁ, huṁ hūṁ, heṁ haiṁ, hoṁ hauṁ, haṁ haḥ. Kṣaṁ, kṣāṁ, kṣiṁ, kṣīṁ, kṣuṁ, kṣūṁ, kṣeṁ, kṣaiṁ, kṣoṁ kṣauṁ, kṣaṁ kṣaḥ. Haṁsoham.*

MEANING: "AUM *haṁ*, etc. . . . I am the Swan [the embodiment of knowledge]."

PURPOSE: To destroy the power of evil spirits and ghosts, to remove the influence of evil deeds or the effects of poison.

REFERENCE: *Uḍḍīśa Tantra* 166–68. [587]

The Calming-of-Anger (krodhaśānti)

TEXT: AUM. *Śānte praśānte sarvakrodhopaśamani svāhā.*

MEANING: "AUM. At peace! and pacifying! All anger be calmed! *Svāhā.*"

NUMBER OF REPETITIONS: Twenty-one.

PURPOSE: Calming the anger of man or the elements.

RITUAL USE: Utter this *mantra* over some water, and wash the mouth.

REFERENCE: *Uḍḍīśa Tantra.* [588]

*The Fire-*Mantra (agni-prajvālana)

TEXT: AUM. *Citpiṅgala Hana Hana, Daha Daha, Paca Paca Sarvānājñāpya svāhā.*

MEANING: "AUM. Yellow fire of the mind! hurt, hurt! burn, burn! eat, eat! Invoke him who knows all. *Svāhā.*"

PURPOSE: Producing fire.

REFERENCE: *Mahānirvāṇa Tantra* 6.142. [589]

The Fire-extinguishing Mantra (agni-stambhana)

TEXT: AUM. *Namo Agnirūpāya mama śarīre stambhanaṁ kuru kuru svāhā.*

MEANING: "AUM. To thee I bow. Do, do stop the action of Fire on my body. *Svāhā.*"

NUMBER OF REPETITIONS: 108.

PURPOSE: To render the body immune to fire.

RITUAL USE: Take the fat of a frog, mix it with the sap of the *ghṛtakumārī* plant, and rub the body with it.

REFERENCE: *Uḍḍīśa Tantra.* [590]

The Prevention-of-Sleep (nidrā-stambhana)

TEXT: AUM. *Namo [Bhagavate] Rudrāya nidrāṁ stambhaya. Ṭhaḥ, Ṭhaḥ, Ṭhaḥ.*

MEANING: "AUM. I bow to the glorious lord of tears. May he paralyze sleep. *Ṭhaḥ, Ṭhaḥ, Ṭhaḥ.*"

NUMBER OF REPETITIONS: 108.

PURPOSE: To suppress sleep.

RITUAL: Crush the roots of the *bṛhati* and *mulethi* plants, filter through a cloth, and smell while repeating the *mantra*.

REFERENCE: *Uḍḍīśa Tantra.* [591]

The Śiva Mantra *of Five-Letters* (pañcākṣara)

TEXT: AUM! *Namaḥ Śivāya.*

MEANING: "AUM! To Siva I bow."

DEFINITION: This is one of the chief *mantras* used by all Hindus. It has different forms according to the qualifications of the worshipers. The number 3 is the number of the cosmos. The number 5 is the number of life. The five letters of the Siva *mantra* represent the symbols of the fivefold aspects of all the forms of the world of life, beginning with the five elements.

PURPOSE: Spiritual realization as well as worldly achievement and warding off danger and fear.

NUMBER OF REPETITIONS: 108, thrice or five times daily.

REFERENCES: *Śiva Purāṇa, Śiva Āgamas, Brahma-jābāla Upaniṣad* 2.4. [592]

Haṁsa-mantra, *the Thought-Form of the Swan of Knowledge*

TEXT: AUM *Haṁsaḥ So-ham Svāhā.* [593]

Haṁ is the Seed-of-Ether (*ākāśa bīja*).

Sa represents the Sun.

MEANING: "AUM! I am he; he is I. *Svāhā!*"

DEFINITION: This *mantra* should be repeated with the rhythm of breathing, uninterruptedly, from one dawn to the next. It can be uttered by everyone.

NUMBER OF REPETITIONS: 21,600.

PURPOSE: To attain the four objects-of-human-life (*puruṣārtha*): righteousness, pleasure, prosperity, and liberation.

The Thought-Form of Eight-Syllables (aṣṭākṣara) *of Viṣṇu*

TEXT: AUM *Namo Nārāyaṇāya.* [594]

MEANING: "AUM! Obeisances to the Abode of Man" (i.e., he from whom are obtained knowledge and liberation).

DEFINITION: A *mantra* for use, like the Gāyatrī *mantra,* at the three daily devotions; to be repeated three times.

PURPOSE: Obtaining liberation.

The Thought-Form of Fifteen-Syllables (pañcadaśī) *of the First Goddess* [8]

TEXT: *Ka-e-ī-la-hrīṁ, Ha-sa-ka-ha-la-hrīṁ, Sa-ka-la-hrīṁ.* [595]

MEANING:

Ka = lust
e = womb (or speech)
ī = the substance of lust
la = thunderbolt-bearer (or the earth, or Śiva)
hrīṁ = a cave (the seed-*mantra* of the Goddess)
ha = Śiva
sa = energy
ka = wind (or lust)
la = lord-of-heaven (Indra) or Śiva
ha = cloud (or Śiva)

(*sa*, *ka*, *la*: *Sakala* = everything)

DEFINITION: This *mantra* represents the power of the Self, the power of enchantment of the world.

NUMBER OF REPETITIONS: To be repeated twenty-one or 108 times.

PURPOSE: To attain all the desires and liberation.

REFERENCES: *Devī Upaniṣad, Nityāṣoḍa, Śikārṇava, Varivasyā-rahasya,* etc.

8 The *Lalitā-triśatī,* a hymn to the Goddess, is based on the seed-letters of this *mantra.*

The Yantras, *or Magic Diagrams*

YANTRAS are geometrical figures made from linear elements intended to represent, in a synthetic form, the basic energies of the natural world, which are the deities. They are the visual equivalents of the *mantras* or thought-forms. "The *yantra* has the *mantra* as its soul. The deity is the soul of the *mantra*. The difference between the *yantra* and the deity is similar to that between a body and its soul." (*Kaulāvalīyam*, quoted in *Śabda-kalpa-druma*. [596]) *Yantras* are believed to be the basis of the natural, or true, ideograms from which writing is derived. "Writing (*lipi*) is of five kinds: through gesture (*mudrā*), images (*śilpa*), and the flow of the pen, through designs [made with rice powder] or engraving on wood." (Quoted in *Śabda-kalpa-druma*. [597]) All the elementary geometrical figures—point, straight line, cross, circle, triangle, etc.—have a symbolical value corresponding to basic notions. They can be combined in more or less complex figures to become the representations of particular forces or qualities embodied in some aspect of creation. There is no shape, no movement, which may not be reduced to a combination of these elemental forms. The magic diagrams constructed with their help truly analyze and represent the creative forces of the cosmos which we call divinities.

Yantras, though drawn on the flat, must be conceived as solids. The flat drawing is a mere suggestion of the three-dimensional figure which the *yantra* is. The three-dimensional *yantra* is itself but a static image of the moving, living combination of forces represented in a particular divinity.

The *yantras* are the necessary basis for all attempts at symbolic representations, all sacred forms, all images, all sacred architecture, altars, temples, and ritual gestures. They are used in most kinds of worship, the deity being evoked by drawing its *yantra* and calling its subtle name.

Yantras can express the inner aspect of any form of creation. The nature of men and animals as well as that of gods can be expressed through *yantras*.

"There are, in the world, innumerable *yantras*. Every shape, every leaf, every flower is a *yantra* which, through its shape, its color, its perfume, tells us the story of creation." (Devarāja Vidyā Vācaspati, "Tantra men Yantra aur Mantra," *Kalyāṇa*, Śakti aṅka, p. 390. Hereafter called "Mantra-Yantra-Tantra.")

Hence "Viṣṇu should always be worshiped in water, fire, a heart, a discus, or the *yantra* which represents him" (*Nāradīya Saṁhitā* [598]), or "in black-pebbles (*śālagrāma*), jewels, *yantras*, images, and symbolic drawings on the ground." (*Gautamīya Tantra.* [599])

"The Goddess is to be worshiped in the sex emblem, a book, a symbolic drawing on the ground, an image, water, or a stone." (*Yoginī Tantra.* [600])

Once we know the traditional meaning of their geometrical elements, we can easily read the outward meaning of all *yantras*. The inner meaning, which is the nature of the deity, is, however, difficult to grasp and can be normally experienced only through the vision of its radiance gained by the practice of yoga. The secret of the *yantras* is one of the most guarded forms of Hindu esoteric teaching, since the power of a *yantra*, when it is made alive through the proper ritual, is believed to be limitless.

The Constituent Elements of the *Yantras*

The Point (bindu)

The point is an all-pervading spatial concept. Any movement, any shape, can be conceived as made of points. The nature of space, of ether, is location, that is, the possibility of defining particular places or points. The all-pervading, extensionless mathematical point thus expresses the nature of ether. The point can also represent the limit between different orders of existence and the origin of manifestation. When a nonmanifest stage of existence becomes manifest, its manifestation must begin somewhere, in some point of space, at some point of time. There must be an instant when it has not yet any extension but has begun to have location. This first instant when a thing does not yet exist and yet has already begun is adequately represented by the point, which can thus be defined as the "limit of manifestation."

The Straight Line

When a point moves independently of any external attraction its movement is a straight line. The straight line is taken to represent unhindered movement, that is, the principle of all development.

The Triangle

Development assimilated to a rising or a movement in an upward direction can be represented by a vertical arrowhead or tongue of fire. The triangle with its apex upward is also taken to represent fire, identified with the male principle, the *liṅga* or phallus, symbol of Śiva the Progenitor or of the Cosmic-Person (*puruṣa*). All upward movement is characteristic of the fiery element, of which mental activity is the subtle form. Its numerical symbol is the number 3.

The triangle pointing downward represents the force of inertia which pulls downward, and tends to suppress activity. It is associated with the element water, which always tends to come down, to equalize its level. It is the passive aspect of creation and thus is represented by the *yoni* or female organ, the emblem of Energy (Śakti) or Cosmic-Nature (*prakṛti*). Other symbols associated with the element water are the arc of a circle, the crescent, and the wave. The corresponding numerical symbol is the number 2.

The Circle

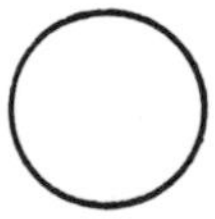

The notion of the circle arises from the revolutions of the planets. It is the symbol of all the returns, all the cycles, all the rhythms, that make existence possible. The circular movement is characteristic of the *rajas* (revolving) tendency which is the nature of perceptible manifestation. An inner circle, however, can represent the withdrawing of manifestation, the coiled energy which, when awakened, allows all beings to cross the sphere of manifest forms and reach the stage of liberation.

The Hexagon

The circle is sometimes taken as a symbol of the element air, though the conventional symbol for air is the hexagon. Movement is the characteristic quality of air, but it is a disorderly, inordinate movement represented by the multiples of the prime numbers 2 and 3, which are the numbers of inanimate nature.

The Square

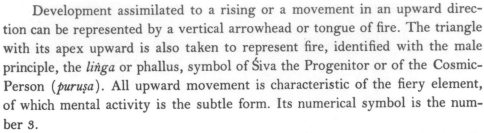

"The notion of extension is connected with that of many-sidedness. Among many-sided figures the one with fewest elements [apart from the triangle] is the square. The square is taken to represent the earth. It is the symbol of the element earth." (Devarāja Vidyā Vācaspati, "Mantra-Yantra-Tantra," p. 390.) The number 4 is the numerical symbol for the square.

The Pentagon (Star)

All inanimate life is believed to be ruled by the prime number 3 and its multiples by 2 and 3. Life, sensation, appears only when the number 5 becomes a component of the inner structure of things. The number 5 is associated with Śiva, the Progenitor, the source of life. The pentagon is thus associated with love and lust as well as with the power of disintegration. It is a necessary element of most magic *yantras*.

The Cross

When the point develops in space it expands in the four directions. The cross is the symbol of the expansion of the point in space as well as of the reduction of space to unity. It thus shows the dominion of one power over multiplicity.

The Svastika

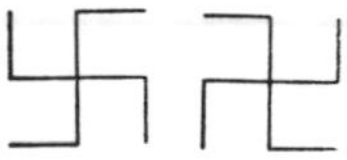

The knowledge of the Transcendent is said to be "crooked" because its understanding is "not straight," not within the realm of human logic. The simple cross represents not only the reduction of space to unity, but the field of external manifestation which, from the central point, the *bindu*, symbol of ether, expands in the four directions and the four perceptible elements.

This, however, is not true from the point of view of transcendent Divinity, which cannot be brought back to unity. This is shown by the crooked branches of the auspicious *svastika* which, although connected with the material center, now point to the undetermined immensity of space.

Knowledge of the transcendent aspects of Divinity can be reached only indirectly, through the right- and the left-hand ways. Hence the two directions in which the branches of the *svastika* can be crooked. Used everywhere as an auspicious sign, the *svastika* is meant to remind man that the Supreme Reality is not within the reach of the human mind nor within man's control.

The Star Hexagon

The star hexagon (in fact a dodecagon) is one of the most common elements in *yantras*. It is made of two triangles penetrating one another.

We have seen that the upright triangle represents the Cosmic-Person (*puruṣa*) and the triangle pointing downward stands for Cosmic-Nature (*prakṛti*). When these unite and are in a state of balance, they form the star hexagon, basis of the wheel symbol of the third-tendency or revolving-tendency (*rajas*) from which the universe is manifested. The circle by which the hexagon is surrounded represents the field in which the two triangles unite, that is, the field of time. When the two triangles separate, the world is destroyed; time ceases to exist. This is shown by the hourglass shape, the drum of Śiva.

The Lotuses

All symbolic numbers representing particular entities are shown in the *yantras* as circular flower patterns called lotuses.

The Principal *Yantras*

*The King-of-*Yantras (yantra-rāja)

The King of Yantras is described in the *Mahānirvāṇa Tantra.* "Draw a triangle with the Seed of Illusion (the character *hrīṁ*) within. Around it draw

two concentric circles. Draw in pairs the sixteen filaments and, besides, the eight petals of a lotus. Around them is the Earthly City, which should be made of straight lines with four entrances and should be of pleasing appearance. In order to cause pleasure to the deity the worshiper should draw the *yantra* either with a gold needle or with the thorn of the *bel* tree on a piece of gold, or silver, or copper which has been smeared with either the *svayambhū, kunda*, or *gola* flowers, or with sandal, fragrant aloe, *kuṅkuma* or red-sandal paste." (*Mahānirvāṇa Tantra* 5.172–76.)

The purpose of this *yantra* is to create contacts with supranatural worlds. With its help, the worshiper can gain all worldly and supranatural powers.

In the center of the *yantra*, the character *hrīṁ* stands for the divinity of fortune, Lakṣmī.

Around her is the fiery triangle [1] which draws into its ascending movement the coiled-energy (*kuṇḍalinī*), the circle surrounding it. The sixteen filaments of the lotus represent the attainment of perfection (sixteen is the perfect number); the eight petals represent the all-pervading ascending tendency, that is, Viṣṇu.

The outer circle is creation, the circular movement of which all things are born. The power over the manifest world is shown by the square, symbol of the earth. On the four sides are the four gates leading from the earth to the worlds beyond.

To the north (i.e., on the left) is the gate to the way-of-the-gods (*deva-yāna*). To the south (i.e., on the right) is the gate to the way-of-Ancestors (*pitṛ-yāna*). To the east (upward) is the gate to the priestly solar way, and to the west (downward) is the gate to the royal way, the way of the lord-of-the-waters (Varuṇa). The four gates lead to these four directions, forming the cross, symbol of universality. This cross further develops into a double *svastika* which indicates the return to the principle through both the left-hand and the right-hand way.

The Yantra "*Guarded on all Sides*" (sarvatobhadra)

Described in the *Gautamīya Tantra* (30.102–108), this *yantra* is said to be the instrument of the fulfillment of all wishes, in the present and the future, in the visible and the invisible world.

1 Woodroffe describes the feminine form of this *yantra* with a watery triangle, pointing downward. (In an article in Hindi in *Kalyāṇa*, Śakti aṇka.)

"Its name, which means the 'evenly square,' is that also of Viṣṇu's chariot. It shows the state of balance between activity and rest, acquisition and renunciation. He who from all sides is equal to himself, within and without, flourishes and bears fruit. He who sits firmly on his life's chariot, guarded on all sides, perfected on all sides, is free from danger." (Devarāja Vidyā Vācaspati, "Mantra-Yantra-Tantra," p. 389.)

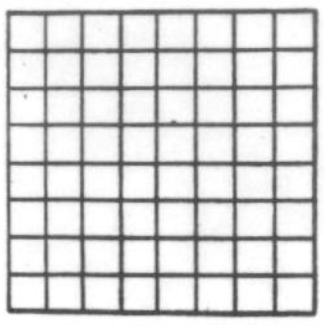

This *yantra* has eight squares on each side. It is therefore a Viṣṇu *yantra*, corresponding to the *sattva* quality, to the right-hand way.

The Remover-of-Desire (smara-hara)

The description of this *yantra* is given in the *Śyāmāstava Tantra*, verses 18 ff. Made of five triangles, it is a Śiva *yantra*, five being the number corresponding to the procreative and destructive principle. The triangles represent fiery *liṅgas*, phalli of fire.

"Through the power of this *yantra* man can conquer Lust (Kāma). The seeker who grasps its lesson remains well guarded, so that no enemy may move him with the weapons of lust, anger, greed, delusion, pain, or fear. [It is an instrument of magic accomplishments and] its worshiper can go wherever he pleases in this and other worlds without meeting obstacles. Truly this *yantra* helps man to defeat the power of lust and the delusions of life." (Devarāja Vidyā Vācaspati, "Mantra-Yantra-Tantra.")

The Remover of Desire is used for destroying external enemies as well as for man's conquest of himself. Its use as an instrument of black magic is explained in the *Yantra-cintāmaṇi* (7.5).

The Remover of Desire (Second Form)

This *yantra* has also another form, explained in the *Kālī Tantra*. "Here also are five triangles, but they are within one another. Two of the triangles are female, watery, and three are male, fiery. Each stage of manifestation is alternately fire and offering, devouring and devoured, male and female. This is also true of the successive sheaths which envelop the individual soul to make a living being. The inner circle is the coiled energy (*kuṇḍalinī*) which, when awakened, permits the crossing beyond the five spheres of manifestation inwardly or outwardly. The outer circle shows the creative power of fire giving rise to manifestation from the midst of the primeval waters." (Devarāja Vidyā Vācaspati, "Mantra-Yantra-Tantra.")

The eight-petaled lotus is the preserving principle, Viṣṇu, which gives stability to the manifest world. Around it is the square, the earth, with the four gates and the double *svastika,* the meaning of which has already been explained (pp. 352, 355).

The second form of the Remover of Desire is shown above. For other *yantras,* see pages 358–61.

The Yantra-*of-Liberation* (mukti)

This *yantra* is described in the *Kumārīkalpa Tantra.* It is made of a square, a fiery triangle, a watery triangle, a hexagon, and a circle, inside one another. The whole is surrounded by an octagon and a square with the four gates. In the center is the Seed of Illusion. It shows the different principles which the living being has to overcome in his effort to attain liberation.

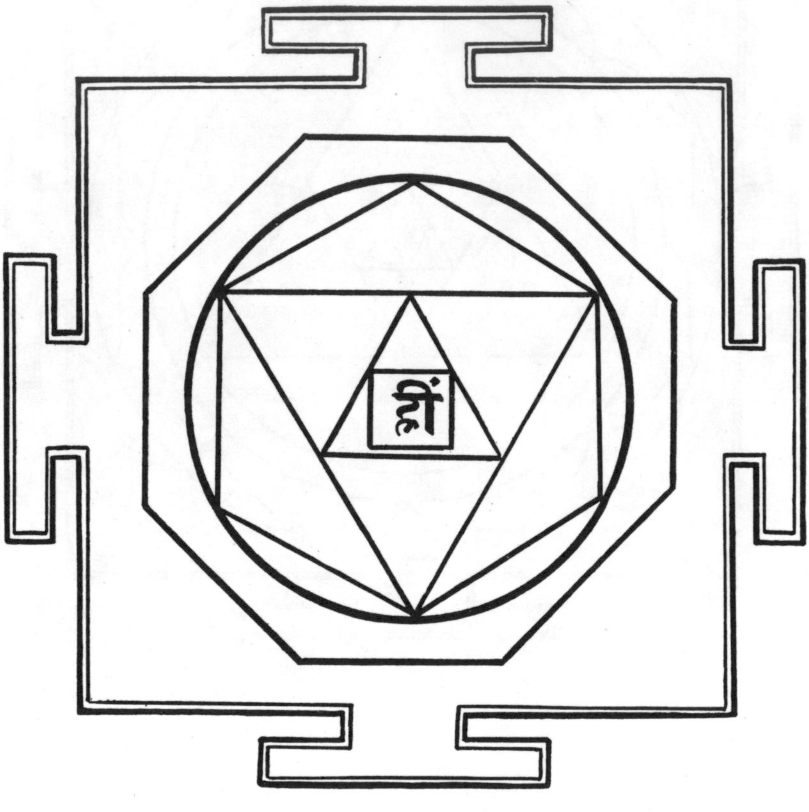

The Śrī Cakra

The Śrī Cakra,[2] or Wheel of Fortune, which represents the Universal Goddess, is one of the principal *yantras* used to represent divinities.

2 An inscribed version is illustrated with the Sanskrit texts, in the appendix.

The Gaṇapati Yantra

The Gaṇapati *yantra* points at the identity of the macrocosm and the microcosm.

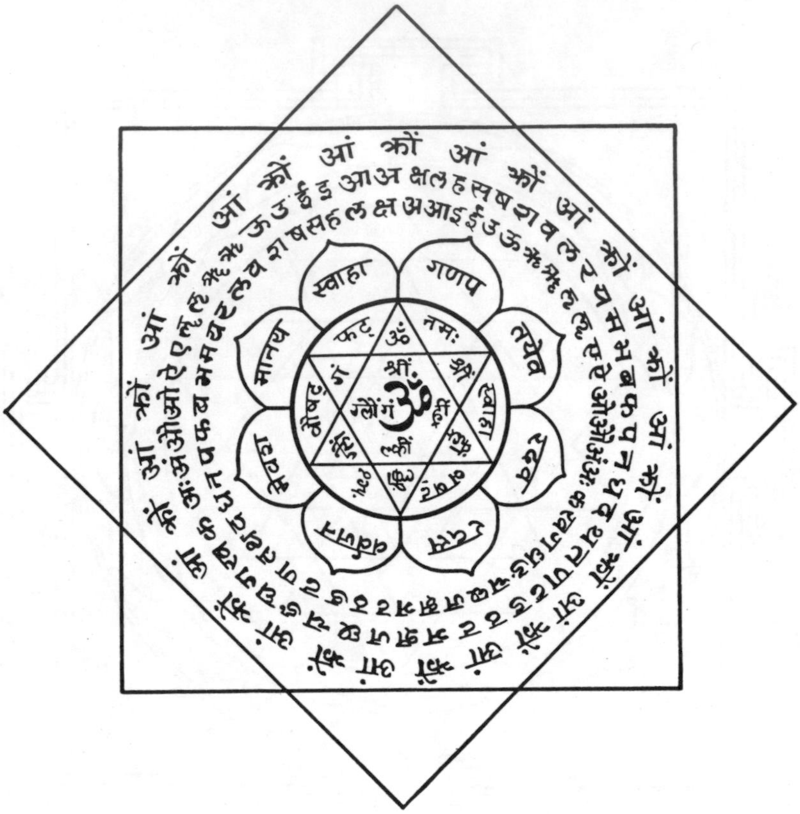

The Viṣṇu Yantra

The Viṣṇu *yantra* expresses the all-pervasiveness of *sattva,* the ascending quality.

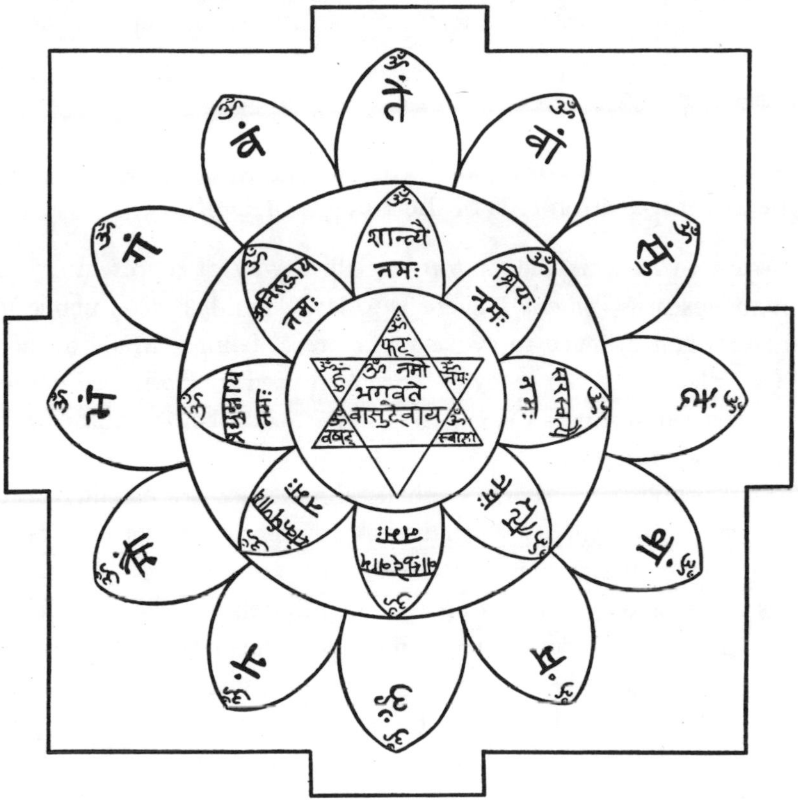

The Images (mūrti) *of Deities*

The Principal Elements of the Images of Deities

IN ADDITION to *mantras* and *yantras*, the third way of representing deities is through gestures (*mudrā*). There is a large number of symbolic gestures used in ritual and believed to evoke supranatural beings. Many of the *mudrās* through which a deity can be evoked are also used in the sacred dance. Some gestures represent qualities characteristic of particular beings whose images will show these gestures.

Certain proportions having symbolic significance are essential features of images as well as of temple architecture. A different canon for each category of being is given in the technical treatises on image-making. The proportions of images and sacred architecture show some relation to those by which musical intervals (*svara*) are formed. Thus musical sounds also are connected with deities. Diagrams, gestures, symbolic proportions, and attributes are therefore the main elements of the image of a deity.

The Purpose of the Images

THE PURPOSE of the image of a deity is to represent, through a combination of forms and proportions, some fundamental aspect of the universe and its presiding consciousness which is not directly perceptible to our senses.

"The idea behind the cult of images is to worship the invisible through the visible. Nowhere do people worship mere wood, stone, or metal. It is the all-pervading, and therefore always-near, Divine Essence, invoked by the power of utterances and rites, which becomes the object of worship in the image. It is through the particular that the notion of the totality arises in the mind." (Karapātrī, "Liṅgopāsanā-rahasya," *Siddhānta*, II, 1941–42.)

"So that the worshiper may accomplish his spiritual destiny, shapes are imagined as the images of the Immensity which dwells in all qualities, although itself beyond qualities, beyond comprehension, beyond form." [601]

The Forms of the Images

THE IMAGE of a deity is thus a form used to concentrate the mind on an abstraction. This image is called a "materialisation" (*mūrti*). Its attributes can be grouped in different ways. The images which combine essential features in greater number are the main deities. Those which present only a few attributes are spoken of as minor deities.

Deities are usually shown with many arms and heads, particular features and headdress, and ride on an animal which is their vehicle. They also carry different accessories and attributes. Images which show only slight differences in the position of accessories or the nature of gestures are classified as various aspects of the same deity.

The value of an image lies in its form rather than in its substance. There are, however, certain deities whose image should preferably be made of a given material (gold, silver, bronze, stone, etc.). Images are sometimes classified according to the material of which they are made.

"Images are of eight kinds, being made of stone, wood, metal, clay, and precious stones. They can also be painted or be merely mental." (*Bhāgavata Purāṇa* 11.28.12. [602])

Image Worship

HOWEVER far we reach into the history of Hindu thought we find a coherent use of images to represent abstractions. The whole of Hindu iconography is built on a code of symbols based on the assumption that there exists a natural affinity between forms and ideas. The images of deities are conceived as the application of symbolic equivalences just as is also the case for *yantras* and for writing. The Indian code of symbols appears to have come down from very ancient times. Its origin is lost in remote ages of prehistoric mankind.

When we find, among the "primitive" or the "civilized" peoples, icons, idols, strange images, to which particular efficacy or magical power is attributed, we can usually trace their origin to ancient symbols or symbolic tales the meaning of which has been partly forgotten. Any attempt to derive the meaning and implication of Hindu deities from arbitrarily reconstructed primitive belief does not account for the logic and the systematic use of the symbolic attributes;

it does not help us in any way to understand the significance of the images, and leads us to a wrong perspective of religious history.

The idea that the Hindu gods with their numerous limbs, their forms often partly animal, are monstrous beings, born of the fear of primitive man bewildered by the mystery of nature, could hardly have been put forward by people conversant with the Hindu language of symbols. If some deities have features which appear to us surprising or monstrous, this is because we fail to grasp their significance. It is merely the need for more complex, more elaborate, symbols which has taken the images away from simple anthropomorphism. Hindus are usually aware that images are symbols, and they do not consider the images of their "gods" as actual living entities endowed with magical powers.

Strangers are surprised when they see the huge clay images, modeled and adorned with love and skill, then worshiped with great display of ceremonial and devotion, thrown later into rivers and ponds and lying uncared for until they melt away. They fail to understand that this negligence arises because the image is only an instrument which has no value once it has filled its purpose. Even the permanent images installed in temples have to be thrown away and replaced when broken and worn.

The follower of yoga, adept in a technique which permits a direct experiencing of subtle entities, does not require images or myths.

"The yogi perceives the Giver-of-Peace (i.e., Śiva) in his own heart, not in images. Images are meant to meet the need of the unrealized." (*Jābāladarśana Upaniṣad* 4.59. [603]) Yet, "because the unrealized have not the capacity of worshiping divinity in its true form, they should accept the help of images. This is why images are necessary." (Chalāri's commentary on Madhvācārya's *Tantra-sāra Saṅgraha*. [604])

The error of the iconoclasts is to believe that a mental image is less an idol than a physical one. In fact, the external form of the image is rather a help to the understanding of its relative value. It is among the most violent iconoclastic religious groups that we find the most material, childish, anthropomorphic conceptions of God. To have any meaning, the objection to images should refer not only to those that are material but also to those that are mental.

When an image, or the story of an incarnation or a prophet, or any other manifestation of divinity comes to be regarded as a material reality or a historical fact, instead of being understood as a symbol, it has lost an essential part of its meaning and of its value and has become an object of idolatry and superstition.

From very early times there have been religious groups which opposed the representation of abstract principles in the form of personal gods or the use of mental or material images of divinities, since they considered this unnecessary and dangerous. Such religions as that of the Jains, for example, prefer to worship saints or sages as the visible form through which we can grasp transcendent reality. Early Buddhism followed the same path. Since the objection referred more to the mental image of divinities than to mere symbols of stone, it never led to the discarding of all icons; a predominance of aesthetic elements and the worship of living beings and their pictures replaced the more imaginative representations of supranatural beings. Among the Hindus the appearances of deities among men are not believed to be primarily historical facts, although they may center around the story of a particular historical figure. Divine manifestations are the outward expressions of cosmic laws. The very characteristics of divinity are permanence and universality. Whatever divine manifestation may be envisaged it must take place at all times and on all planes, in every aspect of the physical and the subtle world, in every microcosm as in the macrocosm. If a universal principle manifests itself in a living individuality this cannot be a mere historical accident. In each universe, for each cycle or subcycle, the same "incarnations" of Divinity take place, just as the same entity (Vyāsa, "scribe") will write the Scripture in the different ages, though it may be manifest through distinct individuals, whose character and functions will, however, be one. Vyāsa and all the other principles of divine manifestation exist also in ourselves as elements of the structure of our own being, and we may very well understand that this inner aspect is the more real one and the myths of the living Vyāsa and the historical avatars are only symbols.

The Worship of Deities

The Object of Worship

No code of worship is suitable for all men. Everyone should worship the deity which represents the stage of abstraction that is nearest above him, the stage which he can understand and which can directly help him. There is no purpose in man trying to contact the more remote aspects of divinity, neglecting those within his reach. The task is beyond his power, and the effort is just as unnecessary as trying to climb a staircase without touching the steps.

Our worship goes to the higher gods but through the hierarchy of all the degrees of their manifestation. There is no short cut, and we cannot come into contact with the less manifest aspects of divinity without the help of the more manifest forms any more than we can enter the inner sanctuary of a temple without going through the outer enclosures.

For people who believe in a divine origin of creation there can be nothing in the universe that is not of divine nature, which is not of the substance of divinity. Whatever form we worship, whatever the purpose of our worship, that worship goes to the gods.

Whenever we look toward the higher aspects of anything, what we perceive is the reflection of a divinity; it is for us the form of Divinity and may be worshiped as such.

Divinities thus appear to adapt themselves to the need of the worshiper, even though it always remains impossible for man to adapt himself to the ways of divinities. The willingness of the gods to make themselves accessible is emphasized everywhere in the Hindu Scriptures.

"Whenever a devotee wishes, with unwavering faith, to worship me in a particular form, I take that very form." (*Bhagavadgītā* 7.11. [605])

"I take, to welcome them, the shape in which they worship me." (*Bhagavadgītā* 4.11. [606])

"Whichever the form in which they like to conceive you, that form with true mercy you take." (*Bhāgavata Purāṇa* 3.9.11. [607])

"As he is worshiped, so he becomes." (*Mudgala Upaniṣad* 3.3. [608])

Any object, any living creature, any action, any quality, can be taken as the image of divinity and worshiped as such. The realized sages bow to everything, calling it a god.

"The All-Powerful Divinity dwells as the living individuality in [all living things]. Hence [the wise] bows before a horse, a man of low birth, a cow, or an ass." (*Yājñavalkya Upaniṣad* 7. [609])

Divinity dwells in speech as the power to protect,
in the in-breath and the out-breath as the power to take and give,
in the hands as the power to act,
in the feet as the power to move,
in the anus as the power of riddance.
In the world of the elements, it dwells in rain as the power to quench,
in thunder as strength, in cattle as wealth.
It dwells as light in the stars,
in sperm as the power of generation, and in sex as pleasure.
It dwells in ether as [the support of] all.
And where it dwells, there it must be worshiped.
(*Taittirīya Upaniṣad* 3.10. [610])

In the *Viṣṇu Purāṇa* the gods invoke Viṣṇu as the Cosmic Being found in his entirety in every aspect of the world.

You are everything, earth, water, fire, air, and space,
the subtle world, the Nature-of-All (pradhāna),
and the Person (puṁs) *who stands forever aloof.*

O Self of all beings!
From the Creator (Brahmā) to the blade of grass
all is your one body, visible and invisible,
divided by space and time.

We worship you as Brahmā, the Immense Being, the first shape,
who sprang from the lotus of your navel to create the worlds.

We, the gods, worship you in our selves,
we, the King of Heaven, the Sun, the Lord of Tears,
the Indweller, the twin gods of agriculture,

the Lord of Wind, the Offering, who all are your shapes
while you are our Selves.

We worship you in your demonic shapes, deceitful and stupid,
wild in their passions, suspicious of wisdom.

We worship you in the genii, the yakṣas,
with their narrow minds obdurate to knowledge,
their blunt faculties covetous of the objects of words.

O Supreme Man! We bow to your fearful evil shapes
which wander at night, cruel and deceitful.

O Giver-of-Rewards (Janārdana)!
We worship you as the Eternal Law
whence virtuous men, who dwell in the heaven,
obtain the blissful fruit of their just deeds.
We bow to the Realized (Siddhas) who are your shapes of joy;
free from contacts, they enter and move within all things.

O Remover-of-Sorrow (Hari)! We bow to your serpent shapes,
lustful and cruel, whose forked tongues know no mercy.

O Pervader! We worship you as knowledge
in the peaceful form of the seers,
faultless, free from sin.

O Dweller in the lotus of the Heart! We bow to you
as the self of Time which, at the end of the ages,
infallibly devours all beings.

We worship you as the Lord of Tears,
who dances at the time of destruction,
having devoured gods and men alike.

O Giver of Rewards! We worship your human shape
bound by the twenty-eight incapacities,[1]
ruled by the powers of darkness.

1 The twenty-eight incapacities (*badha*) are defined in the *Sāṅkhya Kārikā* (49–51) as the limitations (*aśakti*) of the five senses of action and the five senses of perception (weakness of sight, of hearing, etc.) and the mind (madness); then the lack of happiness (*tuṣṭi*) coming from one's nature, circumstances, times, and chance, as well as detachment from the objects of the five senses of perception; then the eight accomplishments (*siddhi*) which are obstacles to the liberation of man: thought, speech, and learning, suffering on the spiritual, mental, and physical planes, happiness, and generosity.

We bow to you as vegetal life (mukhya rūpa),
by which the world subsists and which—six in kind,
trees, [creepers, bushes, plants, herbs, and bamboo] —
supports the sacrificial rites.

O Universal Self! We bow to you under that elemental shape
from which beasts and men have sprung,
gods and living beings, ether and the elements,
sound and all the qualities.

O Transcendent Self! We bow to you as the Cause of causes,
the Principial shape beyond compare,
beyond Nature (pradhāna) *and Intellect.*

O All-Powerful (*Bhagavān*)*! We bow to your shape*
which the seers alone perceive and in which is found
no white nor other color, no length nor other dimension,
no density nor other quality.

Purer than purity it stands
beyond the sphere of quality.

We bow to you, the birthless, the indestructible,
outside whom there is but nothingness.

You are the ever-present within our bodies as within all things,
as the intrinsic principle of all.

We bow to you, resplendent Indweller (*Vāsudeva*)*! the seed of all that is!*
You stand changeless, unsullied.

The Supreme stage is your core, the Universe your shape.
You are the unborn, Eternal.

(*Viṣṇu Purāṇa* 3.17.14–34. [611])

Concentration on any form leads to the vision of the principle beyond that form. Any mental or physical attraction, whatever its nature, facilitates the first stages of concentration and thus the objects of our desires or love are the proper images for mental worship.

Commenting on Patañjali's aphorism "by meditating on any object of liking" (*Yoga Sūtra* 1.39 [612]), Vyāsa says: "Whatever may be the object of a man's liking, let him meditate upon that. If the mind settles upon that particular object, it may also later settle on something else" (*Yoga Sūtra Bhāṣya* 1.39 [613]).

For most people, in the first stages of spiritual development only objects of great physical attraction have a strong enough appeal to take the mind away from the mechanical agitation of everyday preoccupations. This is how erotic emblems come to be considered useful instruments of mental liberation. In modern religious developments both in India and in the West, these are often replaced by fetishes, which have the same value transposed.

Though every aspect of creation may be an object of worship, in each order of things certain forms, kinds, functions, individualities, are the particular points where divinities seem more easily accessible. Certain plants and animals, certain features of the earth, certain stars or constellations, are by their nature the embodiment of certain qualities and are thus considered sacred. Such are, for example, the *tulasi* plant, the sacred fig tree (*aśvattha*), the rivers, the mountains, the cow, the elephant, and also the priest, the king, the teacher, who are honored like divine beings and are worshiped like Indra, Śiva, or Viṣṇu.

The Kinds of Worship

"WORSHIP is of three kinds: that performed daily, that offered on particular occasions, and that made for the attainment of special aims." (*Rudra-yāmala Tantra.* [614]) The daily rituals as well as the rituals ordained for certain days of the year should be performed by everyone. They are man's religious duties, his participation in the cosmic life and its cycles.

"A man must have a chosen deity, but he must also honor the family deity, the village deity, the village guardian angel, the village genie (*nāga*), on the prescribed occasions." (Vijayānanda Tripāṭhī, "Devatā tattva," *Sanmārga*, III, 1942.)

On the other hand, worship performed to obtain the realization of a desire has no compelling character and is done only by those who feel the need for it. Yet if we use worship as the instrument of gain, whether spiritual or material, it is essential to know which kind of divinity we should propitiate and through which procedure. The divinity worshiped and the technique of worship are different if the aim of worship is to achieve a particular result, obtain a particular quality, reach a particular stage of worldly or spiritual accomplishment. When the saint prays to obtain liberation, the thief to succeed in his enterprise, the soldier to kill his enemy, although each may address his prayer to the same divine name, the divinity which may acknowledge it is in fact a different stage of being, a different god.

When we invoke an abstraction in the hope of saving our life or winning a war, our prayer is wrongly addressed because an abstraction can have nothing to do with the forms and interests of the manifest world. It cannot answer prayers, much less favor worshipers. Only the minor deities, the subtle beings who are part of the inner life of things, can co-operate with man in such matters, and it is these deities which should be approached through the proper ritual channels. A forest deity, however, will have no power to help man in spheres of abstract realization.

Man becomes what he worships. His desire is the essential form of his becoming. Kṛṣṇa, the embodiment of love, says in the *Bhagavadgītā* (9.25 [615]):

"Those who worship the gods become gods; those who worship Ancestors become Ancestors, those who worship the elements master the elements, and those who worship me gain me."

In the *Bhāgavata Purāṇa* a list is given of the deities who are to be worshiped for particular aims.

"He who wishes for the illumination of knowledge should worship the Immensity (*brahman*).

"He who wishes for the pleasures of the senses should worship Might (Indra), the king of heaven.

"He who desires children worships the lord of progeny, Prajāpati.

"He who desires luck worships the Power of Illusion, Māyā.

"He who desires intelligence worships the Sun (Sūrya).

"He who desires wealth worships the spheres of the elements, the Vasus.

"He who desires virile power worships the divinities of life, the Rudras.

"He who desires food worships Aditi, the mother of the gods.

"He who desires a place in heaven worships all the gods.

"He who desires a kingdom worships the Universal Principles, the Viśvadevas.

"He who desires power worships the Means-of-Accomplishment (Sādhyas).

"He who desires a long life worships the celestial physicians, the Aśvins.

"He who desires strength worships the Earth (Ilā).

"He who desires stability worships the World-Mothers (Loka-mātās).

"He who desires beauty worships the celestial musicians, the *gandharvas.*

"He who desires a woman worships the nymph Urvaśī.

"He who wishes for domination worships the Supreme-Ruler (*parameṣṭhin*).

"He who desires fame worships the lord of the sacrifice (*yajña*).

"He who desires a treasure worships Pracetas [Varuṇa, the lord of the waters].

"He who desires knowledge worships Śiva, the lord of sleep.

"He who desires a happy married life worships Peace-of-the-Night (Umā), the consort of Śiva.

"He who desires [firmness in his] duty worships the Highest-Praise (Uttama-śloka), that is, Viṣṇu.

"He who wishes for numerous descendants worships the Ancestors (*pitṛ*).

"He who desires protection worships the virtuous-ones (*puṇyajana*).[2]

"He who desires strength worships the divinities of wind, the Maruts.

"He who desires a throne worships the Lawgiver, Manu.

"He who desires magic powers worships the goddess of witchcraft, Nirṛti.

"He who desires lust worships the Offering, Soma.

"To be free from desire, a man should worship the Supreme Person, Para Puruṣa.

"Whether a man is realized or is a seeker or is still in the grip of attachment, he should, with intense devotion, worship the Supreme Person." (*Bhāgavata Purāṇa*, 2.3.1–10. [616])

The Stages of Worship

WORSHIP can be of different forms. It can be mental or external, collective or individual. It can begin with abstract contemplation and end in outward ceremonial or the reverse. The external worship of the yogi is only the instrument that leads to abstract contemplation.

"The highest stage is that in which the Immense Presence is perceived in all things. The middle stage is that of meditation, the lower that of hymns and rosary. Still lower is the stage of external worship." (*Mahānirvāṇa Tantra.*)

"The worship performed by the initiated is of two kinds, internal and external. Internal worship is ordained only for those who have renounced the world. Both internal and external worship are necessary for others." (*Tantra Saṁhitā*. [617])

"The worship of images of stone, metal, jewels, or clay leads the seeker of liberation to rebirth. Hence the man who wishes to renounce the world should worship only in his own heart and fear external forms of worship so that he may not have to live again." (*Śilpa Śāstra*, p. 27. [618])

2 I. e., the *yakṣas*.

In the final stage of realization, the yogi does not perceive anything but an Immense Presence pervading all appearances. At this stage no outward ritual exists any more. All physical and mental functions have themselves become ritual, that is, have ceased to have any purpose other than to support the contact between the yogi and the object of his contemplation. When life itself becomes a hindrance, the lingering remnant of an already past existence, the yogi has ceased, for all practical purposes, to be a human being.

Ritual

Life as a Ritual

IN THE Hindu conception of life there is no separation between sacred and profane activity. The whole of human existence is considered a participation in the cosmic symphony. Life is a priesthood. There are no indifferent actions. All our gestures, all our deeds, bear consequences; hence they should be controlled to conform with the harmonic pattern of the universe.

There is a ritual for bathing; there is a ritual for taking food; there is a ritual for love, for procreation. There are rituals to be performed at sunrise, midday, and sunset and all the crucial points in the cycle of seasons and years. There is a ritual for breathing, a ritual for dressing, a ritual for study. There is a fire ritual, a ritual for each change of status, and rituals for all the important events of life.

All our actions are forms of divine worship and should, therefore, be accomplished with composure, order, and precision.

"Worshiping him through his actions, man attains liberation." (*Bhagavad-gītā* 18.46. [619]) In Sanskrit, there is no distinction in words between physical action and ritual action; all action is considered a form of ritual.

The Rituals of Worship

THOUGH the very act of living can be made the instrument of all realization, there are also other forms of ritual which we may call external, to differentiate them from the inner vital ones, and which constitute special techniques aiming at creating contacts between this world and other worlds. Through these man can obtain the help of deities and other supernatural beings who guide him in his efforts toward spiritual as well as material progress.

The different worlds stand in harmonic relation to one another and, through ritual action, they can be made to respond, just as stringed instruments respond when one of their harmonics resounds. Ritual is thus an application of the science of subtle correspondences. Its value cannot be estimated in terms of worldly appearances but only from the results it may bring through the awakening of inner or outer energies.

Because of the concordance between the macrocosm and the microcosm all rituals have a simultaneous action on the energies which rule the inner functions of the human body and those which, as the deities, govern the functions of the universe. Besides their value in propitiating the deities, rituals have thus a physical and a psychological effect. These two functions of worship are inseparable. Ritual is a form of magic art through which, with the help of sounds, forms, rhythms, gestures, flowers, light, incense, and offerings, the mind of the worshiper is carried away from its material preoccupations toward a world of divine beauty, while the deity, also enchanted, is brought nearer to him.

The two main forms of external ritual are individual-worship (*pūjā*) and ritual-sacrifice (*yajña*).

The Technique of Worship

THOUGH certain forms of inner illumination may permit contacts with the higher states of being we call deities through the mere strength of an inner desire, such contacts remain accidental experiences which cannot be renewed at will and the exact nature of which cannot be controlled. There is therefore no purpose in doing away with the technique and ritual of worship, which greatly facilitate such contacts.

Even mental forms of worship should follow a systematic ordinance, for man by his own mental power alone is not normally able to reach divinity. The bridge of ritual, whether external or mental, is essential to establish contact and to maintain it.

The invisible worlds are of many kinds, and since the effect of rituals cannot be directly detected, they may create wrong contacts and have results quite contrary to those wished for. Rituals are therefore dangerous instruments, and no alteration can be made in their form except by competent technicians.

"I [Kṛṣṇa] am the enjoyer and the master of all ritual; hence those who do not know my inner nature will fail." (*Bhagavadgītā* 9.23. [620])

A famous story, retold in the *Mahābhāṣya*, concerns the divine craftsman Tvaṣṭṛ, who made a great sacrifice to obtain a son who would destroy Indra, the king of heaven. Because he made a slight error in accent, the words *Indra śatruḥ*, intended to mean "Indra, the enemy," came to signify "the enemy of

Indra," and it was Vṛtra, his son, who was destroyed. (See also *Śatapatha Brāhmaṇa* 1.6.3.1.)

The Place of Worship

THE CHIEF temple of the Hindu is the universe. It is in the forests, the mountains, on the banks of rivers, under the shade of certain trees, or in his own house that he performs all the daily ceremonial of worship, all prayer, all meditation.

"The best places are holy grounds, river banks, caves, sites of pilgrimage, the summits of mountains, confluences of rivers, sacred forests, solitary groves, the shade of the *bel* tree, valleys, places overgrown with *tulsi* plants, pasture lands, temples of Śiva without a bull, the foot of a sacred fig tree or of an *amalakī* tree, cowsheds, islands, sanctuaries, the shore of the sea, one's own house, the abode of one's teacher, places which tend to inspire concentration, lonely places free from animals." (*Gāndharva Tantra* 7.)

There are buildings which, by their structure and proportions, create a favorable environment for worship. Hence the importance of the laws of sacred architecture in the construction of houses, of the rooms consecrated for worship, or of temples.

Temples are, however, of secondary importance. They are not, as in some religions, the meeting places of the faithful but are the homes of deities, places where a particular aspect of Divinity is honored, worshiped by priests who are its servants. People go to the temple as they go to visit a saintly man or a sacred place or a renowned scholar. They pay homage to the image and offer flowers and incense. But if there were none of these sanctuaries Hindu life and its rituals would in no way be affected. In fact, certain classes of Hindus are not supposed to enter some parts of the temples (just as women cannot, during office, enter the inner sanctuary of a Roman Catholic church), but this in no way implies that they do not perform rituals or that they have a religious life less intense.

The Main Features of Individual-Worship (*pūjana*)[1]

RITUAL WORSHIP is conceived by the Hindu as a complex and elaborate art. Though there are forms of collective worship, most worship is an individual

1 The rituals of worship described here belong to the Tantric form, which is meant for everyone. Other rituals vary in the gestures, *mantras*, and accessories used but are not basically different.

ceremonial in which the worshiper, alone with the deity in an undisturbed chapel, practices a complex ceremonial with flowers, incense, holy water, and offerings, which aims at creating a sort of intimate and aesthetic relationship considered to be a useful prelude to mental concentration. In the ceremonial of worship the image is treated as a noble guest visiting the house. The worshiper enacts a complete ritual, which may last for hours, in which the guest is welcomed, his feet washed, a seat offered. The god is then bathed, perfumed, clad in new garments. He is offered flowers, food and drink, and *betel* nuts, then allowed a rest, given presents, and bidden farewell.

Each of the elements used in this performance is said to have a symbolic meaning on which the worshiper should concentrate his thoughts.

The most important features of this form of worship are: (1) the purification-of-the-elements (*bhūta śuddhi*) constituting the subtle and physical body of the worshiper and their dedication, (2) the consecration of the different parts of the body to distinct deities with the help of seed-*mantras* (*nyāsa*), (3) breath-control (*prāṇāyāma*), (4) mental-concentration (*dhyāna*), (5) mental worship, (6) repetition of *mantras*.

The Purification and Dedication of the Body

The dedication of the body of the worshiper to the deity is a necessary prelude to ceremonial worship. In this rite the worshiper purifies and consecrates each part of his person so that he may become fit to appear before a god.

"No man should worship a deity so long as he himself has not become a deity. If the repetition of sacred utterances is performed without previous dedication of the parts of the body to the different deities, this repetition of *mantras* is demoniacal and without useful effect. To worship a deity, a man must become the Self of that deity through dedication, breath control, and concentration until his body becomes the deity's abode." (*Gāndharva Tantra.*)

1. The first step is the purification of the worshiper and of the accessories of worship.

"The purification of the person of the worshiper consists in bathing. The purification-of-the-subtle-elements (*bhūta śuddhi*) of the body is done through breath control and through the dedication of the six main parts of the body to the six deities to which they correspond. After this the other forms of dedication are performed.

2. "The purification of the place of worship is done by cleaning it carefully, adorning it with an auspicious ornamentation made of powders of five colors, placing a seat and a canopy, using incense, lights, flowers, garlands, etc. All this must be done by the worshiper himself.

3. "Purification of the ritual utterances, the *mantras*, is done by repeating the syllables which compose them in the regular order and then in the reverse order.

4. "Purification of the accessories is done by sprinkling water consecrated with the basic *mantra* and the weapon-*mantra* (*astra-mantra*, i.e., the sound *phaṭ*) and then displaying the cow-gesture (*dhenu-mudrā*).

5. "Purification of the deity is done by placing the image on an altar, invoking the presence of the deity through its secret *mantra* and the life-giving breathing-*mantra* (*prāṇa-mantra*), bathing the image three times while reciting the basic *mantra*, then adorning it with garments and jewels. After this an offering of incense and light should be made." (*Kulārṇava Tantra.*)

Removing Obstacles

"The worshiper should bow with respect to the deities of the doors, first at the eastern door of the house of worship, then, successively at the southern door, the western door, and the northern door. After this he should bow to his chosen deity present in the form of its *yantra*." (*Nigama-kalpalatā* 14.)

If the sanctuary has only one door, the worship of the deities of the three other directions should be done mentally. "The sacrificial house should be entered with the right foot" (*Śivārcana Candrikā*); with the left foot if it is a left-hand sacrifice.

"The worshiper should remove obstacles of celestial origin by the godly look (looking with wide-open, unblinking eyes). Obstacles of the intermediary world are removed with the help of water consecrated with the *astra-mantra*. Terrestrial obstacles are avoided by doing three taps with the heel of the right foot." (*Śāmbhavī Tantra.*)

The Praise of the Deity

"Just as gold is freed from its dross only by fire and acquires its shining appearance from heat, so the mind of a living being, cleansed from the filth of his actions and his desires through his love for me,[2] is transformed into my transcendent likeness. The mind is purified through the hearing and uttering of sacred hymns in my praise." (*Bhāgavata Purāṇa* 11.14.25. [621])

The glorification of a deity is something different from meaningless praise. The *Bṛhad-devatā* (1.6 [622]) says: "The praise of something consists in the

2 Kṛṣṇa speaks.

utterance of its name, the description of its shape, the proclaiming of its deeds, the mention of its family."

"We cannot know a thing without knowing its merits, its qualities. All knowledge or science is based on a form of praise. A dictionary is but the praise of words. The works of science are filled with glorification. Everything which is an object of knowledge is as such a deity and is glorified in the Scripture that deals with it." (Vijayānanda Tripāṭhī, "Devatā tattva," *Sanmārga,* III, 1942.)

Meditation

"Meditation is of two kinds, gross and subtle. In the subtle form meditation is done on the 'body of sound,' that is, the *mantra,* of the deity. In the gross form meditation is on one image with hands and feet. . . . The suprasensory can seldom be reached by the mind; hence one should concentrate on the gross form." (*Yāmala Tantra.*)

"The worshiper should engage in meditation, gradually concentrating his mind on all the parts of the body of his chosen deity, one after another, from the feet to the head. He can thus acquire such an intense state of concentration that during his undisturbed meditation the whole body of the chosen deity will appear to his mind's eye as an indivisible form. In this way the meditation on the deity in its formal aspect will gradually become profound and steady." (Śiva Candra Vidyārṇavā Bhattāchārya, *Principles of Tantra* [ed. Woodroffe], II [1916], 134, or p. 874 [1952 ed.], quoted with slight changes.)

Japa, the Repetition of Mantras

"Japa, as the repetition of a mantra, has been compared to the action of a man shaking a sleeper to wake him up." (Woodroffe, *The Garland of Letters,* p. 211, with slight changes.)

"Once the image of the chosen deity has been formed in the mind by concentration, the seed-mantra should be repeated, withdrawing the mind from all other thoughts. . . . Japa is of three kinds, audible, articulate but inaudible, and mental. . . . When concentration by this means is perfected, the consciousness of the worshiper is transferred to the deity represented by the utterance and he ceases to have an individuality distinct from that of the deity." (Baradā Kanṭha Majumdar, *Principles of Tantra* [ed. Woodroffe], II [1916], 77–78, or pp. 648 f. [1952 ed.], quoted with slight changes.)

The two lips of the worshiper are the two causal principles, Śiva and his power, Śakti. The movement of the lips is their coition (*maithuna*). The sound which springs forth from them is the point-limit (*bindu*), the sperm, the point from which manifestation arises. The deity engendered is thus in a way a creation, a son of the worshiper.[3]

The Accessories of Worship

The Water

Water is used at every stage of worship not only as an instrument of purification but also as the element pervading all life and thus a symbol of pervasiveness.

"The water offered to wash the feet of the deity represents the perception of Existence-Consciousness-Experience pervading all forms and names.

"The water offered as a gift symbolizes the perception of the Ultimate Principle pervading the subtle world.

"Perception of the Principle-pervading-perception-itself is the water offered to rinse the mouth.

"The bathing of the image symbolizes the perception of Consciousness and Experience (joy) pervading the three fundamental qualities.

"A form of meditation in which the lady of lust, Kāmeśvarī, who embodies the Conscious, is seen as the object of all thought is called the 'consecration of water.'" (Karapātrī, "Śrī Bhagavatī tattva," *Siddhānta*, V, 1944–45, 192.)

The Ornaments

"The different ornaments placed on the image symbolize the attributes of divinity, such as to be without disguise, never to wither, to be free from anxiety, to be immortal, etc." (Ibid.)

The Perfume

"The offering of perfume stands for the perception of Consciousness pervading the element earth of which the worshiper's own body is made." (Ibid.)

The sense of smell is the sense connected with the element earth.

The Flowers

"The flower offering stands for the perception of Consciousness pervading the element ether." (Ibid.)

3 See Woodroffe, *The Garland of Letters*, p. 211.

The Incense

"The offering of incense stands for the perception of Consciousness pervading the element air." (Ibid.)

The Lamp

"The offering of light stands for the perception of consciousness pervading the element fire." (Ibid.)

The Edibles

"The offering of food stands for the perception of the principle of immortality." (Ibid.) Food is that which sustains life.

The Rice

"The rice offering stands for the perception of Existence-Consciousness-Experience in all things." (Ibid.)

The Lauds

"The offering of praise stands for the dissolution of words into the Word principle." (Ibid.)

The Waving of Lights

"The waving of lights stands for the discarding of the object of thought which is the inanimate world." (Ibid.)

The Obeisance

"The obeisance stands for the dissolution of all thoughts into the Principle-of-All." (Ibid.)

Right- and Left-hand Ways

THE PANTHEON with all its deities, its legends, its complex iconography, does not represent conflicting creeds but illustrates the path of human realization from the lower to the higher forms. It is a picture of spiritual progress; its external forms lead each man, according to his strength and pace, toward the ideal but remote goal of abstract contemplation. Once the living being has attained this goal and reached the state of complete identification, he never returns into the realm of existence. This is the *samādhi*, the "identification," of the yogi, from which he never awakes though his body may remain alive as an unconscious automaton for a certain length of time.

All the forms of manifestation lead to Divinity but through distinct paths. These paths may be classified into three main categories, the way of immobility or nonaction, the way of cohesion, and the way of disintegration.

The way of nonaction rejects equally all good and evil, all forms of religion or irreligion. This is the path of the yogis who have mastered their own selves.

"Giving up all forms of religion, take shelter in me [Kṛṣṇa] alone." (*Bhagavadgītā* 18.66. [623])

Then comes the way of cohesion, that of the *sattva* (cohesive) quality, which aims at purifying man from the bondage of Nature (*prakṛti*), the chains of his instincts. This is the way of the virtuous, of the pure, of the man of renunciation, also known as the right-hand way.

The path that corresponds to the disintegrating-tendency (*tamas*) uses the power of Nature, the passions and instincts of man, to conquer, with their aid, the world of the senses. This way leads directly from the physical to the abstract because, as we have already seen (pp. 56 f.), the descending tendency is at both ends of the manifested. This is the way of the mystic and also the left-hand way, which may utilize even eroticism and drunkenness as means of spiritual achievement.

Rituals internal or external can be of the Vedic (right hand) or Tantric (left hand) way.

"My worship is of three kinds, Vedic, Tantric, and mixed.[4] A man should worship me in whichever of these three ways he prefers." (*Bhāgavata Purāṇa* 11.27.7. [624])

"The lord-of-tears (Rudra) has shown in the left-hand doctrine that spiritual advancement is best achieved by means of those very things which are the causes of man's downfalls." (*Kulārṇava Tantra*. [625])

This way can be dangerous, but it may also bring quick and wonderful results. According to the Tantra, the main scripture relating to this path, it is the only method which may bring actual results in the difficult conditions of the Age of Strife, the Kali Yuga, in which we live. It requires several lives of fearful asceticism to reach the feet of Divinity through the right-hand way. We thus see the moralist, the pure, the puritan, wither in the practice of useless virtues which may bring them worldly praise but a too slow rate of spiritual progress. Passion alone, when astutely directed, can overcome egotism and pride and

4 Kṛṣṇa speaks.

sordid calculation. Alone it has the momentum to draw man away from the bonds that chain him to his interests, his beliefs, his virtues, his reputation.

One of the cardinal principles of the left-hand way is to secure by its practice both liberation and enjoyment. This is possible by the identification of the individual self, when in the state of enjoyment, with the universal Being.

"Through enjoyment one gains liberation; for enjoyment is the means of reaching the Supreme Abode. Hence the wise who wish to conquer [the spirit] should experience all pleasures." (*Kulārṇava Saṁhitā* 5.219. [626])

"Enjoyment is the grasping of the form of what is perceptible. It is the realization of the quality of what is desirable or undesirable." (*Yoga Sūtra Bhāṣya* of Vyāsa [627])

Both the taking of food and sexual union are divine acts which cannot be in themselves objectionable. The notion of impurity is the progeny of ignorance, which, having lost sight of the divine character of particular actions, pretends to lower them into mere physical functions. Thus man the god falls from his divine status to that of man the beast. It is the work of the "hero" to undo the instincts born of ignorance and harmonize himself with the divine Law, to look at himself as a divine instrument which he must study and help to function and not as his own property that he is free to ill-treat.[5]

When use is made of sexual elements, the way of disintegration is usually connected with the cult of the female principle. But there are other forms of the left-hand way connected with the cult of Gaṇapati and Skanda. In its higher forms the left-hand way is connected with the cult of Śiva envisaged as the destructive and procreative principles. The right-hand way is, however, usually a form of the cult of Viṣṇu, embodiment of the cohesive tendency.

In left-hand worship five supports are used. As the Sanskrit names of all of them begin with an *M*, they are called the five *M*'s. They are wine (*madya*), meat (*māṁsa*), fish (*matsya*), gesture (*mudrā*),[6] and copulation (*maithuna*). In the higher yogic practice these become "drinking of the wine which flows from the center-of-the-thousand-petals at the summit of the head; killing lust, anger, greed, delusion, and other evil beasts; cooking the fish of deceit, calumny, envy, etc.; showing the gestures of hope, desire, and contempt; and enjoying the lustful beauties found along the spinal cord. These five actions lead man to inner perfection." (Karapātrī, "Pañca 'Ma' kāra," *Siddhānta*, III, 1942–43, 290.)

5 See Baradā Kantha Majumdar, *Principles of Tantra* (ed. Woodroffe), Introduction, II (1916), 133, or pp. 707 f. (1952 ed.).

6 *Matsya* and *mudrā* are in some texts replaced by excrements (*mala*) and urine (*mūtra*).

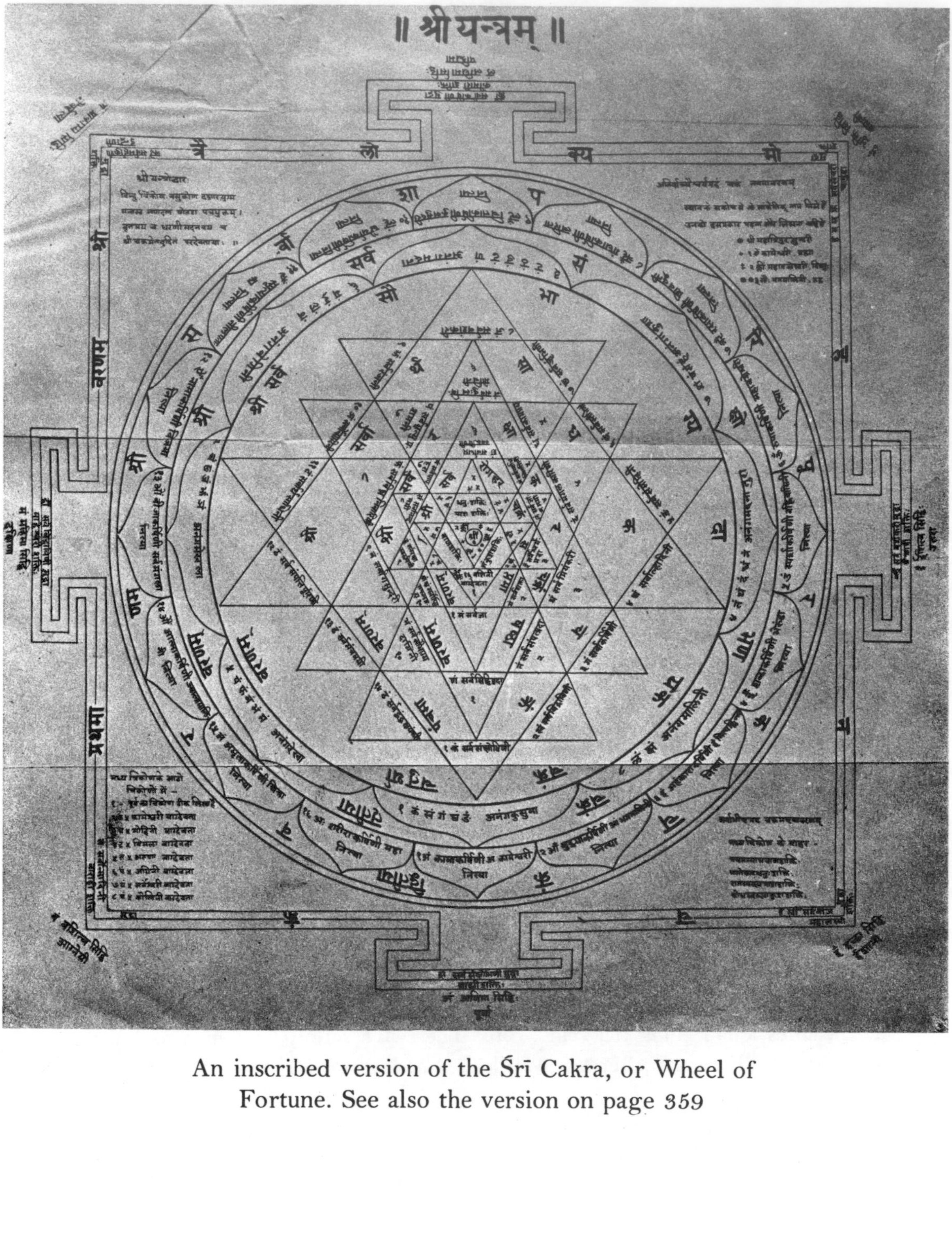

An inscribed version of the Śrī Cakra, or Wheel of Fortune. See also the version on page 359

Selective Bibliography

Throughout the text, there are numbers in brackets [ ] following the quotations translated from the Sanskrit. These numbers refer to the Devanagari transcripts included in the previous edition of this book but removed from the present text. Scholars who are interested in receiving these transcripts may write to the publisher.

A. SANSKRIT TEXTS [1]

1. *Vedic*

Aitareya Āraṇyaka. Edited by A. B. Keith. Oxford, 1909.

Aitareya Brāhmaṇa. Ānandāśrama ed. 2 vols. Poona, 1931.

Atharva Veda Sanhitā. Edited by R. Roth and W. D. Whitney. Revised by Max Lindenau. Berlin, 1924.

Atharva Veda Sūkta. In the *Atharva Veda* (*Saṁhitā*) (q.v.).

Devī Sūkta (*Ṛg Veda* 10.125). Often reprinted in editions of the *Devī Mahātmya* (q.v. in VI).

Gopatha Brāhmaṇa. Calcutta, 1872.

Jaiminīya Upaniṣad Brāhmaṇa. D. A. V. College, Lahore, 1921.

Kapiṣṭhala-kaṭha Saṁhitā. Edited by Dr. Raghu Vira. Lahore, 1932.

Kāṭhaka Saṁhitā. Edited by S. D. Satvalekar. Aundh, 1943.

Maitrāyaṇī Saṁhitā [*Kṛṣṇa Yajur Veda*]. Edited by Leopold von Schroeder. 4 vols. Leipzig, 1881, 1883, 1885, 1886.

Maitrī Saṁhitā. See *Maitrāyaṇī Saṁhitā.*

Pañcaviṁśati Brāhmaṇa (Ms.).

Puruṣa Sūkta (*Ṛg Veda* 10.90).

Ṛg Veda. See *Ṛg Veda Saṁhitā.*

Ṛg Veda Bhāṣya of Sāyaṇa. In: *Ṛg Veda Saṁhitā.* 5 vols. N. S. Sontakke, Poona, 1935–51.

Ṛg Veda Saṁhitā. Edited by S. D. Satvalekar. Aundh, 1940.

Saṅkhyāyana Brāhmaṇa (Ms.).

Śatapatha Brāhmaṇa (The White [or Śukla] Yajur Veda, part II). Edited by Dr. A. Weber. Berlin, 1855.

Taittirīya Āraṇyaka. Mysore, 1902.

Taittirīya Brāhmaṇa. Ānandāśrama ed. 3 vols. Poona, 1938.

Taittirīya Saṁhitā (*Kṛṣṇa Yajur Veda*). Edited by Dr. Albrecht Weber. (Indische Studien, 11, 12.) 2 vols. Leipzig, 1871–72.

Vājasaneya Saṁhitā (The White [or Śukla] Yajur Veda, part I). Edited by Dr. A. Weber. Berlin, 1852.

1 The Sanskrit quotations translated in the text are taken from both Indian vulgate printed editions and manuscripts, which sometimes differ appreciably from critical printed versions. Transcripts of the Sanskrit texts, identified by bracketed numbers accompanying the translations, are given in the appendix. In the Bibliography, printed editions are recorded wherever possible for the convenience of readers.

II. *Upaniṣads*

The following abbreviations of works containing these texts are used in this section:

M U — *Major Upaniṣads*, with the commentary of Śaṅkarācārya. 4 vols. Gītā Press, Gorakhpur, 1945.

Śaiva U — *Śaiva Upaniṣads*, with the commentary of Upaniṣad Brahmayogin. Adyar Library. Madras, 1925.

Śakta U — *Śakta Upaniṣads*, with the commentary of Upaniṣad Brahmayogin. Adyar Library. Madras, 1925.

S V U — *Sāmānya Vedānta Upaniṣads*, with the commentary of Upaniṣad Brahmayogin. Adyar Library. Madras, 1921.

T M U — *Ten Major Upaniṣads*, with the commentary of Upaniṣad Brahmayogin. 2 vols. Adyar Library. Madras, 1936.

V U — *Vaiṣṇava Upaniṣads*, with the commentary of Upaniṣad Brahmayogin. Adyar Library. Madras, 1923.

Y U — *Yoga Upaniṣads*, with the commentary of Upaniṣad Brahmayogin. Adyar Library. Madras, 1920.

Advaya-tāraka Upaniṣad. In *Y U.*

Aitareya Upaniṣad. In *T M U; M U.*[2]

Avyakta Upaniṣad. In *V U.*

Bhasma-jābāla Upaniṣad. In *Śaiva U.*

Bhuvaneśvarī Upaniṣad. In *Śakta U.*

Bṛhad-āraṇyaka Upaniṣad. In *T M U; M U.*

Chāndogya Upaniṣad. In *T M U; M U.*

Darśana Upaniṣad. See *Jābāla-darśana Upaniṣad.*

Devī Upaniṣad. In *Śakta U.*

Gaṇapati Upaniṣad. In *Śaiva U.*

Garuḍa Upaniṣad. In *V U.*

Gopāla-pūrva-tāpinī Upaniṣad. In *V U.*

Gopāla-uttara-tāpinī Upaniṣad. In *V U.*

Īśopaniṣad. In *T M U; M U.*

Īśopaniṣad, with Kaulācārya Satyānanda's commentary. Edited by Arthur Avalon [Sir John Woodroffe]. 2nd ed. Ganesh and Co., Madras, 1952.

Īśopaniṣad Vijñāna Bhāṣya of Motilāl Śarmā Gauḍ. BCE Press, Jaipur, 1931.

Jābāla-darśana Upaniṣad (or *Darśana Upaniṣad*). In *Y U.*

Kaivalya Upaniṣad. In *Śaiva U.*

Kali-santaraṇa Upaniṣad. In *V U.*

Kalyāṇa, Upaniṣad aṅka (including Kaivalya, Nīlarudra, Devī, Gaṇapati Upaniṣads). Gītā Press, Gorakhpur, 1949.

Kaṭha Upaniṣad. In *T M U; M U.*

Kena Upaniṣad. In *T M U; M U.*

Kṛṣṇa Upaniṣad. In *V U.*

2 Cited as Adyar ed. and Gītā Press ed., respectively.

Mahā-nārāyaṇa Upaniṣad. Edited by Col. G. A. Jacob. Bombay Sanskrit Series, 35. Bombay, 1888.

Maitrāyaṇī Upaniṣad. In *S V U.*

Maitrī Upaniṣad. Adrien Maisonneuve, Paris, 1952.

Māṇḍūkya Upaniṣad. In *T M U; MU.*

Mudgala Upaniṣad. In *S V U.*

Muṇḍaka Upaniṣad. In *T M U; M U.*

Nārāyaṇa Upaniṣad. In *V U.*

Nīlarudra Upaniṣad. In: *Unpublished Upaniṣads.* Adyar Library. Madras, 1933.

Nṛsiṁha-pūrva-tāpinī Upaniṣad. In *V U.*

Nṛsiṁha-uttara-tāpinī Upaniṣad. In *V U.*

Praśna Upaniṣad. In *T M U; M U.*

Rāma-pūrva-tāpinī Upaniṣad. In *V U.*

Śvetāśvatara Upaniṣad. In *Śaiva U; Kalyāṇa,* Upaniṣad aṅka. Gītā Press, Gorakhpur, 1949.

Taittirīya Upaniṣad. In *T M U; M U.*

Tāra-sāra Upaniṣad. In *V U.*

Tripurā-tāpinī Upaniṣad. In *Śakta U.*

Yājñavalkya Upaniṣad. In: *Saṁnyāsa Upaniṣads,* with the commentary of Upaniṣad Brahmayogin. Adyar Library. Madras, 1929.

III. *Purāṇas*

Agni Purāṇa. Ānandāśrama ed. Poona, 1900.

Bhāgavata Purāṇa (*Śrīmad Bhāgavata*), with Hindi commentary. Śyāmakāśī Press, Mathura, 1940.

Bhaviṣya Purāṇa. Venkateśvara Press, Bombay, 1910.

Brahmāṇḍa Purāṇa. Venkateśvara Press, Bombay, 1912 (Part I), 1919 (Part II).

Brahma Purāṇa. Ānandāśrama ed. Poona, 1895.

Brahma-vaivarta Purāṇa. Ānandāśrama ed. 2 vols. Poona, 1935.

Devī Bhāgavata [*Purāṇa*], with *Devī Bhāgavata Ṭīkā.* Vavilla Ramasvami Śāstri and Sons, 1930. (Ed. in Telugu script.)

Devī Purāṇa. Bombay, 1919.

Garuḍa Purāṇa, with Hindi commentary. Prahlada Das, Benares, n. d.

Kālikā Purāṇa. Venkateśvara Press, Bombay, 1908.

Kalki Purāṇa. Calcutta, 1890.

Kūrma Purāṇa. Venkateśvara Press, Bombay, 1927.

Liṅga Purāṇa, with *Śivatoṣiṇī* (commentary). Venkateśvara Press, Bombay, 1925.

Lomaśa Saṁhitā. In the *Padma Purāṇa* (q. v.).

Mārkaṇḍeya Purāṇa, with Hindi translation. Mathura, 1941.

Matsya Purāṇa. Venkateśvara Press, Bombay, 1934.

Maudgala Purāṇa. Gaṇapati Lalji and Sons, Poona, n. d.

Nārada Purāṇa, with Hindi translation. Moradabad, 1940.

Narasiṁha Purāṇa. Bombay, 1911.

Padma Purāṇa. Lucknow, n. d.; Ānandāśrama ed., 4 vols., Poona, 1894.

Saura Purāṇa. Ānandāśrama ed. Poona, 1924.

Śiva Purāṇa, with Hindi translation. 2 vols. Mathura, 1940.

Śivatoṣiṇī. See under *Liṅga Purāṇa*, above.

Skanda Purāṇa, with Hindi commentary. 16 vols. Navala Kiṣore Press, Lucknow, 1913.

Śrīmad Bhāgavata. See *Bhāgavata Purāṇa*.

Sūta Saṁhitā. In the *Skanda Purāṇa* (q. v.).

Vāmana Purāṇa. Venkateśvara Press, Bombay, 1903.

Varāha Purāṇa. Venkateśvara Press, Bombay, 1902.

Vāyu Purāṇa. Ānandāśrama ed. Poona, 1905.

Viṣṇu Purāṇa, with Hindi translation. Gorakhpur, 1940.

Viṣṇu-dharmottara Purāṇa. Venkateśvara Press, Bombay, 1913.

IV. *Epics*

Adbhuta Rāmāyaṇa. Gītā Press, Gorakhpur, n. d.

Bhagavadgītā, with Śaṅkarācārya's commentary. Gītā Press, Gorakhpur, 1931.

Harivaṁśa. Citraśālā Press, Poona, n. d.

Mahābhārata. Bhandarkar Institute, Poona, 1927–33.

———. Kumbakonam ed. Bombay, 1906–14.

———. Svādhyāya Maṇḍala ed. Aundh, 1926.

Rāma-carita-mānasa of Tulsī Dās, with commentary by the editor, Vijayānanda Tripāṭhī. Leader Press, Allahabad, 1940.

Rāmāyaṇa of Vālmīki. See *Vālmīki Rāmāyaṇa*.

Vālmīki Rāmāyaṇa. Sasti Pustaka Mālā, Benares, 1936.

V. *Tantras and Āgamas*

Agastya Saṁhitā (Ms.).

Ahirbudhnya Saṁhitā. Adyar Library. Madras, 1916.

Bagalāmukhī Tantra. In *Śākta Pramoda* (q. v.), p. 307.

Bhairavī Tantra. Ibid., p. 253.

Bhuvaneśvarī Tantra. Ibid., p. 197.

Chinnamastā Tantra. Ibid., p. 225.

Dattātreya Tantra Saṁhitā. Venkateśvara Press, Bombay, 1951.

Dhūmāvatī Tantra. In *Śākta Pramoda* (q. v.), p. 281.

Gāndharva Tantra. Kashmir, 1934.

Gautamīya Tantra (Ms.). Also a printed version: Bombay, n. d.

Kālī Tantra (Ms.). Ibid.: Calcutta, n. d.

Kāmakalā-vilāsa [of Puṇya Nanda]. Translated by Arthur Avalon [Sir John Woodroffe]. Tantrik Texts, X. Luzac and Co., Calcutta and London, 1922.

Kamalā Tantra. In *Śākta Pramoda* (q. v.), p. 355.

Kulārṇava Saṁhitā (Ms.).

Kulārṇava Tantra. Tantrik Texts, V. Luzac and Co., Calcutta and London, 1917.

Mahānirvāṇa Tantra. Edited by Arthur Avalon [Sir John Woodroffe], with English translation. Ganesh and Co., Madras, 1927.

Mahāsundarī Tantra (Ms.).

Nārada Pāñcarātra. Venkateśvara Press, Bombay, 1905.

Nigama-kalpalatā (Ms.).

Pārameśvara Saṁhitā. Srinagar, 1953.

Piṅgala Tantra (Ms.).

Prapañcasara Tantra. Tantrik Texts, III. Luzac and Co., Calcutta and London, 1915.

Rudra-yāmala Tantra. Calcutta, 1937.

Śākta Pramoda. Venkateśvara Press, Bombay, 1931.

Śakti Saṅgama Tantra. 4 vols. Baroda, 1932.

Śāmbhavī Tantra (Ms.).

Sātvata Tantra. Chowkhāmbā Sanskrit Series. Benares, 1939.

Śoḍaśī Tantra. In *Śākta Pramoda* (q. v.).

Śyāmāstava Tantra (Ms.).

Tantra Saṁhitā (Ms.).

Tantra-sāra. Chowkhāmba Sanskrit Series. Benares, n. d.

Tantra-sāra Saṅgraha of Madhvācārya, with Chalāri's commentary. n. p., n. d.

Tantra Tattva-prakāśa (Ms.).

Tārā Tantra. Bengal, n. d. Also in *Śākta Pramoda* (q. v.), p. 123.

Tripurā-bhairavī Tantra (Ms.).

Uḍḍiśa Tantra. Mathura, n. d.

Vaikhānasāgama of Marīci. n. p., n. d.

Varadā Tantra (Ms.).

Viśva-sāra Tantra (Ms.).

Yāmala Tantra (Ms.).

Yoginī Tantra. Calcutta, n. d.

VI. *Various*

Aparādha-kṣamāpaṇa Stotra of Śaṅkarācārya. In: *Bṛhat-stotra-ratnākara*, I. Nirṇayasāgar Press, Bombay, 1952.

Architecture of Mānasāra. Translated by P. K. Acharya. Oxford University Press, London, [1934].

Aṣṭādhāyī of Pāṇini. Various eds.

Aśvattha Stotra. In *Bṛhat-stotra-ratnākara*, II (q. v., under *Aparādha-kṣamāpaṇa Stotra* above).

Bhāmatī of Vācaspati Miśra. Nirṇayasāgar Press, Bombay, 1938.

Brāhmaṇa-sarvasva (Ms.).

Brahma Sūtra Bhāṣya of Śaṅkarācārya. 4 vols. Benares, 1930.
Bṛhad-devatā. Harvard Oriental Series, V. Cambridge, Mass., 1904. (English translation by Arthur Anthony Macdonnell, in vol. VI.)
Bṛhat Kathā-mañjarī. Nirṇayasāgar Press, Bombay, 1931.
Bṛhat Parāśara Horā. Calcutta, n. d.
Bṛhat-saṁhitā. Vijayanagar Series. Vijayanagar, n. d.
Dharma Śāstra of Nārada (Ms.).
Dhātu-pāṭha of Pāṇini. In *Aṣṭādhyāyī* (q. v.).
Devatāmūrti-prakaraṇa and *Rūpa-maṇḍana*. Calcutta, 1936.
Devī Māhātmya. Madras, 1943.
Grahayāga-tattva (Ms.).
Hara-carita-cintāmaṇi. Kashmir, n. d.
Hayaśīrsa Pañcarātra (Ms.).
Jaṭādhara (Ms.).
Kalpa Sūtra of Paraśu-Rāma (Ms.).
Karma-locana (Ms.).
Karpūrādi Stotra. Translated by Arthur Avalon [Sir John Woodroffe]. Tantrik Texts, IX. Luzac and Co., London, 1922.
Karpūra-stava. Ganesh and Co., Madras, n. d.
Kāśīmukti-viveka of Sureśvara (Ms.).
Kathā-sarit-sāgara. Nirṇayasāgar Press, Bombay, 1930.
Kirātārjunīya of Bhāravi, with Mallinātha's commentary. Benares, n. d.
Kumārasaṁbhava of Kālidāsa. Nirṇayasāgar Press, Bombay, 1893.
Lalitā-sahasra-nāma, with Bhāskararāya's commentary. Adyar Library. Madras, 1925.
Lalitā-upākhyāna. In the *Brahmāṇḍa Purāṇa*, Part II (q. v. in III).
Mahābhāṣya of Patañjali. Various eds.
Mālatī-mādhava of Bhana Bhūti. Various eds.
Mānasāra (Ms.). See also *Architecture of Mānasāra*.
Mantra Mahārṇava. Venkateśvara Press, Bombay, 1925.
Mantra Mahodadhi. Bombay, n. d.
Manu Smṛti, with Kullūka Bhaṭṭa's commentary. Nirṇayasāgar Press, Bombay, 1933.
Meghadūta of Kālidāsa, with Mallinātha's commentary. Edited by Pandit Sri Narayan Sastri Khiste. Kāśī Sanskrit Series, 88; Kāvya Section, 14. Benares, 1931.
Nandikeśvara Kāśikā. Grantha ed. Chidambaram, 1888.
Nāradīya Dharma Śāstra. See *Dharma Śāstra* of Nārada.
Nāradīya Saṁhitā (Ms.).
Nāṭya Śāstra, with Abhinava Gupta's commentary. 4 vols. Baroda, 1926.
Nirukta of Yāska, with Durgācārya's commentary. Nirṇayasāgar Press, Bombay, n. d.
Nityāṣoḍa (Ms.).
Paraśurāma Kalpa Sūtra. See *Kalpa Sūtra* of Paraśu-Rāma.
Puṇyāha-vācana. In: *Dānakhaṇḍa* of Hemadri. Calcutta, n. d.

Raghuvaṁśa of Kālidāsa. Nirṇayasāgar Press, Bombay, 1886.
Rūpa-maṇḍana. See under *Devatāmūrti-prakaraṇa*.
Śabda-cintāmaṇi. See *Śabdārtha-cintāmaṇi*.
Śabda-kalpa-druma, compiled by Raja Radhakanta Deva. 5 vols. n. p., 1892.
Śabdārtha-cintāmaṇi. 3 vols. Agra, 1865.
Śaiva Siddhānta-sāra. Benares, n. d.
Sāṅkhya-sāra of Vijñāna Bhikṣu. Calcutta, 1862.
Sāṅkhya-tattva-kaumudī of Vācaspati Miśra. Benares, n. d.
Sarvānukramaṇī. Edited by A. A. Macdonnell. Clarendon Press, Oxford, 1886.
Siddhānta-kaumudī of Bhaṭṭojī Dīkṣita. 6 vols. Calcutta, 1926.
Śilpa Śāstra. Lahore, 1928.
Śiva-mahimna Stotra. Ganesh and Co., Madras, 1953.
Śivārcana Candrikā (Ms.).
Śivārcana Siddhānta (Ms.).
Śiva-tattva-nidhi (Ms.).
Sūrya-siddhānta. Calcutta, 1860.
Uṇādi Sūtras of Pāṇini. In *Aṣṭādhāyī* of Pāṇini (q. v.).
Vaiyākaraṇa-mañjūṣā. Chowkhāmbā Sanskrit Series. Benares, n. d.
Varivasyā-rahasya. Madras, n. d.
Varuṇa-dhyāna (Ms.).
Viṣṇu-sahasra-nāma Bhāṣya of Śaṅkarācārya. Gītā Press, Gorakhpur, 1934.
Yantra-cintāmaṇi. Venkateśvara Press, Bombay, 1930.
Yoga Sūtras of Patañjali. Sacred Books of the Hindus. Allahabad, 1926.
Yoga Sūtra Bhāṣya of Vyāsa. Ibid.

B. MODERN WORKS

VII. *Studies*

Dikshitar, V. R. R. *Purâṇa Index*. 3 vols. Madras, n. d.
Dowson, John. *A Classical Dictionary of Hindu Mythology*. . . . Trübner's Oriental Series. 3rd ed. London, 1891.
Dumézil, Georges. *Les Dieux des Indo-Européens*. Paris, 1952.
Fausbøll, V. *Indian Mythology in Outline according to the Mahâbhârata*. Luzac and Co., London, 1903.
Gopinâtha Rao, T. A. *Elements of Hindu Iconography*. 4 vols. Madras, 1914.
Kalyāṇa. Gītā Press, Gorakhpur. Issues: Śakti aṅka, 1938; Śiva aṅka, 1937; Upaniṣad aṅka, 1949; Veda aṅka, n. d.; Vedānta aṅka, 1937; Viṣṇu aṅka, n. d.
Karapātrī, Svāmī (Svāmī Hariharānanda Sarasvatī). "Ganapati rahasya." In: *Śrī Bhagavat tattva*. Benares, 1938.*

* In Hindi.

Monier-Williams, Sir Monier. *A Sanskrit-English Dictionary*. Oxford, 1899.

Motilāl Śarmā Gauḍ. See *Īśopaniṣad Vijñāna Bhāṣya* in II.

Rāma dāsa Gauḍ. *Hindutva*. Benares, 1939.*

Renou, Louis, and Jean Filliozat. *L'Inde classique: Manuel des études indiennes*. 2 vols. Imprimerie Nationale, Paris, [1949]–53.

Woodroffe, Sir John (pseud. Arthur Avalon). *The Garland of Letters*. Luzac and Co., London, 1929; Ganesh and Co., Madras, 1951.

______. *The Greatness of Śiva*. Ganesh and Co., Madras, 1953.

______. *Mahâ Mâyâ*. Ganesh and Co., Madras, 1929 and 1954.

______ (ed.) *Principles of Tantra*, with an introduction by Baradā Kānta Majumdār. Luzac and Co., London, 1916; Ganesh and Co., Madras, 1952.

______. *The Serpent Power*. Ganesh and Co., Madras, 1931.

______. *Shakti and Shakta*. Luzac and Co., London, 1929.

______. *The Wave of Bliss*. Ganesh and Co., Madras, 1954.

______. See also *Īśopaniṣad* (in II); *Kāmakalā-vilāsa* (in V); *Mahānirvāṇa Tantra* (in V).

Yogatrayānanda. *Śiva-rātri*. Calcutta, 1910.*

______. *Śrī Rāmāvatāra kathā*. Calcutta, 1911.*

VIII. *Articles*

Places of publication: *Kalyāṇa*, Gorakhpur; *Sanmārga*, Benares; *Siddhānta*, Benares.

Devarāja Vidyā Vācaspati. "Tantra men Yantra aur Mantra." *Kalyāṇa*, Śakti aṅka, 1938, p. 387.*

Durgādatta Tripāṭhī. "Deva guru Bṛhaspati." *Siddhānta*, IV, 1943–44, 54–66.

Giridhara Śarmā Caturvedi. "Paśupati evam Prajāpati." *Kalyāṇa*, Śiva aṅka, 1937, p. 41.*

______. "Śiva Mahimā." *Kalyāṇa*, Veda aṅka, p. 40.*

______. "Śiva Mahimā." *Kalyāna*, Śiva aṅka.*

Gopinātha Kavirāja. "Linga rahasya." *Kalyāṇa*, Śiva aṅka, 1937, p. 476.*

Hīrānanda Śāstrī Gauḍ. "Tārā rahasya." *Kalyāṇa*, Śakti aṅka, 1938, p. 224.*

Karapātrī, Svāmī (Svāmī Hariharānanda Sarasvatī). "Ahamartha aur Ātmā." *Siddhānta*, II, 1941–42.*

______. "Bhagavān Kṛṣṇa aur unke parivāra." *Siddhānta*, V, 1944–45.*

______. "Kṛṣṇa tattva." Ibid.

______. "Liṅgopāsanā rahasya." *Siddhānta*, II, 1941–42.*

______. "Maheśvara." *Sanmārga*, 1946.*

______. "Panca 'Ma' kāra." *Siddhānta*, III, 1942–43, 290.

______. "Śrī Bhagavatī tattva." *Siddhānta*, V, 1944–45.*

______. "Śrī Śiva tattva." *Sanmārga*, 1946.*

______. "Śrī Śiva tattva." *Siddhānta*, II, 1941–42.*

* In Hindi.

______. "Śrī Viṣṇu tattva." *Siddhānta*, V, 1944–45.*

Motilāl Śarmā Gauḍ. "Daśa Mahāvidyā." *Kalyāṇa*, Śakti aṅka, 1938, p. 89.*

______. "Veda-kā svarūpa vicāra." *Kalyāṇa*, Vedānta aṅka, 1937.*

Rāmacandra Śankara Takki. "Parā aur aparā Śakti." *Kalyāṇa*, Śakti aṅka, 1938, p. 477.*

Rāmacandra Śarmā, B. "Some Aspects of the Vedic Gandharva and Apsarases." *The Poona Orientalist*, XIII, 1948, 61 ff.

Śaṅkara Tīrtha, Svāmī. "Bhagavān Hiraṇyagarbha." *Siddhānta*, III, 1942–43.*

Vāsudeva Śaraṇa Agravāla. "Śiva kā svarūpa." *Kalyāṇa*, Śiva aṅka, 1937, pp. 492, 497–98.*

Vijayānanda Tripāṭhī. "Devatā tattva." *Sanmārga*, III, 1942, 682.

Woodroffe, Sir John. "Ṣaḍadhva." *Kalyāṇa*, Śakti aṅka, 1938, pp. 583 ff.

* In Hindi.

Index

A

Abandonment, *see* Vaitaraṇī
Ab-bīja, 314
abdhi-jau, 129
Ābhāsvara(s), 302, 303
abhicāra yajña, 90
Abhimānī, 88
Abhinandana, 294
Abhi-rūpa, 314
Abhiyutākṣika, 105
Ābhoga, 120
Abhra, 92
Abja-hasta, 89
Abja-ja, 235
Abja-yoni, 235
able-ones, *see* śakinīs
ab-loka, 67
Abode-of-the-Clouds, *see* Meghaveśman
Abode-of-Delight, *see* Nandana
Abode-of-Joy, *see* Śambhu
Abode-of-Life, *see* Viśvāyu
Abode-of-Treasures, *see* Vasu-sthalī
absolute-might, *see* aiśvarya
abstraction, degrees of, 332
Ācāra Tantra, *see* Tantras
Accomplished, the, *see* Susiddha
acids, digestive, 70
action, 32, 45, 47, 67, 241; fruits of, 28n.; organs of, 26n.; *see also* karma; kriyā
active-notion-of-individual-existence, *see* rajas-ahaṁkāra
activity, 23, 45; *see also* Cyavana; kriyā; rajas
Acyuta, 154
Adam, 236
ādāna, 22
Adharma, 121, 138
ādhibhautika, 48, 49, 50, 81, 83, 85
ādhidaivika, 48, 50, 81, 83
adhiṣṭhātrī, 276
Adhokṣaja, 154
Adhvaryu, 340
ādhyātmika, 48, 49, 50, 81, 83
Ādi-kavi, 235
Aditi, 87, 95, 96, 104, 109, 112ff., 122, 125, 170, 178, 371
Āditya(s), 70, 79, 80, 82, 83, 92, 112ff., 128, 246, 255, 302, 341; Sun as, 96, 97, 238, 261, 340
Adolescent, the, *see* Kumāra
Adorned-with-Skulls, *see* Kapālinī
adri, 66
Adri-jā, 266
Advaya-tāraka Upaniṣad, *see* Upaniṣads
Advice, Giver of, *see* Nārada
Ādyā, 270
ādya-bīja, 343
ādyā vidyā, 153
Āgama(s), 163, 188, 189; *see also* Tantras
Agasti / Agastya (Puranic spelling), 116, 121, 317, 322f.
Agastya Saṁhitā, *see* Saṁhitās
Agha, 178
Aghora, 212
Āghṛṇi, 124
āgneya-prāṇa, 204
agni / Agni, 45, 48f., 63f., 85, 86, 87ff., 199, 228, 315, 319, 340, Pl. 6; Kapila as, 183; as Lust, 312; as regent of direction, 130f.; and Rudra, 195; and semen, 226, 227, 298; three spheres of, 80f.; Viṣṇu as, 170
Agni (ṛṣi), 318
Agnibāhu, 319
Agnideva, 318
Agnidhra, 319
Agnihotra, 69, 90n.
agni-prajvālana, 347
Agni Purāṇa, *see* Purāṇas
agni-stambhana, 347
Agra-samdhānī, 134
Agravāla, Vāsudeva Śaraṇa, *see* Vāsudeva Śaraṇa Agravāla
agriculture, 185f., 326
Aha / Āha, 86
Ahalyā, 108, 110, 236
ahaṁkāra, 26n., 212, 233
aham-tattva, 51, 52, 243
ahargaṇa, 67
Aharpati, 97
āhavanīya-agni, 90n., 248, 340
Ahi, 107
Ahiṁsā, 182
Ahirbudhnya, 105
Ahirbudhnya Saṁhitā, *see* Saṁhitās
Ahiṣṭhana, 135
āhlādinī-śakti, 258, 261, 264
Ahura (Mazda), 121, 140
āhvana, 341

C

D

Girl-of-Sixteen, *see* Ṣoḍaśī
Giver-of-Existence, *see* Bhāvanī
Giver-of-Food-and-Plenty, *see* Annapūrṇā
Giver-of-Joy, *see* Śaṅkara
Giver-of-Offerings, *see* Havismat
Giver-of-Peace, *see* Śaṅkara-Śiva
Giver-of-Rewards, *see* Janārdana
giver-of-seed, *see* bījavan; bījin
glauṁ, 343
Glorified-in-a-hundred-Sacrifices, *see* Śatakratu
Glorious, the, 54, 57; *see also* Virāj; virāṭ
glory, *see* yaśas
gluttons, *see* praghasa
goat, 97, 322; one-legged, *see* Aja-ekapāda; she-, *see* ajā
God, 198; unity of, illusory, 35f.; & the universe, 37; *see also* Īśvara
god(s), 4, 8f., 27, 81f., 332, 363f.; age of the, 145; as entities or powers, 8; false, 10; number of, 79, 82ff.; thirty-three, 79ff., 82ff.; *see also* deva; sura
Goddess, Supreme / Universal, 32, 253ff., 359; *see also* Śakti
goddess-of-fortune, *see* Lakṣmī
goddess-of-the-spheres, *see* Bhuvaneśī; Bhuvaneśvarī
Goddess-of-tears, *see* Rudrāṇī
God the Father, 24n.
god-of-rain, *see* Parjanya
God the Son, 24n.
God's-Friend, *see* Īśa-sakhi
gola, 355
Golden-bodied, *see* Suvarṇa-kāyā
Golden-City, *see* Hiraṇya-pura
golden color, 88, 159, 175
Golden-Embryo, *see* Hiraṇya-garbha
Golden-Eyed, *see* Hiraṇyākṣa
Golden-Fleece, *see* Hiraṇya-kaśipu
Golden-Garland, *see* Hema-mālā
Golden-Vesture, *see* Hiraṇya-kaśipu
Gold-maker, *see* Hiraṇyakṛt
go-loka, 177
Gomatī, 308
Good-Archer, *see* Sudhanvan
Good-Behavior, *see* Sunīti; Suśīlā
Good-Looks, *see* Suruci
Good-Star, *see* Su-tārā; Su-tārakā
Good-Taste, *see* Su-rasā
goose, 237
Gopāla-pūrva-tāpinī Upaniṣad, *see* Upaniṣads
Gopāla-tāpinī Upaniṣad, *see* Upaniṣads
Gopāla-uttara-tāpinī Upaniṣad, *see* Upaniṣads
Gopatha Brāhmaṇa, *see* Brāhmaṇas
Gopati, 97
Gopinātha Kavirāja, 230
goptṛ, 104
Gotra-kāra, 321
Go-vana, 178
Govardhana, 111
Govinda, 154
graha, 316
Graha-pati, 97
Graha-rājan, 97
Grahayāga-tattva, 100
grahī(s), 288
grāma-devatā(s), 301, 307
grāma-kālī(s), 301, 307
Grass-robed, the, *see* Śākambharī
Gṛdhu, 314
Great, the, *see* Mahān
Great Bear, 105, 317, 319, 323
Great-Captain, *see* Mahā-sena
Great-Courage, *see* Mahā-vīryā
Greatest-of-Poets, *see* Kavitama
Great-God, *see* Mahā-deva
Great-Goddess, *see* Maheśvarī
Great-Leader, *see* Vināyaka
Great-Lord, *see* Bṛhaspati; Maheśvara
Great Master, *see* Bṛhaspati
Greatness, *see* Mahimān
Great-One, *see* Bṛhatī
Great-Poet, *see* Kavitara
Great-Seers, *see* Mahā-ṛṣis
Great-Veil, *see* Mahā-vila
Great-Yogi, *see* Maheśvara; Śiva
Greece, 24n.
Gṛhya Sūtras, 299
Gṛtsa, 121, 314
gruel-eater, *see* Karambhād
guarded-on-all-sides, Yantra, *see* sarvatobhadra
guha / Guha, 298, 299
guhā, 49, 50
Guhyā, 274
guhyaka, 135, 137
guṇa(s), 23, 24, 26ff., 216, 231, 241, 253; *see also* rajas; sattva; tamas
Guṇakeśī, 110
Gupta(s), 298
Gupta-cara, 180
guru, 331

H

hā-i, 344
Haima-vatī, 266
hair, lock of, 157

Hope, *see* Āśis
horse(s), 128; Indra's, 109; sacrificial, 75; Sun's, 95; *see also* aśva; Haya
Horse-headed, *see* Hayaśiras; Hayaśīrṣa
Horses: Joyful, *see* Haryaśvas; Multicolored, *see* Sabal-āśvas; Simple-natured, *see* Saral-āśvas
Hotṛ, 340
Howling-Ones, *see* Rudras
hṛdaya, 45, 47
hrīṁ, 342, 354, 355
hṝṁ, 155
Hṛṣīkeśa, 154, 259
huṁ, 343, 344
huṁ!, 277
Humility, *see* Sannati
hunger, 274f.
Hunter, *see* Mṛgavyādha
Hutabhuj, 89
Hutāśa, 89
Hymns-of-Praise, *see* Khyāti; Māhātmyas

I

i, 344
"I," the, 18f.
I-ness, 33, 212; *see also* ahaṁkāra
icchā, 199, 340
icchā-śakti, 39
Icchā-vasu, 136
iḍā, 216
Idaṁ-dra, 108
Iḍaviḍā, 135
ideation-wording-utterance, *see* paśyantī-madhyamā-vaikharī
identification, *see* samādhi
identity, 17
ideograms, 3
idhma, 340
Īdṛś, 106
ignorance, 30; *see also* avidyā
Ikṣumatī, 308
Ikṣvāku, 96
Ilā, 371
Ill-Omen, *see* Ariṣṭa
illusion, 7, 22, 28ff., 35, 50; *see also* māyā
illusionist, *see* māyin
Ilvala, 323
image(s), 362ff.; forms of, 363; materials for, 363; phallic, 230–31; purpose of, 362f.; *see also* mūrti
Immense, the, *see* Prabhūti
Immense-Being, *see* Brahmā
Immense-Grove, *see* Brahma-vṛnda
Immensity, 7, 35, 50; *see also* brahman
Immortal-City, *see* Amarāvatī
immortality, 16; physical, 52; *see also* amṛta
Immortals, *see* Maruts
Immovable, the, *see* Dhruva
Impermanent, the, 44, 45, 46, 51, 55
Impetuous, *see* Caṇḍa
impulse: *see* Utsarga; inner, *see* antaścara; outer, *see* bahiścara
impurity, 383
Inaccuracy, *see* Vitatha
incapacities, *see* badha
incarnations, *see* avatars
incense, 381
indestructibility, *see* akṣara
Indestructible Person, 6, 45, 46, 47, 50, 55, 64; *see also* akṣara puruṣa
Indirā, 262
individual-bodies, *see* piṇḍas
individual-existence, *see* asmat
individuality, 18, 32, 33, 35, 51, 52, 53; first, 46; knot of, 53; *see also* aham-tattva
individual-plane, *see* ādhyātmika
individual-worship, *see* pūjā; pūjana
Indonesia, 323
Indra, 17, 45, 47, 49, 51, 57, 66, 79, 80, 81, 83, 91, 101, 104, 106ff., 114, 115, 119, 123, 126, 128, 130, 162, 194, 213, 260, 262, 287, 288, 294, 315, 322, 323, 324, 339, 342, 343, 371, 375f.
aspect of Śiva, 199, 278; desire for nonexistence, 197f.; dethroned by asuras, 141; elephant of, 283; happiness of, 146; relation to Agni, 88, 89; Trita &, 138
Indra-dhanus, 110
Indra-the-Great, *see* Mahendra
indrajāla, 315
Indrajit, 110
Indrāṇī, 104, 109, 287
Indranūja, 127
Indra-sāvarṇika Manu, 319, 327
indriya, 27, 51
indu / Indu, 100, 108
indweller, 45, 47; *see also* praviṣṭa; Vāsudeva
inertia, 22; *see also* tamas
infinity, 198f.; one &, 7
Inflamer, the, *see* Darpaka; Dīpaka
Inflamer-of-the-Creator, *see* Kandarpa
Inherited-Share, *see* Bhaga
Initiation, 283; *see also* Dīkṣā
inner-faculties, *see* antaḥkaraṇa
Inseparables, *see* Nāsatyas
Inspiration, *see* Kratu
Inspired, the, *see* Vipra
Instigator-of-Cycles, *see* Saṁvartaka

O

S

BOOKS OF RELATED INTEREST

GODS OF LOVE AND ECSTASY
The Traditions of Shiva and Dionysus
by Alain Daniélou

THE HINDU TEMPLE
Deification of Eroticism
by Alain Daniélou

WHILE THE GODS PLAY
Shaiva Oracles and Predictions on the Cycles of History and the Destiny of Mankind
by Alain Daniélou

SHIVA AND THE PRIMORDIAL TRADITION
From the Tantras to the Science of Dreams
by Alain Daniélou with Jean-Louis Gabin

A BRIEF HISTORY OF INDIA
by Alain Daniélou
Translated by Kenneth F. Hurry

INDIA: A CIVILIZATION OF DIFFERENCES
The Ancient Tradition of Universal Tolerance
by Alain Daniélou

THE COMPLETE KAMA SUTRA
The First Unabridged Modern Translation of the Classic Indian Text
Translated by Alain Daniélou

THE PHALLUS
Sacred Symbol of Male Creative Power
by Alain Daniélou

YOGA
Mastering the Secrets of Matter and the Universe
by Alain Daniélou

VIRTUE, SUCCESS, PLEASURE, AND LIBERATION
The Four Aims of Life in the Tradition of Ancient India
by Alain Daniélou

GODDESS IN INDIA
The Five Faces of the Eternal Feminine
by Devdutt Pattanaik

SHAKTI
Realm of the Divine Mother
by Vanamali

SHIVA
The Wild God of Power and Ecstasy
by Wolf-Dieter Storl, Ph.D.

KALI
The Feminine Force
by Ajit Mookerjee

THE PATH OF THE MYSTIC LOVER
Baul Songs of Passion and Ecstasy
by Bhaskar Bhattacharyya with Nik Douglas and Penny Slinger

HOW GANESH GOT HIS ELEPHANT HEAD
by Harish Johari and Vatsala Sperling
Illustrated by Pieter Weltevrede

KARNA
The Greatest Archer in the World
by Vatsala Sperling
Illustrated by Sandeep Johari

RAM THE DEMON SLAYER
by Vatsala Sperling
Illustrated by Pieter Weltevrede

Inner Traditions • Bear & Company
P.O. Box 388
Rochester, VT 05767
1-800-246-8648
www.InnerTraditions.com

Or contact your local bookseller